A Different Shade of Orange

For Bob Slayton, my good friend, with whom I have been able to share many experiences, including a memorable time in Alabama, and continue to share each month with you in our gang of four

Bob J.

Michi Nishiura and Walter Weglyn
Multicultural Publication Series

Arthur A. Hansen, Series Editor

Other Published Titles

Song of Anger: Tales of Tule Lake
Barney Shallit

Between Two Adversaries:
Korean Interpreters at Japanese Alien Enemy Detention Centers
During World War II
Hyung-Ju Ahn

Behind the Orange Curtain:
Religious Pluralism in a Southern California County
M. Margaret Tanaka and Cheryl Amarasuriya Eberly, Editors

Silent Scars of Healing Hands:
Oral Histories of Japanese American Doctors in
World War II Detention Camps
Naomi Hirahara and Gwenn M. Jensen

Forgotten Patriots:
Voices of World War II Mexican American Veterans of Southern California
Charlene Riggins and Miguel A. Garcia, Editors

Twice Orphaned:
Voices from the Children's Village of Manzanar
Catherine Irwin

A Different Shade of Orange

Voices of Orange County, California, Black Pioneers

Robert A. Johnson
Charlene M. Riggins

Library of Congress Cataloging-in-Publication Data

Johnson, Robert A., 1932-
A different shade of Orange : voices of Orange County, California, black pioneers / Robert A. Johnson, Charlene M. Riggins. -- 1st ed.
p. cm. -- (Michi Nishiura and Walter Weglyn multicultural publication series)
Includes bibliographical references and index.
ISBN 978-0-930046-25-5 (pbk. : alk. paper) 1. African Americans--California--Orange County--Interviews. 2. Orange County (Calif.)--History, Local. 3. African Americans--California--Orange County--History. 4. African Americans--California--Orange County--Social conditions. I. Riggins, Charlene, 1951- II. Title.
F868.O6J64 2009
307.2089'96073079496--dc22
2009000038

Published by Center for Oral and Public History
California State University, Fullerton

Cover design: Monty Starks and Dwight Blair
Technical assistance: Leslie Nash
Printed by Short Run Solutions

Table of Contents

Part Three: Appendices

Foreword

Arguably, the most iconic photographic image linking Japanese Americans to African Americans in the post-World War II era is that which appeared in *Life* magazine of Yuri Nakahara Kochiyama, the Nisei (US citizen offspring of Japanese immigrants) social activist, cradling the head of Malcolm X, the revolutionary civil rights leader and black nationalist, in her arms as he lay dying on the Audubon Ballroom stage in New York City's Harlem on February 21, 1965, after being shot by assassins' bullets. Five years earlier, Kochiyama (1921-), a close friend and associate of Malcolm X, had moved to Harlem with her Nisei husband Bill, a WWII veteran of the heralded all-Japanese American 442nd Regimental Combat Team, and their children.

During the mid-sixties, another Nisei woman, Michi Nishiura Weglyn (1927-1999), was also living in New York City, in a posh Park Avenue apartment on the Upper East Side of Manhattan, with her husband Walter (1926-1995). Five years younger than Yuri Kochiyama, Michi shared a similar background with her. Both were native Californians (Yuri was born in San Pedro in southern California, while Michi's birthplace was Stockton in northern California), both were incarcerated with their families in concentration camps during World War II (Yuri in Jerome, Arkansas, and Michi in Gila River, Arizona), and both came of age comparatively unaware of political affairs and issues such as racism and oppression.

Notwithstanding the contrasting New York neighborhoods in which Yuri and Michi resided, by the early 1970s, Michi was following in Yuri's footsteps along the path that led to her being labeled by some as the "Mother of Japanese American Redress." Frank Abe, the noted Sansei (third-generation Japanese American) writer and filmmaker, called her the Rosa Parks of the Redress Movement. It was on December 1, 1955, in Montgomery, Alabama, that Parks earned her moniker as the "Mother of the Modern-Day Civil Rights Movement" by refusing to give up her seat to make room for a white passenger. This act of civil disobedience led to the Montgomery Bus Boycott and catapulted boycott leader Reverend Martin Luther King, Jr. to national prominence in the Civil Rights Movement. Michi's act of resistance responsible for her being compared to Parks was writing a book, *Years of Infamy: The Untold Story of America's Concentration Camps* (1976)—the first major work about the World War II Japanese American experience from the perspective of one of the 120,000 victims. It armed the Japanese American community with the facts needed to question their eviction from their West Coast homes and their detention in interior facilities. In the words of the late Clifford Uyeda, a national redress chair for the Japanese American Citizens League, "it was Michi's book that really gave the Nisei documented proof of why they needed to fight for redress." *Years of Infamy* indeed laid the groundwork for the redress and reparations movement of Japanese Americans which climaxed in the Civil Rights Act of 1988. This point was made anew by the Japanese American National

Museum at its 2008 annual dinner when, in commemoration of the twentieth anniversary of this milestone, it selected Michi Weglyn among its honorees.

Well before her passing in 1999, Michi and her husband Walter made it clear in their words and deeds that their efforts for civil and human rights were inspired by the powerful example set by the leaders and the rank and file in the black community, as well as their allies in other communities of color, such as Yuri and Bill Kochiyama. The Weglyns paid tribute to these two friends by setting up a fund in their names to support college scholarships. Small wonder, then, that at the time of Michi's death a shocked and saddened Yuri declared: "I admire her very deeply."

Two African Americans friends whom the Weglyns admired very deeply were the comedian Bill Cosby and the actor Harry Belafonte, both civil rights activists. This situation came to my attention in 1990 when Dr. Milton A. Gordon, an African American, was appointed to succeed Dr. Jewel Plummer Cobb, also an African American, as the president of California State University, Fullerton (CSUF). Apparently moved by the anomaly of their heading an institution whose enrollment of black students was quite small within a county whose black population, percentage-wise, was even smaller, Michi Weglyn urged me to explore having either Cosby or Belafonte being awarded a Doctor of Humane Letters at Cal State Fullerton. Within two years, in 1992, Cosby was so honored by CSUF's nearby sister institution in Los Angeles County, California State Polytechnic University, Pomona. Its president, Dr. Bob H. Suzuki, in the following year, conferred the same honor on Michi Weglyn. During the balance of her life, Michi periodically proposed that I nominate Harry Belafonte for a Doctor of Humane Letters at Cal State Fullerton, with the proviso that he could use the celebratory occasion as a platform for making a serious civil rights speech (as he had already done when granted an honorary doctorate at other colleges and universities). I profoundly regret that I did not follow through in a timely manner on Michi's recommendation. Still, I am sure that it would have pleased her immensely to know about the publication of this present volume on Orange County's black community, *A Different Shade of Orange,* particularly since it is graced by Prefaces written by the esteemed African American leaders of three distinguished county institutions of higher education.

* * *

The Michi Nishiura and Walter Weglyn Multicultural Publication Series aims to memorialize the humanitarian legacy of the Weglyns. Their estate has made the series financially possible, while their lives have invested it with palpable meaning and high-minded purpose.

As a twelve-year-old, Walter Weglyn secured the last space on a transport that in 1939 brought two thousand German Jewish children to a special children's camp in Rotterdam. To stay alive, he was forced after Holland fell to the Nazis to flee from one shelter to another, eleven in all. Thereafter, a kindly Dutch diplomat's wife, who nightly buried him under a goat stable, saved his life. German aerial bombings in the Lowland killed most of the refugee children, and of those spared, only Walter and one other child survived the war. So also did his parents, who had been interned at Theresiendstat concentration camp in Czechoslovakia. Walter Weglyn, whose wartime odyssey was later featured along with Anne Frank and other Holocaust victims in Harvey Shapiro's book *What Evils Men Do*, arrived in the United States in 1947. While living at Columbia University's International House in New York City, he met Michi Nishiura, who had come there when personal misfortune forced her to withdraw from Mount Holyoke College in Massachusetts to become a costume designer. After Michi was diagnosed with tuberculosis and temporarily confined in an upstate New York sanitarium, Walter proposed to her. Following their 1950 marriage and the establishment of their home in Manhattan, Walter embarked upon his long and successful career as a perfume chemist and Michi pursued her profession in broadcast television (including an eight-year stint as costume designer for the popularly acclaimed *Perry Como Show*) and also wrote poetry and painted.

Then, after the war in Vietnam and the Watergate scandal opened the actions of the US government to increasing scrutiny and criticism, Michi began to question the decisions responsible for interning herself, her family, and her ethnic community during World War II. Unsalaried and without the aid of grant monies, she spent years systematically searching through the archival records in repositories like the National Archives and the Franklin Delano Roosevelt Library, to find evidence proving that "military necessity" was only a pretext for the racist wartime policy of mass detention for people of Japanese ancestry. "Persuaded that the enormity of a bygone injustice has been only partially perceived," Michi explained her decision to write *Years of Infamy*: "I have taken upon myself the task of piecing together what might be called the 'forgotten' or ignored parts of those years." The release of this book in 1976, in the words of Phil Tajitsu Nash, "finally gave redress advocates the facts they needed to press their righteous claims in the courts and in Congress." Michi was greatly assisted in the research and writing of her seminal book by Walter, who was outraged by the incarceration experience of Japanese Americans (as he also was of the treatment of African Americans in the South, where he lived before settling in New York). "Walter is my most exacting critic and mentor," Michi was quoted as saying. "I was able to write *Years of Infamy* because of the critical feedback he gave me, and his determination that I must expose the lies used to justify that atrocity." Truly, as the writer Frank Chin and the oral historian Paul Tsuneishi pointed out in their obituary of Walter Weglyn for the *Rafu Shimpo* (Los Angeles Japanese Daily News), Walter was "passionately committed to others who were disadvantaged or suffering oppression everywhere . . . [and] shared his wife's zeal in Asian American civil rights issues."

In 1993, while both of the Weglyns were still alive, President Bob Suzuki of California State Polytechnic University, Pomona, announced the establishment of the Walter and Michi Nishiura Weglyn Endowed Chair in Multicultural Studies. As an addendum to his moving tribute to Michi written shortly after her April 25, 1999, death, Phil Tajitsu Nash remarked that because she had been a person of action as well as ideas, one very fitting memorial to her would be for admirers to think of ways to build ongoing institutions such as the endowed chair at Cal Poly

Pomona and to further their own vision of a better world. It is in this spirit that the Michi Nishiura and Walter Weglyn Multicultural Publication Series is dedicated.

Arthur A. Hansen
Series Editor
Center for Oral and Public History
California State University, Fullerton

First Preface

It is an honor to be invited by Dr. Arthur A. Hansen, Professor of History Emeritus at California State University, Fullerton, to contribute to the Preface for this important book on the history of African Americans in Orange County, along with my distinguished higher education colleagues, Dr. Michael V. Drake, M.D., Chancellor, University of California, Irvine, and Dr. Jerome Hunter, Chancellor, North Orange County Community College District.

In order to put this history of African Americans in Orange County in perspective with my own personal experiences as an African American growing up in America, I would like to begin by sharing these with you.

I grew up on the south side of Chicago, which was basically the African American section of the city. However, my neighborhood was an integrated working-class area of the city, which was important for my development. My parents had five children—three of whom graduated from college—which was an outstanding achievement at that time. My sisters graduated in education and I graduated with a Ph.D. in mathematics, and collectively, the three of us have over 100 years of education.

When it came time for me to attend college, I had an athletic scholarship to a Historically Black College (HBCU), Xavier University of Louisiana in New Orleans. My father had migrated from New Orleans to Chicago in the early twentieth century and I wanted to go back to see what it was like in New Orleans and the South. The South was totally segregated at that time, and it was an eye-opening experience for me. It began when I boarded the train in Chicago. The train had separate cars for African American passengers and for white passengers, and usually there would be a railroad car or two between those passenger cars in order to separate both groups from the other.

During my years in New Orleans, I sat at the back of the bus, sat in balconies of theaters, ate in black-only restaurants, and suffered all the indignities of being African American in the southern part of the United States. I often look back at my years in New Orleans as some of the most important years in my life because it taught me what it was like to be a second-class citizen in my country. Hence, I knew about the South, but not about California and Orange County.

In the twenty-two years I have lived in California, I have come to have a much more realistic image of the state and southern California. When I was hired as vice president for academic affairs at Sonoma State University, I had an image of California as a young state, free and open to everyone without consideration of ethnicity. Since moving to Orange County, I have African American and Hispanic friends who have told me how they were treated growing up in this county and I was shocked. To me, it sounded like the South of my college years.

For the Preface for this book, it is important that I tell the story of the search process that led to my appointment as the president of California State University,

Fullerton, in 1990. This is a story that is very relevant to the theme of this book—African Americans in Orange County.

In the spring of 1990, I was invited to be interviewed for the position of president at California State University, Fullerton. This was quite an honor, and my wife Marge and I were excited about the possibility. Shortly after the candidates were publicly announced for the interview, I received a phone call from a person who said he lived in Orange County. He said that I should drop out of the interview process because as an integrated couple, we would not be welcome in Orange County. This was a real surprise to both of us—after all, this was 1990. That was our introduction to Orange County. We decided to go to the interview and give the campus, the community, and the California State University (CSU) Board of Trustees the best interview we could and not look back. At the end of the day of the interview, we knew that we had given the best interview we could and returned to our home. I give great credit to the campus, the community, and the CSU Board of Trustees for making the decision to follow the appointment of one African American president with a second African American president in Orange County. I also want to say that the person who made that phone call I mentioned earlier was wrong.

Over the past nineteen years, we have been welcomed by both the campus and the Orange County community. During the years we have been here, we have seen significant change in the diversity of the campus, our local community, and the county at large. Cal State Fullerton students reflect the change in diversity in Orange County, southern California, and the state of California, and the majority of our students are now from underrepresented categories. We are the only four-year Hispanic Serving Institution (HSI), of which I am aware, in Orange County.

When I became president of Cal State Fullerton in 1990, we had about 630 African American students enrolled and the university graduated 67 during that academic year. We now have more than 1,300 African American students, with more than 200 graduating in 2008. While this is an improvement, we still need to increase this number significantly. Further, it is my understanding that we are the first university west of the Mississippi to establish an internship program with Howard University to hire their Ph.D. graduates. Howard University is recognized for its excellence in graduating African American students with Ph.D. degrees. We had two Howard University Ph.D. interns with us in 2008. All of these changes bode well for the future of African American students at California State University, Fullerton, and for African Americans in Orange County.

I have had the pleasure of reading this book by Robert Johnson and Charlene Riggins about the history of African Americans in Orange County in advance of its publication. Many of the stories contained in this book remind me of living in New Orleans while in college and confirm what my African American and Hispanic American friends have told me about the Orange County of their youth. I would recommend this book as a must-read for everyone in Orange County, southern California, the state of California, and the nation. Having read the book, it also highlights what great changes have been made in the county by everyone working together to create a better life for all. However, these improvements must continue until we can assure equal access for everyone.

Milton A. Gordon
President
California State University, Fullerton

Second Preface

The themes of this oral history of black Orange County will ring true for many African Americans who moved, just as I did, from an all-black community to grow up in predominantly white communities here in California and in other western cities in the 1950s and 1960s. The stories in this book are similar to my own experiences growing up in Sacramento, as well as to those of friends I have since met who were raised in Berkeley, Modesto, Walnut Creek, or similar places.

These stories demonstrate how the law and the courts made a difference in the quality of education, housing, jobs—indeed the lives—of African Americans in Orange County. These histories personalize the effect of the law and the courts. For example, the strength and conviction of Dorothy and Lincoln Mulkey led them to file a suit in which the US Supreme Court overturned a California state constitutional amendment that allowed housing discrimination. World events also touched the lives of African Americans in Orange County: Ed Caruthers faced the question of whether to boycott the 1968 Olympic Games in Mexico City and then witnessed the negative reactions to John Carlos and Tommie Smith raising black-gloved fists; affected by the death of Dr. Martin Luther King, Jr., Ernestine Ransom became active in the Southern Christian Leadership Conference as well as University of California, Irvine, where she helped with outreach; and Everett Winters and Ervin Smith brought their civil rights experience to create or grow local civil rights organizations.

Finally, these are also personal stories of survival and success despite the adversity of racism and the extreme disadvantage that flows from it. Successes have many measures, from education to jobs to community and friendships forged, despite the disadvantages of racism. The authors of *A Different Shade of Orange*, Robert Johnson and Charlene Riggins, have been able to meld these personal stories, with all their differences, into a cohesive and significant history of blacks in Orange County.

As Chancellor at UC Irvine, I am also delighted that we have been able to contribute to this important work through the efforts of Professor Emeritus Spencer Olin, who has, for over thirty years, studied, taught, and written about American and California history. He, Professors Hansen and de Graaf, through the former *Journal of Orange County Studies* and indirectly, this book, have helped contribute to a closer understanding of the experiences of blacks in Orange County.

Michael V. Drake, MD
Chancellor
University of California, Irvine

Third Preface

Several years ago, Ruby Dee and her late husband, Ossie Davis, toured a play entitled *From the Inside Out*. A central point of the dramatic presentation was that the best way to learn about people was not through external observation, but through personal interaction, their habits, their cultures, and their own words. *A Different Shade of Orange: Voices of Orange County, California, Black Pioneers* is an excellent example of how light can be shed on the meanings of our complex existence when individuals simply share snapshots from their personal lives.

The tradition of oral history is strong in the African American community, and from the perspective of some, has its roots in the African storyteller, the Griot. The African American community in Orange County has traditionally been a small, not well-understood minority. In many instances, we have also been a "silent minority." Prior to this current publication, there has been no book-length, historical study of the African American community in Orange County. This publication, then, is past due and welcome.

When I first came to Orange County in 1964, there existed a fairly well-defined "black" community in the southwestern part of Santa Ana. There were black churches, barbershops, restaurants, a barbecue stand, and social organizations such as the Orange County Partners for Progress, the Orange County Democratic Black Caucus, the Orange County Opportunities Industrialization Center, the Orange County Urban League, and the Orange County Military Retirees. In recent years, African Americans in Orange County have become much more integrated and dispersed. Many of the organizations identified here now only exist in the minds of those who earlier experienced them. The compilation of essays in *A Different Shade of Orange* replaces these fading memories with fresh, new accounts of a variety of people with a variety of perspectives and experiences in Orange County.

As we read through the information provided in this volume, we should be reminded that there are many other stories of African Americans in Orange County that are not being told. Dr. Arthur Hansen and the California State University, Fullerton, are to be commended for providing the leadership for this informative and valuable historical document—the first of its kind. They and others also are encouraged to continue this meaningful endeavor.

Jerome Hunter
Chancellor
North Orange County Community College District

Acknowledgments

To acknowledge the help in publishing this book, we will start with its history. This book is the outgrowth of Bob Johnson's desire to write a book on the migration of African Americans to Orange County in the mid-twentieth century. In 2003, during a monthly dinner, former Orange County Fair Housing Council board members Edward Muehl, Leon Napper, and Robert Slayton strongly suggested that he write about the history of fair housing in Orange County and its legacy. That made sense because of Bob's having been deeply involved with the black community for almost thirty years, starting in 1966, a little more than a year after the Fair Housing Council's founding in 1965.

Having decided to write the history, Bob contacted the then department chair of Afro-Ethnic Studies Department at California State University, Fullerton (CSUF), Professor Wacira Gethaiga, whom Bob and his wife Lois knew from Gethaiga's Chapman University days. In 1975, Professor Gethaiga had co-edited a book titled *Harvest,* containing oral histories of minority people in the county. Bob also contacted Professor Lawrence de Graaf of the History Department of CSUF, then the leading expert on the history of the black community in Los Angeles (and whom Bob lunched with daily many years earlier when both were Glendale High School students). Professor de Graaf and his students had done numerous oral histories with black people in Los Angeles and Orange County.

Professor de Graaf introduced Bob to Professor Art Hansen, then director of CSUF's Center for Oral and Public History (COPH), and his staff. Bob soon started the first of twenty-two oral histories. COPH's administrative assistant, Kathy Frazee, and its archivist, Stephanie George, guided Bob through the interview process and all of the post-interview paperwork. Their time and effort was greatly appreciated. Bob's work benefited greatly by having an extremely talented transcriber, Suzanne Walter. Sometime in this process, Stephanie George suggested that COPH publish these oral histories in book form for its Michi Nishiura and Walter Weglyn Multicultural Publication Series. Professor Hansen, the editor for this series, agreed with this arrangement. Charlene Riggins, an adjunct professor of Afro-ethnic studies and history at CSUF and an oral history consultant then in the process of co-editing an earlier volume in the Weglyn series, *Forgotten Patriots: Voices of World War II Mexican American Veterans of Southern California*, came on board to co-author this volume. Charlene and Art Hansen then enlisted Monty Starks, a CSUF graduate student, to assist in the production of *A Different Shade of Orange.*

It became clear that the Orange County black community story, as expressed by the interviewees, was broader than simply one of migration. The stories included their life in the county after having arrived and the lives of their children. We also realized that earlier interviews in the COPH collection that had been conducted by Professor de Graaf, Lillie King, Mae Ussery, and Wendy Barker had great value and should be included in the book. In addition, we converted two DVD interviews conducted by Eli Rena and Rusty Kennedy of the Orange County Human Relations Commission and Yvette Cabrera of the *Orange County Register* newspaper into oral history form and edited these, as well as an interview conducted by Monty Starks, for inclusion in the present volume.

The production of this book was a team effort that involved more than the two authors and Monty Starks. We want to thank Professor Hansen, Kathy Frazee, and Susan Sang for the many hours they spent proofreading the manuscript and making suggestions to the authors regarding readability and historical authenticity. For this project, Kathy Frazee and Monty Starks learned the computer program Adobe *InDesign* and then assembled the manuscript for the printer. That was not an easy task. Thanks also to Stephanie George for recovering oral history manuscripts and along with Kira Gentry, COPH's graduate assistant, converting the older typed transcriptions into digital form.

We also want to acknowledge the institutional support at CSUF provided by Dr. Natalie Fousekis, director of the COPH; Dr. Bill Haddad, chair of the Department of History; and Dr. Thomas Klammer, dean of the College of Humanities and Social Sciences. In addition, thanks go particularly to Professor Wacira Gethaiga, former chair of CSUF's Afro-Ethnic Studies Department, who allowed Bob Johnson to organize his experiences and knowledge of racism in Orange County by inviting him to be a visiting lecturer in his classes once every semester. Bob also thanks his real-life, often in-your-face, fair housing mentors, Dr. Ralph Kennedy, Col. James Allen, James Hillman, Richard Petherbridge, and Ken Caines. Four decades ago, by their knowledge and deeds, they helped Bob Johnson begin to understand the issues regarding race relations in America.

We want to thank President Milton Gordon of CSUF for his intellectual and monetary support of this project as well as for contributing a preface, and also Chancellors Michael Drake and Jerome Hunter for their respective prefaces, and Professor de Graaf for his afterword. We want to thank all of the people who volunteered to be interviewed and opened their lives to the world, as well as those relatives who helped us obtain photographs. Most of all, we want to thank our spouses Lois Johnson and Chester Riggins, Jr., who, though supportive, have had to suffer, as in the past, by having to lose us to "the book."

Editorial Note

The purpose of this manuscript is to create a coherent and interesting volume by using people's own words to give the reader a collective sense of what it was like to be black and living in Orange County in the 1930-to-1980 time frame. If, for research purposes, the reader wants the entire oral history from the complete transcription or wants to hear the audio tape, these are available from the Center for Oral and Public History at California State University, Fullerton.

Most of the material that was not related to Orange County or not relevant to the person's life in this county was removed from the original oral histories. On the average, roughly half of the material was removed without the customary ellipses. Other material was removed because it was redundant or very often said in other oral histories. Material the editors knew was in error or in question, like dates and places, was deleted. Material was removed because it was somewhat disconnected or had no relationship to the person being black. For example, information such as "we went to the beach" is relevant because in many areas in California black people were disallowed from using public beaches, whereas in Orange County, they could frequent any beach. Some material was removed simply to reduce the length of the interview.

It is important for the reader to know what similarities were in the lives of the black interviewees and their white (and other non-white) neighbors, and that they are much greater than the differences in their lives. This may have been true throughout America, but was true to a large extent in Orange County. With this understanding in mind, we often removed material relating to what "everyone" did and retained the material relating to differences in lifestyle and even more so, retained material regarding the society's differing treatment of blacks and whites. Also retained was contrasting material pointing out surprising similarities like the lack of segregation in the schools, on the beaches, and in the parks.

Most of the interviews were conducted by white interviewers in an Orange County setting. Because the interviewees were either raised in predominantly non-black communities or had spent most of their adult lives in Orange County, in most cases their speech was in standard rather than vernacular English. In introductions, footnotes, and sidebars, the term *black* was most often used to denote race. This was because the majority of the people interviewed used the term *black*, and not very often used "colored," "African American," "Afro-American," or "Negro."

Some articles and conjunctions were added to clarify the material or make for easier reading. Sometimes the question was modified to fit the person's response in order to make sense of the response. Changing the sequence of the interview material was only done in the Dorothy Mulkey interview because of the difficult and possibly confusing nature of the civil rights issues involved. Changing wording or reconstructing a sentence was seldom done and only done when the editing was necessary to make sense out of the material. Explanatory material via footnotes and bracketed notes were utilized very sparingly.

General Introduction
Black Orange County, 1930-1980

"Black people in Orange County? There aren't any black people in Orange County." That was true, after sundown in the Orange County towns of Orange and Brea in the first half of the twentieth century, and those words are still being heard. During that early time, there were only handfuls of black people in areas surrounding the county seat, the city of Santa Ana. But change took place in the second half of the century. The tiny black community grew in both population and influence in the life of Orange County. Roughly 2 percent of this county of three million people, around 60,000 people in the 2000 federal census, considered themselves black or mixed-race, including black. As of the publication date of the present book, this change is also exemplified by the presence of African Americans in all aspects of community life, including the county's two major universities, led by President Milton Gordon of California State University, Fullerton, and Chancellor Michael Drake of the University of California, Irvine.[1]

Professor Lawrence de Graaf, in the Afterword of this volume, compares the unusual history of Orange County's black community to those of other African American communities in large metropolitan areas of California and the US. The fact that descriptions of Orange County in this book only go back to about 1930 does not present a problem. As mentioned, there was hardly a black community before that time. The Great Migration, where Negroes in the South were drawn to jobs in the northern states following our entrance into World War I, had little effect toward increasing the black population of Orange County during the war and the decade after. Therefore, the history, which our interviewees describe in this volume, starts in the 1930s as black families trickled into Santa Ana, and to a lesser extent, Fullerton, and other cities surrounding Santa Ana. But it wasn't until the 1960s that the trickle turned into a small stream.

In spite of the jump in the number of black personnel at the Tustin and El Toro marine bases, data shows that as late as 1960, the percentage of black people in Orange County was less than one-half percent, the same as recorded in the US Census of 1950. This changed in the decade of the 1960s. Industrial job growth, civil rights organizations, and laws covering employment and housing, allowed increasing numbers of blacks to move into Santa Ana and the suburbs. By the mid-1970s, integration of the suburbs was fueled by black families moving from outside of the county and from the Santa Ana "ghetto." By 1980, the black population of Santa Ana had leveled off and the black population of the rest of the county was fast moving toward the present plateau of 2 percent of the total population.

---

[1] Most often the editors of this book will use the term *black* in their own writing to describe a person who identifies with being a colored, Negro, black, African American, or mixed-race person. Use of the term *black* more closely parallels the language used by those being interviewed even when discussing their early lives at a time when the terms "colored" and "Negro" were most frequently used. [See Editorial Note]

Knowing the population demographics provides a context in which the reader can understand the lives of these black Orange County pioneers and their children who moved into this almost all-white county. [2]

In this book, each chapter is comprised of oral histories, the story of each individual's family. We could have chosen to design the book chapters around subject areas such as church, school, housing, and the workplace, but instead we chose to keep the book in the narrative form of the interviews, which we think is generally more interesting to readers. Keeping the family stories together also allowed us to use names and photos without creating confusion in the reader's mind. We have kept a few stories that occurred outside of Orange County because they are great stories involving the interviewee. In our editing process, we have tried to do this without unduly sacrificing the book's historical value.

All of the persons interviewed are African Americans with the exception of the Kennedys from Fullerton. The individual sagas have been chronologically ordered by their arrival in Orange County in each of the book's two parts. The first part includes only those persons whose first Orange County home was in Santa Ana. The second part includes only those who first lived outside of Santa Ana, which we call the suburbs. Because some of the people interviewed moved in to and out of Santa Ana, their story may include both Santa Ana and suburban experiences. Some, like Gladys Smith and her family, first came to Santa Ana and then, as quickly as possible, moved to the suburbs. Others, like Earl Dearing, came to the El Toro Marine Corps base in what is now Irvine and subsequently moved to Santa Ana and stayed there. Some people, like Jessie Allen, moved out of Orange County and eventually moved back to the county. Connie Duffy Farlice never came back to Orange County.

Our choice to include oral histories of people who lived in the suburbs, as well as Santa Ana, was to provide balance to the Orange County story. The total number of black people in the suburbs was roughly equal to the black population of Santa Ana until a spike in the Santa Ana black population in the late-1960s to mid-1970s. We chose to interview both, not only because of the equal numbers, but because often their views and experiences were quite different, even when both were imbedded in neighborhoods that were predominantly Mexican American.

Blacks living in the suburbs, with the exception of those dwelling in a single neighborhood within each of the two north Orange County cities of Fullerton and Placentia, were surrounded by white neighbors, and their children went to almost all-white schools. Often, the black child was the only African American in the class or even in the school. Although this situation created some difficulties, the children learned to navigate in relative comfort, and even to excel in a white world. For parents like Ken and Jo Caines, this was what they wanted for their children. Some children, as they grew into adulthood, remained close to the white world, even marrying into it; others moved in and out or chose to live in both; and some chose to leave Orange County or associate primarily with black friends.

---

[2] Population details, from the years 1920 to 2000, concerning the nineteen largest cities in Orange County, are found in Appendix II. The 2000 Census shows that of the fifty major metropolitan areas in the United States, Orange County has the most dispersed (spread out) population.

Children growing up in the suburbs, and even in Santa Ana, faced a very different world from their parents. Interviewee Zeph Jones was senior class president of Santa Ana High School in 1950, in spite of the fact that there were few black students in the entire school. Chris Caines, whom we interviewed, and Robert Clemons, the son of interviewee Bob Clemons, were student body presidents of their almost-all-white high schools around 1980. Interestingly enough, these latter two high schools were in the city of Orange, formerly a "sundown town." Because the children's histories so often contrasted with those of their parents, we have placed some emphasis on their lives even though their stories are mostly told through their parents' voices and extended into and beyond the 1980s. But, before black families could bring their offspring to the suburbs, they first had to deal with the discrimination they faced in finding a job and in moving into a white neighborhood.

Most, but not all of the people interviewed encountered discrimination at one time or another in obtaining the housing of their choice. For those who had no trouble when coming into the county, discrimination often occurred later when they wanted a more desirable location, either in Santa Ana or the suburbs. When the Mulkeys chose an apartment to rent outside of the "Negro area" of Santa Ana, they were turned down by the owner. In 1963, they sued and that case, *Reitman v. Mulkey*, went to the US Supreme Court in an important and successful effort to invalidate a state anti-fair housing initiative, Proposition 14. But even after a successful effort to move into an apartment or home in a non-black area, some people experienced problems with neighbors, as in the case of Josh White, who was shot at. But these problems most often subsided when the white residents got to know their new black neighbors.

Up until the 1960s, a problem more critical than housing was the lack of good jobs for black people. Orange County's employment was primarily based on agriculture, and blacks simply were not hired for these jobs, because of the availability of better qualified and/or less expensive Mexican, white, and Asian labor. Two exceptions were 100 black strike breakers brought in from Los Angles in 1917 to harvest sugar beet fields and 1,500 Jamaicans hired near the end of World War II to work in La Habra and Irvine. World War II provided some jobs in construction, but most of the jobs in the county until the 1960s were menial and service-oriented (e.g., shoe shining, janitorial, and in the case of women, working as domestics). There were some black businesses that served mostly blacks such as barber shops and restaurants as well as those that served the entire community in areas of building maintenance and cooking.

This narrow range of options changed with industrialization in the 1960s, led by aerospace and electronics companies like Autonetics, Hughes, Aeronutronic-Ford, and Collins Radio. Workers were needed and government contracts depended on these companies providing equal job opportunities for black people. This meant professional-level job openings in business, engineering, and teaching and resulted in the formation of the effective Equal Opportunity Employers Association. Everett Winters tells about how, under black leadership, the organization was formed and its role in breaking down racial barriers and encouraging blacks to work in Orange County. Without work, there was no reason to move to the county. Johnny Williams, one of the early black school teachers hired in Santa Ana, said, "In my family, wherever you find a job, that's where you stay." That is, as Williams might have added, if you are not denied housing where you chose to live.

Bob Clemons's motivation to continue working as an engineer in Orange County was that it was less expensive to purchase a home in the city of Orange than to change jobs and live in a black suburb of Los Angeles. So, job openings, good wages, and lower housing prices resulted in more people having the motivation and financial means to live in Orange County suburbs. Also, motivators included the good schools and a crime-free environment that could be found in the county. On the other hand, Orange County's deserved reputation of being ultra-conservative and libertarian with strong ties to the John Birch Society was an inhibitor to blacks moving into the county. These political realities were reinforced by racial discrimination, making it difficult to rent or purchase housing in the Orange County suburbs. Many who worked in Orange County would drive every day from their home in Los Angeles County.

But some black families did move. As more black people came to live in the county, their numbers ignited the fears and prejudices of the majority of white citizens, resulting in an increased number of cases of racial discrimination. In the early 1960s, the local National Association for the Advancement of Colored People (NAACP) and the American Civil Liberties Union (ACLU), organizations led by people like Everett Winters and Richard Petherbridge, provided legal help based on newly instituted fair housing laws for families seeking housing outside of the "ghetto." The Orange County Fair Housing Council was formed in 1965 in response to the passing of the aforementioned Proposition 14 that invalidated California's fair housing laws. The work of the council is described by early members Gladys Smith, Ralph and Natalie Kennedy, and Jo Caines.[3]

When black persons began moving into suburbia, there were increased incidents of racial profiling and police harassment. This was particularly true regarding blacks being pulled over in traffic. The number of these incidents depended on the city, the looks, dress, age of the driver, and the car being driven. When Wacira Gethaiga was a student at Chapman College in the city of Orange, he was stopped numerous times, whereas marine corpsman Earl Dearing could not recall ever being stopped due to profiling or harassment. Everett Winters

[3] The term "ghetto," as used in this book, is limited to describing three areas in Orange County: Santa Ana, Placentia, and Fullerton. In Santa Ana, the ghetto of the 1920s was northwest of First Street and Bristol Avenue and, in time, expanded south. In Placentia, the ghetto was formed in the late 1950s and early 1960s and was primarily composed of two streets, Missouri and Kansas Avenues, located immediately west of what is now the 57 Freeway. The black community in Fullerton in the mid-1920s grew from the 100 and 200 blocks of East Truslow Avenue to the south and east. The ghetto in Santa Ana, near the peak of black migration to the city, had only one census tract out of 104 that was close to 50 percent black (48.2 percent of a tract population of 2,626 in 1970). The ghetto in Placentia, in the 1960s, was predominantly black, but in Fullerton the ghetto maintained a mixed-race population. So, when the term "ghetto" is used in this book, its primary meaning is an area where the largest percentage of African Americans have congregated, and where housing is obtainable without having to deal with discrimination.

tells about county sheriffs following or stopping him and other blacks in spite of the fact that the officers knew who they were. He also tells about the FBI tracking him in the 1960s. Because of issues like racial profiling, the Orange County Human Relations Council was formed. This predecessor to the present county-sponsored Human Relations Commission is described by one of the people on its formation committee, Joshua White. Less ambiguous was the access to some government facilities and public accommodations in the 1930s, 1940s, and early 1950s.

Although not mentioned in Mary Owens's oral history, her uncle, Neff Cox,[4] worked in the city of Brea but was not allowed to stay there overnight. Ernestine Ransom tells a similar story about helping her mother clean houses in the late 1930s and having to leave the city of Orange before dark. There is no record of any law, ordinance, or resolution to this effect in either city, but it was "common knowledge" that it was not legal for blacks to stay after dark. The penalty for doing this has not been documented.

In the case of swimming in the Orange City Plunge, a public swimming pool located in Hart Park, non-whites had one day in which they could swim. Discrimination was also present in the case of public accommodations, such as restaurants, movie theaters, and clothing stores. Most, but not all of the restaurants in the 1930s and 1940s in Santa Ana would not serve blacks. Also, most clothing stores would not allow blacks to try on clothes. When Connie Duffy was told she could not try on a hat, her mother made her leave and refused to ever again shop at that store. Regarding the movies, one of the three (later, two of the four) theaters in Santa Ana and the theater in Orange made blacks and "Mexicans" sit in the balcony. But, these examples of blatant discrimination are not the whole story. [5]

Generally speaking, in the 1930s and 1940s, most Orange County towns were not "sundown towns" in the literal sense. Of course, racial profiling and housing discrimination were present in all Orange County cities, as in most cities of America. But, unlike cities like Los Angeles and Chicago, there was free access to beaches and parks as well. Connie Duffy Farlice's brothers even had jobs as life guards in Newport Beach. The major county park, Irvine Park, was a favorite place for all races to celebrate occasions or simply have picnics and was mentioned often in the interviews. Blacks were buried in the same cemeteries as whites.

Most black families in the early days simply did not have the money to eat out, and the teenagers—white, Mexican, and black—when going to the beach, would bring their own lunches. Black boys and girls were free to play with Mexican and white friends. Although Zeph Jones maybe had a few more fights because of racial slurs, he, being a football player, did not find that much of a problem. Ernestine

---

[4] See Oral Histories OH 1726 (Thompson) and OH 1720 (Jaster). Neff Cox was a boot black in Brea during the day, was very well liked, earned enough money to bring his relatives to Orange County, but had to go back to Fullerton before dark each night. Cities like Brea and Orange are called "sundown towns."

[5] The term "Mexican" was commonly used to differentiate Anglo Americans from Latin Americans, because Latinos/Hispanics considered themselves white. But, since most of the Latinos in Orange County in the early days were from Mexico or their parents or grandparents were from Mexico, the term "Mexican" was used as an identifier. For example, Connie Duffy Farlice speaks of her best friend as a Mexican girl and not at all in a derogatory way.

Ransom, who came to Orange County as a teenager, liked it in Santa Ana because she did not have to participate in fights like she did in the all-black areas in which she previously lived. Connie Duffy Farlice can only remember one racial slur.

Generally speaking, before the 1960s, because there were so few black children in neighborhoods and schools, black children had few black children to relate to, and therefore, blended into the white and Mexican communities. Each was not perceived as a threat or an outsider, but as simply another player in games, student in school, or friend in the neighborhood.

Sports teams were integrated and no restrictions were placed on where they could play. In the late 1930s and early 1940s, the Duffy boys played sports at Santa Ana High, Bill going on to play for UCLA. Brig Owens, the famous Washington Redskin football player, as with six of his brothers, was an outstanding athlete. This was in the 1950s and 1960s at the mostly white Fullerton High School. Another exceptional athlete from Fullerton was Thomas Berkley, who came with his parents to live in this city in 1931 while he was in high school. His sister, Ruby Berkley Goodwin, was in her late twenties at that time and through studies at Fullerton Junior College, she began her writing career.[6] Thomas Berkley became a famous attorney and publisher of the *Oakland Post* and Ruby became well known as an author. Ruby's son Robert went from elementary school through Fullerton Junior College and became one of the first black script writers for Hollywood movies and television. Although all of the Berkley family members who settled in Fullerton were deceased before the final group of oral histories were taken, it is important to note that they were forerunners to a number of those interviewed who were also involved in writing, television, and theater production. This included interviewees Jo Caines at TV station KOCE and Adleane Hunter, who made theater production her lifetime profession

Parents, particularly in Santa Ana, mostly socialized with other black families and sometimes were members of fraternal orders like the Masons, as were Warren Bussey and John Smith. Although the church was the major institution in the black community, only one pastor was interviewed. But, almost all who were interviewed were asked about their relationship with the church. In contrast to their parents, the second generation had broad social outlets with friends of all races and did not depend as much on the black church. Although there was always interracial dating because the black community was small, interracial marriage only became common in the 1970s and beyond. As often as not, the children of those who were interviewed married someone of another race.

In determining which interviews to include in this book, there was an attempt to choose a wide spectrum of interviewees, including almost an equal number of women and men doing a wide variety of work. If in the selection of the interviewees there is an unbalance, it is tipped toward the notable or exceptional. Notable, for example, are Ed Caruthers, the Olympic silver medal winner in the high jump during the 1968 Olympics, and as already mentioned, Dottie Mulkey, famous for her involvement in the landmark case, *Reitman v. Mulkey.* Many

[6] Ruby Berkley Goodwin wrote the popular autobiography *It's Good to be Black* (1953), the story of her experiences as a child in the small town of Du Quoin, Illinois.

selected for inclusion in this book are also notable, in a local sense, because of the outstanding work they have done in the county. But, possibly the tilt towards these exceptional people is justified in that the Orange County black community, considering its small size, has been exceptional in many areas of the community at large. But, this should be expected of people who had the grit and courage to move to Orange County and deal with being black in a white milieu, and also have the intelligence and education to compete as equals in school and the workforce in this highly competitive Orange County society.

Part One

My First Orange County Home Was in Santa Ana

Introduction

Constance Duffy was born in 1922, in an early-1920s-style narrow frame house her father, Willis Duffy, had contracted with Simon Fluor to build. This is the same Simon Fluor who, in time, created the huge corporation, Fluor Construction. Their home was the first house west of the southwest corner of Bristol and Fourth Street in Santa Ana, in roughly the center of a twelve-block area, in which the majority of Santa Ana's black population lived. Her father had come to Santa Ana in 1913 or maybe a little earlier. He had a bootblack business, then worked for the Elks Club, bought and sold property, and eventually had his own barbecue business. Connie Duffy Farlice's story provides us with a picture of what it was like in the 1920s-30s growing up as a black child in the midst of mostly white and Hispanic neighbors.

Santa Ana is near the geographic center of Orange County. Though it is not the largest city in area, throughout the twentieth century, Santa Ana had the largest population in the county. In 1889, when its citizens chose to separate from Los Angeles County, Santa Ana was picked as the seat of the new County of Orange. From its beginnings through the first half of the twentieth century, most of the land surrounding Santa Ana was utilized for farms and orchards. The farm workers were inclined to live on the outskirts of town near their work in the orchards, fields, and sugar beet processing and orange packing plants. The Mexican American workers lived in barrios like Logan in the east, and Delhi in the southeast, but a greater number of Latino families lived in the west part of the city.

It was also in the west, near the Duffys, where a majority of the black families coming into the city were absorbed. The county directory of 1926 shows a scattering of black families, among mostly white families, on the west side. In the area from Second Street north to Fifth Street, and one block east and two blocks west of Bristol, there were ten black family units along with a small number of Mexican American families. Four blocks further west and on Eighth Street. stood the Second Baptist Church and its parsonage. South and west of the church lived the majority of the Hispanic workers. The 1926 directory showed only five other black families in Santa Ana: one downtown, one on the east side of town and the other three just outside of the Bristol and Fourth twelve-block area. The estimated African American population in Santa Ana near the end of 1925 was fifty-five; this was up from twenty-two, according to the census of 1920.[1]

Unlike most men in the Mexican[2] community, blacks in Santa Ana did not work in the fields; instead, they held traditional service jobs typical in many areas of America where the black population was small compared to the dominant white community. Of the fifteen males listed in the directory as heads of households, three worked as bootblacks (shined shoes), three were porters, two were janitors,

---

[1] See Appendix II for U.S. Census population data on major Orange County cities, in ten year increments, from 1920 (or date of incorporation) to the year 2000.

[2] The term "Mexican" is used throughout this oral history by the interviewees, to identify Hispanics. There was no attempt to differentiate between citizens and non-citizens, nor was the identification intended to be pejorative.

and one was a cook. Also included was Reverend Hill from Second Baptist and Connie Duffy's father, Willis, who was listed as: Steward, Elks Club. The work of the other four "colored"[3] men was not included in the directory. By 1930, when Connie Duffy was eight years old, the black population of Santa Ana had risen to 109, out of a total population of 30,322, still mostly residing in the west part of town.

In 1930, Baxter Young graduated from Santa Ana High School and proceeded to work as a bootblack and dishwasher. Later, he worked as a janitor, and finally, he worked in construction when jobs opened up at the end of the Depression. Earlier, in 1926, Bernice Young's father, Edward McKinney, had come to Santa Ana. He had a shoe-shine stand and before his family came the next year, he had built a home. From that first job as a bootblack, he, like his son-in-law, took on work as a janitor.

Wives also worked outside of the home. The most common job was cleaning white people's homes, not only in Santa Ana, but also houses from Newport Beach to the city of Orange. In the 1930s, the children also made a little money by shining shoes or helping in their parents' cleaning businesses. It was not hard work like picking cotton in the southwestern United States. In fact, Connie Duffy had fun waiting tables for her father at the Elks Club's weekly dinner.

By 1940, the black population of Santa Ana had increased to 158. He was still a small number, but the total population of the city had barely increased during the decade of the 1930s. Once World War II started, better jobs opened up, particularly in the construction of the military bases, and by the end of the 1940s, the black population had increased to 433. Again, while not a large number of people, it did represent a much larger percentage change than in the city as a whole. Roughly half of the African American population was still located in the west part of Santa Ana. Was this by choice?

In the early 1950s, renting or purchasing a home on the west side meant moving into an expanding integrated neighborhood, one that was still mostly white, with decent schools and few social problems. Living near Fourth and Bristol also meant living near the black churches and other black families. Except for a paucity of good jobs and your child being the only black kid in his or her class, life was not bad. But, for new marine families, relatives, and blacks who had job opportunities, moving to west Santa Ana was not a choice. Realtors steered black families who wanted to purchase homes to west Santa Ana. Steering is a polite word for refusing to show homes outside of the designated Negro areas. Apartment house owners and managers more and more refused to rent to blacks who tried to find housing in their all-white parts of town. In 1950, property owners could still be sued for allowing non-white persons to live in property or purchase property covered by racial covenants. But this was not something new.

The area north of downtown Santa Ana for many years had been reserved for white folks of means. New housing developments were covered by racial housing covenants that, by law, prohibited people not of the Caucasian race from living there. The best known of these neighborhoods,

[3] Black families in the directory had a "(c)," designating "colored," following their name.

along Victoria Drive, was formed in 1925. By 1935, living in this segregated neighborhood were the families of prominent people like publisher R. C. Hoiles, his son Clarence Hoiles, and lima bean grower Anton Segerstrom.[4]

As increasing employment opportunities in Orange County's small, but new, industries opened in the 1950s, there was a greater desire by black families to live in areas outside of those designated for them by white realtors and builders. By 1952, the racial covenants were no longer enforceable and in 1959, the Unruh Public Accommodations Act was expanded to include rental housing. Although these changes had little effect far outside of the area designated Negro, this area, block by block, expanded south of the Duffys' original neighborhood, which itself became increasingly black. By 1960, the black population of Santa Ana had increased to 1,759, which was a four-fold increase during the decade of the 1950s.

Finally, starting in the 1960s, major industrialization of the county began. This took many forms, but the major players were in aerospace and electronics, and like the US Marine Corps Air Station, El Toro, the majority of these companies were located outside of Santa Ana. But still, pressure exerted by the white housing industry and the fears of white property owners was to confine blacks to the "ghetto" in Santa Ana. Therefore, while incoming blacks took jobs outside of Santa Ana, due to racial discrimination, they were pressured to live in southwest Santa Ana. Some fought this situation, but others chose to live there rather than file lawsuits and become unwanted persons in all-white neighborhoods. For some, like the family of Gladys Smith, living in Santa Ana was a temporary housing solution. Her husband was an engineer who worked in Newport Beach. Frustrated by not being able to rent outside of Santa Ana and not knowing any better, the Smiths moved into the Myrtle Street apartment complex. Due to his changing jobs, her husband had to make a number of business trips to the Bay Area. In Gladys Smith's words, "The first weekend he was gone I heard somebody was knifed down the street, and I was scared to leave the apartment. Then I think the next month he was gone and somebody got shot. So when he came home, I said, 'We gotta move, we gotta get out of here!'" They got their rental deposits back and moved to a safer apartment complex, but still in Santa Ana. Later they moved to Tustin and then to Irvine.

The process the Smiths went through was not unusual: "My first Orange County home was in Santa Ana and then . . . " So, as black families moved into Santa Ana in relatively large numbers, small numbers of black families moved to the "suburbs." The result was an expanding black population in Santa Ana in the 1960s that now included people like Everett Winters and Gladys Smith's husband Ervin Smith. Both men had the civil rights experience needed in working with others to help create or enlarge viable organizations like the local National Association for the Advancement of Colored People (NAACP), the home-grown Equal Opportunity Employers Association, and the Orange County Fair Housing Council. But, of all those who moved into Santa Ana, the most significant person

---

[4] *Santa Ana Register*, January 28, 1925. The racial covenant covering the Victoria property deeds read, "No person or persons other than a member of the Caucasian race shall be permitted to use or occupy any portion of said land, except a family servant." Also, "The above mentioned conditions, covenants and restrictions shall be inserted in any deed hereinafter made, conveying any lot, piece or parcel of land front or abutting upon said street."

was a woman who, in 1963, upon having served in the US Navy, moved into her first home in Orange County, her husband Lincoln's parents' home. It was Dorothy Mulkey who soon after that move made history by filing a law suit against a Santa Ana apartment house owner unwilling to rent to her and her husband because of their race. She and her husband, with the help of the NAACP and the American Civil Liberties Union (ACLU), pursued the case for four years.

The result of the *Reitman v. Mulkey* housing discrimination suit, which was settled in the US Supreme Court, was the restoration of fair housing laws in the state of California. The impact was so important that it was enough to discourage other states, which might so choose, from eliminating fair housing laws. With regard to Orange County, the Mulkey suit, along with other lawsuits and a change in white attitudes (possibly due to the fear of lawsuits being stronger than the fear of black neighbors) resulted in a greater movement of black people both into and out of Santa Ana. In the 1960s, as in the 1950s, there again was a four-fold increase in the number of black residents. But, by 1974, the percentage of African Americans in the city began to decline and by the early to mid 1980s, the total number of black people living in Santa Ana peaked at roughly 8,300 residents.[5]

In this introduction, the demographics of the movement of black people into the city of Santa Ana have been outlined through the use of oral histories, directories, and census data. To follow, in Chapter 1, the reader can find the stories of Santa Ana, pre-World War II, and African American pioneers. Chapter 2 is devoted to the stories of those persons who grew up in Santa Ana after WWII, while Chapter 3 relates the stories of adults who first came to Santa Ana during the times of major growth in the 1960s.

[5] U.S. Supreme Court, *Reitman v. Mulkey*, 387 U.S. 369 (1967).

Chapter 1
Growing Up in a Small Black Community

Constance Duffy and Zeph Jones were born and raised in Santa Ana. Connie left for college in 1940 and Zeph for the US Army in 1952. Although there was roughly a ten-year difference in their ages, they both experienced growing up in an environment not much different from white kids living in small-town Middle America. With the exception of having to sit in the balconies of two movie theaters and not being allowed to eat at most restaurants, there was very little they and their Mexican American friends couldn't do that the white kids could. So, outside of the home, they lived with their Latino, white, and few black friends in a white world.

Vern Napier was only a year old when his family arrived in 1942. They first settled on the west side of town, and by the time Napier was school-age, they had moved to the east side, where there were only a few Negro children—maybe four in his school—some of Mexican descent and the rest white. By the time the family moved back to the west side, Napier was a teenager who found some difficulty navigating in the emerging black community. So, although living in Santa Ana a decade later than Zeph Jones, like Jones and Duffy, he found himself comfortable in the mostly white world.

Of the people interviewed for this chapter, the oldest were Bernice and Baxter Young. Baxter came from El Centro, California, where he went to segregated schools with blacks and Mexicans Americans together. When his family arrived in Santa Ana, in 1929, he entered Santa Ana High School as a junior. This was difficult for him because he had never gone to school with whites and certainly not a school of 1,400, which had only two African American boys. Bernice Young came to Santa Ana two years earlier than Baxter, but as a twelve-year-old. From the oral history, the racial makeup of Bernice's previous schools and neighborhoods is unclear, but both Mr. and Mrs. Young, as adults, were comfortable being a part of Santa Ana's small black community. After all, Baxter had his own barbershop there.

Ernestine Ransom, who is about the same age as Connie Duffy Farlice, is the daughter of a Baptist pastor. She grew up in Oklahoma and Arkansas, moving to Topeka, Kansas, from where the family moved to Santa Ana in 1937, when her father assumed the pastorate of the Second Baptist Church. She was fifteen years old when they arrived and she entered Santa Ana High School. Although she was one of the few blacks at school, she had gone to an integrated school in Topeka and liked the fact that she did not have to engage in fights like in Kansas, due to her being a newcomer in numerous black schools she attended in Arkansas. Mrs. Ransom's mixed-race growing-up cumulated in her positive high school experience and allowed her to be comfortable, as an adult, in both the black and white communities.

CONSTANCE DUFFY FARLICE[1]

Constance Farlice was born in Santa Ana in 1922 in the Duffy family home at 4th and Bristol. Her father worked for many years at the Elks Club, along with owning his own barbecue business. Her brothers were outstanding athletes and had exceptional careers after college. They, like Connie, chose to live outside of Orange County in spite of the fact that their mother and father continued to live in the 4th Street home after their children had left. Mrs. Farlice lives in Los Angeles; both of her brothers have passed away. Photo ca. 1940.

What were your parents' names?

My mother's name was [Victoria] Minnie Canniville Duffy and my father's name was Willis Kiel Duffy. My mother was from Charleston, South Carolina. My father was born in Glasgow, Kentucky.

Tell me about your father's life before he met your mother.

He had quite a history. My father actually ran away from home. He was a product of a young girl that worked for an attorney in Glasgow. Of course, he was white and the young girl was black. His two white aunts were raising him, but they made it very clear that they didn't care anything about him. So when he got to be seven years old, he ran away to Bluegrass Country; he used to run over there to watch the horses. So he asked the men working there—they had seen him a lot—could he live there because he didn't have anyplace to live. They accepted him and he stayed there.

It happened that Lucky Baldwin, who is quite famous, took a liking to my dad and kind of reared him. So he became a jockey for Lucky. Then, as he began to travel with Lucky to the various places where the horses were running—I know he used to mention Saratoga Springs, New York, and even San Francisco, and I can't recall the other places, but he used to talk a lot about them. Of course, Santa

[1] Oral History No. 3540. Interview date: April 4, 2007, at the home of Duffy's daughter Viki Ward in Los Angeles, California. Interviewer: Robert Johnson.

Anita, here in southern California, was Lucky's home. He had a ranch there called the Santa Anita Ranch, and that is where the racetrack is today. Daddy stayed there and was raised there. He said he came out here at about the age of eighteen with Lucky.

He stayed there with Lucky, and then went to Santa Ana [in 1913 or earlier].[2] [Later he answered] an ad. They wanted a chef and steward at the Elks Club. That had to be about 1918. He accepted that position. And then he had his own catering business. He had a large barbecue business that he put on annual barbecues—they were really nice—at what then was Orange County Park. It's, I think, Irvine Park now. He met my mother through a mutual friend in Los Angeles, and in 1919 or 1920, I believe, they married and he brought my mother to Santa Ana to live and built her a home there. That's where my younger brother and I were born, in that house; 1306 West 4th Street was the address.

Tell us about your mother.

My mother was from Charleston, South Carolina, and she was educated and raised by the nuns in a school in Rock Castle, Virginia. She was there because she was orphaned. She was the youngest of ten. They all passed but one sister, Gertrude. But Gertrude went to the school and told the nuns that she had her little sister, who was my mother, and she wanted to bring her up there with the Catholic nuns. They were Catholic anyway. She was raised right there.

Oh, incidentally, the nun who is a saint in the Catholic Church, St. Katherine Drexel, was my mother's catechism teacher. She built the school and it was called St. Francis DeSales. She also built Xavier University. She was one of the Drexels, and she dedicated her life to helping the Negroes and Indians, which they were called in those days.

My mother was fortunate to be able to live there, and Gertrude, my aunt; she was the mother to all the girls because she brought in the Indian and the black girls. She stayed there, and there was a lady by the name of Miss Ferguson, who was a wealthy white lady. She wrote the nuns and asked, "Please send me one of your girls. I want a traveling companion. She'll have everything. She'll have her own living quarters." Fortunately, she loved animals. My mother had to have a dog. She loved dogs. So she went to live with Miss Ferguson in Cape May, New Jersey, after she graduated from St. Francis DeSales. She stayed with Miss Ferguson during the flu epidemic of 1918.

My mother got the flu, she was very ill, and the doctor suggested that she go to a warmer place, California or someplace, where she would be safe, because they said she would never survive another winter. So she went to teach. She taught for the nuns in—I think it was in New Mexico someplace. I think she was there a very short time, maybe two years or so, and she went to visit her schoolmate, who also went to St. Francis DeSales. She was living in Los Angeles, so she invited my mother to come and spend some time with her. My mother said, "That's good. I've never been to California."

---

[2] Before working for the Elks Club, he had a shoe shining business. His ad was placed in the *Santa Ana Daily Register* on October 11, 1913.

So, anyway, she went. She was a single woman. And there's where she met my dad. She married my dad and they settled there in Santa Ana. Let's see. I think my oldest brother was born in 1920, so it was probably 1919. They were married here in Los Angeles at Vermont and Western, a Catholic church. It was a good marriage for them. My mother gave up everything, the New York life that she had had, which was wonderful. She gave up everything to go to this small town. She didn't socialize. She went, of course, to our church, which was the St. Joseph's parish. And she had three children. She had my brother Jerome, myself, and my younger brother Bill.

And you said Jerome was born in what year?

Well, it had to be '20 because he was eighteen months older than I, and I came in '22. And Bill came in 1926. I understand she lost one in between us. Jerome, the oldest one, was born in the hospital because my dad thought that would be safer. But, Bill and I, we were born right there in the house. We kept that home, and my mother stayed there even after my father passed. It was twenty-five years after Daddy passed that my mother passed, but she stayed right there in the house.

Did you know who built that house?

Yes, Fluor Construction. Because we knew the Fluors well. I went to school with a girl by the name of Lillian. She married the oldest Fluor [child], Bob Fluor. He was a junior. My father, I have to say, was a very well-loved man in Santa Ana. He knew everybody. The chief of police, everybody used to come by the house. The one we enjoyed the most was—we called him Old Man Irvine, the one that owned all the Irvine property. He used to come because my dad used to make wine and home brew in the cellar, and Mr. Irvine would come, with a chauffeur, and he and my dad would go downstairs into the basement. We called it the cellar. The young son—it must have been his grandson—used to stay upstairs with my brother Jerome and I, and we would play games like checkers. And we'd be up there until Mr. Irvine came back up with his stash, and he would go on.

During Prohibition.

That's right. Even the chief of police was enjoying it. My father was really very well loved, very much liked. He was a wonderful, wonderful man. He was very charitable and helped his own people. The blacks that moved in, he saw to it that they got jobs at the Elks Club with him, the ladies and the men. Some of the white ladies that worked for him, they used to tell me, "I don't like working for your dad because he's too fussy." But he used to put a pan of Lysol and water by the door. If they left the room, whether they went to smoke a cigarette or use the restroom, he made them put their hands in this when they came back, and they didn't like that. Then there was plain water to rinse.

I worked with him, too, now and again, when I wasn't in school. I finished St. Joseph's in Santa Ana in 1936. I started high school, which was nine, tenth, eleventh, and twelfth, at Marywood Girls Catholic High in Anaheim. There were only about fifteen or sixteen in my graduation class, and I was the only black in the whole school. They didn't know too much about us at that time, but the nuns were just wonderful. I enjoyed my four years there. It was a very happy time for me.

Then one of the nuns, Sister Saint Basil, God bless her, she made arrangements for me to go to Immaculate Heart College, which was then in Hollywood. The high school's still there. I finished there in '44. I got my Bachelor of Science degree, and I still thank Sister Saint Basil. She's long gone, but to this day I'm grateful to her and the nuns at Immaculate Heart and Marywood for giving me my education.

Since we're talking about the schools, how did you get across town to go to St. Joseph's? Wasn't that on the other side of town?

Yes. I had a bicycle. We all rode bicycles. In fact, I can tell you something that was most enjoyable in my childhood. During the summers, we used to ride. My dearest friend lived in Placentia. Pauline DeLeon, God bless her. We still correspond. She lives in Anaheim. We used to ride our bicycles—there would be a group, maybe ten of us—down to Newport Beach, spend the day in the sand, and ride home at sundown. There were no freeways. A car would come by and we'd hear "chuk, chuk, chuk, chuk," and then they'd say "aoooga, aoooga." That was the horn. And we would all go to the side, and they'd go "chukking" through. I think the fastest they could go may have been twenty-five or thirty-five in those days.

So would she come from Placentia down to your house? And then you took what, Main Street?

Yeah, we'd go either Main or Broadway—I think primarily Main—straight into Costa Mesa. Then in Costa Mesa they had some kind of a water fountain, and we were told this was health water. It would revive you and make you younger. And, of course, we had to stop in Costa Mesa. That was a very small area at that time. Then we'd cross over the little bridge, and into Newport Beach. Lido Isle was kind of new then, and my daddy dedicated Lido Isle. It's a man-made isle. We could swim over to Lido Isle and swim back to Newport Bay. We stayed at the bay side. I don't think we ever went to the ocean, not much until I was much older.

And you had no problems as one of the few black children?

Nobody paid any attention to us. We had some dear friends. In fact, they had the mortuary in Santa Ana, the Browns. In fact, as a graduation gift from Marywood, she gave my class a whole weekend at her home. That was my graduation gift, and that was at Newport Bay. So I brought my whole class from Marywood there for the weekend.

How did you get to Anaheim, then, to high school?

The nuns had a large old-time limousine then. There were five of us from Santa Ana, and they would pick us up in Santa Ana and bring us home in the evening. The same girls that rode with us, we went through grammar school together. We went through St. Joseph's and then the five of us went to Marywood.

Were the children from school your closest friends? Or were the neighborhood kids your closest friends?

They were not my closest friends, just classmates. My dearest friend was the girl next door, because in my area there were predominately the Mexicans, and my dearest friend was a girl, Celia Sifuentes, that lived next door to me. We remained friends. Celia, she was ten and I was eleven when she moved next door. I didn't have too much connection with the girls from school because they lived on the other side of town. Of course, I just associated with the Mexican kids because that was my neighborhood.

Or your friend from Placentia. How did you meet her?

Pauline? We went to high school together. She was in Marywood. We went the four years, and we became fast friends, and we are to this day, bless her heart. She's very dear to me. It was no surprise to have her come up on a Sunday afternoon on her bike from Placentia. Her dad had an orange ranch there. We had a lot of fun.

When you were small, in your neighborhood, would you play in the street, or would you go to the park?

Well, my dad had his barbecues lined up almost weekly through the summer for different organizations there in Santa Ana. The only one he turned down was the Ku Klux Klan. He told them, "No, I'm not going to bother. You can get somebody else." But the churches and different people had annual barbecues for their employees, so Daddy put them on. We spent a lot of time at Irvine Park. We used to ride the horses. They had horses, they had ponies. We spent a lot of weekends there.

And the family drove a car to the park?

Oh, yes. My mother had a 1925 Studebaker, and she would drive. But my dad had a wonderful business partner. His name was Tony Barrios. He was a Mexican—wonderful, wonderful man. Tony and my dad, they had a little truck. They used to go out to the Japanese farms to buy their produce. They didn't have frozen foods then. If they were going to have a big barbecue, they'd go out. That's another thing—my brothers, my youngest brother mainly, we used to love to go out there with him because they used to give us things. The Japanese people were so wonderful. This was before they were evacuated, of course. They were such dear friends, and they liked my dad. We would take the little truck and go out there.

It was near where Disneyland is now. Disneyland was an orange grove, and when I went to school, we turned right there on—that was Harbor, and when it crossed Manchester, it became Palms, and the school was on Palms and Broadway, right in the middle of Anaheim. Incidentally, there was an article in the paper one time where some man said he was an old Orange Countian and that he remembered when Disneyland had boysenberries. It was not boysenberries, it was oranges. And the day we had a freeze—1938 I think—and the poor man lost his grove. When we passed that corner, the fruit was coal black. It had frozen. We felt so sorry, because you had to have smudge pots.

He had the pots, but I think he couldn't afford the oil. He was burning rubber tires and all kind of things, and we prayed for him when we got to school. We felt so bad. This poor man lost his grove. That's when they fenced it up and it went for sale for a long time. Then I remember when they said Disney bought it. We said, "What is he going to do with that grove?" But in the center of that grove was a hollow area where if it rained it would be like a lake in there, and we said, "It's got a lake in it. What's Disney going to do with that place?"

Tell me what you would do when you were little.

My mother and my dad kept me kind of busy. My mother taught me to sew, and I used to thank God I did because I had five daughters and I was able to make their clothes. I took sewing, I took dancing, and I took what in those days was called Expressionalism. I entertained around Orange County, in the senior citizen groups and the churches and things. I used to recite for them. I started around twelve to fifteen, and I think when I got to be eighteen I kind of dropped off along the way to go to school. But I entertained quite a bit. I took dancing.

Where did you take dancing lessons?

The lady's name was Miss Getty, but it was just downtown Santa Ana, in the second story building there. I took tap dancing. I never took ballet or anything. I wasn't that dainty. But I did take tap dancing. I loved it, and I did a few little programs. Then at the West End Theater I sang. They had what they call a show, and whoever won would get twenty-five dollars. I won and I got my twenty-five dollars. I sang "I Must Have Been a Beautiful Baby." I'll never forget that. How long ago that was.

Which of those theaters didn't allow blacks downstairs?

That was the one on Spurgeon and 4th, I think. One time there was a movie I wanted to see, and my mother said, "Okay, come on. We'll go." When we got there, they said, "You have to sit upstairs," and my mother said, "No. If we have to sit upstairs, we won't go." So we just didn't go. We never frequented that theater. We always went down on Broadway to the West Coast or the other one.

How about sports? Of course, your brothers were so well known in sports. How about yourself? Were you pretty good?

Well, when I was younger I was on the varsity for both basketball and volleyball in high school. I was terrible at tennis. Never could grasp it too well, although I played for years after. I took music, too. My mother, oh, she was adamant on that. My oldest brother became quite a musician. In fact, I have a son that plays at weddings and funerals and everything. I never was good. My poor mother spent all this on me, and I think often—I pray for my dear piano teacher, Mr. Garstang. God bless him. He was so patient with me. In fact, I have to laugh now at the

Red Cars

The "Red Car" was the name used for the street-cars (electric light-rail trains or trolleys) owned and operated by the Pacific Electric Railway. A person could ride a Red Car from eastern Santa Ana to downtown Los Angeles or to Long Beach. The railway tracks followed Fourth Street west through downtown Santa Ana, past Fourth and Bristol Street to Artesia Street (now Raitt Street). From Artesia, the trains traveled northwest on a straight line through Garden Grove, Stanton, and Cypress in Orange County, to the Watts station in Los Angeles County. At Watts, trains branched straight north to downtown Los Angeles or straight south to Long Beach. Another rail line ran from Fourth and Main Streets in Santa Ana to the city of Orange, while still another ran from Fourth Street, south past the Delhi beet-sugar plant and the World War II Santa Ana Army Air Base, eventually arriving in Huntington Beach. From there, trains went to Newport Beach and Long Beach.

annual recital. I played the same song I think for four years in a row. I never could get above it. It was the "Flower Song." But he was such a dear man, God bless him. I never excelled, but today I sing in a choir and I *can* read music.

I taught for a couple of years in Watts at a Catholic school, St. Leo's. I taught the first and second grades. After I finished school and got my degree, I wanted to go into hospital work, but I couldn't get in. For some reason, the nun that taught me, Sister Agatha—God bless her, too—she wouldn't recommend me to get into a program. This is my first time to really—maybe second or third time—to feel prejudice. She recommended everybody else in the class, and they all went to St. Vincent's Hospital. So I had a pastor, Father Birch at Holy Name Church there where I attended, and he said, "Well, listen, I got a job for you." I had worked with the Catholic youth anyway, through college. I was living in the westside of Los Angeles.

And then would come home on weekends?

On the weekends, yes. The Red Car, Pacific Electric, was our main transportation, the main vein to go through Orange County, because the servicemen used it. It went right by my house in Santa Ana. It used to go right down 4th Street and it ended there in downtown Santa Ana. But it accommodated the servicemen. There were fifty thousand boys there, stationed in Santa Ana, out near Costa Mesa. It was the Santa Ana Army Air Base, that's what it was called. That was another thing—the Mexican boys, most of them went into the service, and they were the orange pickers for Orange County, and when they left, nobody was picking the oranges.

When the Japanese were evacuated, I was in college. I had three darling friends; we went to Immaculate Heart together. They were there one day and gone the next. We corresponded for years, and now they were in camp. As I say, they put the big Santa Ana Army Air Base out there, and there were so many boys—they liked Orange County. They either brought their wives out or married local girls. So the people who had the oranges, there was nothing to do but tear the orange groves out and build these real inexpensive little homes. I don't know if they're still around, or not.

People just got rid of the oranges. My father used to say, "Oh, what a crime to kill these beautiful trees." And people that my father knew well used to bring us crates of oranges that they would pick before the trees were destroyed. And we had two orange trees, a Valencia and a Navel.

At your house on 4th Street?

Yes. They're still there, I guess. They produced beautifully. Of course, everybody in the neighborhood grew some kind of fruit. We had plums and—oh, Daddy planted peach trees, orange trees, lemon trees, guava trees, and of course the orange trees, and fig trees. All through the years we had a lot of fruit. And the neighbors had fruit, and we exchanged. It was so nice.

You mentioned that there were a couple of other times that you experienced discrimination or racism.

Yes. One, when I finished St. Joseph's. There was an organization called the YLI, which is Young Ladies Institute. Everybody in the class, when you graduated from eighth grade, were invited to join this organization, and I was the only one not invited. Then my mother investigated, and they said Negroes were not allowed. And that was a Catholic organization. I understand now the president of it is a black lady. But, anyway, I was hurt. I think that was the first big hurt that I felt, and here I was an eighth grader. But I overcame it. I went on into Marywood and enjoyed my years. I was very active in drama, and I had the lead, I must say, in everything I went in, because I was a dialectician and they used me a lot. Then when I went to Immaculate Heart, I was instrumental in starting the drama organization.

I was extremely active in there. It was four very happy years for me there. In the operettas and in the stage plays, I was always in all of them. I never felt that I was black. We had one girl I'll never forget. She was from Honduras, Central America, and it was when the movie with Jennifer Jones was made, and they came to the school to pick [a black girl to play a role] —she was definitely a black girl, but she didn't want to be, which was okay. She wouldn't speak to me. The whole four years she never spoke to me. One girl said to me one day, "How come you don't look Negro, she does, and she says she's not and you say you are?" I said, "Well, that's up to Alicia." They picked her to be in it. She was in the classroom and answered the question when the nun asked the question in the movie. She had a big part, big part.

Was there another thing that happened?

After you finish and you get your Bachelor of Science degree, you can become a medical technologist, but I could not achieve that until I had a year as an apprentice in a hospital under qualified technologists. I couldn't get in. My daddy was the chef for the nuns at St. Joseph's Hospital there in Orange. The nuns had a convent and he was their chef. So Sister Superior, Mother Josephine, she said, "Duffy, didn't your daughter take a course in science? Is she working?" And my daddy said, "I don't think she's working in her field." Sister said, "Well, we need somebody very badly at St. Luke Hospital in Pasadena." So the nuns called me, I went for an interview, I went there to work, I trained, and I passed my state board all at St. Luke in Pasadena.

And your brother did some acting, because I found a newspaper article that showed him and an older man.

Jerome. Yes, he did. He did some acting there in Santa Ana. Jerome was a very brilliant and versatile gentleman, I must say. My brother was really something.

Tell me about your brother.

Well, Jerome, he had a lot of hurt, but he was an outstanding athlete. He held several high school records for years. I was busy going to school so I wasn't always around to hear about them, but I heard about them later. Jerome held the 220 low hurdles and the 440-yard dash high school records for many years. He was really an outstanding athlete. Then when he finished high school, he went to Santa Ana Junior College for a couple of years, and then he went up north to Cal Berkeley, where he entered the ROTC there. He liked the army, so he went into the service.

He went immediately and it seemed to me that he went overseas. It was right in the midst of the war. He married Juanita [she was black]; when he came back they married. She had three pregnancies, Juanita, all boys, because she traveled with him, and all three of them died at the age of forty-eight hours. Then he adopted three. He said, "Well, maybe God wants me to take three others," so he did. Vincent, Maria, and Vicky he adopted. God, they're so precious.

Maria was Korean and white, and the nuns wanted Jerome to take her. She was talking and walking when he got her. Vincent was Korean and black, and Vicky was Chinese and black. As my brother traveled around, he would adopt these little children. He would send children back here. Vincent, the oldest one, grew up to be a big husky kid. They sent him to Catholic schools, and in high school he was the only freshman that was on the varsity football team, because he got so big and strong. Vincent, today he lives out near Bakersfield. He married a Mexican girl, and they have two sons.

And Jerome retired from the military? Was that his career?

That was his career, and he retired as a full colonel. Juanita traveled with him. He got several awards in Germany, I understand. He was always getting awards. He was quite an achiever. Like his wife always said, "Jerome always wanted to be in charge." And I said, "Yes, even as a young boy he was in charge."

His son—he had two of his own and the three he adopted—his oldest son, Billy, is a basketball agent. He has Yao Ming—quite a few. I understand he's in Africa now looking for some more players. Billy said he had thirty-two underneath him. So he's quite a guy. Bill Duffy is his name.

Where did you learn to swim?

At Newport Bay, right there. In fact, my brothers threw me in. They said, "You've got to learn." I was kind of young, so—there were no homes there hardly at the time. There was a little thing that you could walk way out, like a little walkway way out in the middle of the bay. My brothers would take me. One would be under my arms and one with my feet and swing me out. So I had to learn. I learned to swim there. I was, I guess, in high school.

Did you get to swim in Santa Ana or in Orange?

My brothers and I went to the Santa Ana High School pool. We went in and I guess—I don't know this, but I guess we were the only blacks in the pool at the time. Whether they didn't want us in there or not, they never said anything to me or my brothers. But we all became pretty good swimmers. My brothers both were lifeguards, at Newport I think, during summer vacations. They were paid.[3]

So your brothers, they didn't go to Catholic schools, though.

A short time. But they didn't have sports then. Both of them started St. Joseph's, but Bill went to Willard. That was a junior high then. And Jerome went to Santa Ana High. Both of them, I believe, graduated from Santa Ana High.

Tell me about Bill now. What sports was Bill in?

Bill excelled in football. He went to UCLA, and he played on the team there. There was a certain amount of discrimination there because there were not that many blacks on the team, and the [new] coach, Red Sanders [from the University of Tennessee], he didn't

Swimming Policy in Pre-World War II Orange County

Unlike Los Angeles County in the 1930s and 1940s, black children in Orange County enjoyed the summer pleasures of swimming at the beaches of their choice in the Pacific Ocean and Balboa Bay. That was true of Santa Ana's pools as well, but not true of the Orange city plunge at Hart Park. The "plunge," as the swimming pool in nearby city of Orange was called, had a "Mexican Day" on Mondays. It was the only day Mexicans were allowed to swim. It is claimed that the pool was drained that night and was closed on Tuesday for cleaning and re-filling.

Although it is possible that other plunges in Orange County were segregated, such as the Anaheim Park pool, the beaches were not. Connie Duffy Farlice states that her two brothers were lifeguards in the 1930s (she thinks at Newport Beach). In 1920, a black man, Henry Brooks, was one of the two Huntington Beach lifeguards. Brooks was the adopted son of Ella Casselle, the "lone colored resident" of Huntington Beach. There was also the dramatic rescue of a white woman by a young "colored boy," Henry Maunder, off of the Balboa jetty in 1933. For his heroic deed, he was given the highest Boy Scout honor, the Award for Life Saving, in 1935. Maunder later became a volunteer on the Newport Beach life-saving squad, and was first vice-president of the Newport Harbor Union High School student body.

[3] Unlike Los Angeles, there did not seem to be a problem for black people bathing at Orange County beaches.

like my brother, and he didn't allow him to play. He did all kinds of things to hurt him that I did not know about until later. But at his funeral—I had a memorial mass said for him—one of the gentlemen got up and said how heartbreaking it was for Bill. He wanted to be a dentist anyway, so he went two years to UCLA, and then he went to Howard University in Washington, D.C., and that's a black university.

And that's where he got his dental training.

Dental training there. He had met this girl at UCLA. Her name was Faye Hopkins, and he and Faye married, and they both went to live in Washington, D.C., for his time there at Howard. They had one child, little Lori, a daughter. Then when he came back he started his practice with a very elderly dentist who was a pioneer in Los Angeles, Dr. Claude Hudson. He went into practice with him as an apprentice. Then he went on his own.[4]

Why did you and your brothers not come back to Orange County?

I think the main reason was because we began to be established elsewhere. I never went back to Santa Ana to live. I passed my state board when I was at St. Luke, so I did have a license. I would go periodically to stay with my parents in Santa Ana, and then I would work at St. Joseph's at that time.

Going back to your childhood and teenage years in Santa Ana, where did you shop for clothes or gifts?

Downtown Santa Ana. I shopped at Rankins. My mother had a charge there. That was a family-owned store there. Everything came from Rankins.

Did you have any trouble in buying clothes?

Only one time. I went to a smaller store and I was going to buy a hat. Everybody wore a hat in those days. And she wouldn't let me try it on. So my mother said, "Well, that's all right. We won't get one here today." But Rankins, no problem. My mother had a very grandeur manner—she was right from New York City, so Mama looked good, and there never was any question at Rankins. I don't even recall having a feeling that I wasn't welcome there the whole time we shopped there.

But the other store?

That store, no, she wouldn't let me try the hat on. So we never went there again. We just stayed at Rankins.

How about restaurants?

We never went. Because since Daddy cooked all the time and my mother cooked at home, we never went out to eat. They always joke about that. They say that's

---

[4] H. Claude Hudson had a new medical building built in 1929 on Central Avenue in Los Angeles. It was designed by the noted black architect Paul Williams. Hudson became a leader in the Los Angeles chapter of the National Association of the Advancement of Colored People in the mid-1920s, and for a number of years was involved in numerous important civil rights cases.

why the people, like from Louisiana, they're all such great cooks because they couldn't eat out. They'd eat at home. But they would go from home to home. Now, my dad took us up to San Francisco one time, and on the way we stopped in a place and they gave us breakfast. They were very nice. That was one of the first times that I'd ever been in a restaurant. This was high school days.

Did you visit relatives in Los Angeles, or anyplace else? Or did you go on motor tours to different places?

Not too much when we were young. That came in later years. But we had very dear friends in Los Angeles, and that was a big thing. My godmother was my mother's dear friend, and I got to spend a whole week up here in Los Angeles when I was in grammar school *and* high school with my godmother and her family. That was really our only vacation. They came to visit in Santa Ana and spent some time with us. Mainly, my friends there in Santa Ana, the Mexican people, were my friends. We went to the show every Sunday. That was a big deal.

That cost a dime to go. I'll never forget. I was short; I was kind of small, so the young man that took the tickets at the door, he said to me one day, "You've been getting in for a dime ever since I've been here. I know you're older than you say." I said, "Do I look older?" He said, "No, but I think you ought to be paying fifteen cents." I think it went from ten cents—it might have gone to a quarter, which was quite a jump. I can't remember. I said, "Well, I'll start paying more next time." I think I got in for a dime for years, when I was probably eighteen.

Did you ever go to Lake Elsinore?

Oh, yes. My dad had a place there at Lake Elsinore [Riverside County]. I don't know whether Daddy owned that or a friend of his owned it, but we used to go there and stay. I'll never forget, I almost drowned in there, and my cousin pulled me out. Because our friends from Los Angeles would come and we'd all be there at Elsinore and spend time. That was the only place we'd go for vacation. I almost forgot that.

So you had a car, though, and would drive out there?

Our mother had the 1925 Studebaker, and we drove down there. I can think about the Studebaker now with the isinglass curtains you pull down and snap on, and the wheels had bright yellow spokes, wooden spokes in the wheels.

Did your family visit other homes, or did people come over to your house? What was your parents' social life?

Well, you know, they didn't have a lot of it because of segregation and different things. But there was a family in Anaheim by the name of Craddock. Bob Craddock had a bootblack and magazine stand over there.[5] They used to come over, Mr. and Mrs. Craddock. And my mother and dad, they would play cards or something some

[5] Being a bootblack was a common job for blacks. It was a steady job that put the person into the Negro middle class.

nights. My brothers and I would just go in the back and play our games. But that wasn't very often. They didn't have a big social life. But my mother worked very much with the PTA in grammar school, at St. Joseph's. Whatever they had, she helped.

My dad did the Holy Name breakfasts. He used to donate that. He was not allowed to join the Knights of Columbus, which was the big Catholic organization at that time. You would never have known that my father was black. He had blue eyes and red hair. So they told him, "Well, we'll let you in." He said, "No, I don't want to join. But I'll donate." So he donated his time and fixed the breakfasts, the Holy Name breakfasts, and everything. Now, they've changed.

But because he could have passed was the only reason that they would have allowed him.

Yeah. They told him if we don't, they won't tell what you are. My father said, "Why would I want to be in something like that? No." He was not ashamed of what he was. He wanted to be what he was, of course.

It sounds like both your mother and your father had a lot of pride.

That's right. My father was not fortunate enough to get much of an education. He was a self-made man. But my mother was a very well educated proper lady. They used to say, "Mrs. Duffy." And she would say, "I'm Mrs. Duffy." And they'd say, "Oh, your husband's the one over at the Elks Club." "That's my husband." They treated my mother with great respect, when they found out who she was, of course. So she taught us this, to be proud of what you are. Don't try to be anything else. Naturally, I don't want to be anything else anyway. But, always be proud because you have a great heritage. Nothing in this world to be ashamed of.

That's great. Oh! Then you married.

Oh, yes. I met Robert. He was born in New Jersey, raised in Brooklyn [New York] and Cleveland, Ohio, and he was strictly an easterner. He never lived in the South. He was a musician, and he was a staff arranger at RCA Victor, as a matter of fact, when he died. We married in 1948 at Holy Name Church there in Los Angeles. There was a big social life for me in Los Angeles. In fact, Jackie Robinson was at UCLA at the time I was going to Immaculate Heart, and every weekend at Kerkhoff Hall [on the UCLA campus], they had a dance. So my social life was full if I didn't go to spend the weekend with my mother and dad. And I regret that I didn't go more often. There was always a dance, and it was kind of like a formal dance. We had a lot of fun.

You liked dancing, but did you get a chance when you were in Orange County, when you were in high school, to go to any dances?

Rarely, no. In fact, in Santa Ana almost none. I had several Mexican boyfriends. They were real nice guys. They lived in the neighborhood, and they would take me to the show or take me out to dinner. When I'd go home on the weekend, they'd be there. Or one of the boys from Los Angeles would come down to Santa Ana to see me. We would go like to a drive-in. You could drive in and order and you'd sit in your car and eat it. We'd do that. Never went inside. But Santa Ana didn't have any drive-ins. In Los Angeles, there were plenty, so we always went.

Let's say you had a date with one of the neighbors—so you would ride your bicycle or something to the movie theater?

They'd borrow their parents' car. One young man that I dated in Los Angeles, his mother had a beautiful Cadillac, so he would pick me up in that and we'd go.

But in Orange County, if you had a date, then did you get fed afterwards?

We went to each other's homes, I think, more than anything. Or if we went like to the beach during the day, we'd take our own lunch, and we might buy drinks down there. But the Mexican boys were the only ones I went with in Santa Ana, the only ones, God bless them. They were my neighbors. We celebrated everybody's birthdays. I got to make the cake. We had a lot of fun. We really did.

For the recording, why don't you tell me the names of your children?

I was lucky. I actually had seven children. Bobby was the oldest, Robert Arthur, Jr.; Victoria Louise; Constance Marie—we call her Candy; Deborah Jean; Joanne Estella; and Antoinette Lynn. But the fifth one was stillborn. I had seven pregnancies. I have six living children. Quite a few grands and great-grands now.

Your father worked for the Elks Club; where was that?

He was the steward there at the Elks Club. It was on Sycamore, right across from the Santa Ana City Hall. He went every morning on the Red Car, which went by our house. It was very popular then. Daddy caught it right in front of the house. He took it downtown and got off there, and he just had a block to walk. If I wanted to go downtown, I'd walk. It wasn't that far. I think it's a little over a mile. Of course, if I went with my mother, she would drive, because she had the car.

Did you ever go to your brothers' track meets or football games?

Oh, yes; when Bill was playing at Santa Ana High. Jerome left home kind of early, so I saw him run track. Then he went up to Cal Berkeley. I don't think he was in sports too much up there. I think he was just studying.

So he got an academic scholarship.

Absolutely, and then Bill played football. Oh yeah, we always went to the Santa Ana Bowl and Bill played football there. My mom and dad and I would go together.

Bill went into the service. What did he do in the service?

I don't know, but he was one of the Tuskegee Airmen. They just got honored in Washington, D.C., sixty years late. He never had any flying time. He was lucky in that respect, I guess. He is responsible for a large exhibit in the Palm Springs museum for the Tuskegee Airmen. He had that done.

Can you tell me what you see, looking back, with regard to the positives and negatives in growing up in Orange County?

Well, as a child, I never felt anything as far as my race. My mom and dad were very conscientious about that. I'm sure that was because of them. And it was only when I was in eighth grade when I was not able to join the organization. But after that, my mother said, "These are the things you learn in life. You rise above it; you make the best of it, and learn a lesson from it." And I did. So that's when I went to Marywood, which was wonderful, that school in Anaheim.

Well, as a positive, I can thank my dear friend next door, Celia. And my mother kept me active in music and dancing. My life seemed to be very full. And I sometimes worked with my dad, waiting tables. Because every Tuesday, it seems to me, the Elks had a big banquet, and when I was in high school and was living at home, I would wait tables for him. I loved that. The men would tip me. They'd hand me a dollar bill, and that was nice. But they were all very friendly, very nice. I never heard anything, or never had anyone say anything to me that was in a derogatory vein, I must say, until that happened at Marywood.

Do you feel that growing up in such a diverse—except for blacks—community was helpful in the rest of your life? Would it have been better if you could have lived in a middle-class black community?

No, I really don't. I really didn't feel anything because I didn't know any different. I just knew that the whites that I went to school with, I didn't socialize with them because I had the Mexicans. We were right there in a Mexican neighborhood, and you talk about sweet people, they were just wonderful. I loved them and they loved me, as far as I know. I always went with Mexican boys through high school. I enjoyed life, and I didn't feel any different. I didn't feel that I missed anything. The only time I got to see any blacks was when I came to Los Angeles for my week's vacation. Then, actually, they weren't black. They called themselves Creole. So I never really got to be with real black people until I guess after I married.

You know, the Creole people, they don't segregate themselves as much as they used to, but they did. They claimed, and they were, French-Spanish. But most of them looked white and worked as whites. I had many friends that worked as white. They call us black but there are many people who don't look black at all. There's a French word, *passe-moi*, which is pass for white. And many do. In fact, I can name some in the movies, big stars, who were of black descent. A lot of them just went on the other side for jobs. That's the reason. Sometimes they turn their backs on everybody else, and other times they socialize with them. Once in a while somebody got married, and they'd have a big reception, because they always loved to entertain. People from Louisiana love parties and dances. And they would come and just have the best time. Of course, then go back in their white community.

Your dad was aware of the Klan because the Klan was very strong in the mid-1920s. Did he talk to you about the Klan?

Nothing. I just knew that it was something that hated us. The only people I might have known would be the fathers of some of my classmates, and naturally they're not going to say anything to me. So I never knew anybody that was a member. My dad knew the members and knew who they were.

What did black people say, or do they say now, when you say, "Well, I was raised in Orange County"?

They say, "There weren't any black people down in Orange County then." I say, "I beg to differ with you. I was there. I was born there." Because the people that would come out here from Louisiana, the only thing they did in Orange County—they'd go out there to go crayfishing, because they all loved crayfish. Or they'd go someplace to fish. But nobody ever lived down there. Then all of a sudden, there began to be a little bit of integration—but mainly the Louisiana people, the Creole-type people who you wouldn't know who they were anyway.

You mean that came to Orange County from Los Angeles?

Oh yeah, came from different places. There were a lot of them. Some of them that I knew married into influential families there in Orange County and just went on. Nobody knows who they are, so—

Do you have any favorite story about Orange County?

I think I really had a happy childhood. I always loved my schools. And because my parents taught me to concentrate on school, we don't worry about how people think or feel. Like I told you, I never really felt segregation. One girl called me a name one time, in grammar school. I'll never forget. She called me nigger one time, and I slapped her. I've never slapped a woman, or anybody, in my life. I didn't even slap my kids. So Sister Sacred Heart came over and said, "What's the matter?" And I told her, "Margaret called me a name." And she said, "I'll take care of her. You just get back in line." Sister Sacred Heart was just an angel. She's gone to Heaven, too, bless her heart. That's the only person that ever said anything like that to me.

I've worked with a lot of people, very few of my own. In fact, I'm usually always the only one, going to work in the hospitals. And when I supervised the lab in Marina del Rey, I had Japanese, Mexican, Korean, and myself. There were about five of us. And we never worried about race. It never really bothered me, because I didn't ponder on it. I knew there were certain things I had to do, so I went ahead and did them.

Thank you, Connie Duffy Farlice, for sharing your life story with us.

BERNICE AND BAXTER YOUNG[1]

Bernice Young was born Bernice Lela Melvina McKinney, on March 19, 1915, in El Paso, Texas. She was the last child of seven. Her family moved from El Paso to Wichita, Kansas; then Ardmore, Oklahoma; Phoenix, Arizona; and eventually, in 1927, to Santa Ana. Her father came the year before. The primary reason for moving was her father's health. He had worked for the railroad and had injured his back. Baxter Young was born in 1912. His family also came to California, but earlier in 1919, because his father, Joe Young, had severe bronchial asthma. In 1929, they came to Santa Ana. Bernice Young died in 1995 and Baxter Young in 1999. Many of their offspring still live in Orange County. Wedding photo 1932.

What were your parents' occupations?

Bernice: My dad, Edward McKinney, was a master of everything. My mother, Eva Bernice McKinney, (chuckling) was just a housewife. He could do a little bit of everything. He was a carpenter, he was a plumber, and he was a cook. [My dad's first job in Santa Ana] he had a [shoe] shine stand. Then later he got janitorial work where he took care of buildings.

Did they have a hard time finding housing when they got here?

Bernice: Well, he had already purchased a house. It was on West Eighth Street, and it was a duplex, and he took and converted it into a single-living home.

Now, how many other black families were there in Santa Ana at that time?

Bernice: I really don't know. But I remember years later—about, I'd say, five or ten years later—I took a census, and it was only fifty families here at that time. They were caterers and janitors, chauffeurs, and housekeepers.

---

[1] Oral History No. 2389. Interview date: August 22, 1994, at the Youngs' home in Santa Ana, California. Interviewer: Wendy Barker.

What are your earliest memories of Santa Ana?

Bernice: My sister, she was much fairer than I, and we'd go to the restaurant. We just had a little job that we would work; I was agreeable to work, you know, around fourteen, like the age that kids have part-time jobs—and we could meet every Saturday and have lunch. And in this particular incident I'm recalling, she went into the restaurant and was waiting for me, and when I walked in and sit down, the woman came to the table and offered to serve her but said she couldn't serve me. So my sister said, "Well, if that's the case, you're not serving either one of us because that's my sister." And we got up and we walked out.

Now, would it just be things like this, where you tried to go somewhere and they would tell you, or would there be signs up?

Bernice: Oh, yeah. They had signs and things, but we didn't pay any attention to the signs because, you know, sometimes they had it where it's not visible for us to see and we just went in.

Were there stores that you couldn't go in?

Bernice: I never had any trouble with stores.

Okay. What about movie theaters or—

Bernice: Well, movie theaters—they had us sit upstairs, even if you had money to sit in the lobbies. They would plainly tell you that you couldn't sit there. But as I grew older, I thought it was foolish, but that's people's property. We couldn't do anything about it. [The Youngs' daughter said that her parents went to a restaurant and the waitress said, "We don't serve Negroes here," and her mother said, "And we don't eat them, either," and they both got up and left.]

And when do you think that started to change?

Baxter: Thirty-three when we had that earthquake. I tell you what, you couldn't get a job doing anything except shining shoes or washing dishes, but after the earthquake, you could get a job most anyplace. Before then, they would not hire you. And even churches were segregated, but after that earthquake, all the churches went together. They had as many white in the black church as they did blacks and all that. Everything changed after the earthquake. [It was one] of the biggest quakes we've had. We had three people killed right here in Santa Ana. School had been out, because it was six o'clock in the evening. That's why no more people got killed. I was working downtown, down in Santa Ana. People was running and scared and hollering and fainting all out in the street and it wasn't surprising to me because I was used to earthquakes. I come from Imperial Valley where we had all kinds of earthquakes. But a lot of these people here had never been in an earthquake, not that big. We had quite a few buildings shake down here in Santa Ana.

What kind of work were you doing?

Baxter: Shining shoes. That's all you could do. I was working in a barbershop. I was working in Viera and Wilson's barbershop on Broadway between Third and Fourth on Broadway.

Bernice: Across the street from the Broadway Theater.

Now, was the Broadway Theatre segregated, too?

Baxter: All theaters were segregated. They had signs in the windows of all cafés: "We cater to white only." We had one café that didn't have a sign in the window, and that was Tony's Café on the eastside of town; and his wife, she was bitterly against blacks. She wanted to put a [whites only] sign in it but he wouldn't allow it. And that was the only one that you could go in. He was some kind of foreigner. I know he committed suicide down here in the Santa Ana River.

Where did you go to school?

Bernice: I went to Franklin Elementary, Willard Junior High School, and then Santa Ana High School.

How many blacks were in your school? Do you know that?

Bernice: No. I really don't know, because in the different grades they had one or two. It never dawned on me how many was there.

Baxter: When I came here, I was a junior in high school. I came here in 1929, to Santa Ana.

And why did you come to Santa Ana?

Baxter: My father had bronchitis. He coughed all the time, and they said that this climate would be good for his health. That's why we came here. And I went to Santa Ana High School, me and one other colored boy, Freddie Bell. That's all. Fourteen hundred children and we were the only two colored. I wasn't used to it because I had just come from Imperial Valley, where I went to a segregated school where it was nothing but Mexicans and colored. So I was not used to going to school with white kids.

How did they treat you?

Baxter: Oh, most of them treated me fine. I got along with most of them fine. I had no trouble. One or two I'd have trouble with, but I straightened them out and that would be the end of it. [I would] stop them from calling me out of my name, or trying to make jokes, and all that kind of stuff. That's it. I let them know that I was just a human being like they were.

Would you have to get in a fight with them?

Baxter: Lots of times I did. A lot of times. I never had no trouble with the teachers or anything like that, never.

Bernice, did you have the same kind of problems?

Bernice: I just had tongue fights. But I let them all know who I was, and they soon weaned over. And all the sports; I was the only one black person on the sports. The other girls didn't participate. It was two other girls. But I stood ground. I was right with them, and everything they did, I did it. I tried to outdo them because I was a minority. Today, I can meet any of them and they know how to say, "Hello, Bernice," and go on. You see what I mean? You didn't have to fist-fight all the time to make a decision. But I let them know that I wasn't for a whole lot of mess. I was there to learn like they were. Most [people who bothered me] come from the South. They hadn't been educated to the fact. The teachers were very good. In fact, they encouraged me to participate, you know, and do things.

What made you want to stay in Santa Ana as an adult?

Bernice: I was established here then. And we were well-contented. After I got out of high school, it was right into marriage [in 1932], and there I was—if you want to say it—I was stuck raising my kids. I had five children: three girls and two boys. And today I only have three. Five months ago, I lost my baby boy.

Oh, I'm so sorry to hear that. . . . Did your family know [other families] before they got here?

Bernice: No. My father was here for a good while seeking a place for us to stay and everything, to get it ready for us. But he just met them when he got here. And our church [Second Baptist] was small. We didn't have too many people then in church.

When do you think more blacks started coming into Santa Ana?

Baxter: After the Depression, when they started construction work just before the war. A whole lot of construction work opened up here in Santa Ana.

Okay. What was it like during the Depression here?

Bernice: I worked five days a week in different homes. We were talking about these helpers, what do they call them? Hamburger helpers, and all that stuff, that they advertise now? I said, I put that on the market before they came, (chuckling) using the hamburger in so many different ways to stretch it and make it feed five kids. Honey, I had them. Some I haven't even named yet. He was doing janitor work then. (To Baxter) When did you start doing construction work?

Baxter: That was after the Depression. I started doing construction work then, last of '39, '40, on Prado Dam. Well, before I got out of it, I was a cement finisher, but when I first started, I was just a laborer.

Then during World War II, lots of blacks came to Los Angeles. Why do you think people would come here?

Baxter: The work. There was a lot of construction. All these bases were being built. We had the [US Army Air Corps] cadet school. I helped build that. We had the lighter-than-air [base in Tustin]. I helped build that. El Toro, I helped build that. We had Los Alamitos, I helped build that. It was building going on everywhere in Orange County, every place.

It was hard for us to find a house when I first came. My mother and father, when we moved here in '29, there was only one man here at that time would rent to black people. Musselman was his name, and he had quite a few houses, but he was the only one who would rent you a house.

What about later, during the fifties? Did you see more blacks starting to come in then?

Bernice: Yeah, because they was beginning to open up more for those that were qualified to fill these positions like the engineering and all that. We had several from the church that were sent from different places here. But, they were here for a short period of time, for trainees to train, others for the field. But they had to be qualified to fill it. And then some liked it, they stayed. It all depended on the individuals. They started developing more churches. We have every denomination, just about; every type has been started here.

Baxter: And they'd start buying homes here, buying houses. Used to you couldn't buy a house, but it got where you could buy a house [in the] fifties or sixties. You could buy a house most any place then. There was a lot of work going on here.

You said that when you were younger, there was a lot of discrimination in Santa Ana and Orange County.

Baxter: It was discrimination everywhere, just like it was in the South. But here, they tried to make like it wasn't discriminating. It's worse, in a way, because you're being deceived. You go in a place that you think is all right and you find out you're not welcome there. But, if you know that you're not wanted in there, you're not going in there.

I came to California when I was six years old, and I seen enough segregation here to know what segregation is. I went to a segregated school [in El Centro] right here in California. See, I seen them bus kids in those days [1920s]. We had two black kids that lived on the other end of Imperial Valley. They had to bus them right by Central Union High School to El Centro High. A big bus for these two kids, that's all.

Bernice: Well, they did that to our children when we were here in Santa Ana. They made them go clear to Flower Street to McKinley [Elementary] School. And at that time, I was on the membership roll at the school, and I found out all the children they had moved. Now, we had to leave here, pass the school [Franklin], and go way up to Flower Street. And I got all the names and I went up to the district attorney. And I laid everything on the table (chuckling), and I told him I wasn't pleased with it. I said, "My kids have to walk past the school to go to another one. It doesn't make sense." I said, "I don't have one penny to fight no case, but you are here to fight the case for me."

They got to stirring around and laid everything out, and they made every white that was out of the district, too, to move. So then they tried to rezone it where my kids would come back here to the school. But they couldn't, so I said, "Well, if they can't rezone it, then they [the white kids] have to go too." Maybe I made them move, and everybody knew me from there on in. This was in the sixties [actually 1948].

Where did blacks live when you were a kid?

Baxter: They lived everywhere [in the late 1920s and 1930s]. There wasn't a certain district. Anywhere they could buy a house they could live at that time.

Bernice: Yeah, that's right, because some of them lived on the eastside of town, too.

I think you mentioned briefly what kinds of jobs they had.

Bernice: Oh, they had catering. They had a beautiful catering business.

Baxter: Everybody was in the shine business. They were shining shoes, shining cars, shining your clothes, shining your windows. Everybody was in the shine business.

When you were a kid, what kind of things did you do for fun?

Bernice: Oh, we would have little outings, picnics. Orange County Park [Irvine Park] was our main feature at that time. It was a nice park. We would get together, you know, couples, and go out and have a big picnic, ball game, horseshoe pitching. You know, just live it up.

Did you ever go to Lake Elsinore?

Baxter: We went to Lake Elsinore when they had sulfur springs up there. A lot of people went up there for their health.

Bernice: That'd make you feel so good to take a bath, and then go to bed at night and sleep like a baby. (chuckling)

What do you think is the biggest change in the black community in Orange County since you were a kid?

Bernice: They're just doing different things more than ever. It's like we got women in the telephone company, you know, and different firms, secretaries, and things at the various big companies.

What about the sense of community?

Bernice: It was closer together. Just for instance, I can recall a birthday party. Say for instance all the adults, children, they made a big issue of it, and then everybody would come.

Do you think that blacks' attitude toward whites has changed?

Bernice: Oh yes, lots. We get some too that's just as narrow-minded as the whites are. They're beginning to understand, you know, some of the circumstances and try to adjust it. I think through believing in Christ in their hearts that has helped them so much to realize that we are God's children, regardless of our color.

What about the black and Latino attitudes. How do they get along?

Bernice: They get along good. I know we were at fellowshipping with our church and their church and we got to singing "Jesus Loves Me, This I Know." They were singing in Spanish and we were singing in English. And to hear it was amazing (chuckling). And we did that for about a year or two and they came to our church and we go to theirs and have meetings.

Baxter: There's no difference in people. All people are the same. I don't care what color you are, or nothing. We have a daughter-in-law, she's a Mexican girl. She's just like we are, as far as I'm concerned. And her family, we get along. My brother, when he was living, he was married to a Korean girl. So it's no different. Well, look at Bernice there, my wife. Ask her, what is her nationality? Her father was half Irish and Creole. Her mother was full-blood Choctaw Indian. She's a deuce mixture, that's all I can say.

But our society wants to always label everybody.

Baxter: That is the wrongest thing they ever started. My mother was part Indian, but my father was a direct—his ancestors were directly from Africa. So what difference does it make? You're a human being, that's the main thing.

Did your family go to Los Angeles very often when you were growing up?

Bernice: Not too often. Oh, if something was happening in some of the churches that was interesting—maybe some great speaker, you know, that we had known—and then we'd go. That's where my mother was about to go when we had the big earthquake. She was getting dressed to hear some big minister speak. Oh, after we got grown, Baxter and I, we used to go up there to the dances and whatnot.

Baxter: Nightclubs and everything.

Now, were there nightclubs here?

Baxter: No. We had a Red Car, streetcar, used to run right down Santa Ana Boulevard. You could catch it, and in forty-five minutes you'd be in Los Angeles. We had better transportation then than we've got now with all these freeways, because it wasn't crowded. They ran all night and all day; the last one was 2:30 in the morning.

Bernice: We used to take it to downtown [Santa Ana], my sister and I, to shows, movies. When the pictures would change, we would go. Of course, nothing else for us to do, go to see a movie or something. And the guy [street car operator] he knew us and let us off right at the front of our door. (laughter) That's when we used to live in a big, old house over there on Fourth Street. "Okay, now ya'll take it easy." And he'd wait till we got in the house too.

Baxter: Yeah, you could go over there, catch it [the Red Car], and ride downtown for a nickel.

Now, you were a housewife, but your husband was a shoeshine earlier, and then he worked in construction and—

Baxter: I did all kind of work you can mention. I worked in the garages, I washed cars, I polished cars, I did janitor work, I shined shoes, and I was a dye man in the shining. I dyed shoes, dyed leather. And I did all kind of construction work, from laborer on up to cement finisher. And I run a barbershop of my own from 1955 up until I retired here about three or four years ago. Right down on Santa Ana Boulevard, just before you get to Bristol. You'll see a little shop up there now, that barbershop right on this side of Bristol Drug Store. I opened up that shop in 1955. The BY Barbershop. I run it for years. I was a barber.

What was your favorite job?

Baxter: The one that I could make the best living at, that was my favorite job. I changed jobs because I was trying to find something where I wasn't segregated against, somebody trying to keep you down. That's why I changed jobs. And then when I opened up the barbershop, it was my job, my own place. I was the boss. So that's one reason I stayed there so long.

So would you often have problems with the employees at the other jobs you had then?

Baxter: Yes, yes. I should say so; it was just like during the Depression. I was working up there at Hoffman's shoe shop, and he just wanted to boss and make you do unnecessary things, and you had to work long hours with no more pay, and all things like that. I quit that during the Depression when you couldn't even get a job. I quit on account of him, the way he tried to treat you. I told him, "I can work any place I want to." I always figured, as long as I will work and treat people right I can always get a job. And most of the time I had a job of some kind. I'd work any place that people didn't bother me.

Now, did you work in a lot of places where you were the only black or only one of a couple?

Baxter: Yeah, sure. Lots of places like that.

And do you think that they treated you worse because of your race?

Baxter: Yeah. I used to have a pretty high temper and as long as I didn't get into a fight I'd stay there. But when I seen I was going to get in trouble, I'd leave rather than to get in trouble. And I never did like trouble.

And that's another thing we had here before the war [World War II] in Orange County; we had nice policemen. We had a very nice police force and most of your courts—now, I don't say all of them—but most of your courts downtown was strictly to the law and fair with everybody. Some of the judges in those days they would come right out and let you know that you wasn't going to get a fair shake on account of your race. But most of them were fair. They didn't care what color you were.

But after the war, it was worse than it was before the war. We got different policemen. Before the war, I knew almost every police on the force because I worked downtown and I'd meet them and talk with them. Everybody was a friend. They knew you. They called you by your name. But after the war, they got a bunch of Southerners in here and put them on the police force. Every time they'd look up and see a black or a Mexican, they always had something they had to search you, ask you a bunch of questions. But all our old policemen, they quit. They quit the force on that account, because they wouldn't do that.

Do you know people who've had a hard time with the police here?

Baxter: Yeah, and we had it here just like they did in L.A., same difference. I tell you, people is people. I don't care where they live. You never know what people are thinking sometimes. You can live around them for forty years and don't know them. You think you know them, but you don't.

But the job I was going to tell you about—during the war [World War II], I worked civil service at the El Toro Marine Corps base. I was a storekeeper out there. I used to be the head of the ordinance department at El Toro, all during the war. That's why I wasn't drafted, on account of my job. That's before they let blacks into the Marine Corps.

So, what was it like working there?

Baxter: Just another job to me. Only thing, it was so segregated. I'll tell you about these places. We [my brother and I] had to threaten to take the personnel out there at El Toro to court, to the Civil Service Board. We had to threaten them before we got the jobs that we were entitled to. We were the only blacks that worked out there that had guts enough to go up against them. [We] worked out there when the base first opened. We went to work out there as laborers. But when they started to open up different stores in different departments, they would hire [white] people coming in as storekeepers.

Storekeepers made more money than laborers. But we knew everything in the store because we set the stores up. We would put up all the shelves, the bins, and all the material. We had to teach the people they'd bring in there for storekeeper. But yet we could only be laborers; we couldn't be storekeepers. So we went and asked them why we could not get a job as storekeepers, and they just came right out and told us why we couldn't: because of our race. That's all we wanted to know.

They thought it was over with, but it wasn't. So we went over their heads. But when it was all said and done, we got storekeeper jobs. And they even offered me a job higher than the supervisor out there, and I wouldn't take it because I knew all it was was trying to get me into something I didn't know, where they could let me out. You see all of these things after it's over. You know what's going down.

We had one fellow, he came here from Georgia. He was storekeeper at the base in Georgia, and he got transferred out here to El Toro. And when he went out to put his transfer in, why, they didn't want to give him the job that he was doing in Georgia. His job was waiting for him, but they told him they didn't have nothing. He thought they were telling the truth. For about a month and a half he'd go out there every week, and they'd tell him, "No, sorry, we don't have anything." So he was going to join the laborers union and go to work as a laborer in construction work and it just happened he met my brother and me.

We told him he was not to join the union to work labor. Go out there to the base and tell those people out there that if he didn't get his job, he was going to turn them in to the Civil Service Department. He told them that, and they said, "Oh, well, wait. We overlooked the job. Your job is open. You come to work tomorrow." He went to work and he retired from out there. Those are the things we ran up against.

Did the other blacks benefit from that, too?

Baxter: Yeah, the others. You know why others benefited? Because after that, guys would go out there and go to work as storekeepers. They didn't even have to work as laborers.

So you led the way for them. Thank you very much, Mr. and Mrs. Young, for a fine interview.

ZEPH JONES[1]

Zeph Jones was born in 1931 in Santa Ana. His father came to Santa Ana from Oklahoma, and his mother, from Texas. This was in the 1920s. There were few blacks then, maybe ten families, and they lived close to one another. Zeph Jones, except for a two-year army tour, has lived his entire life in Santa Ana. He begins by talking about his father's shoeshine business. Photo ca. 1949.

Where was your father's shoeshine business?

In Orange, just before you get to the circle. Because I remember when I was a kid I used to go over there with him, and help him. When he passed on, I was about six.

Were most of the people he was shining shoes for, white?

Yeah, I would say—the majority during that time.

Do you think that he liked his job, or did he do it because other jobs weren't available?

Well, other jobs weren't available. Gee, that's back in the twenties, and look at things now. The blacks have come some [way since then]; it's better than it was then, but in some cases there's no improvement. This is the nineties and look at the problems that we're having, the racial problems. Oh, I tell you, it's unbelievable.

Your mother was a domestic. Do you know what years those were?

Well, from the time that she came here and got settled until right up until she passed on. She died in 1962.

Did she work for one family for a long time?

[1] Oral History No. 2388. Interview date: May 17, 1994, at Zeph Jones's home in Santa Ana, California. Interviewer: Wendy Barker.

Yeah, she worked for, I remember, Mrs. Jordan, and the Segerstroms that own South Coast Plaza. She had her steady customers, and then she'd go and work on parties and special occasions. I remember her catching the bus because that was the only transportation; we didn't have a car and she couldn't drive. She'd catch that bus about 8:00 in the morning and I guess she wouldn't get home until 4:00 or 5:00 in the evening, I think, unless they had a special party or something like that. Then she would work the weekend.

Do you have brothers and sisters?

Oh, yeah, but let's see, I have three sisters that's living and one sister that's dead. I had three brothers and all three of them are dead. See, my mother was married twice. When she married my dad, he had four kids by a previous marriage.

Then they had children together?

Yeah, my younger sister and myself. My grandmother lived next door and she used to take care of us kids.

How did it make you feel that she was working and away from home all the time with some other family? Did that bother you?

No. It put food on the table. Heck, because my dad had died.

Was there any other kind of work available for black women at that time besides domestic work?

Not that I know of when I was a kid, because most of it was domestic work. I don't recall any of them working in factories or other type of jobs.

The other black families that you knew, were their mothers also domestics at the time?

Yes. Some catered parties. They'd go out and cook at their customers' homes. They didn't prepare many meals at their own homes.

Bootblacks

Folks that shined shoes were called bootblacks. A twenty-first century view may be that shoe shining is demeaning, but for many black men in the early- to mid-twentieth century, this work provided a steady job and a middle-class existence in a time when racism made it difficult to find work of any kind. Neff Cox, who shined shoes in the town of Brea, which he had to leave before dark, owned a home and made enough money to bring his mother and two siblings from Alabama to his neighborhood in Fullerton. When he died in 1941 "the whole town [of Brea] turned out to pay respects at his funeral."

Samuel "Pappy" Drake operated a shoe-shine stand in downtown Santa Ana before he passed away in 1909. He had lived in Santa Ana since 1887. Tom Walker came to Santa Ana in the early 1920s and, like his friend John Wilson, shined shoes in front of downtown Santa Ana barbershops. In the mid-1920s, their wives were members of the prominent circle of black Fullerton and Santa Ana women. In 1925, Thomas Bell came from Los Angeles to open a branch of the Red Cap Shoe Company, a combined shoe repair and shoeshine business. Some considered him the first black businessman in Orange County.

Did your parents have a hard time finding a place to live when they moved to Orange County?

Not that I know of. I remember when I was a kid we lived on Fourth Street, and then after he [my father] died, then we moved to First Street. My mom bought the place on First Street. Those are the two houses that I remember.

I know a lot of blacks have had a hard time finding a place to rent or to buy because of redlining.

Well, see, I was born and raised here in Santa Ana. I didn't realize how prejudiced it was until after I grew up. We went to an integrated school: blacks and Mexicans, white, we all went together.

Are there any family stories that you grew up listening to about your family in Orange County, about their early years?

Well, I know my mom used to tell us about how she used to pick cotton, you know, long hours, [in Texas] when she was a kid. I guess they lived on a farm and they raised their own livestock and stuff. I didn't know too much about my dad.

Your family was one of the first black families in the county. What was that like for them?

Like I say, as a kid, we went to school and no problems. Just certain places we couldn't go, you know—restaurants, we couldn't go to. And I remember two theaters, and boy, if I knew then what I know today, I'd never have accommodated it. But, as a kid you don't; free ice cream and there was a series every Saturday. We had to sit upstairs, you know. We couldn't sit downstairs. It was a fleabag. The State theater and the Walker's theater, and they were owned by the same person, and we had to sit upstairs.

They had ushers upstairs, and, you know, I was a kid. I didn't care. You get a free ice cream; see the series, Flash Gordon and Captain Marvel. It wasn't the best. It had rats running across all over the place. And, like I say, if I'd have known then what I know now—you hurt them in the pocketbook, just don't accommodate those places.

Movie Theaters

In 1930, two major movie theaters in Santa Ana, the Fox Broadway Theatre and the Fox West Coast Theatre, were owned and operated by the Fox West Coast Theatre movie chain. This chain continued ownership throughout the 1930s and 1940s. The oral histories in this book indicate that the two Fox theatres did not segregate, but theatres owned by Charles Walker required that blacks and Mexican American movie goers sit in the balcony.

When do you think that changed and they weren't segregated anymore? Do you remember?

Well, I remember Mr. Bell's daughter [Lorraine Bell]. He was a businessman. He owned one of the biggest shoe-shining parlors and he repaired shoes, shoeshine and everything. I think just about every black kid during that time when I was a kid worked for him. This was during World War II, and the service people were big tippers. His daughter broke up the segregation in the restaurants. Because she went to one of the nicer restaurants here in Santa Ana and they wouldn't serve her. So she sued them and she got a judgment. It was either in the late forties or the early fifties. It was one of the nicer restaurants on Main Street.

So she sued them and won?

Yeah, oh, yeah, and then everybody else – hey, they didn't want to follow suit, you know? I remember a place across the street from the State theater on Fourth and Birch. Boy, they served the best chili dogs. We called it the greasy spoon. We could buy food on the outside, but we couldn't go inside and eat.

Would they have a sign or was it just common knowledge?

They would tell you. I don't remember seeing any signs.

Did your mom ever say you have to act this way or you have to act that way?

No, I don't remember her saying anything like that. I know when I was in grammar school I used to fight a lot because if somebody called me a "nigger," he belonged to me? Then I found out that, heck, anybody could be a nigger; there are all kinds, no matter what color you are. I didn't fight much after I got older. But when I was younger, I did, especially in grammar school; you know how kids can be cruel. You'd have to put them in their place.

When you were a kid, there were not many blacks. Do you recall a time when more blacks started coming?

There was an air force base. It was where we used to work during the summer [Santa Ana Army Air Force Base]. There were lots of service people that were stationed out there [during World War II]; but then El Toro [Marine Air Base], too. They came here and were stationed here, and lots of them just made their home here. Well, I'd say that in the fifties lots of blacks came.

I think L.A. [Los Angeles] was much more the focus than Orange County.

Yeah. Well, heck, Orange County—they [people from Los Angeles] kind of think this is like Alabama or Mississippi, you know, like the Birchers, and heck, they think that's the way blacks are being treated. Because I talked to lots of my friends—"Oh, Orange County? You got them there. How do you survive? How do you make it?" This is the way they looked at Orange County.

What other kinds of things do you remember about Santa Ana when you were growing up?

Oh, the old Santa Ana Bowl. I used to go to lots of ball games there. They used to play softball there. Bristol Street [Drugstore] used to be on the north side and we used to stop in there and get sodas, sundaes, and ice cream at the soda fountain.

We used to go to movies a lot. Go to two movies in one day; oh, that was really exciting. I think at that time the movies ran 20, 25 cents, something like that. I used to sell bottles and rags for show money and spending money. We kind of made our own fun. There wasn't that much to do, but we always had something—lots of fun. We lived across the street from an orange grove and, heck, we never did buy oranges.

Okay, then another thing that really stands out. We used to pack a lunch and we'd cut across the orange grove and go to Monte Vista and Townsend [streets], and there was—like a creek. We used to go there and catch crawdads. We'd take liver or bacon, and catch crawdads by the tub full. Bring them home, mom would fix them. Good eating; very good eating. Yeah, that was really fun.

What schools did you go to?

Franklin grammar school and then I went to Willard. At the time, there were only two junior highs, Willard and Lathrop, and only one high school, Santa Ana High, and that's where I went to school.

Were there very many Latinos then?

Where we lived we were the only black family; the rest of them were Mexicans. We were the only black family in the area.

How do you think that the blacks were treated at school? Were they discriminated against at school?

I didn't notice it that much. They could have been but—I played lots of sports and I was senior class president. In 1950, I believe.

Is that the first time a black had ever been class president?

Gee, I don't know. There weren't too many blacks there at that time, and I was co-captain of the football team because I was really into sports. I played with Reverend Donald Moomaw [an All-American lineman on the UCLA Bruins football team in the mid-1950s]. He's a minister now. Heck, he was [US President] Ronald Reagan's pastor. And then I played with the astronaut, Jerry Carr. Matter of fact, Jerry used to live over here on Eighth Street, and we used to go over there and have cookouts. I played with Herschel Musick. His uncle was the sheriff at the time. I belonged to some clubs. You know, I was accepted.

Where did most of the other blacks live?

Kind of scattered, because we lived on First Street. Matter of fact, I was born and raised on First Street in the 1900 block. Dr. [G. Emmett] Raitt delivered me. That's when the doctors used to come out to the home and deliver. That's one of the reasons that they changed that street. See, the main street used to be Artesia, and then they changed it to Raitt. Because Dr. Raitt was the greatest doctor, boy, I'll tell you.

What ethnicity was he?

Oh, white. You know doctors now, heck, all they want to look at is your bank account, what kind of insurance you've got. You could be lying there, heck—but Dr. Raitt, "Doc, I need your service." Well, he'd be right there. "Well, I've only got three or four dollars." "Well, okay, give me what you've got and you can pay me later." He cared about the people. It wasn't the almighty dollar. Yeah, Dr. Raitt was a great man.

What kind of jobs do you think most of the blacks had then?

I remember my uncle and a few others used to work at the Elks Club in maintenance, dishwashing, and I guess some were cooks. Some of the people worked out at El Toro, out at the base there. Some of them cooked, and gee, chauffeured. Things got better as the years progressed.

When you were a kid, were there certain places that you went for recreation, or that you couldn't go?

Well, I remember, let's see, the swimming pool at the Hart Park [in the adjacent city of Orange]. We couldn't go and swim together. You know, like there was a certain time that minorities could go and the whites; they wouldn't let you swim with them.

What do you think is the biggest change in the black community since you were a child?

Oh, I think, if you have the money, you can buy just about anywhere without too much of a problem.

Have you ever had incidences where you went into a store and they gave you a hard time or you felt discriminated against?

Maybe they might have been a little slow about waiting on you. It probably was there but I probably just didn't pay it much attention. We went back to the South, [in 1965]. We were up in the Smoky Mountains in North Carolina, and they still had signs "Blacks" and "Whites" for the restrooms. I had never seen that before.

How did it make you feel when you saw that sign?

I just wasn't used to it. Heck, after I'd been in California all my life and never had run into nothing real bad, you know, nothing like that. Anyway, it makes you feel, God dang, like you're not a human being. Gee, it's terrible.

At any time did your family ever go to Lake Elsinore?

Oh, yeah! My aunt had a place in Elsinore [Riverside County]. This is when Elsinore used to be like a resort, and we used to go on holidays and go and fish or boat riding or just a picnic. We used to go up and stay maybe overnight or a weekend. Yeah, that's when it was real, real, nice.

What was it about Lake Elsinore that was attractive?

Oh, just going out and picnicking and having a good time, wading in the water, or swimming and boating.

When you went, was it mostly just your own family or would there be groups of families that would go together.

It would be groups, just friends and neighbors. Hey, well, like Fourth of July or something like that. "Let's go." Pack a lunch and go to Elsinore and spend the day or the weekend.

Did you go to Los Angeles very much as a kid?

Yeah, that's when the [Pacific Electric] Red Car was running. Oh, gee, the cheapest transportation there was. I spent enough money that I should own one of those. Because, see, my wife, Laura, lived up there and I used to go up and see my honey. I used to spend lots of time on the Red Car.

Were there certain things that you went to L.A. for that weren't available in Orange County?

Yeah. Heck, go to clubs or something like that, and then we had relatives. My brother and sister lived up there. Because after I bought me a car – I bought me a '40 Ford in 1950—I used to take my mom up there, because my brother would barbecue for Mother's Day.

Did they have clubs here [in Orange County]?

Well, no, they didn't have anything. They'd have [in L.A.] those musicals and the talent. We used to spend lots of time at the Lincoln Theater. We'd see Helen Humes and Johnny Otis and Sammy Davis. They were just starting out.

And they didn't come to Orange County to work?

No, no, not down here. We used to go to the Lincoln, the Orpheum, and then there was another one that just had live talent; it was just like a concert. You'd sit there and listen to the music. They'd have comedians and people singing, just kind of a variety. Wrestling matches—oh, that was a must. We loved wrestling. They had the wrestling at the Olympic [Auditorium].

Where did they [wrestle] here?

Well, the drive-in. I guess it would be Anaheim Boulevard. There used to be a big, old, tin building and we used to go in there and watch the wrestling match. Oh, we used to follow it real close. Even if it was fake, they'd put on a good show.

You were a mail carrier for thirty-five years. What year did you start?

Nineteen fifty-four.

What made you decide to go into that?

Well, I made up my mind, because I was in the service. See, I got married before I went overseas, and then we had one child. I wanted to get into something that had security and a steady income. I had a family to support, and so the post office was my choice and things worked out.

What were the businesses on your routes?

Well, there used to be a big Coca-Cola business. Pepsi Cola used to be across the street from my aunt's house and Coca-Cola used to be right here on First and Raitt. I think they left in the fifties. There were lots of barbers, especially on First Street. Those are more or less about the same: lots of mechanics, electrical and body and fender businesses.

When you were growing up, because there weren't a lot of blacks, you must have had a lot of friends of different races?

Sure. That's why I really couldn't see things that were really bad, except we had to sit upstairs in the theater and restaurants we couldn't go into. Didn't have the money anyway.

Was there a strong sense of community within the blacks that were here when you were a kid?

Well, yeah, picnics. The lady you really got to interview is Bernice Young. She was quite active in the community and she used to be in charge of getting up these programs in church.

What church did you go to?

I was raised in the Baptist. She would always be in charge of the youth groups. I remember we would go to Irvine Park, before they built everything up, and have big church picnics and bicycle riding and boating, lots of food and homemade ice cream.

But you socialized more with blacks, or more with whites, or more with Mexicans?

I would say with Mexicans. Because I was raised around them, we played around together—went to ball games and different events. I'd say the Mexicans a little bit more. We'd have misunderstandings, but not like today where you get into a beef and they blow you away. Then you just duked it out and everybody would go their own way.

Do you think that things are worse now?

I think crime and everything is worse now. Gee, we could leave the house and wouldn't have to lock up. We got broke into once since we've been here, but we never did when we lived on First Street. They wouldn't have got anything anyway except a handful of bills.

You were here in Santa Ana when the Watts riots [in 1965] took place. What did people say about it?

Well, I think people just got tired of the style of living and being pushed around.

Did the blacks in Orange County feel that they had it better here?

I don't know if they felt that they had it better, but I don't think they really wanted to associate themselves with the riots there in Watts.

As a black man, have you ever had times when the police gave you a hard time or you were stopped or anything?

Well, I think you get the feeling that even if you just drive into a mostly all-white neighborhood, they watch you. They watch you closely. I mean, because of your color. I feel that they're judging a few blacks, or all, by a few wrongdoers. I think they figure we're all like that and that's something I don't really like. Heck, I just went over to my niece's house a couple of weeks ago and she lives over on [mostly white] South Baker. I could see this patrolman. He followed me. And then I drove into her driveway and backed out and parked on the side and he was down there watching on the corner. I don't think that they should finger someone or think that all of them are going to do wrong. Just because you got a few wrongdoers, you can't judge all by one. The same way when you go to your department store, they follow you around.

Why do you think more blacks haven't come to Orange County?

They think Orange County is still the Birchers [John Birch Society, an ultra-conservative political organization with a strong membership base in Orange County during the 1960s].

Do you feel that or is that just the reputation that Orange County has?

The reputation. Because I was born and raised here and you're just as free here as you are there.

Or are things really different here? Like opportunities for jobs?

Well, my friend, he's built himself up to a lawyer now and he's going for a judgeship. He says that his color has held him back. He feels as though he should have been promoted and he qualifies. Whites come in and they promote them before they do him. He's bitter about that.

Thank you, Mr. Jones, for your time and hospitality.

ERNESTINE RANSOM[1]

Ernestine Ransom was born in Muskogee, Oklahoma, on March 12, 1923. Muskogee is located near the Arkansas-Oklahoma border. She doesn't remember much about Muskogee, because she was quite young when her family left there. She talks about her teenage years living in Santa Ana and her involvement in civic affairs, often being the only black person. After the death of civil rights leader Martin Luther King, Jr. in 1968, she became involved with Southern Christian Leadership Conference (SCLC) and University of California, Irvine (UCI). Ms. Ransom lives in the same Santa Ana retirement development as her two remaining sisters, and is still involved in both UCI and community affairs. Photo from high school graduation, 1941.

Can you tell us about your parents?

My father was a Baptist minister and my mother and my dad had thirteen children. I'm the eleventh of the thirteen and grew up with nine, around Oklahoma. Because my father was a minister, he was traveling from church to church. I called him a circuit minister. We moved in a lot of areas in Oklahoma; Arkansas; McGehee, Arkansas; Van Buren, Arkansas—I think about those, but I was still a young child.

I was born in 1923 and I came to California in 1937. We had moved from Arkansas to Topeka, Kansas, and we stayed there a while. He had a church there, and then my father came out to California to a convention. He wrote back and said, "There are two churches available," one in Santa Ana and the other [also in California] was in Blythe or Needles or someplace. And he said, "They have cotton down there." My sister and I said, "Oh, my God. I hope he doesn't get that. I don't want to pick any more cotton." So he chose the one here in Santa Ana, and that's when we came, in 1937, November.

When you said "no more cotton," that meant pastors didn't make very much money at the time, so the family probably had to work.

[1] Oral History No. 3241. Interview date: April 28, 2004, at Ms. Ransom's home in Santa Ana, California. Interviewer: Robert Johnson.

That is very true, yes. It's my understanding that my mother took in laundry; she did laundry. And everybody was working.

Your father's name was T. J. Anderson? And he came to what church in Santa Ana?

Second Baptist. At that time, it was located on Raitt. The street name, Artesia, changed to Raitt, but at that time it was 8th and Artesia.

But then he only stayed at Second Baptist a couple of years. What did he do after that?

He went back to Oklahoma, and that's where he died

Did your family have any trouble finding housing in Santa Ana?

Well, being the minister's family, they had a location just adjacent to the church. The church owned the property, and at that time, they used to have parsonages for ministers. Most of the black people, when I first came to Santa Ana, lived on two streets. On 1st Street, one or two, but everybody else lived on 2nd Street in Santa Ana. Then they started to spread out a little bit.

Tell me what happened in the neighborhood. Did the kids play on the street a lot and play baseball or games?

When I was seventeen and eighteen, Franklin [Grammar] School was on 4th Street, and that's where we would go mostly. Or we would go to Santiago Park for church picnics and things like that. We didn't play in the streets or anything. We always went to a school ground, and there was volleyball or baseball down there. We rode our bicycles a lot. And we would have church picnics at Santiago Park, [then] later, at Irvine Park. The only pool was at Santa Ana High School, and we *had* to take swimming because that was required. Because we lived so close to the beach everyone needed to learn how to swim. There was no pool for any recreation except at the local school. There were ice skating rinks or skating rinks, but we had a very difficult time in skating. The police were always there and they made it difficult for us [because we were black], and we would leave.

How about downtown Santa Ana [one mile away]?

We just went down for necessities, and that was it. I guess we stayed pretty close to our own community, among ourselves. There were two black churches at that time: Second Baptist and the Methodist (AME) church. Well, I forget the name of the movie [theater] right there on Main Street, but we naturally were in the balcony of the movie. They had a balcony, and that's where we sat, were required to sit.

Were there any other places you couldn't go?

Those are the areas that I remember not being able to enjoy. I was quite involved with school activities, the high school band, so we did things together as a group from the school. But as a group from the community, those are the things that I remember. I remember once that a lady, Mrs. Wyatt, who was quite an educator, took us to see Marian Anderson at Santa Ana High School, a group of us from our church.[2] Of course, naturally, our seats were the furthest back and way up, but at least we got to see Marian Anderson. That's the beginning of my enjoying music of all kinds, as well as theater.

Was it a good place to be a teenager, do you think?

It was a good place for *me* because we [blacks] were close to each other. We [the black community] were very small in number, at that time, so we knew everybody. The things that we did were mostly church-related. I didn't learn to even dance. If there were dances, my father being a minister, I couldn't go, unless we sneaked and went. I can remember my mother giving me permission to go to my high school prom. Not mine, but I went to a friend's in Long Beach [about twenty miles west of Santa Ana in Los Angeles County]. Evidently, we also had relationships with the black community of Long Beach, and I can remember going over there a lot for different things.

There was no embalming for blacks when we first came. They would get someone from Long Beach to come over and pick the bodies up and take care of them, until Brown's Mortuary started. Regarding the older blacks, nobody but Brown's Mortuary would take care of them.

Blacks were buried where?

Oh, they were buried at the Santa Ana cemetery as well as Fairhaven. My mother's buried at Fairhaven. They were buried here, but they just didn't do the embalming.[3]

You asked me about how I felt about growing up. I've been accused of seeing the world through rose-colored glasses. I've always enjoyed where I was, and I think of where I came from. As we would move from school to school, and they were mostly black schools, I would always have to fight, and I was so glad to get into an integrated situation here and had no more fights. So I've always enjoyed my life in Santa Ana.

Were there any other black students at Santa Ana High?

There may have been about five of us, mostly girls. There was one young man in my class. I was the only black in the high school band, so I've just really sort

---

[2] The concert took place on February 16, 1938, and was covered on the first page of the *Santa Ana Register* newspaper the next day in an article titled, "Voice of Marian Anderson Makes S. A. Music History." The selections included, Schubert's "Ave Maria," opera selections, songs, and Negro spirituals. Quoting the reviewer, ". . .a program that will go down in history, probably, the finest musical event that this community has ever experienced." The following year, Marion Anderson was prevented from singing in the Daughters of the American Revolution (DAR)-owned Constitution Hall, in Washington, D.C., because of a whites-only clause. Public outrage, led by Eleanor Roosevelt, resulted in a free outdoor concert, before 75,000 people and a national radio audience, on the steps of the Lincoln Memorial on Easter Sunday, April 9, 1939. This was a milestone in civil rights history.

[3] The adjacent Santa Ana and Fairhaven cemeteries are the two largest cemeteries in Santa Ana.

of been by myself, involved in things as the only black. My life has been like opening doors, or whatever you want to call it. I also was involved in drama at the school because I wanted to be. I loved drama so I would assist in handing out the costumes. Definitely sports. Again, the only one in my class—baseball, basketball, field hockey.

What did you do after high school?

I wanted to be a nurse, so I went to Los Angeles, to LACC [Los Angeles City College], and worked in Los Angeles County Hospital after the school for a little while. Walked in one night and the nurse asked me if I wanted to help her alcohol down a patient who had died. That was my first experience with death, and I walked out, and that was the end of that relationship. I did not become a nurse and I did not work with patients, although now I'm working at Fairhaven Memorial [Cemetery as service director].

So you went to L.A. City College. Did you finish there?

The war broke out, and I came back and started working at Douglas Aircraft for a while. I put the conduits in the C47s and I did some riveting. Then I got married in '44 to Earl Davis Ransom. After my marriage, we moved to Los Angeles and stayed there for a while. Then we came back to Santa Ana and we had two daughters, Jacquelyn and Francyne. We stayed with my mom for a while. Practically every new black person that came to town met my mother. She was called Mother Anderson. She found them work, as well as stayed at her place until they were able to find another place. She had a place on 4th Street in Santa Ana, and she turned the garage into housing. Little by little at that time, you could see blacks moving further out, but not very far: 7th Street, 8th Street.

Did you work outside of the home?

No, I didn't. He [my husband] worked at the Balboa Bay Club. That was after Treesweet cannery. The war came and after the war jobs started changing, and blacks began to see that there were openings at other places. I'm not sure—I think it was J. C. Penney, another company that he worked in. We were divorced in '72. Jackie was in college. They had both graduated from high school. Francyne was working. Jackie graduated from Long Beach State College. Then after I went to UCI, Francyne went back to college and got her degree from UCI.

When the children were growing up, were most of your friendships with people in the church?

By that time, I had been active in the state convention, and we had been involved in camps with the American Baptist. The YWCA opened up and organized a Phyllis Wheatley Club. That was when integration was happening. My girls were involved in Y Teens and I was a Y Teen counselor. But when they were growing up, I had joined First Baptist Church Santa Ana and was active there. I'm not sure whether I was the first black, but anyway, I was very active in that church. My oldest daughter, Jackie, got married in that church. Francyne was active with children in church school. Then we would go to the retreats and camp, and we were integrating.

I was chosen to be a part of that integration that was happening with the universities. That's how I got involved with the UCI Extension. We were inviting people of all situations—doctors, lawyers, housing people, as well as people like me, housewives, whatever—to talk. And we did that once a week. We went to Santa Barbara [a beach resort city 100 miles north of Los Angeles], and speakers were there from all over, and all the universities were [represented] there. The white speaker was telling the blacks his problem, and the black speaker was telling the whites their problem. And it was hell. You heard people saying, "Get the guns out." I mean, it was really bad. Our group was so glad to get together, because those other groups were so loud and everything. That's where I learned that loud voices don't always mean a fight. Some people scream because they need you to hear them, and if you don't hear them, their voices get louder. That was quite an experience.

You were so much involved in community things, that that more or less formed your education and made you a person that UCI and others wanted to be involved with their program. Is that saying it?

That is probably saying it. The thing that happened—one of the women in the community said, "Come with me because I'm not able to speak up like you would. They're trying to get all the money, and we need some for our community." So I went, and I spoke up. There happened to be a professor there that was in charge of this, from UC Irvine, and I got a call. He said, "I heard you at the group, and I wondered, how would you like to become the counselor for EOP [Educational Opportunity Program] at UC Irvine? This is what I'm organizing." You've got to be kidding, I get paid for doing something that I've been volunteering [to do] all my life?

That's how I got to UC Irvine, through that invitation, and through my activities, like you say, in the community. I just happened to be vocal and he wanted me to be their counselor. These were [mostly black minority] students coming from all different neighborhoods that we would choose. Some of the students were from northern California, as well as here. Most of my activities were within the university, except that we would go to different schools and tell them about the program. "Here you can get your education now because we want you to catch up," quote, unquote.

Were you in touch with the feelings of the black students towards Orange County? Did they have any idea what they were coming to?

No. At first, I guess I wasn't in touch by my actions, because I can remember one of the students that came from northern California said to me that I reminded him of a woman that was his Sunday school teacher. He said, "She'd take me to church on Sunday, but if you walked on her land on Monday, she would cuss you out." I was very hurt by that remark because I *was* a Sunday school teacher, and I guess that's the way I came across. They had all kinds of meetings, all the time, out at UCI. Black Student Union. I guess I spoke up in one of the meetings. Whatever I said, he turned to me, "You don't remind me of that Sunday school teacher anymore." I guess I had *my* way and my time to be. Period. At that moment, I guess, is when I gained his respect, because I did speak up. I don't even know what I said or why. They used to tease me because, at the time, the dress was different, the hair was different. They would say, "Sister, why don't you come home?" [chuckles] Finally, I got the natural and I came home. [laughs]

I went out to UCI in '68 and walked across campus and I saw one black student, and I said, "How many do you have?" He said, "You've seen it." So there was only one black student out there. Then we came aboard, and the blacks started coming in, as well as the Mexicans. It was not easy, because the staff didn't know how to relate. When I was hired, they said, "You're on your own. You can make it or break it. It's up to you."

We recruited, and we brought them in. We had to teach them how to use a bank account, everything. They would have discussions with us, and we would listen to their concerns. We gave them their rooms and their roommates, and we listened to the regular staff's concern about what they were doing. They would group in groups. They couldn't accept the fact that they were grouped. That scared them for some reason. So it was a learning experience on both sides.

When I went and met Chancellor [Daniel] Aldrich, he asked me, "What can the university do for the community?" And I could not answer him because I didn't have any expectations of what the university could be. I was learning. That was the first time I'd been in a situation like that.

Looking back, do you feel that UCI has had any effect?

We were involved. I was involved with a group of young students who were in social science, who wanted to be active in the community. That's how the Southwest Community Center in Santa Ana was organized. It was due to UCI students.

What were your feelings in the sixties about Orange County's really sharp political turn to the right?

It was difficult for me to read the *Register.* I was not a strong person in politics. I was aware, but I guess my feelings are not something that are out there and I'm screaming with them. I do it my way. I was aware. When we first came to Santa Ana, my mother and I came over to Orange to clean somebody's house, and that's when I learned that we had to be out of the city before dark. My mom told me and evidently somebody told her. She just said, "We have to be out of here before dark." So we rushed to clean the place and get out of there. That was the city of Orange. As you talk and share this with other people, whites, they tell you about *their* communities, that it happened there also.

We stayed in Santa Ana until 1971. Then I moved to Orange. I bought a duplex in the area of Chapman and Cambridge. I love the city of Orange, even though I have that history. That was very funny, talking about an experience. When I first bought my duplex, I used to drive home, push the garage door, open it and go in the house, and sit inside and suck my thumb, I say, and contemplate. Then one day I looked around at the people on the street, and I realized, hey, what is this? You belong here, you own property. It wasn't until [after] a few months, [that] I could accept the fact that I was in Orange, of all places, the place where I wasn't supposed to spend the night when I was growing up. I love the city of Orange now. I'm still involved with Orange Housing and Development [non-profit corporation].

Did you have any trouble buying that duplex?

It was very interesting. I saw the place at night, and I didn't find out until later, when people show you homes at night, they don't want the neighbors to know that they're showing that property to the blacks. I didn't have any trouble, but the tenant moved out just as I moved in. When I moved in, I wanted to go next door and see how things were and look the place over and see if they needed any improvement or anything. She did not want me to go in. "Oh, you can't see this." That's because they had already started packing and they were on their way out. The real estate agent got me another tenant. He was a policeman of Orange and a very good tenant. Not even in the city of Orange did I have any problem. It was just within *me* the first few weeks, childhood memories.

I did look at some other property, and they definitely said they were not going to sell to blacks at that time. The agent apologized and said she didn't have anything to do with it; she didn't know anything about it, but we did go to look at a place. Again it was at night. Talking to other people who had taken real estate, if they show you the property at night, that means that there's possibly a problem.

Sundown Towns

The term "sundown town," in its most literal meaning, is a municipality that disallows black people in that town after the sun goes down. It was made clear by US Supreme Court in cases such as Buchanan v. Warley *(1917) that laws and ordinances cannot be enacted denying any person the right to equal protection under the 14th Amendment. Individuals could discriminate but not the government. This being the case, we do not find ordinances or resolutions that prohibit blacks from being in a town after dark. Nevertheless, in the first half of the twentieth century, it was "common knowledge" that there were "laws" to that effect in Orange County cities like Brea and Orange. Therefore, few black people were inclined to challenge these non-existent laws, which might be enforced by police—for example, through jailing the person under a vagrancy law. James Loewen, in his book* Sundown Towns *(2005), states that eyewitnesses tell of sundown signs in more than 150 communities in 31 states. Most read something like, "Nigger, Don't Let The Sun Go Down On You In (the name of the city)." The authors of this present book have disclosed no hard evidence that signs like this were posted in Orange County, but we do know while the Klan was in control of the Anaheim city council in late 1924, the letters K.I.G.Y. (Klansman I Greet You) were painted on the main streets of the city (by police themselves or by their consent, according to the* Anaheim Bulletin*).*

We talked about the SCLC [after Dr. Martin Luther King's death].

We were very active with the nuns from St. Joseph. They were part of our group. People from all over Orange County became active in the SCLC activities that we were doing. I stopped going to the meetings when I started working. The last activity that I was involved in was out on one of the store lots where we were signing people up to register.

Tell me about your children's education, social life, dating, schools.

Jackie was the first and very active at Willard Junior High School. Actually, she was chosen president. She was *very* involved. That was interesting that *she* won the election as president, but when I went to take her picture, the white vice-president was in the office with her. She did not have that office all by herself. She had to share with the loser. She was very active all through high school. Most of her activities were integrated. Actually, she didn't go to her senior prom because she was up for scholarships, and I didn't want her to because the person who wanted to take her was a white student, and I didn't want anything to happen to keep her from getting scholarships. I didn't know what the attitude would be. She did go out with this young white man, but he came by the house and was interviewed. They wanted to go to Los Angeles. I asked him what he would do if anything happened, if somebody jumped them. We just put him through it. And he said he would take care of her. So we let her go. [laughs] That was quite interesting.

Francyne, on the other hand, was altogether different. She was totally involved with African Americans all her life. That's the difference between the two. I can remember when we were integrating the camps up at Thousand Pines [in the San Bernardino Mountains], someone asked me if we wanted to move to Long Beach. I asked Francyne, and she said, "If we move into a black community, yeah." It didn't matter for me and Jackie, but for her, it was definitely that.

I don't think either one of them did much dating. There wasn't much dating among the minority students. They had friends, both Mexican as well as white, but there wasn't much dating. They had parties, house parties, a lot of house parties.

Did they get married ?

Yes. Jackie married a young man that she met over there [at Long Beach State]. No children. He was black, yes. She did a lot of going to fraternity parties here in Orange County. I forget the name of the fraternity, but she was the most popular one. Jackie was married twice. She divorced her first husband and married Ryan, who is white, her second marriage. She died in '91 with cancer. Francyne has one child, a son, Myron. She lives in Mission Viejo and works at Santa Ana, in the financial aid office, Santa Ana College.

But you had said Francyne was more comfortable with black people; yet she stayed in Orange County.

Oh, yes. (laughs) I see what you're saying. Now it's probably still the same. She knows people, but most of her friends are African American. I guess if you grow up here, that's what you see, and you don't realize that you've missed anything else. We go to Los Angeles—at that time Jackie was little and she said, "Oh, Mother, look at all the Negroes." Because we didn't see that many in Orange County.

You went to a predominately white church. You worked at UCI. You have friends all over the community. Do you find that most of your friendships are with black people or with white people?

I think most of my friendships are with black people. But, it's a combination of the two. I'm living in a community here, I lawn bowl. There are two of us [blacks] that are lawn bowling. For a long time, I was the only one. Because I like activities, I like traveling, I like theater. So the things that I'm interested in, a majority of whites are interested in the same things.

What have been the positives and negatives of living in Orange County?

I think the positive was when we *were* in this community, because we did things together. But as we started to prosper after the war, and housing opened up because those were the things we were working on—opening up—and people started moving out [of Santa Ana], we lost our voice almost, especially, the political clout that we did have when we were all together. I think that's the negative. And we don't see each other as often as we used to. To me, I think that would be the negative, that we've lost something by spreading out. We are also leaving Orange County, moving, of all places, [back to the] South. A lot of the blacks are going south again, because property's cheaper there. I've had friends move to Alabama—I mean, really south—Texas, go back to Texas and other areas. They love it. They have these big homes that they're enjoying. They left the property here with their children.

Most of the people that I've worked with and grew up with, I see them every so often. We'll see each other at funerals or some big event, but otherwise, not very often.

Events like at UCI maybe, some talks?

Yes. I'm on the retirement board out there, so I meet every two months, but this is with the university staff that has retired. They have lectures out there every month on Wednesdays in the University Club, and when I'm available, I can go to lunch and then listen to a lecture on different topics. I see people like that at the basketball games. I'm still involved with that, and I still have season tickets for the drama department. I see the students out there and I read about the activities, but I'm not involved in them. I am definitely retired.

My two sisters live here in Lake Park [a development in Santa Ana] with me, and that's good because we're the last three of my family. We used to be scattered all over and went to the last funeral, of my brother, back in Virginia, and realized that our family's getting smaller and we're all in this community. My daughter Francyne graduated UCI. Her son, Myron, graduated at Chico State. I think the exciting thing is he just moved back to Orange County. Just last year he bought out near Mission Viejo [south Orange County city]. I'm glad to have him back.

Are you glad that you stayed in Orange County, overall, or do you wish maybe you should have lived somewhere else?

No, no, no. I like it here. I love traveling so I travel, but I like it here. This is where I grew up.

Thank you very much, Ernestine Ransom, for being very open and letting me interview you for the Cal State Fullerton Center for Oral and Public History.

VERNON NAPIER[1]

Vernon Napier came to Orange County from Tulsa in 1942, when he was less than one year old. His elementary school experience was at an integrated school on the east side of Santa Ana. He feels that he sees the world differently from how he would have had he attended a largely black school, as he did as a teenager. Mr. Napier is a philosophical person who deeply interprets the complexities of his life throughout the interview. He still lives in Santa Ana. Photo from high school graduation, 1960.

Mr. Napier, please tell us about your parents.

My father, Vernon Napier, was born in Eufaula, Oklahoma, in 1913, [and was] raised most of the time there on a farm. He was one of twelve kids. My mother, Rosetta, was an only child, born in Tulsa, Oklahoma, six years later. They met in Tulsa after my father's family had moved to that area. After a two-year courtship, they were married, and after two years of marriage, I was born. My father was a shoemaker. He came to California for employment at what is now Orange County, or John Wayne Airport, which was then a military installation.

Did they come out together?

He came out, preceded her by three months or so, and then my mother and I came out after he had gotten himself established here in Santa Ana. That was 1942. Being less than a year old when they came here, this is the only place that I've known as home.

My mother was a domestic. She worked at that until well into her forties. She participated in the choir at church, at Johnson Chapel AME, and my father became an usher and then a deacon in that church, I do believe. My mother died at fifty-eight years old, and my father died at seventy-six.

---

[1] Oral History No. 3227. Interview date: March 10, 2004, at Mr. Napier's home in Santa Ana, California. Interviewer: Robert Johnson.

Your grandmother, on your mother's side, Legenia Gardner, was written up in the paper [*Orange County Register* Obituary, February 14, 1998]. Did she come first?

No. It might have been during the war, but it might have been after. She also worked as a domestic for a long time and participated in the church. [My grandmother and my parents] got along quite well, and they had an awful lot of things to pass along to myself and, by then, my two brothers. We were given an upbringing in the church, and it would be kind of surprising that we're not staunch churchgoers today, but I don't know. That's kind of a complicated thing.

Where did you live when you first came here?

My parents moved to the 1300 block on West Second Street in Santa Ana, which is in a house that's just a half a block from Johnson Chapel AME today, about a half block west of Bristol. I didn't attend school until my parents moved to the east side of town, which was 308 South Standard. We attended grade school there. It was a pretty good blender. There were an awful lot of different ethnic groups going to that school, and there was very little concern about ethnicity in the schools at that time. At least, I wasn't sensitive to that.

Were there some black children in that school?

Very few; I could count maybe four in the entire school. It was quite a mixing pot there, but we got along pretty well. I was tall for my age back then, and my friends tended to be older than I was, because we could do basically the same things.

Did you move then?

Yes. First of all, to reiterate, my father came here and for the next twenty-five years of his life he was preparing to move back to Oklahoma, so he never bought a piece of property. He was poor. But we didn't know that. We never got into buying property until I was an adult and I went in with him and bought a piece of property on a partnership basis so that my mother would have a house. All the time she was dreaming about a house, and my father says, "Well, we're going back to Oklahoma." But she wanted a house and he wanted to move back to Oklahoma, and she would say, "You're never going to get there." And he didn't. But he had his dream. So we moved around a bit. We went from the east side of town to the west side of town to a house back on the same block that we lived on when we first came out here from Oklahoma. I was into my teenage years by then. We were always thinking about the fact that my father and mother were going to move, and we didn't know where we were going to live, because we didn't want to go to Oklahoma. So that was one of the uncertainties of our life, early times.

As things turned out, it was pretty good, because we met quite a mixture of people. But in our moving, I could see a social difference. Once we came back to the west side of town from the east, there were more blacks in the neighborhood, and we really didn't fit in that well. We were kind of an oddity because we didn't see the same problems with people. My younger brother, being six years younger, was influenced by that group of people when we came back into the west side of town. For all his life he had that influence from them, a mentality that he gleaned from his friends around him. It was troubling to see how differently he looked at the world through his entire life.

You lived mostly with the whites and mixed race people for your early years. When you moved back to southwest Santa Ana, there were enough black people that they sort of hung around together?

Right. There were social groups, and I really wasn't a part of the social groups because I didn't come up that way. Then one of the redeeming factors was the fact that one of our neighbors, when we came back to the west side, walked up and asked if I wanted to be a Cub Scout. I thought that was the coolest thing in the world, so the parents decided, well, we're going to put him in Cub Scouts. I was in the Scouts all the way through Boy Scouts, and through the Explorers, and I met this menagerie of people again.

So I really had no sensitivity about all this until the Little Rock [school integration] incident. There were all these questions that came up that we had never even confronted before. We looked at it and went, "My God, there's a hassle going on." My parents then took us aside and told us about race riots and stuff in Oklahoma when they were younger and how things had happened; horrendous things had happened that we didn't know anything about.[2] That was our introduction to the problems with racists. Now, as you know, in Santa Ana, there was stuff boiling around us all the time, but we were just little kids and we didn't really know what was going on.

Let's talk about that some. Did you used to go to the movies? And if so, did you have to sit in a certain place?

No. I never experienced that. I do recall that the Mexican kids were suffering from the label of being *Pachucos*. That was the story back then. They wore their pants like my son wears his pants, low and all that, and they slicked their hair back. You had to be aware because they would always have, supposedly, a razor in their pocket or something and were going to "getcha." The biggest threat that we knew as kids, was these kids who were members of gangs. I thought for a long time the only gangs were Latino gangs, and as your horizons grow, you see things different, but at that time—

Ourselves, as far as accommodations were concerned, we were never put in a situation by our parents where we would be—I think we might have been protected by our parents, looking back at it. The only things that I remember were the questions about swimming in the public pools. I remember vaguely a hassle about the Orange Plunge and the Memorial Park pool [in Santa Ana]. While I don't think we were ever denied access to the Memorial Park pool, we were, at one time, denied access to the Orange Plunge. The Orange Plunge was something that was kind of a sinister thing. You don't go to the Orange Plunge, I can remember that.

[2] These were the bloody Tulsa riots in 1921. As many as 300 blacks were killed and 1,256 residences were destroyed, mostly in the black community.

How about the beach? Did your family go to the beach at all?

We went to the beaches; we would go to Newport. We would go especially to Balboa, because we would walk on the jetties. We would go fishing on the jetties and surf fishing down in the Wedge, I think it was; my father, that was one of his big pastimes. He enjoyed fishing. We would have wienie bakes and do our marshmallows and stuff. I don't remember any restrictions there.

I didn't realize that, like I said, there were so many problems and stuff, violence, coming up. I think it was a benefit to live in a society like we live in, to come up the way we did, because it allowed us to make judgment of people based on their actions and not their ethnicity. Even at the time of the Civil Rights Movement, a lot of the people in the Civil Rights Movement had a different background and different experience than we had. A lot of the things that they were discussing and talking about, we were being confronted with for the first time.

At sporting events in, let's say high school, did the black kids all sit together, or did people sit with their friends, black or white?

It was pretty much a closed situation. So when you ask about people closing up together, I think if people aren't in a situation where they're raised, not by design but just by circumstance, to be around other people, they're going to be aware of that and they're going to close themselves up to feel comfortable. And I think this goes both ways. So I look at that as just being a normal reaction.

Oh, let me ask you about the neighborhood. Did you play baseball out in the street, or did you always go to a park?

When you look at kids depicted today playing, we were basically that way. It was in the street or wherever we could go to have a good time. Our parents supported us at doing what we did, and we carried that tradition on to our kids.

Did you play football on people's lawns?

Oh, yeah. We played football, we played baseball, we broke a couple windows, got ourselves into trouble. I got banged on the head one time and split my head open and had to have stitches and all that. That was just a normal childhood. Did some dangerous things that we look back at now and, oh, my God, I lived through that!

How about at Santa Ana High School? Did you play sports?

I was involved in football, basketball, and I ran a little track. I was in the band; I was in percussion. My senior year, on a dare, I became the drum major of the band, and the football coach was ticked off because I did that. So here I was, instead of playing football, I was sitting on the sidelines as a drum major. But I did pretty well at that. In my time in the Boy Scouts, we had marched in parades, and I think there was a ten-year period in my life where I never saw the Santa Ana Christmas Parade, [because] I was always in it.

So after we got through with Boy Scouts, I went into Civil Air Patrol. We had a drill team in Civil Air Patrol, and again a very integrated group of people. That's when I thought I was going to make the step into the military to become a pilot, but then I found out that I was too tall. I was brokenhearted. And I got away from aviation, which was my first love, and still is, and got involved in cars and stuff like that and became a "gear head."

Where would you buy things? Would you just walk or take the bus to downtown Santa Ana?

Downtown Santa Ana was the big shopping center at the time; most of the time we walked. There was a period of time my father didn't own a car, so when we were younger we would walk to town and go to the movies and all that. It was quite a deal. The family would go on [an] expedition. We'd get there, and we'd go to Pringle's Drugstore at Fourth and Broadway and have ice cream cones—big doings back then.

On Saturdays, we would attend a free show. All the kids in the whole town would be lined up around the block. There was no segregation or anything, just first come, first served. You'd walk in. It was big doings for us. We were able to, at a pretty young age, walk to town—what we called town, 4th Street—and go to the free show. We'd have a quarter in our pockets and be able to have the goodies and watch the show and come home and dream until the next week. This went on for several years in our younger lives. The town was, to us, a comfortable place, and we enjoyed ourselves and didn't see a lot of what was going on.

How about church? Was that a good part of your social life?

Yes and no. It was, a lot of times, drudgery to go to church for us because the two-hour church service on Sunday was a killer. We'd have to sit still for two hours. Then we got to know some of the ministers as we got older. These ministers would come through, and there were these classic characters that came through that were really interesting to know and entertaining to listen to. And they had a message to give you. That was great.

One of the drawbacks of the church, to me, was the politics and the fact that the church was, in so many people's lives, I think, the top of the social curve. That was the fashion show, the gossip pit. Everything went on around the church. That was the part that I really didn't like. We never were the fashion people. We never had the newest and shiniest car, we never had any of the things to show off, and I don't know whether that's resentment or just being bored with all that. I really don't. It could be a bad point or a good point of my personality. But I just didn't like that.

What was it like as an older teenager in terms of social life—your early twenties, or even your late twenties?

There were clubs that people hung out at, and there were parties and stuff. We were included in most of the parties of our group, our ethnic group, and also parties and clubs of the majority group, because we were members of the society at large. We didn't have any problems with social life. We had a great time.

One of the biggest problems we had was the fact that, after getting involved with cars and stuff, we got into the *American Graffiti* cruising scene, and we must have burned a couple thousand gallons of fuel driving around Santa Ana, Garden Grove, Whittier, and places like that, to the cruising places in our cars. We probably gave up a few Ph.D.'s just fiddling around with the cars. That got to be a big part of our lives. I say "our" lives because by this time my brothers had come of age, and they could get around the same as I, so it became a pastime.

Friday nights you would go down to—there was Russ's and Oscar's and Winchell's Donut Shop. Any one of those three places you would hook up with whoever you're going to be hooked up with that night, and you would go cruising around different places. There was never, at least in my time, there were never fights involved. The biggest thing was to show off your iron, to show what you had. The parties came from the people that you met. People would invite you over to a party or something, and you would go, and that would be the social highlight of the weekend, or whatever. It was, as far as I was concerned, pretty typical of everybody.

Then what happened after high school?

I went to Santa Ana JC [Junior College] for a couple years. I worked for Uniroyal for a couple years, and I got nailed by the draft and I ended up going to Vietnam. I was drafted in '64. I graduated from high school in 1960. I ended up being volunteered to go to Vietnam. That was an experience. I think it was something that, at least the emotions, I think most people need to experience. When I came home, it was something of a negative experience, a humbling experience, or something, [to] be treated the way some people treated you.

So you didn't come back as a hero.

Oh, no. It was funny. We were the first mass troop movement to Vietnam. But at the time we were leaving, there was a band playing, and there were a thousand people or so standing out there on the dock yelling and waving at us and all that. This rain cloud came over, and it just rained all over everything. The band left, the people left, and then the boat didn't get off the dock. We went below deck and came back the next day. The band was there and about twenty people were there, and they all waved us away, and we left. So when we came back, you felt like you were a rat sneaking through the kitchen. It was really different.

I think a lot of people were afraid to go there, so they looked at it and said I'm not going to go, I'm not going to do this because I can't participate. If you look at it, some people had very valid reasons for protest because the history didn't bear out what we were doing. I didn't know that at the time, and I didn't feel that I knew enough about it to protest it. I was just given orders to go, so I went.

You came back here, and what did you do?

I went back to work for Uniroyal. I went to school at night to learn, not on a set curriculum, just to learn some of the things that I needed to learn and apply to what I was doing in my life at the time. I went to Santa Ana College. I went to adult classes at night and got some college credits, but they were not [tied] to a curriculum. Later on, I was working at Uniroyal and experienced my first and last union strike. A friend of mine called me and said, "Would you want to go to work for Jerry Jardine?" I was interested in cars, so I went to work for Jerry Jardine, and that was my first job working in metal fabrication and welding and stuff like that. I worked for that company for six years or so, did every job in their plant, and learned how to do everything. Jerry wouldn't give me the reins to run the shop, so I was ticked off, and went to work for another company.

So you left Jardine and you went to work for Dan Gurney.

That was a race car shop, but I wasn't involved in the race cars. I went to work for the motorcycle division and built motorcycles for police activities. We built the first bikes that were used on the TV series *CHiPs*. We developed a whole line and got these things together and produced the first five hundred motorcycles for police officers, police motorcycles built from 900 Kawasaki, KZ900s.

A spin-off from that was my next job. I worked for another company, basically doing the same thing. I did all the production tooling and scheduling and all the stuff that had to do with running that operation. I had done that over the years until I opened my own company about fifteen years ago, which to me, it was a mistake because it put me in a situation where I was throwing the party and nobody came. Being stubborn, I stuck with it for a long time.

When did you get married?

Let's see. We got married in 1973. I knew Jean Alderson's mother and father and two or three of her brothers before I ever met her. We were all patrons of a place called Jerry's Barbecue on Seventeenth Street in Santa Ana. I, in the days when I was younger, enjoyed going to bars and having a drink. Usually, at those places, you would sit down and there would be a good time had by all, and you would leave that night, and the police weren't sitting out the door waiting for you to come out the door.

Well, Jean came in one night with one of her workmates. It was late one night, and she bought drinks for everybody sitting at the bar. We had a spat over the fact that she was buying me a drink, and we didn't speak for a couple of months. She would come in and steam at me, and I would steam back at her and ignore her and go on. So finally one night we talked, and we started going out together. A year and a half later we got married; then a year after that we had a kid, first kid.

Your wife is white. How did your families take it?

Well, my family, it really didn't make a whole bunch of difference to them. They didn't seem to be concerned about that. My wife's family, they disowned her for the first six months or so. They didn't come to the wedding. Everybody else but her mother and father came to the wedding. In six months or so, we were invited to dinner. I think it was after they heard that she was pregnant. We went to dinner, and then things just kind of wound up and we became closer friends and stuff, and all the problems from before disappeared.

The biggest problem I have right now is that her side of the family sees things on the majority side. They understand what's going on *their* way. My side of the family sees things on the black side. You see things from different points of view, and sometimes you can see where one person assumes and expects things to be one way and another person assumes and expects things to be completely different

I see this in different people all the time. I know people are—the whites in our society feel—so many feel that there are no just restrictions, there are no closed doors, and there's no one really involved in wishing them wrong. Where the blacks, on the other hand, have gotten themselves into the situation where they've given up on the idea that things are going to be straight up. Some of them are very lethal with this. Some of them have given up. My daughters have been involved with characters that you look at and you scratch your head and you feel sorry for them, but you also know that you better not stick your finger out there or they'll bite it off. Because the society that they see is completely different than the society that I see and a different society than you would see in your life

You worked for different companies. Do you feel that being black affected your ability to move up?

Very much so—in a lot of cases, yes. Now, this has a couple different reasons, I think. My own people sometimes project an image that really isn't conducive to the technical world, to the business world. I know who I am. I'm this black guy who's sixty-two years old, who lives in this society that is keyed very much on my appearance. I can easily be the junkman and drive around and people will look at me, and I'm the junkman. If I were to pick up my calculator or to go to the computer and say, okay, I'm going to do this or do this, it doesn't fit the image. I understand that in an image-driven world. I can walk across the parking lot and listen to people lock their cars.

I'm aware of all these things—I mean painfully, sometimes, aware of all these things. A lot of times that's because the image that's projected of me by mass media is detrimental to me in my activities. So I see these things, and I understand them, and I'm sensitive to that. I don't want to be looked at as a clown, I'm not a stuffed shirt, I'm not trying to be somebody else, I'm only me. I'm a guy who was raised here in this town—a rarity, see, in this town. I'm a product of this town. My younger brother had his formative years on the west side of town. On the west side of town, he would be affected differently by those formative years.

I think that my kids, this guy here [Napier's son, Matthew, came into the room], hard worker, he's going to succeed at something. But he, like my daughters, was built to be ships at sea; so when it comes time for them to go, they can go, they can cast off. That's what they're supposed to be doing. My youngest daughter is in New York. She moved back there six months ago from scratch and works two jobs and all that, and she's getting herself up. She just got a degree from University of Arizona and proud of it. She's a good person. But she frightens people around her. Her mother and people around her, like her grandmother, look at her and go, "My God, what's she doing?" But she's an independent person, ready to go out there.

She doesn't need a leader to lead her through things. All she needs to know is where to get the traction to go forward.

And you have how many children?

I have four. The oldest is Amanda, and she's twenty-nine years old now. She's got one daughter. She works for the County of Orange as a welfare case worker or something like that. She went to Western Michigan. She moved back there when she was seventeen to go to Western Michigan. She didn't finish there. She has one daughter now, who is three years old. Amanda plans on going back to school, and she doesn't know exactly what she wants the degree in. But she's a go-getter. She'll succeed at that.

And she married a black person or a white person?

A black person, in Michigan. She has since separated from him. Then I have a number two daughter, which is Amy, who is now twenty-seven years old, and she lives in Wilmington [California]. She's got a son and a daughter. She's a medical insurance writer. They're not getting married. A modern couple, I guess. Then there's Alison, who is twenty-five years old, twenty-four? She is managing a restaurant in New York City, and she figures that she's going to be a semi-permanent resident of New York. She's single.

Did I hear somewhere that one of your daughters is very tall?

Yes. That's Alison, the one that's in New York. She's six foot three. She was a volleyball player in Arizona. She was on the short list of scorers at Arizona in that history of that team. She was an English literature major. And everybody thinks that she should be a model because she's a very attractive young lady at six foot three inches tall, and she's very impressive. She's very independent, and she sees the world as the place to live her life.

About the children. First, where did they go to high school?

The first two went to Valley High School, south Santa Ana. The other two went to Century High School [also in Santa Ana]. In high school, Ally played both volleyball and basketball, and when she got ready to go to college, she was recruited for both sports. Matt followed through in her wake—went to Century High School. He had gone to basketball camps there at Century High School. He played four years varsity there at Century.

How about their social life?

I don't think they really had any real problems with the social aspects of the thing. They made friends, and they have friends today that they went to high school with. Every time Ally comes back in town, she goes and collects her buddies and they take off.

Socially—this guy [Matt] right here, he outdated me when I was in high school. I think they know him by his name and address at the tuxedo shop. He's been to every social function and everything that goes on. I don't think he missed any real high school experiences. And I can say the same thing for my daughters. They really had a good time, if not the most rounded setup. It was a lot like my experience as a kid in this town. There were neighborhoods that I would walk through that people would look at me in disdain, and their eyes would be blue. Now you can walk through the same neighborhoods, and the people's eyes are brown and the same thing's going on.

Were there problems with the police, you being black?

I suspect so, but I didn't really notice any more attention from them than anybody else got. I think that had to do with our activity. A lot of times, the police would stop us only to ask us what we had in that car, how do you make that car work like it's made? We had made some lasting friendships with people that are on the police department. They never were a threat to us.

So we didn't really see harassment there. What we saw was the same thing you see today. It's sometimes misdirection. Sometimes the police are guys that are working on a job that I really don't think that they scholastically or psychologically really qualify for. I think it requires a whole lot more empathy, a whole lot more insight to be a policeman than I see demonstrated. I look at some of these people; I think they've gone to the muscle side, trying to be cops. And they are the minority.

Did you ever have any problems in buying homes?

Again, like my father, I don't think I've ever pushed the issue. The first house was my father and my mother getting a house where they wanted to live. The second house, the first house my wife and I bought, my wife wanted to stay in Santa Ana and the neighborhood that we moved into was in flux.

In this house, we were basically refugees from the old house. We came here because the neighborhood was a nice neighborhood, quiet. By the time we bought here in 1990, the racial situation wasn't really an issue. Besides, I let my wife do the first contact with people, if she'll do that. She doesn't think that's necessary. And half the time people don't know who I am on the phone, so I talk to them and we get things all squared away.

You sound like a white guy.

Yeah. I'm Orange County. That's who I am.

Do you have any stories that you'd like to tell?

We were watching TV one day and we happened to see this guy on the show that was very familiar to us. We had seen him, and at first I didn't really remember where I had seen him. He was a black guy. He was tall like me. And he was the sailing master on this big schooner, Bob Lyon's *Double Eagle* down in Newport Beach. We kept looking at the guy, and about the same time, we came up with, "That guy lives right next door."

And sure as heck, at five o'clock that afternoon we were sitting out front waiting for this guy to show up. He rode the bus from Newport Beach, got off the bus, and walked up and went up the front walk to go to his apartment, which was in the back of my neighbor's property. This particular afternoon, he comes walking up the driveway. "We saw you on TV." And a big smile comes up, and he spoke to us in this accent. He was from the Caribbean.

He was a different person than he looked like on the surface. It was my first experience up close with a black person from a different locale. He had a different point of view to native black people of this society. He didn't really appreciate us as a group too much, and he had seen us over the period of time he was there and didn't approach us because he didn't want to be involved. But then we came together and started talking and became friends. He was an endless source of stories of the sea. He was definitely concerned about his projection of his image as a person. I've met several people like that in my life that have been interesting people that changed my direction.

Are you glad you stayed in Orange County?

I'm glad my father moved to Orange County. I'm the person that I am, who I like, because of my exposure to different people, because of my parents' approach to answering the questions in my life when I was a kid. It gave me the ability to look at things, halfway through high school, and say, well I really don't care what they think. I can be me. I've been raised to be sensitive to what happens with people. I don't like people to call me names, and I don't call other people names. There is no time that anybody has to worry about me using a derogatory term for someone's ethnicity. This is something built in, and I appreciate that.

Those are things that I look at as being thankful for the fact that my father stopped in Santa Ana and went to work here. And for all the things that might have been negative on the surface, I think they're a positive thing and have given me a life that makes me feel that I have some of the keys to how to live life, and I really want to make sure I pass them on to my offspring.

Vern, I thank you for your time and your insights.

Chapter 2
Growing Up After World War II

The following four oral histories involve people who were born in a nine-year time span beginning in 1944, which is one year before the end of World War II. Adleane Hunter, Ed Caruthers, and Jessie Allen were all raised in the South and came to Santa Ana as teenagers in the years 1958 to 1961. They came from all-black schools and found themselves in Santa Ana schools with almost no blacks. Adleane Hunter found the change difficult in that she and her teachers responded to each other in a different way. She had been an excellent student in Florida, but found herself struggling in Santa Ana. Two years later, she had her first black teacher, Miss Darling, who validated and affirmed her. Then in high school, it was a white teacher, Paul Reardon, for whom she worked as a secretary, who was like a father to her and guided her toward college, which led to her life in the dramatic arts.

Ed Caruthers also experienced culture shock, and like Adleane Hunter, he lived in a neighborhood that had a large Hispanic population. One Mexican American youngster in his area became a close friend and many others were also friendly. He had not been involved in sports in Oklahoma, but a junior high school teacher encouraged him to play after-school basketball. When he went to high school, he signed up for football, basketball, and track and field. These were events that led to his high jumping stardom and his future career.

Jessie Allen went to Santa Ana Valley High School when she first came to Santa Ana from Louisiana. She came from an education-oriented family, and not only had she been a good student, but her course work was more advanced in Louisiana. Positive academics, combined with being in a circle with two other black girls—the three being together on the school drill team—made the black-world to mostly white-world transition easier for Jessie Allen.

Connie Jones did not have to deal with the black-to-white culture transition. Although she is younger than the three others in this chapter, and therefore was closer to the rapid increase in Santa Ana's black population, she still grew up, to a large extent, in a non-black world. That is, a world outside of her large black family network and the Second Baptist Church. Her grandmother, Annie Mae Tripp, was a huge presence in her family and in her own life, leading to her present vocation and involvement in church and community.

CONNIE JONES[1]

Connie Jones was born in Santa Ana in 1953 in a little one-room apartment at First and Bristol. She has lived most of her life in the city, except for seven years with her husband while he was in the army. She provides a young person's view of black Santa Ana in the 1960s. Her grandmother, Anne Mae Tripp, was an extraordinary person who had a heart for helping the poor and was the driving force for many years at Santa Ana's Southwest Community Center. Connie Jones, following in her grandmother's footsteps, is presently the director of the community center. Photo from high school graduation, 1971.

Connie Jones, you were born and grew up in Santa Ana; where did your parents come from?

They came from Corpus Christi, Texas, and from Midland, Texas, in the early fifties; my uncle came in '49 and brought the rest of the family here around '51. A lot of the family members came together here, my grandmother and my mom and dad.

Your grandmother on your mother's side.

My grandmother on my mother's side, Annie Mae Tripp; today was her birthday, March 24th. So it's a special day.

Why did they come to Orange County?

For jobs, the opportunity of better jobs. When my grandmother got here, she worked at the [Holly] Sugar Plant, and my mother did nurse's aide work when she came. They heard about Orange County through my uncle, who was in the military and had been stationed out here at El Toro. He went back and told them

---

[1] Oral History No. 3051. Interview date: March 24, 2003, at the Southwest Community Center in Santa Ana, California. Interviewer: Robert Johnson.

the possible opportunities that were here in Orange County, and they chose to settle in Santa Ana, on the east part of town first. Not too far from the sugar plant.

Did they have any problems moving in?

Not really, because they moved in where there were black families already settled. Some moved to the east part and some moved here in the central part of town. When a lot of black families moved into this central part, it was considered Little Texas to them. Most people from Texas moved into the Little Texas area, so there really wasn't a problem as far as them moving in, because it was already a known area for black families migrating here.

Did your parents have any interesting stories that they would tell you about living here in Orange County?

I know we were the central point for different family gatherings and different things that went on. My mother would share the story of where South Coast Plaza [in Costa Mesa] is now, how it was fields of vegetables and things like that. And we'd go down at nighttime and just grab a few things of greens and turnips and things like that right off the fields and just come home and cook them the next day. Stories like that; and going out to the orange groves near the El Toro area and pick oranges and stuff off the side of the road.

When they came from Texas, were they poor?

I guess because they never went without anything to eat, they wouldn't consider themselves poor. The term we use now would be "low-income." I know that they felt that they were low-income. But they were entrepreneurs in many ways. My uncle started a cleaning business, Sears Janitorial. Because he cleaned and did windows, my grandmother and other family members cleaned the houses. They didn't do windows because that gave the opportunity for my uncle to make money. So they had the sense of being entrepreneurs when they came here. They did that on the side, as well as holding an eight-to-five job.

Let's talk about your grandmother [Annie Mae Tripp]. When did she get involved with low-income people, poor people?

I'd say she got involved with them in the sixties when she did domestic work and did parties and things like that out in Newport Beach and Irvine and places like Tustin. There would be things that were left over and people didn't need it. She'd bring it to her house, and she'd take what she had and would share with others, not realizing that she would later become a real advocate for people. She collected things and just shared them, and that was just her way of helping other people.

So she worked for wealthy white people in many cases.

Yeah, wealthy white people that, when they got done doing a party or a dinner party or something, they'd bring the leftovers back. Or if there was an excess of canned goods and clothing and different things like that, she'd bring them back to her house and then disperse them out of her home.

She was sick back in late '69 or '70 or so and had a stroke. She had a dream or a vision of feeding people. Back then, you would consider the people that were homeless and needy—they used the term of "hobo" and "winos" and things like that. So she got together with Jean Forbath from the Share Ourselves program, and she got together with Betty Thompson from Trinity Presbyterian Church and Jeane Vieje from Trinity Episcopal Church, and told them about a dream that she had. And they went around talking to the different ladies group, called Church Women United, and asked if they would commit to serve a meal a month. That was the beginning. It's evolved over the years.

What stands out most in your mind about her?

What stands out most is her ability to go after things and get them, even with just the little education that she had. She had the stamina. And her thing was that, if she came to you and you told her, no, it just meant "not now"; it meant that she could come back. She was a strong Christian, a firm believer in helping and doing things, and I believe that her strong determination is her foundation, and trust in the Lord is what carried this program on in our family. Also, it is because she just believed that "no" wasn't right then. Like you go back for seconds, she'd come back for your second answer. Eventually, her perseverance would get to you, and you'd say, "Okay, Annie Mae, I'll just help you do a little bit." You saw her efforts, so that would make you want to reach in, and make you want others to reach in, and help other people. It was like a domino effect and just hit you, and it just went on and on.

So she got you involved.

She got me involved as a volunteer. She would call me Sister, because my mother died when I was a teenager. She'd say, "Well, Sister, when I die, would you keep this on?" I said, "No way." I said, "This is too much responsibility, too much of a headache." I said, "Oh, no, I wouldn't do anything like this." But as you can see, that was my desire not to do it, but it was the Lord's work for me to do it, so that's why I'm here.

Let's talk a little bit more about you.

I live in Santa Ana not far from [Santa Ana] Valley High School. I spent maybe seven or eight years away from Santa Ana, but when my husband got out of the military, we came back home. I was raised three blocks from here. Went from 1420 West Third Street [from 1953 to 1958] to where my sister still resides on Daisy Street in Santa Ana, Daisy and Myrtle area. Then from there, I got married and traveled with my husband to Germany and Spain and Texas and Kentucky and came back here.

Your husband, where did he come from?

He came from Houston, Texas. His family came here in '69. His dad was a truck driver, and he had a sister that worked and lived in the San Fernando Valley with her family. He went to high school there, and his dad got a job in Anaheim working for a cabinet manufacturer, moved to Santa Ana, and been here since.

Where did you go to school?

I went to Franklin Elementary School, to Monte Vista, and then I went to Smedley Junior High [School], Santa Ana High School, and then Santa Ana College.

Oh, so you went to Santa Ana High; you didn't go to Valley.

Valley was rough in those days. You're talking about '69 to '71. So my mother chose that I could not go to Valley because it was rough. She worked two jobs, so I had to get up and walk to and from school, and she wanted me to be where she felt it was safer.

Can you tell me where you met your husband?

I met my husband at Sadie Reid's Creative Day Care Center in 1969. I was working there with the Neighborhood Youth Corps program under the Community Development Council. He was bringing or picking up someone. I got a ride home with him and some friends. That was before he went in the service. He went in the service in '70 or '71. I was still in high school when I met him. He was in the service eight years.

Tell us about your neighborhoods. Were they pretty much mixed racially where you lived, for the most part?

Right now, it is pretty mixed. Before, I'd say, when we moved there in '79, it wasn't. It was a few black families there. Mostly white families were there. Right now, like I mentioned before, it's mostly Hispanic families and Asian families. I think it's just three of us that are the original homeowners from early back then that are black and maybe five white. And they're retired persons. When we came back from the service, for about nine months I lived on Daisy Street with my sister and my stepfather. Then we bought a home on his G.I. Bill. My husband worked two jobs and went to school, and I worked two jobs, and that's what helped qualify us to purchase a home.

Tell us about your children.

I have three children. I have a thirty-year-old daughter, Delshanna; a twenty-eight-year-old son, Namath; and a twenty-six-year-old son, John. I have five grandsons and a granddaughter that was born five days ago.

So how was it with your children in terms of social life and dating?

The neighborhood was quite integrated. My oldest married a Puerto Rican young lady; my youngest, a Spanish young lady. So I have biracial grandchildren. I'm trying to teach them Spanish, but they just don't want to pick it up fast enough. My youngest grandson loves to play with the Spanish language and try it, but the other ones, they don't think that it's necessary. My children didn't want to pick it up either, and they see that it's hurting now, because that extra Spanish language can help them on the jobs that they're presently in.

What did they do after high school?

My daughter went on to college. She received her master's at UNLV in Las Vegas [Nevada]. She's still there. She's a mediation specialist for Clark County. My oldest son went in the military and he's been in college also. He is, at the present time, working at the prison, federal prison—I believe that's what it's called—in San Pedro area. And my youngest works for an electronics company in Irvine.

Well, how was it for you as a child growing up here? What was *your* social life like?

I was a loner. We had very large family gatherings, and I never wanted to be with a bunch of people. I'd be at home, and my mother would be at work, and she would call and say, "Has everybody reached over there yet?" And I'd say, "No, Connie's still at home." So she'd send someone over there for me to get to our family gatherings, which were normally at my uncle's house. I didn't get involved in doing things socially until high school. I started with Tri-Y, which happened to be the YWCA's program for young ladies in high school, and got into usherettes and sports, girl's athletic things, and that's what started me into volunteering. Halloween we did UNICEF [United Nations Children's Emergency Fund]. So that's what got me going. While in the military, I'd volunteer with the American Red Cross at the different bases, and he's [my husband] the one that got me more involved in going out and doing things. He might be sorry for it now.

Did your grandmother go to church here?

Yes. When living on Third Street, we went to Second Baptist Church, which was three blocks from where I was born and raised. I've been with Second Baptist Church since then. A lot of my family members have moved away to Riverside and Corona and Temecula. A few of them still come here on Sundays to church. And we have part of our family members that are Catholic and belong to Immaculate Heart of Mary and St. Joseph's Church in Santa Ana. So we have a mixture of denominations.

Church definitely was part of social life. As a teenager, on Sunday afternoon, we could go to either El Salvador Recreation Center or to Jerome Recreational Center in between the hours of, say, one and four. You went to Sunday school, you went to church, and then you went to Baptist Training Union in the evening. And that's just about what your social and your Sunday was like. You had to get those hours in there. That set up a firm foundation and has helped.

After the service, what did you do?

When my husband got out of the service, I basically was at home with my children for a while. My aunt, Scotty Biddle, worked for the employment department. I went to see her about getting a job, and I went to the Girl's Club of Santa Ana, and that's where I started working first, teaching arts and crafts. So from teaching arts and crafts there, a position became available at Southwest Center for a cook. They had to have a board meeting and check to make sure it wasn't a conflict of interest for me working for my grandmother. I started out April '79 as a cook here at Southwest Community Center. I started from the bottom up. I went to UCI [University of California, Irvine], Cal State Fullerton, and Long Beach State taking non-profit courses, in the volunteer center taking certificated courses to help get us to where we are here now, especially with the support of the strong board of directors to keep us going.

Did you graduate from college?

No. I can remember—and I was in double-A classes—that the teachers would say, "Well, you really don't have to worry about learning all this because you'll never end up going on to college." So that was a discouragement for a lot of us. I can just take a look now at some of the African American students and black students that I was there with, they went from high school into work and didn't go straight on to college.

I found the same thing, unfortunately, when my daughter was in high school and in junior high school. We went to one particular parent-teachers conference, and she was taking wood shop courses. I don't want her taking wood shop courses. It's still a bitter taste. I volunteered through the school system, PTA, and everything, even when my kids weren't in school. So it's a known thing around here, unfortunately, that they really don't push college to the students, and they don't go to the utmost of what they could do. That's my belief.

It [encouragement] didn't come from the school system, and it didn't come from the community. Most came from family and from church. A lot of people at church were Sunday school teachers, but they were also teachers through the school system. It's much better now because at Second Baptist, I think we have a rate—maybe 70 to 75 percent of our students go on to college and graduate, which is really good. We can give our hats off to Johnny Williams and our pastor for having such a strong youth program to support the kids and keep them going. They're not our future, they're our now.

Did you know Johnny Williams when you were going to school?

Yeah, he was well known at the schools. See, he was at Santa Ana Valley and I was at Santa Ana High. And I think he was here maybe in my senior year or something like that. Actually, I didn't have him as a counselor, but my sisters and cousins and everybody else below us had him. If something went on, they'd call Johnny, and Johnny would call your parents. Dr. McKinney was another one.

Have people who have moved out of Santa Ana maintained their church relations?

Yes, they have. I believe that in most of the churches in Orange County, the congregation members live more than thirty minutes away from where they fellowship.

Is there a lot of networking between black people?

A lot of networking through different sorority clubs, social clubs, fraternities, things like that, and the different issues that come up with the NAACP and National Council of Negro Women, things like that. I just go to a lot of different functions and support a lot of different things that go on, because my plate is already full just with my job and with church. I'm a trustee at church, so that takes a lot of time, too. I try to connect resources and connect people together. We're not the information and referral line, but we'll get a lot of calls here: "Where do we go for this?" Or, "Where do we go for that?" Or, "Where's a black barbershop?" Things like that. So we just answer them.

Since you've seen the world, what's the most positive aspect about living in Orange County?

Being able to help people. There's a sense of caring in Orange County, and it comes from businesses, churches, organizations. I see it on a level of it's not where it should be or could be, but it's better off than some other places that I've been. And I know that our giving per capita in Orange County is not what it should be, but from who I've come across, it's been wholehearted and people have open arms.

Was it a good place to raise the kids, for instance?

I think it was a good place to raise the kids. I do have family members that have moved out of the area to raise their kids in other areas, other areas of the state. Well, say in Riverside County. Basically, most of our family has moved to Riverside area. It was cheaper. They could purchase something in that area. If I was a person that could handle the freeway, I'd have been gone too. Freeways stress me out.

Did anyone in the family move to anywhere else in Orange County?

We still have some family in Anaheim, Garden Grove, Irvine, one or two in Costa Mesa. I'd say maybe out of seventy-five, there are only twenty-five of us still here. So two-thirds of us are gone. And that's how many people gather when we have a function. It's about seventy-five.

Well, what's been the most negative thing about Orange County?

The over-crowdedness, the traffic, and not being able to go places and be accepted. I'll elaborate. You can go to certain areas to do shopping and looking over your shoulder [the salesperson is] watching you move. And that still happens. It's sad to say, and people won't believe that, but it's like that. And shopping in certain areas, you need help and people walk in the other direction. I've been to different parts of the county and shopped and not been as welcomed as I've been with the stores in Santa Ana. I buy, shop, and live in Santa Ana. Customer service is number one. I don't mind paying three or four dollars more, but if you give me the customer service, I'm going to come back to you. And I spend black dollars wherever I can spend black dollars, too. I support my people. If I go to the beauty shop and her items cost more than at a regular store, I'm going to get them from her because I need to help support her. If I don't, who will?

So you do feel a difference when you go to other parts of the county?

Oh, definitely. I definitely do feel the difference. I don't do it now, but years before when they'd stare, I'd say, "Take a picture; it'll last longer." I had a little snappy attitude. The Lord's taken most of that away. My mother always told me, "You need to just close your mouth and just keep on walking." But it's irritating sometimes to find someone [walking] behind you while you're in the store. And you know who they're looking at. There are not many other people in the store. It's disheartening.

Do you have any favorite stories about living here?

I enjoyed when the Black History Parade was done right down in the middle of the community. I enjoyed those days when Miss Helen Shipp started it, because it went down the streets where all of us lived, and that was just enjoyable to see your own in the midst of your own. It has changed since because so many of us have moved away, but those were good times.

I enjoyed the days when we had Girl Scout troops and when I had 4H programs. I enjoyed my church groups and things that we did together. I did a lot of things. My mother always made sure that we were busy doing things, too. Even though she worked all the time, she kept us busy. I enjoyed when the Jerome Center was first opened and we volunteered on the Teen Advisory Board.

Anything else you want to say before we close?

I just appreciate the opportunity that you contacted me to share about what's happened in our lives and what has evolved around Southwest Community Center and Annie Mae Tripp—her bringing her family here, which when she came it was maybe ten or fifteen of them, and I'm the eldest of her thirty-something grandchildren, who have enjoyed life. Her coming here has really been a tremendous blessing for our family, family members that are entrepreneurs and continue to share and do.

Thank you very much, Connie Jones, for letting me interview you.

ED CARUTHERS[1]

Ed Caruthers came to Orange County from Oklahoma City, Oklahoma, in 1958, when he was thirteen years old. He went to Garden Grove and Santa Ana schools. It was in his senior year at Santa Ana Valley High that he became serious about high jumping. He went to the Mexico City Olympics in 1968, rated as the best high jumper in the world. He tells about the potential Olympic boycott and the Tommie Smith-John Carlos black glove drama. Ed Caruthers lives in Fullerton near California State University, Fullerton, and has been an adaptive physical education teacher for physically challenged children in the Garden Grove Unified School District for more than thirty years. Photo is after Pan American Games, 1967.

Mr. Caruthers, tell me about your family's coming to Orange County.

When I was twelve, my mother, Ruth Burgess, along with my step-dad, Leon Burgess, moved to Orange County. I lived in Oklahoma City with my grandmother for one year until my mother got established out here, then they brought me and my brother, Sam, here to live.

My step-dad had a sister who lived in Orange County. I think she had convinced him that he could do better out here, so he decided to move the family and came to Orange County and got a job as a custodian at some banks. And he did okay out here.

The first house we lived in was with my step-dad's sister and her husband. We lived in Fountain Valley. The Santa Ana riverbed was behind the house; it was farmland, orange trees all around the area there. It was kind of a rural area. We had a lot of fun playing in the riverbed when I was young, and running through orange trees, throwing rocks and things out there.

We came out in the summer, late summer, and I enrolled in Peters Junior High School as an eighth grader. After my step-dad had found a stable job and my

[1] Oral History No. 3085. Interview date: January 7, 2004, at Mr. Caruthers's home in Fullerton, California. Interviewer: Robert Johnson.

mother found a little job, they actually moved over to Santa Ana, on Fifth Street, just east of Harbor Boulevard. I didn't have to change schools or districts. It was still in the Garden Grove district [as was the Fountain Valley home].

Were there other black kids at the school?

No. It was quite a shock to me, because back in Oklahoma, most of the schools I attended, especially elementary school, were all-black. So, I was the only black kid that first year at the junior high school, until about the last couple months a little black kid moved in. But I didn't know what to do the first few months. I finally made friends with a Mexican kid who lived near me, and we became pretty good friends. It was cultural shock; there were all kinds of adjustments to be made there being the only black kid at a school.

Were you involved in athletics at all in junior high?

The first few weeks, I wasn't involved in anything—just going to school and just trying to get home as fast as I could. There wasn't any trouble or anything like that, but there was always some word that some kid wanted to beat me up or have a fight with me because I was black, and that kind of thing. Nothing ever became of it. I wasn't involved in sports. Just going to classes and just trying to adjust as much as I could. The teachers were friendly, and for the most part, I had no problems. Most kids were pretty friendly. Most of the little Mexican kids around my area were pretty friendly.

I think it was my math teacher who asked me to stay for an after-school program to play basketball. That was the start of my doing sports. I was never involved in any organized sports, especially back in Oklahoma, nothing there.

In your neighborhood, was there any socialization there?

Once I got home in the neighborhood, there were a couple of Mexican American kids.

Where did you go to high school?

I went to Bolsa Grande High School [Garden Grove], which was a fairly new school. At that time, I knew I was going to be involved in sports. I liked sports based on my experiences at the junior high school, so I signed up to go out for football and played on the "B" team there. Went out for basketball and played on the junior varsity team. And went out for track and did some events there just for fun. Track and field wasn't really a big interest of mine, but everybody else was going out for it from the other teams, so I just went out.

I went there my freshman year and my sophomore year. Then my folks decided they wanted to move into the south part of Santa Ana. They rented a house on Raitt, just about two or three blocks south of First Street in Santa Ana, which was then the Santa Ana Unified School District, and I wound up going to Santa Ana Valley High School.

Did you get more involved in track and field?

Yes, I did. My best sport was football. I loved football, so I was on the varsity football team my junior year there. And I loved basketball. I was on the varsity basketball team. I was a starter my junior year, and went out for track and field. Had a lot more black friends over there, and they were all involved in sports. I think it was '61 when I got there and they had some good coaches. Some of those kids were really outstanding football players. My junior year we wound up going undefeated. My senior year we lost one game out of the whole season

When did you start high jumping?

Well, I actually started high jumping at Bolsa Grande as a freshman, but it was just mostly just a fun thing. The coaches had me doing the long jumping, high jumping, and some running events. Didn't like most of the events, wasn't real successful. My real strong interest in track and field and high jumping was my junior year at Santa Ana Valley. Wound up being the second best jumper on the team. I went about six-two. I was starting to grow a lot more at that time also. But again, my strong interest was still football and basketball.

I finally became more interested in high jumping my senior year, and I started really focusing and watching people that were good high jumpers in the world—the Charlie Dumases and John Thomases, Olympians. I was starting to notice their style, and I decided to change my style after I saw Charlie Dumas, who was the first man to jump over seven feet. He finally became my little idol, so I tried to emulate his style and went from jumping six-two to six-eight my senior year. It was a huge change just by changing my style. I wound up winning the high school state championship.

Did you have a good coach at Valley?

Yeah. As far as track and field, Howard Brubaker was my track coach there. He was a good coach in the sense that he was mostly a track coach and distance running coach, but he knew that he was not a real technician as far as the high jump was concerned. He would pick me up some days, on a Saturday, and take me over to Los Angeles and let me work with Chuck Coker and some coaches for the Striders, which was a track club. So I had the opportunity to work with some people who were more in tune to high jumping.

What was social life like at Valley? You mentioned that there were a number of black kids. Was there any interracial dating?

When I got there my junior year, there were more black kids compared to Bolsa Grande where there were only one or two guys and maybe one or two girls. When I got to Valley, there were many more black kids and the socialization thing was much better for me. I could identify and talk to kids. We could talk about things, our special interests, and I felt that we could relate a lot better.

There wasn't a lot of interracial dating. As a matter of fact, I can't recall any, really, at that time. People were friendly. I don't know why there wasn't that connection. Maybe their home life or something might have had something to do with it. But people were friendly. I never had any problems speaking to people of different races. There were Mexican kids there, white kids. The majority of the school was white at that time. You'd talk to girls, talk to guys; there were no problems that I could basically see. I never experienced any of it.

We'd go to dances. I was a little shy—*very* shy at that time. I didn't really date that much. I really poured a lot of my energies into sports. I really loved sports. It was like my release, my everything. I didn't have a break during the course of the whole year to really do anything other than just be involved in sports. I didn't have a girlfriend until my senior year. As a matter of fact, I had two little girlfriends at that time, one during football season and then broke up with her after football season, and then started dating my future wife at that time who was on the drill team. That was pretty much my extent of dating.

Then you graduated from there and you went to Santa Ana College. Why did you choose Santa Ana?

Well, when I was in high school, in my community, most of the fathers of kids that I knew were doing custodial type work. They weren't doing jobs that were prestigious or jobs that I felt like I wanted to do myself. My own step-father was a custodian at a bank and would take me and my brothers along sometimes to do the scrubbing on the walls, the floor, to clean those things. I knew I didn't want to do that kind of work the rest of my life. Not that there's anything wrong with it. I mean, it was a good honest living and I still appreciated everything that he was doing, but I just didn't want to do that kind of work.

Now, the friends that I had whose fathers were in the military seemed like they had the best kind of life at that time. They seemed like they had more money to spend or better clothes, things of that nature. So from the time I was probably a sophomore or a junior in high school, I was thinking more about military as my future work. I never saw sports as a way of getting an education or doing anything other than just having fun with it.

My senior year, I was pretty much outstanding: All Orange County as a football player, honorable mention as a basketball player, and All American as a track person. I started to receive letters from colleges regarding coming to school on an athletic scholarship, but in the meantime, I wasn't that great a student. Again, my focus was, as soon as I get out of high school, I'm going to join the military. I never thought of college that much. I didn't take college prep type classes. Even though I liked math, I had good grades in math and some of the shop classes and always had good grades in P.E. I just didn't think I could go to college. I didn't think I was college material.

By the middle of my senior year, I decided I was going to try junior college. I didn't think I could go to a four-year school. I thought, well, I'd give junior college one year. I knew I could make it through football because that was first semester, and I just wanted to see how much farther I could go with football.

I played football at Santa Ana College my freshman year. I was a wide receiver and defensive end. I didn't make any All Leagues or anything like that. It was a fair season for me; it was a test. Again, I didn't do well in classes that fall. I actually didn't think I was going to make it another semester, but the coaches were still plugging away and encouraging me, and, "You can do it." I was going to try and play basketball also, and I just didn't think I could hang in there with football, basketball, and track and field. It was almost impossible for me to do it. But I did promise the track coach that I was going to try and stick in there for track.

That's probably the best move I made, really, because I did manage to hang in there to get decent enough grades to be eligible to do track and field my freshman year. Like I said, it was the best thing that ever happened to me because I went through the track season, won everything. Then Chuck Coker invited me to go back to the national championships [in the summer of 1964].

By the way, I did go back to the national championships my senior year in high school. Didn't do well, but it was an experience that was invaluable to me because the next year, my freshman year at Santa Ana College, I knew I wanted to compete in that national championship again. I was competing against the best in the country and I won the doggone thing. I jumped seven-one and won it. I beat John Thomas, who was the Olympian and world record holder, and I wound up beating him on misses. It qualified me to go to the Olympic trials, but not only did it do that, I was the national champion, so it qualified me to compete on the United States track team against the Russians at the Coliseum later on that year.

Oh, those were famous meets. My wife and I used to go to those.

They were some of the best track and field meets that were ever held, other than the Olympic Games. Actually, like you say, they were big meets, competing in the Coliseum before sixty thousand people. I mean, sixty thousand people at track meets was pretty much a big deal back in those days. You can't get that here nowadays unless there's an Olympic Games. But the Coliseum—a dual meet against the Russians—people would come out of the woodwork to see that. I wound up third. The world record holder at that time was Valery Brumel, who had broken John Thomas's record. So I got beat by those two guys and got third.

It also allowed me to travel in Europe, which, up until then, I thought I'd never get out of the country. I wound up going to Europe and competing in some meets in Europe, and it qualified me for the Olympic trials, which were held again at the Coliseum in September of '64. Wound up jumping there, winning that, and next thing I know, I'm on a plane to Tokyo.

I had just turned nineteen years old. It was quite an experience for me. It's a place that I never thought I'd be because I hadn't had that dream. It was just something that was happening to me, it was like an unreal kind of experience. I was glad I was there and things were just happening. Even when I was marching into the stadium in Tokyo with the team, I'm pinching myself and saying, "Am I here doing this?" Because the year before that, I'm thinking about the army. Marching in there with all those countries, with my team, the United States track and field team, it was just unbelievable for me.

The experience was fantastic. Meeting all these athletes from different countries and sitting down and having dinner with them in the cafeterias and watching them do the things that they do was just—it was just invaluable for me. At that time, I was soaking it all in, and it turned out that that was the thing that prepared me for the next Olympics, because I'm just watching these guys and watching what they're doing.

At the same time, I was doing too much watching. We got there a week before the Olympic Games started. My particular event is like the last two days of the Olympic Games, so I was there for probably sixteen or seventeen days before it was time for me to compete. I'm in the village and I'm eating three meals a day, which I normally don't do. I'm still training two hours a day, and I'm doing all these leisure things, playing Ping Pong, pool at the rec room. Then they've got all these different machines around there: ice cream and sodas and things of that nature, which I'm not used to. I weighed a hundred and ninety pounds before I went over there. I got on a scale about two or three days before it was time for me to compete and I went up to a hundred and ninety-eight pounds. I'm saying, "Oh, no." My being over there almost three weeks before the competition kind of killed me.

Anyway, to boil it down, I wound up eighth place. I made it to the finals and jumped six-ten-and-three-quarters, and that got eighth place. I was sitting there watching those guys jump. John Thomas and Valery Brumel went one, two, and they jumped seven-one-and-three-quarters. I knew I was better than that; I knew I was coming back.

Did you continue on at Santa Ana College for another year?

Yes, I did. I was a little more motivated to do a lot more things after I came back. My grades got better and I could focus a little bit more. I knew from then on that I was not going into the military. I wound up doing my track season there at Santa Ana College. Then I transferred to the University of Arizona [in Tucson, Arizona]. At that particular point, my goals were to get a college degree and to go back to the Olympic Games. SC [University of Southern California] and UCLA [University of California, Los Angeles] had wanted me to come over there for track and field, but it was too close to home for me. I still had a bunch of friends around here in Orange County. I felt like I knew what my goals were and I needed to be away from this area to reach those goals.

Well, the other thing that happened to me before I went to Tucson is I got married. I was nineteen, twenty years old, and I'd been dating my future wife at that time for about a year and a half. She had graduated that June, and I thought, well, I'm going to go to Tucson and be down there for three years. My good friend and her sister wound up getting married, and I think I had that little pressure, "Well, when are you guys going to get married?" We decided to get married the first week of September, and I was off that next week to Tucson. My wife was there with me. I was going to be focusing on school and track and field.

There were black people there, a little black community, so you could get a haircut and food and things like that. I think the cultural kind of thing was there, church. It wasn't much of an adjustment. I had all the facilities and everything I needed down there to work toward my goal, and that was to get back to the Olympic Games. I started training differently. Weight training was a big help, nutrition, studying technique, and things of that nature. So it took me about a year to have all this stuff mesh. So '67 was a fantastic year for me; I pretty much won everything. I think I only lost two meets that year, and one was the national championship

I almost broke the American record; the bar just dangling on and fell off. I never had any luck with that. I went through Europe, competed against the Italians, the Polish, England, several other countries, and won all my events. Therefore, after the end of the season, *Track and Field News* ranked me the number one high jumper in the world.

After that, came back to Arizona. I still needed some more time to get my degree. I actually played football that fall, because I still had a love for football. Then when the track season started in '68—by the way, going back to that NCAA thing in '67, Dick Fosbury was there. He was a sophomore at Oregon State, and he had his style of jumping [head first, with his back toward the ground] then. He went six-six that day. That was the best he did at that time, six-six. And I jumped seven-one. I looked at it, everybody looked at it, and we kind of laughed at that time. I didn't have much of a conversation with him, just said hi and that kind of thing.

Anyway, in '68, I went through most of the meets. Had not quite the season I had the year before, but won most of my meets, jumping seven-one, seven-two. The issue of boycotting the '68 Olympic Games was starting to come up early in the season. It had started up in the Bay Area. Harry Edwards, he was a track and field athlete himself at San Jose State. He had had the ear of most of his teammates up there—Tommie Smith, John Carlos, Lee Evans—and I think he had convinced most of those people that this was something that the black athletes should do for issues dealing with the civil rights, and what have you, in the country at that time.

So as I would go to some of these meets, there would be meetings or discussions regarding this issue. At this particular time, my mind for four years was set on getting back to the Olympic Games, and I just couldn't see giving up that dream and that goal. I let it be known early that I was going to go to the Olympic Games, and there wasn't going to be anything to stop me if I made the team.

1968 Olympics

The 1968 Olympic Games in Mexico City were exceptional, not only in terms of athletic performances, but also regarding the socio-political issues affecting the games: apartheid in South Africa, human rights issues in Mexico, and injustice in the USA.

Forty countries around the world threatened to boycott the games if South Africa, a white-dominated and segregated country, was allowed to enter a team. South Africa was not allowed in. In 1967, San Jose State sociology professor Harry Edwards led the movement of blacks to boycott the Olympics over justice issues. The boycott failed, but during the games, the 200-meter champion, Tommie Smith, before the medal ceremony, gave one of his black gloves to third-place winner John Carlos. And together, during the playing of the National Anthem, they raised their gloved fists in a black-power salute. This resulted in their being suspended from the team and banned from the Olympic Village. Most people in the black community saw the Smith-Carlos action as a heroic act and the image of their salute is burned into their memories.

I think that in most of the discussions at those meetings, everybody pretty much felt the same way, that a dream of going to the Olympic Games was something that was ingrained in everybody, and they just didn't want to give it up. Once Harry Edwards and the other people who were in favor of this thing felt that the boycott was not going to happen, the second thought was to do something in the way of some demonstration at the Olympic Games. Most athletes, mostly black athletes, were somewhat in favor of doing something in that regard. I even thought about doing something myself. But it was mostly in regards to wearing something. Most of the black athletes had decided that they'd wear black socks. The Tommie Smith-John Carlos thing was something that, I think, having talked to them, they came up with almost on the spur of the moment. I think they had black socks on, but I think one of them had a pair of black gloves. They decided to do that on the spur of the moment, the salute with their black glove type of thing.

I was in the dorms, the Village, just kind of getting my rest and was watching TV when it happened, and [I observed] the shock and the amazement of how people reacted to it, especially the officials. They felt it was a slap in the face of the country and subsequently voted them off the team and threw them out of the Village.

I think for some of us, it seemed like an overreaction, but that was the way it was.

Yeah. We felt that way, too.

You're saying that the black athletes reacted more to the fact that they were kicked off the team than almost anything else.

Yeah. They were pretty angry about that particular part, because they didn't really feel it was being disrespectful to the country. When you look at those two guys that were up there, they were still but they had their hands up and with their black glove on. Listening to their own explanations, the explanations from Tommie Smith and Carlos, they didn't feel they were being disrespectful. They just wanted to demonstrate in some way to show the social ills that were in the country at the time. And when we talked to them about it, that's what their thoughts were.

And they were hurt later on, almost unemployable.

Oh, I'll tell you, it was brutal, especially for John Carlos, who is more vocal than Tommie Smith. John Carlos, he disappeared, as far as I was concerned. I hadn't run into him or couldn't find him for several years until I found him selling clothes down in Los Angeles on one of the streets down there, in one of the little clothing stores. [I had] to listen to the tragedy of his life afterwards, including his wife at that time committing suicide.

By the way, how did you do in the meet?

I was favored to win it, having been the number one high jumper in the world the year before and having had some outstanding performances. Dick Fosbury perfected his style during the course of that year. I beat him at the Olympic trials up at Lake Tahoe and thought I was going to beat him—of course, I felt like I was going to beat everybody at the Olympic Games. He was probably a little bit more "on," is what we call it, that particular day. I had a hard time keeping my focus, I guess; so many things going on. My wife was pregnant at the time, and I'd called her two days before and she was in the hospital. Then the boycott thing was going on. I'm not using these as excuses or anything, but it was just those kinds of things. Of course, I knew what to do this time compared to the '64 games—diet and training and all those things that are involved with the Olympic Village and being prepared. So I was more prepared. I wound up going seven-three-and-three-quarters, tied the American record, or just about the American record. But Dick Fosbury broke the American record that day with seven-four-and-a-half. So we finished one, two and beat all the Russians and everybody else.

Being on the victory stand was a fantastic feeling. To be on the victory stand, and if I had to be beat, to be beat by another American so I could listen to the [US] National Anthem, was probably the second best thing that could happen, if I had to lose. It was fantastic. I was up there listening to the National Anthem, proud of what I had accomplished, and proud to be an American, and proud that four years prior to that I was at the Olympic Games and I'd set this as my goal—to get back and to be on the victory stand. It was a fantastic feeling, just a great feeling.

What made you decide to come back to Orange County?

Well, you know, I actually loved the weather, the county, my wife was from here, I was from here, and a lot of my friends were still here. When I was down in Arizona, my basketball coach that I had at Bolsa Grande High School was down there working on his doctorate degree. He was still an administrator in the Garden Grove district. I'd have dinners with him, and he'd say, "Come on back to Orange County and be a teacher at the Garden Grove High School District. You'd be at Bolsa Grande, your old high school."

I actually had the teaching job before I went to Mexico, because that summer, my high school coach that I mentioned, had convinced me to come to Garden Grove and teach. My folks were still living here at that time. They're still here today—two brothers and my mother's still here.

How did you get into adaptive P.E.? Was that from the beginning?

Well, what happened was, I was drafted by the Detroit Lions in the spring of '68. So they asked me if I was going to play football or go to the Olympic Games. I said, "No, there's no way I'm going to play football with you people until this thing is over with my track and field." So after I went down to Mexico and did what I did down there, I came back and started teaching. I thought, well, I still love football. After my first year of teaching, I decided I was going to go back to Detroit and sign a contract and try to play football. Went back in that summer of '69, was there through about November. I was on the taxi squads, that kind of thing. Got hurt a little bit and decided just to give it up and come on back and start teaching again.

When I finally came back in November, I went over to the district office, just trying to find any old kind of job. They were getting ready to start a new program called Adaptive Physical Education for physically challenged kids. Got started and liked it. It wasn't something I wanted to do at the time. I wanted to coach. It still afforded me the time to coach. I coached La Quinta High School track and field and basketball, and I could travel around to two or three schools and do the adaptive program. I enjoyed doing it. There were a few students that made little progress, but the progress they made was really enjoyable and exciting.

That's how I got started. I didn't think I'd be doing this for thirty-some years, though. That's the most puzzling part to me, because I thought I was going to be a college track coach. After a couple years, my goal was set to be a junior college track coach, but things just kind of happened with my relationship with my wife, and things of that nature, that prevented me from making a whole lot of changes. I had my two daughters, and I wanted them to stay here. It didn't work out.

I still assisted working with the junior college kids. It's a little higher level and more motivated people to work with. I feel like I'm a technician type of a person, and I wanted to work with people who were more interested in being good. So I have the better of two worlds here, the way I look at it. I've got some really highly motivated kids to work with in track and field, and then I've got the specially challenged kids that—a little progress, but a lot of fun when they make some progress.

Where did you live when you came back?

We moved in to Santa Ana and stayed with my in-laws for about two months until I started teaching and got a few paychecks. We moved into an apartment on Townsend Street in Santa Ana. You talk about ghetto, that's a big ghetto, but it was a cheap apartment. I knew I wasn't going to be there long; I knew I wanted to have a house and that type thing. I had made some money with the football thing, so I could afford to buy a house. The first house that I bought was in Fountain Valley, a really nice house, about two years old. A family that was leaving the area [was] going back up to Idaho or someplace, so I bought the house from them.

Any problem in purchasing the house?

Yeah. When you think about racism or being a little prejudiced, this is, I think, the first time I'd actually experienced blatant type of prejudice in Orange County. I mean, I may have been prejudiced against, may have had something happen, but didn't know it. But this was the first time that it just absolutely hit me in the face.

With the neighbors?

Yes. We had looked in Santa Ana for housing, thinking that we wanted to stay there in the beginning. And I said, "No. Let's move out of this area." So we looked out in Fountain Valley, which was kind of like a nice little growing community at that time. Again, we found this house, a really nice little house. We went by to look at it. The realtor picked us up at our apartment and took us by there to look at it. We liked it the first time. We had to get out of the car, and the neighbors had to see us going into the house. The owners weren't there at the time. We looked at a couple more houses, but we decided that we liked that house. Everything was right. They just wanted somebody to come in and assume a loan.

So we made an offer on the house. We went back and looked at it a second time, and the neighbors saw us again. Went back and looked at it a third time and made an offer on the house. The realtor took the offer to the people, and they accepted it. But I guess when they accepted the offer, they didn't know we were black and the neighbors had come over and indicated that we were black. Then the owners tried to get out of selling us the house. Because the realtor gave them the offer the first time, they accepted it. He came back and said they accepted it. He had to go back over for some reason, and then the owners said, "No, we're not going to sell it because they're black."

So the realtor came back to us, and it was almost like he was in shock. He was white, and he had indicated that that's the first time that had ever happened to him. He apologized, and he was sorry, and suggested that we get an attorney.

In 1968, there was already a federal fair housing law.

Right. So he suggested that we get an attorney and fight it. I think what happened was, as I recall it, he went back to the people and told them that we were going to get an attorney and fight it, so they decided to go ahead and sell us the house. Well, we had some reservations about the house, because we knew it was the neighbors and not necessarily these people. They were getting out of town. We didn't know how many neighbors were involved or how vicious or how involved they would be. We thought it over. We decided we were going to take the house. We made up our mind we were going to go ahead and do it. But there were a lot of reservations about it, because I had a young daughter at that time, and I had another baby on the way, for that matter. This was before I decided to go back to Detroit. I was going to be in Detroit and my wife was going to be here. She was pregnant and just had another baby. But we wanted that house.

So I was back in Detroit most of the time. My wife was here, and I was calling every other day to make sure she was all right. Had her sister live with my wife just to make sure that we were okay. I was gone for about a month. I had moved her in, bought the house, put new furniture in it and everything, and made sure she was okay. Of course, her father and mother and my mother and step-father were close by, just in case they needed anything.

Nothing really happened while I was gone, but as soon as I got back and decided I wasn't going to go play football anymore, we started to get letters in the mailbox indicating that niggers could move into the neighborhood, you could do this and you could do that, but you'll never be in our hearts. It was just all kinds of little letters. Rocks were thrown at the mailbox and things. I had a one-year-old and another little baby, but nothing really happened to them at that time.

We got things like that for about a year, until the neighbors really started knowing us. After about two years, I was over at their house for dinner, they were over at my house for dinner, and nothing really that severe ever happened again in that neighborhood. Granted, there were a couple little things. When the kids went to school, there'd always be some little something, but nothing real blatant or to the point where I just had more fear for their safety.

I was there for about six or seven years. I had neighbors next to me, like I said; we were over to their house for dinner. Had neighbors across the street—they had boats and things, and we'd all go out to the Colorado River and skiing and everything else. I still to this day don't know who the neighbors were that wrote the letters and all that kind of stuff, and told the owner of the house that they didn't want us to move into it.

We sold the house after being there for about six or seven years. I'd had my two daughters, and I felt that we wanted a different house, a bigger house, and we wanted to move over to Orange. It was a new tract, brand new houses. We picked out the lot and everything; [we] had an opportunity to watch them build the house, which was fantastic. We loved the house. Shortly after it was built, I was able to afford to have a swimming pool built for my kids, and they enjoyed that.

No trouble moving in?

No trouble moving in. The neighbors were friendly. Two teachers on both sides of me, so we had that. One was a track coach from Foothill High School, so we knew each other. Down the street, kids were playing, and no problems. A lot less worries back then than nowadays with kids being out in the streets playing and having fun. Neighbors—again, I'm over at their house for dinner and they're over at my house for dinner; nothing unusual.

The girls didn't have any problems?

No problems. They were going to elementary school and they were in the Brownie troops—nothing that they ever came home and said anything to me about. I thought that they were just having a great time growing up at good schools. They had nice little friends and some overnight sleeps at their house. It was good.

After being there for about three years, we decided—well, if we were ever going to get a bigger house where the kids could have their own room, I could have an office, my wife could have a sewing room or whatever she wanted to have, we'd have to move into another house. So [we] looked at this house. It was a thousand square feet bigger, everybody had all the space they needed, and decided to make that move.

Right near Cal State Fullerton.

Yes, Cal State Fullerton. Had a few friends that lived in the Fullerton area, so we were a little closer to them. And the schools were great. All the colleges and everything around—I thought for sure my kids would be going to all these colleges around here. Our older daughter, Sheri Jonné, wound up going to Cal State Fullerton and graduating from there. So I thought this was perfect.

And the other daughter?

Chara's goals were different. She wanted to do something different. She wound up getting accepted at UCLA, so went there for her four years and graduated as a civil engineer. When she graduated, she got a job right away for the City of Los Angeles as a civil engineer. Worked there one year, but during the process of going to school at UCLA, she met her future husband there. He was an Australian. He moved back to Australia and convinced her to move there, and I had to fly over to Australia for a wedding

And your older daughter, what did she major in?

Sheri Jonné always wanted to be in law enforcement, so she went to Cal State Fullerton and majored in police sciences. She wanted to be a policeman or highway patrolman. Didn't work out too well here in the state of California, so she had a friend who was over in Las Vegas, Nevada, who said there were a lot of opportunities over there. So she moved over there, and about six months after she moved over there, got hired as a gaming officer. She went through their program, and she's been a gaming officer over there for about four or five years.

During the time that she was in college, she signed up in the army reserves. When she went to Nevada, she was in their reserves there—or National Guard. I think it's the National Guard. During the process of going to some seminars, she met her future husband [also a white man], who was at one of these training sessions also. They got married [a few months ago] just before she was shipped out to Iraq.

Have you ever had any encounters with the police?

I've been stopped by the police, but I can't really say it was like harassment or anything. The one time that I even came close to something of that nature was when I was in high school. I was a senior in high school, I had my first car, I was out late at night, and it was just me by myself. I was pulled over by the police officer, and I asked him why. He said that some black person had just done something. He didn't say he thought I was the one that did it, but then he made me park my car, put me in the back of the car, took me to the police department, took all my information and everything, and put me in a holding cell. About an hour later, he came back and said, "Okay, you're not the person." Put me back in the car, drove me back to my car, and that was it.

Are you glad you came back to live in Orange County?

Yeah. I love Orange County, and I am *very* glad I came back. I think my kids —they're thirty-one, thirty-two years old now—I think that they've enjoyed living here in Orange County. I think we've had a pretty good life here, just normal, and I didn't want anything more or less.

Work-related, people are always helpful or courteous, for the most part. I've enjoyed my work. I would like to have had maybe a few more black people around. There are no black people in this neighborhood, other than myself. But I don't think I've missed out on anything, because I still have black friends and I have white friends. Probably still associate a little bit more with the black ones when it comes to holidays and those things. But I don't have anything real negative.

Mr. Ed Caruthers, thank you very much for allowing me to do this interview. I've really enjoyed it. It was very good. You were very open.

JESSIE ALLEN[1]

When she was sixteen, Jessie Allen came with her family from Louisiana to Santa Ana. Two years after graduating from high school, she went to Southern University, in Louisiana. Following graduation, she came back to Santa Ana and went to work for the Social Security Administration in Long Beach. She moved to the city of Columbia, Maryland, a planned community, and lived there for a number of years. She moved back to Santa Ana to take care of family members. Most of her family is in Orange County, but she misses life in the DC area. Photo courtesy of Jessie Allen.

Tell me about your parents and where you were raised.

My mom started out as a schoolteacher after completing eleventh grade. There was a desperate need for teachers for black children because it was a segregated school situation, and there were few colored teachers graduating from colleges at that time. They started her teaching elementary school. When I was born, she stopped working.

My father was a master mechanic for Swift Packing Company when he got out of military service. When I was two years old, we moved to Lake Charles, Louisiana, and I was there until I was in the tenth grade. My father worked at Swift in Lake Charles until Swift closed down. When Swift offered him a place to move with the company, he decided that it was not a place he wanted to rear children, so we ended up in southern California with an aunt and uncle. My uncle was assistant minister at Johnson Chapel AME Church here in Santa Ana. We lived in the 1300 block of West Third Street. It was 1960, so I was sixteen. They were trying to boost the enrollment, so I got assigned to Valley High School. My class that graduated was the first class to take all three years at Valley.

---

[1] Oral History No. 3067. Interview date: October 24, 2003, at the Southwest Community Center in Santa Ana, California. Interviewer: Robert Johnson.

In the pre-enrollment phase, when I had to go in and talk to the counselor, I'd been in an all-black situation, a totally segregated situation in the South. I thought I had a really good education. The counselor at Valley took a look at my record, and her first reaction was, "This is amazing. You come out of a southern situation and a southern school, and you've had some courses that our kids haven't had yet." And that was because the math teacher there in the junior high school and the high school was a friend of the family. My father and mother were sticklers as far as you having to learn, so education was very important to them. It was interesting to me that she would have that kind of reaction, because it was as if the message to me was, "You're further advanced than what our kids are." And I found that out as I got into some of the courses, particularly in English and in math.

Valley, at that time, most of the kids were white. Is that right?

Most of the kids were white. There were four blacks in my class—two girls and two boys. I was in the class with Dan Griset [later, mayor of Santa Ana]. And because there were so few of us, we kind of mingled together. The only thing that helped us get out of our own little black circle was that the two black girls there decided we were going to join the drill team. The teacher in charge of the drill team was a military person, and her whole thing was, if you can do it, no problem. It took a little while for the girls to understand it, but the black girls just decided we were going to do this. We were really shocked when we made it.

What did you do after high school?

I graduated from Valley in 1962, took a year off. There are five of us in our family—the first three of us, a year and eleven months apart. So I worked. I took some courses at Santa Ana College and then in 1964, I went to school at Southern University in Baton Rouge [Louisiana]. It's a family school. We have a tradition of supporting black colleges. As the oldest of five children, I needed to be exposed to a little bit more outside.

I can remember a college here in this area [Southern California College in Costa Mesa], a Christian college, recruiting me and telling me that though they wanted me as a student at the school, I could not live on campus because it would not be acceptable. Reverend Walter Cooks was one of the gentlemen who was really pushing me to go there, and I'm assuming now, looking at it later, just using me as a test case to see what would happen. The school was known for having international students. It was very interesting that there were no blacks there. They wanted me to come as a black, but because I'm "high yellow," as they say down South, I would blend in very well. That was one of the statements I got. But still, they were not ready for me to live in the dorms with the other students, and it wasn't because I lived close. It was just that they didn't want me to live in the dorms. Very interesting for a Christian college; kind of bothered me for a long time. I think it still bothers me.

Was there any social life outside of school?

The social life was totally the church, totally Second Baptist. I was very much immersed in the Christian education program in terms of being one of the youth leaders and working, as I mentioned to you earlier, with Ernestine Ransom there as the youth director. We went away to conventions and conferences during the school holidays. We were always gone somewhere. And the church provided a lot of social activities. In terms of dating in high school, the four of us in the class were just too close as friends to even think about dating each other.

Did you marry?

No. I had plenty of opportunities. I was engaged to marry a gentleman in 1990, and three months before, he had a heart attack and died. I had some good times and some great friends, some really great friends. Because of the kind of work I did, I was in a man's world most of the time, with attorneys and doctors, so that I have a great relationship with some friends. I have one friend now, Bob Shepherd, that I have known since I was in high school. He tells folks when he does concerts —because he's a baritone and has been doing a lot of work with our church and our convention—that he tried his best to marry me and I had other plans.

Well, my other plan was, as an oldest child, I needed to go to school so I can help my parents put my other sisters and brother through school. And that's basically what I've done. Then we started with the second generation of helping them get through school. And, as I said, education is something real big for us.

I heard that the majority of the young people from Second Baptist go to college and graduate. Is that true?

They do, yeah. Thanks to Johnny Williams, I think. This year we sent fourteen kids off to college in this year's graduating class, out of a total of sixteen, I think. We've got them scattered all over the country, from Hawaii to Louisiana. As a matter of fact, one of the girls chose to go to my school. Never been down South before, and I've really been worried about her. My brother made a visit down there so he could check on her, and her mother and I talk at least once a week to make sure she's doing okay.

Because of culture shock, it's a big difference going from Santa Ana High to an all-black college in Louisiana where they are very protective, though not as protective as they were when I was there. It was probably the best experience for me, really, going away, because it was easy for me to be able to move away from home in the seventies and stay away as long as I did, for thirty-some years.

When did you leave Orange County?

I graduated from college in 1967. In the last year of school, because I was on the honor roll and a member of a national honor society, we started getting recruited. Many of us, recruited from several different federal agencies, as well as private companies. I got recruited by Ed Conkler, who was the recruiter for the Los Angeles District Office for Social Security Administration. He knew that my family lived in Santa Ana, and the classes there in Los Angeles were getting full, so he asked me if I would switch from Los Angeles and come into Santa Ana to train. He said, "It's going to be a difficult situation for you." I'd been involved in all kinds of activities on [the Southern University] campus anyway, from the standpoint of closing the campus down just to get some of the things we wanted, thanks to Mr. Julian Bond, as a matter of fact. But I just wasn't ready to fight when I got home. I didn't expect to fight because I thought things had changed enough. This is California; things ought to have changed by then.

By the time I got to Santa Ana, I ran into the John Birch Society. This was even before training started. At the time, I didn't realize what I was getting myself into. The first day out on the desk, after going through all the training, after being encouraged to stay in the program when I thought I just couldn't do it, a gentleman came up who had lost his wife. He was coming to file for death benefits. He didn't want to be interviewed by me at all. It was very interesting, because the man who was training me, who I was sitting with at the desk, was retired military. He said, "You know what? If you don't talk to her, you're not going to talk to anybody."

The man was in deep grief, and I always had a problem with the mortuary bringing them over right after they finish arranging so that they could get their money, and I understood that from an economic standpoint. But the man broke down, and he was so embarrassed to break down in front of me and apologized all the way through. Toward the end, he said, "Well, this wasn't as bad as I thought it was going to be." I was sitting there going, "Well, why don't you just tell me what the problem is." And he couldn't tell me what the problem was. He was a native Orange County person. That stuck in my mind. That was the first time for me to see a man cry, because my father, if he was going to cry, he was never going to cry in front of us, his children.

Did you then take a job with the Administration?

JOHN BIRCH SOCIETY

The John Birch Society, like the Ku Klux Klan three decades earlier, proclaimed that they were not a racist organization. In spite of that assertion, this anti-Communist society locked arms with racist individuals and organizations that used the Birch Society's rhetoric to justify their opposition to civil rights. For example, Dr. Martin Luther King was portrayed as having Communist ties in addition to the Society attacking him as a law breaker. Two prominent black men, Nobel Peace Prize winner Ralph Bunch and Congressman Adam Clayton Powell, were accused of being "leaders in a Communist drive to infiltrate government." These demeaning distortions implying that Negroes were being duped by the Communists set well with white racists, but obviously not with the great majority of black people.

Anti-Communism was very strong in Orange County, in part because of a large number of people working in the defense industry, as well as at the marine base at El Toro. The best known of the John Birch members in Orange County was the retired marine pilot John Schmitz. He led the fight, in the California State Senate in 1964, for eliminating fair housing laws (like the Unruh and Rumford Acts) through the passage of Proposition 14 and continued that fight unsuccessfully after Prop 14 was ruled unconstitutional by the US Supreme Court.

I did. I worked for them for thirty-two years. There were openings here in Santa Ana, and I was told by the manager here that the public would not accept me there in the office. There were no black employees in that office at the time, and this was '67. So I ended up in Long Beach [Los Angeles County].

Did you live in Orange County?

I stayed right here in Santa Ana and commuted to Long Beach for the five years that I stayed there. I tell folks now I don't know anything about downtown Santa Ana, because we just didn't go into downtown Santa Ana. We didn't feel welcome in downtown Santa Ana. Our parents didn't think we were safe in downtown Santa Ana. It's interesting now that my niece went to a school the last two years in the old West Coast Theater building. When I walked in there for one of her graduating exercises, I said I had never been in that building. I never knew what it was. It's such an ornate, beautiful building inside where they hold their church services. I just never came downtown.

Where did you shop? Were there markets here?

The Santa Ana Food Market is where my mom did her grocery shopping. Mom worked in Newport Beach. Mom took a job when my youngest sister, Gladys, went to school. Mom started cleaning houses in Newport Beach. So she would stop on her way home so that we didn't shop except at Santa Ana Food Market.

How long did you stay at the Social Security office and live in Orange County?

I got recruited out of that office by Social Security's legal department in 1972 and moved back to Maryland in 1972 and stayed there five years. When I was going back to Maryland, Social Security's Human Resources staff was trying to find someplace that was going to be very much like what I had here in southern California. They were putting me in a community like Irvine, they thought.

Well, the community I was in was a community planned by James Rouse. Rouse is the epitome of fairness of any man I could find. His idea was to develop a community of villages where there was housing for everyone, regardless of your economic standing—90 percent of the residents were federal employees—where everybody could live together. He would put apartment buildings, condos, and single-family homes all within one block. Every village would have its own grocery store, pharmacy, and any other kind of basic needs type store. So he developed this little town, Columbia, Maryland, the epitome of equalness, as far as he was concerned when he developed it.

How would you compare Columbia to Irvine? They were both planned communities.

Irvine, looking at it now, is more affluent than Columbia will ever be. One, because of the mix in population. The housing costs are so much lower in Columbia than Irvine. Irvine, I think, has outgrown what I thought was the intent, and what a lot of us thought was the intent when it first started—as a haven for a mixture of people.

You had Section-8 housing [for low-income people] in Columbia?

Section-8 housing. As a matter of fact, next door to my condo—mine sat on the top of the hill, the highest place, a man-made mountain overlooking one of the man-made lakes. Right next door was Section-8 housing and as close as the next block was single-family [housing].

The feeling I had with places like Columbia is that they were integrated both economically and racially, and planned that way.

Exactly. I thought, on paper, Irvine was planned to be the same way, not so much in the village structure but planned in the same way, as a haven for people trying to get away from the negativeness, I guess, or the conservativeness of Orange County. Trying to just get into Irvine, where they could express ideas.

Because of the university.

Yes, because of the university. That it would be free for all races to move in, and economically free, because of the university as well as the students and everything else. And it's an ideal setting. But it has grown beyond that, as far as I was concerned. If I were coming into Orange County as an employee now, I don't know that there's anyplace I would want to live, unless maybe Fullerton, around the university. It seems to have gone beyond the idealism of fairness and equalness.

I was out there when the university [University of California, Irvine] set up its first office for minority students. I was very much involved in them setting that up. My friend Ernestine Ransom was the first director out there, so I was helping her a lot out there. And I don't see that. I understand the melting pot situation, but it's not a melting pot because you still have that strata there, and you can't go beyond that into the next one, because of economics more than anything else, I think. I haven't been back long enough to know how it relates to minorities moving. Minorities, meaning Hispanics, more than anything else. I don't see Irvine as accepting of the different types of Hispanic populations that you have here in Santa Ana. I don't see them as accepting as I think Columbia would be.

You were involved with the Southern Christian Leadership Conference (SCLC) [in the late 1960s].

The SCLC, under Reverend Kilgore in L.A., wanted to make some inroads into Orange County, because they knew about the problems in Orange County, and they felt that perhaps they could do something. [In Orange County were] Reverend Nichols, a Jewish rabbi, which was amazing; members of the First Baptist Church in Santa Ana; as well as a group of international students at Southern California College. I think Reverend Kilgore had been at one of the benefits for Biafra. Ernestine, because she had been around Orange County for such a long time, mentioned some of the problems they were having. So he [Reverend Kilgore] sent out one of the fieldworkers, Reverend O. C. Smith, to start setting up a chapter here. We started with voter registration. It was amazing the complacency of the blacks here, as if what we do here won't make any difference one way or the other. Because we had such a tough time, they [the SCLC] were trying their best not to give up on Orange County, but I think they did, to the point where I ended up being assigned to L.A. County as part of their program with the young people.

Ernie [Ransom] and I thought we could do the same thing. We started with Second Baptist kids. Black people were just not interested. I think they'd gotten to the point where they thought it just didn't matter. Some of these people were folks that we knew very well, including my own parents. Mom said she'd been that route already. I can remember her saying, "Look, I fought in Louisiana. I'm just too tired to do this now, and I've got to work now, and I've got to do this and I've got to do that." The whole idea was, we're trying to make a living and there aren't any things open. My dad went to work at Balboa Bay Club. Here was a man who had been working on huge trucks, master mechanic, going all over the country for Swift, and he went to work at Balboa Bay Club as part of its maintenance department, because that's the only job he could get in this area. He ended up working there so that he could get us through school and could at least get us into a house.

Is that because we didn't have many industrial jobs at the time?

We didn't have many industrial jobs, and even those we had were not open to blacks. My brother, Robert, graduated as an engineer. He started out with Rockwell, and he's still with them. He came back [from Southern University] at a time when they were hiring blacks and they were trying to integrate. Hired on at Rockwell in Anaheim and has been with them through all the name changes. My middle sister, Patricia, is a teacher here, and she's been teaching here for thirty years at the same school in Santa Ana, Abraham Lincoln, not far from where we live. One sister, Beverly, is in Chicago. She is an accountant with United Airlines. All of them went all the way through the Santa Ana school system. And the youngest sister, Gladys, did all of hers here, and she's a nurse. She lives in Anaheim.

Did they marry black people or white people?

All black.

You had told me that one time you took a history class at Santa Ana College, from John Schmitz. [2]

Oh, yes. That was before he got deeply into the John Birch Society. He was a very conservative person, but a good instructor, a very good instructor. I couldn't accept some of his ideas, so I didn't do very well in his class, because it was so foreign to what I grew up with and what I had learned. And I didn't know that he

---

[2] John Schmitz was a marine pilot and anti-Communism teacher at El Toro, an instructor at Santa Ana College, a member of the John Birch Society while an Orange County Congressman, and presidential candidate on the American Independent ticket, after Governor George Wallace of Alabama was shot.

was headed in that direction. I think I had gone to Maryland when he was running for an office, and [I thought] "I know that man." Then I realized where I knew him from. "Oh, he went that deeply into it."

What were the views of black people in Long Beach and in Los Angeles regarding Orange County?

They wanted to know how I got here. Everybody would say, "You live in Santa Ana? Why? Why'd you go there after being where you were? It's just like being in Louisiana." I said, "Well, that's where family is, and you have a tendency to go there." I did go to plays and things like that in L.A. County. I like black theater; there's no black theater here. I said, "So I just went where family was." Though I laid my head down at night here, I was in L.A. County, for social activities and everything else. So I didn't participate that much [here], except to go to church. It's essentially the same way now.

What was their reluctance to move here?

Most of the blacks in L.A. County, particularly Los Angeles, at that time had come from the South. As a matter of fact, there was a huge Louisiana Club in Los Angeles, and their attitude was Orange County was just like being down South, was just like being in Louisiana. They didn't want to experience that. They didn't get a chance to know the Segerstroms like we did. [White people] would get involved in some of our [church] fundraisers and things like that, because Ernestine's mother had worked for them in the kitchen.[3] So they participated with us. But they [blacks in L.A.] didn't see this as any place that they wanted to be because of what it was before.

When did you come back to Orange County permanently?

I hope this isn't permanently. June of 2000, I came back. My mother was ill. My youngest sister, Gladys, has multiple sclerosis and she was diagnosed right after they had adopted a baby, a newborn. In black families, the oldest child is responsible for everybody. The youngest sister was always my responsibility, so her children became my responsibility, that kind of thing.

I miss the interaction with black people that I had on the East Coast. I miss the seasons on the East Coast. If I could have gotten Gladys to move back there, I would still be back there, really. It's a different environment. Just going to church is not what's doing it for me at all. I don't see enough of a black society here like I had in Maryland and in Washington. The black book clubs and plays, and things of that nature, I don't see here. And I feel really separated from the community here. And I'm trying, I'm trying to get involved. Everybody has to come in from Riverside County. Our church has very few people that live in Santa Ana. They're all from outside the county.

---

[3] John Segerstrom brought his family to Orange County, and starting with 20 acres of leased land, the family became major dairy farm and lima bean producers. In the 1960s, the family developed the giant South Coast Plaza shopping center on portions of their Costa Mesa and Santa Ana land. Ernestine Ransom's mother worked for a caterer, who provided food for families like the Segerstroms. This was a common way that black people made contact with wealthy white people.

With regard to any other negatives or positives of living in Orange County, can you just talk about those, please?

I'm trying to think of the positives. From the standpoint of social, I don't see any. I developed some very close friends—some friends I still have on both sides, black and white. My secretary from the field office in Long Beach and I still have breakfast once a month. As I said, Ernestine Ransom was very influential in my family, and I would not have had that had I not come to Orange County or gone to Second Baptist. I think I may not have had the opportunity to develop some of my attitudes had I not had the Orange County perspective to put into play. When I look at my life totally, it's not very different from Louisiana. I'm still trying to figure out how it's going to be as I come back and get involved. I think a lot of it made me stronger in the sense that I knew what to expect in certain situations. When I think about the kind of support system I had here, it was good to have it at the time.

From the negative standpoint, I still see such a separation and a division. I see a separation starting all over again, just by sitting here at the desk at the Southwest Community Center seeing the differences. I didn't expect to see it, and it shocked me the first time I heard it. "Well, she's just from El Salvador," or, "she's just this and that." It bothers me. We have a second grader in our family, and it bothers me that she feels that she has to know Spanish to live here.

I'm still idealistic where I think we can all live together and try to get along together. I think it's going to be tough for us, though, as we become more Hispanic-oriented. I'm afraid that there's going to be a real negative kind of division, like we saw down South, in Santa Ana, with the whites on one side and the Hispanics on the other side. I tell some of my Hispanic friends, "You're becoming the blacks of this generation, and it's real tough, but you're going to have to experience some of the things that we experienced."

Do you have a favorite story about Orange County?

One of the stories I tell the kids at church when they talk about "this person doesn't like me," I say, "Remember I had one instructor in high school that gave me a real hard time. That man thought I could do nothing, and I felt so insecure and so negative around him. But, the night I graduated, he came over to me and straightened my hat on my head and fixed my tassel and put his arm around me." I said, "That was the most amazing thing, because I thought this man just didn't like me at all. You can overcome some of everything, but you overcome it one by one by one, and that's the only way you can do it." Your character has to speak for everything.

That's a great story to end on; thank you, Jessie.

ADLEANE HUNTER[1]

Adleane Hunter came to live in Orange County in late December 1961 or early January 1962, and attended Smedley Junior High School in Santa Ana. Her husband, mentioned quite often in this oral history, is Dr. Jerry Hunter, chancellor of the North Orange County Community College District. She was the founder of the Orange County Black Actors Theater (OCBAT), which operated from 1987 to 1990. Ms. Hunter, now working out of Los Angeles, is well known in the field of theater production.

Ms. Hunter, you were a young girl when your family moved to Orange County. Where did you come from and why did they choose Orange County?

Well, we came from south of Miami, Florida, a little town called Perrine, located in Dade County, and they didn't actually choose Orange County—fate chose Orange County. They came to Los Angeles after the pioneer who came to get a job first and get housing.

His name was Seymour Dorsey. Seymour Dorsey was my cousin's husband. My mother came to visit after I came out to stay with my cousin for a summer. Dorsey went to Los Angeles and couldn't find work. He was a construction worker. He joined the union and there was a job in Anaheim. And so, rather than do that commute, there was a small black community in Santa Ana, an area called "Little Texas." He was able to rent a room there. Then he found a house and his wife came out. I came out that summer, and then my mother moved the entire family. She said, "I like it out here," and she just moved everybody, her and five of the kids. So that's how we ended up in Santa Ana. Most folks that left the South, they went to big cities. You didn't come to small places like Orange County.

What were your earliest impressions of Orange County?

[1] Oral History No. 2364. Interview date: May 7, 1994. Interviewer: Mae Ussery.

I was here initially in the summertime, and it was just wonderful to be here with my cousin and meeting new friends, and all that was pretty exciting. I'd come up where everybody in my community was black: all my role models, all of the store owners, and the teachers, the business people, the doctors, everybody. All the significant people in my life were all African American. So when I went to school [in Santa Ana], it was very different for me to have no black teachers. And I think what made it even more difficult was that they didn't respond to me as the teachers I had grown up with for six years. I had been through sixth grade, so I started school here at Smedley Junior High School in 1961, and that was difficult. That was an adjustment and it took me awhile to come to grips with what was going on, and it was just kind of subtle.

How was Orange County different? Weren't all the blacks living in a particular area?

Well, they really were, but where we ended up living was right in the middle of a Hispanic community right off Raitt and Fifth, which is still, I think, predominately Hispanic. We and the lady, who lived next door to us, and another family that we were friends with, were the only blacks in that area. So, no, I didn't live in a black community, I didn't go to a black school, and I found that people were responding to me differently, and I'm sure I was responding to them differently.

What is your fondest memory of your childhood here?

I know what it is, and I think she used to be embarrassed by this because, of course, you know I'm forty-something now. And when I say Mrs. Darling was my first black teacher, of course that tells her age, because she's quite youthful-looking. Do you know Mrs. Darling?

Oh, yes, I did. She's Mrs. Whittaker.

I still call her Mrs. Darling because she was my first black teacher. And I think I was in the ninth grade and I think she was teaching history and I was so thrilled to have her. For me it was a return to something that I was most comfortable with, and a validation and an affirmation of me that I had not had for the two years that I had been here. I was in an advanced placement situation when I was in school in Florida. There were about a dozen of us, because of our being farther along than the other kids in our class, and they had put us all together and had us in this special class for the bright. You know, they didn't call us bright, but we were advanced, and so I was used to getting a lot of strokes and encouragement.

And, of course, they were very proud when I was going to California because the whole thing was, "She's going to go to California and go to school out there." And I was to write them and send my report cards, which I did. And my mother wrote to the school and they would read over the announcement what my grades were. They were so proud because I was going to an integrated school, and it was a big thing. I did well my first two years, but I didn't have the kind of interaction with the teachers that I was used to having. I had uncles who taught at the school [in Florida]. My mother's cousin was the P.E. [Physical Education] teacher. I had family there as well, so I think I probably got more attention than the average kid did, that I wasn't even aware of at the time. But coming to the situation at Smedley Junior High—Mrs. Darling, that's probably the fondest memory for me when I walked in that class and saw her. And she was a good teacher and she was a very nice person as well.

What was your most unpleasant memory of your childhood in Orange County?

I don't know that any of them were major—I mean, in terms of being unpleasant. I don't think I can think of one thing that stands out. For me the impact was something that was cumulative, because it kind of all hit me that I had somehow been dealing with this real hidden kind of subtle racism. Because what I found was that gradually I withdrew in terms of being an active participant in my education. And I just didn't enjoy school as much, so I didn't work as hard. But I didn't understand why that was, and I really think it was because I didn't have the kind of teachers that inspired me. Actually, I had only two that I can remember that made an impression on me, because I felt they genuinely were concerned and were good teachers.

Who influenced you the most during this early period—your parents or your teachers or just who?

Paul Reardon, who was also one of my teachers at Santa Ana High School, and I was his secretary. Outside of school, certainly my mother. I had very strong role models at home, particularly strong, black women. Then my cousin Dinah Mae Dorsey, who again I came out to stay with—because I would live with her on and off, back and forth, sort of—and she was certainly a great influence on me.

But outside of my home, I would say Paul Reardon, in terms of when you're really struggling to make those decisions about what I wanted to do with my life. He chose me to be his secretary. It was a coveted position that everybody wanted, and you had to apply—a typing test and all of that, because you literally ran the Work Experience Program with him. And he was so proud of me. He would show me off. He'd take me to lunch with the companies where he was going to set up the programs. He would take me with him and expose me to the business world, because he really thought I had potential. And I wanted to be an airline stewardess and he used to hate that. He used to say, "Oh, no. It's just a dumb waitress in the sky." He said, "Anybody can do that."

He kind of just took to me like a father. He would call my mother if I did something he didn't like or if he wanted to discuss with her some things he thought I should be doing relative to going on to college. My mother was like, "Well, you just go to community college." She wasn't looking to push me out to a four-year school. She didn't feel she had the resources. And he took it upon himself to contact her and discuss options with her relative to my education. And, of course, what I wanted to do was be a stewardess.

Now is Mr. Reardon a black or a white man?

He's a white man. He was so genuine. And all the kids knew—black, white, blue, it didn't matter—Mr. Reardon was fair. He cared about us all genuinely, and when he saw potential he tried to encourage you. He tried to keep you straight when he saw you going the wrong way. And he had a way of relating to you.

When I got ready to get married, I introduced him to my first husband, and he said, "No, he's not the one." He said, "He's got ego problems," and he just ran down a whole litany of things about him. But he was very accurate. I married him anyway. So when I got ready to marry Jerry, I called him up. I said, "I'm going to marry this other guy. I want you to meet him." And I took Jerry over to his house for dinner, and he took him in the kitchen and talked with him while I visited with his wife. And when he came out he called me in the kitchen and he said, "Now this is the one." He said, "He's got some sense, he's got some money in the bank, he ain't driving a big old car." You know, he hated men that drove the big, old Cadillacs and stuff that was all about big egos that weren't necessarily in line with their ability. So he would get the award. He was *the* most influential person, really, outside of my home.

Okay, did you ever see a play when you were a young child?

No, I didn't. The first play I ever saw was [when] I was twenty-two, *The Dawning of the Age of Aquarius.*

You saw *Hair*? That was your first play?

And I thought it was the freakiest thing. I thought, "Oh my goodness, why are all these people running around without their clothes on? Oh!" I saw it at the Aquarius Theater in Los Angeles. It was an integrated cast. They had a couple of blacks in it. It was so well-publicized and everybody was talking about it. It was about this nudity. You know, people were nude on stage. But that was the first one. That one didn't hook me.

About a year and a half later, I saw *Young, Gifted and Black.* Jerry took me to see it in Los Angeles and I was just overwhelmed. Because not only were there people in front of me performing, it was the material. I had never heard of Lorraine Hansberry at that point, and I had to find out who she was. And I knew this was autobiographical. That turned the tide. Although I went for several years not doing theater, it left an indelible impression on me. And then again, I think because it was so positive. And for me what I saw up there took me back to my childhood. All of a sudden I was able to reconnect with that part of my culture and myself that I had grown up with for twelve years of my life that had been missing. And here it was there in front of me and I could relate to it. I didn't go to any of the school plays when I was in high school. I was part of Girls Athletics; I played sports. I played baseball and volleyball and basketball.

When did you first perform?

In 1972, and I know that because Jerry and I left closing night, went home, went to bed, got up the next morning, Sunday morning, drove to Santa Barbara, and got married. So I closed August 5, 1972, *Amen Corner*—James Baldwin's play, *The Amen Corner.*

And where was this? Here in Santa Ana?

At Santa Ana College, as a favor to Jerry who was teaching there part-time. A group of black students had gone to the dean of the department and complained that they never did productions that had roles for black students other than slaves, subservient kinds of roles. So they protested. And the dean, to placate them, said, "Well, you know, if you want to do something this summer, you can." But the catch was, "We have no money and whatever you do, you have to do it without a budget." And he said it had to be supervised by someone on the staff.

Well, Jerry was a young professor there. All the students knew him and they thought he was kind of cool. Jerry had been a student at Santa Ana College and had done theater when he was there, and so they went to him. Jerry said, "I will supervise. I'll oversee this." And they held their auditions [for *The Amen Corner*] and they didn't get enough students to play all the roles and so he came home one night after the audition—No , we weren't living together, but we went out after and he was saying to me—we weren't living together. Did you hear that?

Okay.

He came after one of their auditions and he was telling me and his sister about the fact that they needed other people, and he was trying to recruit us. And we said, "Oh, I don't want to do that."

And were you a student there?

No, I was dating him and I was working at Hunt-Wesson Foods [in Fullerton] at the time. I spent six or seven years there. I was a general office training coordinator and that's how I met Jerry. But he begged us to do it, literally, because he said, "Come on, and just audition. You can just be in the congregation." So we said okay, fine, you know, nothing else to do for the summer. So his sister and I went and auditioned, and she got cast in the congregation and I got the role of the lead character's best friend. And I thought, "Oh, my God!" But it was fun. So I did that and went on with my life. At that time I was majoring in business. I later went on to major in psychology. I never thought of it, theater, as a career.

It was a great summer. We did *The Amen Corner* not only at the theater there [at Santa Ana College], but we did it in a park at Monte Vista [elementary school]. They put up a portable stage and we performed in the park, because it was about taking it to the community and making it accessible, even then. And that's a big thing now.

Did you have any favorite actors or singers and artists?

Yes. I'm embarrassed to say it, too. It was Elvis Presley. He was the king. I got a spanking when I was—I had to be thirteen. In my family, the philosophy is, my mother said, "Well, you never get too brown." But I went to see *Blue Hawaii* with my little cousin, and after the movie I was supposed to come home. But I was so smitten I just couldn't leave. I stayed and watched it again. I stayed there watching *Blue Hawaii*, dreaming about Elvis. I was in love with Elvis.

And then they did a movie that featured the Supremes and James Brown and all of them. It was some movie, the Motown deal. And that was another movie I remember watching again and again and again. But yeah, it was through the movies and not a lot of that because Sundays were reserved for church.

Saturday was the day we did things around the house. You cleaned and cooked and washed, did all your chores: stripping wax off the floor, defrosting the refrigerator, and all of that. That took up your whole day. And then on Sunday it was church. And oftentimes if there were services in the afternoon, pastors' anniversaries, church anniversaries, other churches visiting you, and to visit other churches, we had to go. So that took your whole Sunday.

What church were you a member of?

Community Temple. It was a nondenominational church. It was very by-the-book. My mother now goes to New Spirit but my stepfather's still there, yeah. The other church that I know we used to visit frequently was First Mission Baptist. Reverend Hollings was here. Who's not deceased was Reverend Carrington [of Friendship Baptist in Fullerton], who's now in Yorba Linda. Reverend Carrington was a new minister who had come from Los Angeles and was having services in Eunice Bryan's home. And then they moved into this little gas station that had gone out of business. And I remember going to his church. Other members in Orange County didn't welcome him. They didn't like the fact that he was an out-of-towner, an L.A. slick kind of thing. Well, that was their perception.

Were there any black kids that you came up with at that time?

Oh, yeah, Edna Woods; she sang back-up for Tina Turner. She was one of the Ikettets. So we were like, "Edna Woods!" And we loved Tina Turner. And I know when I saw the film *What's Love Got To Do With It?* I thought about her, because it showed the 1971 concert at the Greek Theater, and I was there. I was there because Edna was there, Edna Woods, and she let us backstage and we got to meet Tina.

Gary [Templeton], the baseball player, lives in San Diego; he was with the Padres. I grew up with Gary. I used to live down the street from him and his sister Gail and all the whole family; and Isaac Curtis. He used to play for the Cincinnati Bengals. Isaac went on to be in *Sports Illustrated* when he was in the eleventh or twelfth grade, which is unheard of. That's how good he was. Sadly enough, I also came along in the seventies when a lot of teenagers were beginning to experiment with drugs. So a number of the kids that I went to school with ended up overdosing on drugs, and some are probably still on drugs or came to some kind of tragic end.

About how large would you say the black community was when you were a teenager?

I went to Santa Ana High. And there were maybe twelve or thirteen of us at Santa Ana High. I mean, you could count us on two hands, literally, maybe three hands.

There weren't many of us at all. [Santa Ana] Valley [High School] was where most of the black kids went.

Well, what have your formal educational experiences been like?

Unlike my daughter, who I encourage and who is very active in a lot of things in school, I think my experience could have been much richer, much broader. And because I wasn't able to make or have the assistance with making the cultural adjustment from leaving an all-black South to an integrated situation, I think I wasn't as prepared to deal with either; we all stuck together because we were alienated. And so I don't think it was as rich as it could have been. I think I was deprived in many ways, because I think I should have been exposed to theater and I should have been exposed to French club and other things that I had no desire to be involved in because I didn't feel a part of my school in that way. And thank God for Mr. Reardon, because had he not chosen me to do what I did with him, I would have no extracurricular activities other than sports. .

I sewed to get through my high school years. I think it was a way to redirect that kind of energy. I became a seamstress and my mother bought me a Kenmore stand floor model sewing machine, a couple of hundred dollars, which was [big] money at that time. I made all of my clothes and I made designer clothes, because I had this energy, I had this creativity, and I had nowhere to direct it. And, you know, Simplicity patterns? I thought, "Oh, no." I needed the Butterwick, the Vogue, and then I would take that and make my own design out of it. And so that's what I did with the kind of energy that I had, because I didn't feel welcomed or I didn't feel it was there for me.

And it was real odd when I moved back to Santa Ana in 1984 and my children were at Santiago School, the elementary school, and I went to the parent-teacher night and I saw a lot of the faces of the white students that I went to school with. They would kind of recognize me, I would recognize them, but we were never friends, we never talked. Now here we were adults now with our own children going to school together. It was a real strange scenario initially. Because I would see some people I knew, and I would remember some of their names. One girl was a cheerleader. But we didn't socialize at all.

You were there but you weren't interacting at all.

Oh, you better believe it. It was apartheid. (laughter) We had it here in Orange County. We had it, and we didn't socialize. We went, we took pictures, and we have pictures from our scrapbooks. We did not stay, we didn't dance. We never liked the bands. The music was not music we would dance to.

When you finished Santa Ana High, where did you go?

Well, then I went to Santa Ana College, and I was in the stewardess program. And I think that gave me a sense of identity and a sense of purpose and belonging. Although I was the only black in that program, I still felt a part of something. And the lady, Mary Lou Finely, who started the program, was wonderful. And then when I got married, I completed the program, but I never went on to be a stewardess.

Then Crystal came, my firstborn. Then I went to work for Hunt-Wesson Foods [in Fullerton] when she was like six or seven weeks old and stayed there for like six years. So, during that period of time, I would go to night school, take business courses, because Hunt-Wesson had an educational reimbursement program. They encouraged you to go back to school, get your degrees. And I was kind of tracked to management. After about six months I was promoted. I started as a secretary to the plant manager, and then from there I was promoted to the plant manager, and then from there I was promoted to training coordinator. They put together a training program to train minority women, to hire them. It was an affirmative action program because affirmative action was big during that time and large companies like Hunt was trying to find a way to hire minorities.

About what year was that?

I think I took the program over in '69 or '70. Well, it wasn't a program. I designed it. I was interviewed and hired by the personnel manager at that time, who was a Caucasian. I did the research and recruited the women and hired and trained them.

So, it really wasn't until I decided to stay home and be a mother—after the second marriage, and decided I wanted to have another child; I would stay home because I didn't want to raise my children through daycare—that I really gave some thought to what it is I really want to do? I went to Fullerton Community College then, enrolled in a full-time program in psychology—because I thought I wanted to be a psychologist—transferred to Cal State Fullerton, decided I wanted to specialize in child psychology, and spent a semester in child development courses and took a creative dramatics course.

That changed everything around. I had so much fun in that course and the professor said to me that I had gotten the only *A* he had given, and he said, "I'm very tough." He said, "Have you ever given thought of going into theater?" And I said, "No, it's just a fun thing to do." I sat and talked to Jerry about it one night, and we talked, and talked, and he said, "You know, you ought to try it. You ought to explore that." This was my senior year. I went back to school that next semester and dropped all my courses that I had signed up for and took all theater courses. And I've never looked back. It was another three years before I could graduate, because I had to take all of this stuff from the ground up. In between I had [my other child] Lawrence.

You said that you decided to go into theater and your husband was very supportive. How did the rest of your family feel about that?

My mother knew I had been a working professional and at any time I wanted to do that, she always used to say to me, "You know Hunt will take you back anytime." Bernice Hurd, and there were some other people there that I knew—I could have said I want to come back and I could have gone back. They were supportive of my going to school; let me say that, because they all chipped in and helped take care of my kids while I was in school.

Why did you start the Orange County Black Actors Theater [OCBAT]?

I was pursuing acting as a career. I really thought I wanted to be an actress, and I had had a little taste of that and I had been bitten by the bug when I started doing *Colored Girls*. The director of this play brought that show to Orange Coast College, brought it in as Artists in Residence. So I had a taste of being somewhat of a professional actress and being paid money and knew how to put it together.

I'd been auditioning for shows at Cal State Fullerton and wasn't getting cast. I had a very close friend, a white male friend, who is a damned good actor, Joe Parrish. And Joe Parrish would get very angry because they wouldn't cast me, and he'd say, "You were the best thing in there." I complained, and I talked to him and my advisor and the dean of the department about these things. I was not happy about it. But by the same token, I also said, "Let me just get what I need, in terms of skills, and get out of here." I felt I had bigger fish to fry, other battles to fight, so I switched to directing. And the first class I ever took in directing, I just took to it like a duck to water. And actually it was a blessing because I love that so much more.

Joe Parrish and I were the best during that year. All of the students would flock to our auditions because they all wanted to work with us. So I had my pick and was empowered in a way that didn't make me feel helpless as an actress, because I wasn't going to get on stage. And that's when I also said, "Well, you know, if you don't sing and dance and you're black, you don't get on stage." Anytime there was a musical, you know, they would give us some part. But straight plays, there were no roles for us. The same problems the students had when I did the show in Santa Ana College in 1972 I was now dealing with at Cal State Fullerton ten years later—the exact same scenario.

What spurred me to start the Black Actors Theater was that experience. I recognized that it was going to be difficult. I wasn't going to Los Angeles to work. I had a family and I didn't desire to live in L.A. And if I want to raise my family, and I want to participate in theater and have it as a career, I was going to have to lay the platform. I was going to have to do something to create that. I had talked to Robert Hooks—I had seen him at a conference and was a co-founder of the Negro Ensemble Company—and Robert said, "Go for it. I'll help you. I'll do whatever I can. That's exactly what you should do."

So when did you first appeal to corporations for financial backing?

By '84 I realized that the kind of criteria a lot of the corporations and governmental funding agencies looked at were demographics. But you had the majority of the black population living in Santa Ana, the county seat. Actually, that's why we bought the home in Santa Ana. Jerry and I talked about that and said, "You know, I think if I'm in Santa Ana, I'll be able to make more progress. I will be able to at least make a stronger argument for funding such a program that I wasn't able to make with the demographics that exist in Fullerton."

Okay, how was all that organized? What was its structure?

Well, originally, it was called the Intercultural Committee for the Performing Arts, the original organization; intercultural, because the concept was to be multi-cultural. I did not want to be guilty of reverse discrimination. In fact, what I wanted to do was provide a new model for bridging gaps and bringing people together. And so the concept was intercultural amongst and between cultures, and we set out to recruit people of other ethnic persuasions to get involved. But what we found was we had difficulty getting non-black people to make a commitment to the organization, because they had so many other avenues and opportunities available to them. So that's why the name change [to OCBAT] came about, because we found ourselves all black, although we weren't originally designed to be that way.

Now, which plays were performed, and why were they chosen?

The first one was *Trouble in Mind* by Alice Childress. That was chosen to make a statement about what the mission of the organization was. And the mission was to provide non-stereotypical opportunities—presentation opportunities for blacks on stage. And *Trouble in Mind* dealt with that. It dealt with negative stereotypes of blacks in theater.

Who were some of the creative people you've worked with?

There's another story that is precious to me. Richard Abraham was a graduate of Cal State Fullerton from the music department; we met because our mothers worked together at Monte Vista Elementary School, in the kitchen. My mother was a supervisor and his mother worked for her, and they would brag about their children. Both their children were in theater. They kept wanting us to get together and we kept saying, "I don't want to meet him," "I don't want to meet her."

And, oh, I have to back up. Our first production was, *Moving On, Seven Decades of Black Entertainment.* That was our signature show. We were in the Olympics with that show; represented the United States. When I was desperate for a musician, I finally said to my mother, "Now, what is that lady's son's name that worked with you? What did he do in the music department?" I said, "I need to meet him." So we met, and it's been a perfect relationship. We've had a great relationship and he's brilliant. We made him an honorary black. He loved it.

Who did your scenery and costumes and things of that sort?

Initially, we would do the thrift store shopping and put together what we could on our own. Wendell Carmichael would help us and then I used Style Leader, which is a company that makes all of the uniforms for the drill teams and the bands for all the schools, and they sell a lot of dancewear and stuff like that. They did our *Colored Girls* costumes. For like *Trouble in Mind*, we bought all that stuff in thrift stores, and often out of my closet. Jerry would come to the plays and say, "Isn't that my robe?" I said, "Yeah." Then at the end, Roxie Roker walked out in my suit. My daughter said, "Ain't that your suit?" If you lived in my house, I'd have all your stuff in the show.

In terms of a house to put on a play, what were your experiences at the South Coast Repertory Playhouse [in Costa Mesa] like?

You know, that's a loaded question. Well, they were negative and positive. It was good for us to go down there and work in a legitimate house that had all of the resources that one could ever want to put on a quality production. At the same time, they weren't used to having people [produce their own plays] in their theater, let alone people of a different color. So it's like having strangers come into your home, and I'm sensitive to that. But also I think it added another dimension, the fact that we were African Americans, and they were not accustomed to having African Americans as audiences let alone as artists. They didn't quite know how to deal with us, so they kind of didn't deal with us. It was like "act as if they're not here and they'll go away."

Was this management or just employees?

These were the employees. David Ems was certainly astute enough and enough of an art administrator and sensitive enough to the climate at the time. So was I, which is why I went down there and spoke to him. I approached him, he didn't approach me. David thought it wouldn't look good if he had said no to us. So he said, yes, I believe thinking that we were going to be this little community group putting on a little community play and that we were going to lose a lot of money and not be able to afford to be able to come back, and all of his problems would be solved. Well, quite contraire, because *Colored Girls* was a very big hit. The critics were screaming for more and the audiences were screaming for more. They only gave us two weeks, and we ran Tuesday through Sunday. Seven shows a week, with the matinees and all, and sold it out, every ticket. David said to me at the wrap-up session, "Well, I guess since it was such a success— if you'd like to come back." But see, he didn't count on it being a success.

So now what do you say when it's a big hit? You can't say, "Well, thank you, that was great, and we'll see you around." You should extend to us an invitation to come back. Well, then what happened was they had difficulty finding time in their schedule to bring us back in, because they didn't usually rent their space. So he tried to find very diplomatic ways of getting around it, and then I was just persistent. I followed up with him until he finally said, "Well, okay, we've got a week we can give you." Then they finally came back with two weeks. So we went back in with our second show, which was *Eubie,* and it was a big hit as well. Because we were not only able to make money in a very short period of time, which is difficult to do, we were able to put on quality productions that didn't necessarily rival his, but we didn't look like amateur people. We did encounter some other altercations, even a couple with some of his staff.

Would you like to share one of those?

I think the one that really stands out as just blatant, a blatant attempt to say, "We don't want you in our theater," was closing night of *Ain't Misbehavin'* when the house manager wouldn't allow me in the theater because he said the place was packed. It was sold out and the ushers were sitting on the stairs, and he said, "There's no room in there for you." Now, you would never say to the producer of a show that they couldn't go into the theater and see their show. It's unheard of. You may put someone else out but you don't tell the producer they can't go into their own show. That sparked some pretty heated dialogue between him and me.

At the same time, although unbeknownst to me, there was an altercation going on with the backstage supervisor-janitor, I guess he was, and George Hammonds, who would videotape our shows for archival purposes. George had parked in the loading dock area, initially, just to go in and unload his equipment. And when he got in, he was already running late, the show had started, so he just set up his equipment and went on shooting the show and thought, "Well, I'll just go move my car at intermission." After he got it all set up and got it rolling, he ran back out to move his car, and this guy was about to have his car towed. He and George got into this shouting match. The guy was saying, "You people—we don't want you people here anyway." He kept referring to us as "you people." Well, then he, the janitor, calls the house manager, who's dealing with me—he and I were having words—and he gets called on his beeper saying that there's this altercation going on in the back with one of my people and then we march around there and they're at it, and so it was a big mess.

Why did OCBAT fold?

Lack of funds and relocation on my part. If you're going to do something like that, it's very vital that you live in that community and be part of the pulse of that community. It's not the kind of thing that you can do and live afar, and that became very clear to me real quick. You know, it was very difficult for me to cut it loose, because I felt like I had just put so much into it. I really wanted to see someone continue it, to carry it on, because it's very difficult to get projects like that off the ground. I mean, it doesn't matter; black or white, starting a theater is a major undertaking. So I'm sure it won't be as OCBAT. I would hope that at some point in time someone will start up another project.

Well, thank you so much. This has been marvelous.

Chapter 3
Coming to Santa Ana during the Time of the Black Community's Rapid Population Expansion

The most significant changes in Santa Ana's black community began in the late 1950s and continued throughout the 1960s. In each of the two decades, between 1950 and 1970, the black population of Santa Ana increased fourfold. Two major elements promoting the change were primarily related to factors that occurred outside of the city. The first was the rapid expansion of jobs and job opportunities for blacks due to industrialization. The second was the discrimination in the rental and sale of housing in the suburbs coupled with black individuals and families choosing not to live in isolation from other black people.

In 1960, college graduate and school teacher Everett Winters came from Kentucky with his family to Orange County in hopes of finding a job outside of teaching. He found a low-level job in the shipping-receiving crating department at Autonetics, in Anaheim, but within a few weeks, he procured a position in administration. Winters saw his housing options only in Fullerton or Santa Ana and he chose a home in a new tract that opened up in Santa Ana. Four years later, in a situation similar to the Winters family, Gladys Smith and her engineer husband, Erv, came to Orange County. He had taken a job at Aeronutronic in Newport Beach, and they had little choice but to live in Santa Ana, because of discrimination they experienced in their attempt to find housing near his place of work.

In 1964, Grambling State University graduate Johnny Williams left Louisiana where teaching salaries were very low, and after a short stay in too-cold Chicago, came to Santa Ana. With the help of a marine, he obtained housing in a Minnie Street apartment in southeast Santa Ana. This was an all-white neighborhood, of mostly enlisted marine families. The county welfare director, Grandville Peoples, deemed this as the area with the greatest number of social problems in the county. A year later, the Williams family moved to southwest Santa Ana.

Whether it was by necessity or by choice, the Reid and the Shipp families settled in Santa Ana. In 1965, the Shipps had decided to move from Florida to California. Helen Shipp's husband, Felton, found work at Delco Batteries in Anaheim, near Santa Ana where his brother was pastor of Calvary Baptist Church. Sadie Reid's husband Ezrom, employed by the firm Telemetrics, was transferred from Los Angeles to their plant in Santa Ana. Like the Reid family, Lincoln Mulkey chose work in Santa Ana, as a postal worker, and the Mulkeys chose to live there as well. Because of Lincoln's work, he knew good apartments from bad. They chose three apartments outside of the ghetto and suffered discrimination in attempting to rent each of the three. This was the beginning of the famous *Mulkey v. Reitman* lawsuit.

2

1 **The Alexandria Boot Black Stand**

W. K. DUFFY

Formerly at the Rossmore Barber Shop

First-Class Work Guaranteed

Special Attention Given to Ladies' and Children's Shoes

416 N. Main St. Santa Ana, Cal.

4

3

[1] 1913 Willis Duffy shoeshine stand ad in the *Santa Ana Register* soon after Duffy came to Orange County. [2] Connie, 7, with her brothers Bill (left) and Jerome. [3] The Duffy family, Connie, Jerome, and Bill behind father Willis and mother Minnie, about 1941. [4] Baxter and Bernice Young, 19xx. (Photos 1-3, courtesy of Connie Duffy. Photo 4, courtesy of Bethel Young Reeves.)

1

3

2

[1] Franklin School. Barbara Young (daughter of Bernice and Baxter Young), front row second from left, and Zeph Jones top row next to the teacher. [2] Santa Ana high football co-captains Herschel Musick, nephew of the Orange County sheriff James Musick, and Zeph Jones. [3] Zeph Jones in front of his home in Santa Ana. (Photos courtesy of Zeph Jones)

1

2

3

4

[1] The Educational Extensional Club. From l. to r.: Ernestine Ransom (with glasses), Bernice Young, author Ruby Berkley Goodwin from Fullerton, Mattie Davis, next Goodwin's cousin, next Mrs. McCarthy, Tessie McAllister, and Goodwin's sister Francis. [2] Ransom in about 1941. [3] Ernestine Ransom's mother and sisters. From l. to r.: Ernestine's mother (Mother Anderson), Ruth Fox, Bessy Crawford, Ruby Denham, Ernestine Ransom, and Christine Green, in the early 1950s. [4] Vern Napier with his wife Jean and three daughters, l to r, Alison, Amy, and Amanda. (Photos 1-3 courtesy of Ernestine Ransom, Photos 4-6 courtesy of Vern Napier).

2

[1] Left to right, Connie Jones, her grandmother Annie Mae Tripp, and Yvonne Tripp, who also is Anne Mae's granddaughter. [2] Recent photo of Connie Jones and Jessie Allen working at the Southwest Community Center. [3] Members of Sunday school at Second Baptist about 1964. Back row: Ernestine Anderson Ransom, Regina White Ford, Francyne Ransom Bryant Verlin Burton, Larry Fulcher, Ione Curtis, Percy Burton, Johnny Williams, Rosette Williams, Beatrice Fields, Lois Curtis Augustine. Second row: Jeannetta Sterling, Gladys Allen Dixon, Cheryl Hatchett, Tommy Fields (behind Cheryl Hatchett), Melvina Miller, Anthony Fields, Hortense "Peaches" Henderson, Samuel Henderson, Jr., Sandra Burton (behind Henderson Jr.), Patricia Allen, Reginald Fields, Aaron Fields, Katie Berry Allen (behind Aaron Fields). (Photos courtesy of Connie Jones and Jessie Allen).

1

2

3

4

5

[1] Ed Caruthers clearing the silver medal height at the 1968 Olympics in Mexico City. [2] Caruthers congratulating gold medalist Dick Fosbury. [3] Caruthers with his mother Ruth Burgess. [4] From left to right: Caruthers (co-Grand Marshall); his daughter Sheri Jonné; 4x400 gold medal winner in the 1964 Olympics Ulysses Williams; four-time gold medal winner in diving, Pat McCormick; and Caruthers'daughter Chara Lora, at the Orange County Black History Parade in the late 1980s. [5] Adleane Hunter with Hinton Battle at the Eubie opening night, 1987. (Photos 1-4 courtesy of Ed Caruthers, Photo 5 courtesy of Adleane Hunter.)

1

2

3

4

5

6

[1] Santa Ana community activists and volunteers in Everett Winters political campaigns. Front: Rayford Rodgers and Ray Johnson. Back: Clarence Lee, Everett Winters, Rudy Francis, Jess Berry (with the glasses), unidentified, and Columbus Hamilton. [2] Recent Winters photo. [3] Dottie Mulkey (Right), US Navy football cheer leader in 1960. [4] With second daughter Sheryl in Santa Ana in 1966. [5] Dottie with Sheryl (l) and first daughter Michelle, 1970. [6] Dottie and husband Lincoln, Christmas Day, 1974. (Photos 1-2 courtesy of Everett Winters and 3-6 Dottie Mulkey)

1

2

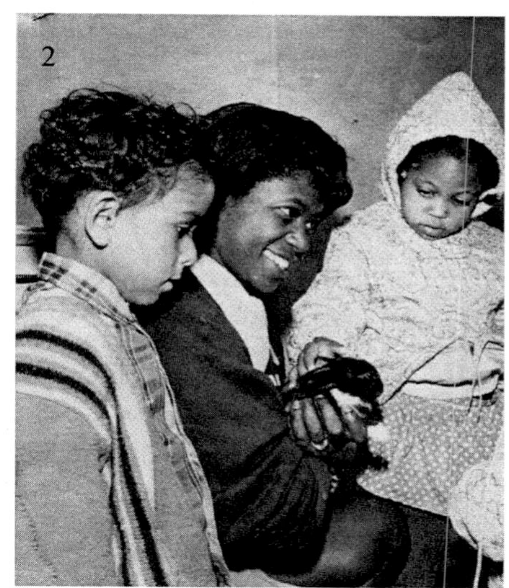

3

4

5

6

[1] Gladys and Ervin Smith in 1968. [2] Sadie Reid Benham with children at the Creative Day Care Center. [3] Sadie Reid was invited to the White House in 1980 and met Jimmy and Roselyn Carter. [4] With Santa Ana school board members: (from left) Jim Ward, Mary Pryer, Joan Wilkinson, Sadie, and Jim Richards, sometime in the mid 1980s. [5] Helen Shipp with her husband Felton. [6] Helen Shipp speaking at a Black History Parade.

1

2

3

4

[1] Leon and Mary Owens with daughter Karen and son Darren (1966). [2] 1969, Mary and Leon Owens in Washington D.C. with Darren, Sharen, Karen, and cousin Robin in Leon's arms. [3] Natalie and Ralph Kennedy with Cesar Chavez in 1957. [4] Ralph and Natalie with son Rusty, 1967. (Photos 1-2 courtesy of the Owens family and 3-5 the Kennedy family.)

1

2

3

4

5

[1] John Smith, a young marine. [2] John Smith, on the right, was Superior Court clerk for Judge James W. Cook, seated. This was the third Superior Court judge for which he was the clerk. [3] City of Placentia active reserve police officer John Smith, about 1966. [4] Josh White with his friend Jess Berry (in the white coat). [5] The Reverend James Carrington in the pulpit in the early years of his ministry. (Photos 1-3 courtesy of John Smith. Photo 4 courtesy of Josh White. Photo 5 courtesy of Rev. James Carrington.)

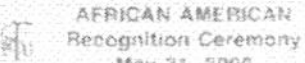

5

[1] Professor Wacira Gethaiga and CSUF President Milton Gordon at the university's 35th year celebration in 1993. [2] Gethaiga speaking at the African American Recognition Ceremony in the year 2000. [3] Jo Caines, a 19 year old at NYU. [4] Husband Ken and Jo Caines, at one of many events in which they were involved. [5] The Caines family; from left to right: Chris, Leslie, Jo, Clark, and Ken. (Photos 1-2, courtesy of Professor Gethaiga and Photos 3-5 courtesy of Josephine Caines.)

1

2

3

4

4

5

[1] Jim McKay, a single guy about 1970 and [2] pilot Jim McKay. [3] McKay with his wife Loralee. [4] Bob Clemons with his and his wife Lois's first three children; left to right: Gina, Robert, and Sherry shortly before they moved to Orange County from Watts in 1969. [5] Barbara Youngblood and son Ty at a 2008 volunteer luncheon. (Photos 1-3 courtesy of Jim McKay. Photo 4 courtesy of Robert Clemons. Photo 5 courtesy of Barbara Youngblood.)

[1] 

[2] 

[1] Choir of the Johnson Chapel AME. Below right, Angeline Carter. First row, from left: Rosetta Napier, not known, Tessie McAllister, Lillie Mae Walker, and Catherine McCarthy. Top row, from left: Harold Ross, Marcellus Lang, Willy Walker, Mattie Lang, Elnora Ross, and Legenia Gardner. Early 1960s. [2] Helen Shipp teaching at a church women's fellowship. (Photo 1, courtesy of Vern Napier. Photo 2, courtesy of Helen Shipp)

EVERETT WINTERS[1]

Everett Winters was born in Henderson, Kentucky, near the Kentucky-Indiana border on June 27, 1934. Through high school, he went to segregated schools, in spite of living in an integrated neighborhood. He chose to go to a predominantly white, but integrated, college, which provided him with even greater exposure to the world he would settle into in Orange County. While in college, he was involved with marches and sit-ins through the NAACP, leading to a lifetime of work in civil rights, both professionally and as a volunteer. Everett Winters now lives in Dallas, Texas, having retired as the Executive Assistant to the President & Director of Affirmative Action, Southern Methodist University. Photo ca. 1960.

Tell us something about your early upbringing, particularly as you feel this might have influenced your later life.

I'm a native Kentuckian born in Henderson, Kentucky, June 27, 1934, the seventh child of Elijah and Martha Winters. I was educated in an all-black elementary school and an all-black high school. I mention that because of what I think is significant later in my life. When I was making some choices as to where I might go to continue my education, I had scholarship offers at Kentucky State University and Tennessee State University, then predominantly black colleges. I eventually decided that I wanted to go to an integrated institution and I selected Evansville College in Evansville, Indiana [eight miles north of Henderson]. At the time that I enrolled at Evansville [in 1953], there were seven black students out of a total of 3200 students. I had some adjustments to make, and I think that those adjustments have been particularly meaningful to me in my later career and perhaps to some extent with the upbringing of my family, and probably caused my move to the state of California.

---

[1]Oral History No. 1684. Interview dates: May 25, 1982, June 1, 1982, and June 8, 1982, at California State University, Fullerton. Interviewer: Lawrence de Graaf.

I was determined to enjoy the fruits of my education and I decided that I was going to become involved in as many of the student activities as I possibly could. I ran for a student government office and I came in second, which has occurred throughout my career in terms of being elected to some type of an office. Obviously, I had to go out and do quite a bit of campaigning, had to solicit other persons to campaign for me and with me, and the fact that I did come in as a runner-up was very meaningful. But there were other adjustments, in terms of being the only black person in the Thespians and having persons try to determine what kind of roles would Everett be playing. Even at that early age, I had decided that I did not want to just have roles only black people could play. I wanted to be a full participant and I was allowed to do that.

Was this the first exposure you had in your life in relating to a predominantly white situation?

I grew up in an integrated neighborhood. Henderson itself was well integrated in terms of housing patterns. My early childhood was spent where in my home, white majority youngsters sat at my table, had dinner. We slept together in the same beds at night. I would go to their homes. It was not unusual for me to have dinner there, not unusual for me to spend the night there. I still have some lifelong friends from that. Until we were about fourteen or fifteen years old, even though we went to segregated schools, there was a very close-knit relationship. Their families would often have exchanges with my family, meaning the adults, and this didn't just happen with the boys; it was happening with the girls who were a part of my family also. Let me mention one other thing that was rather important to me. The movies in Henderson did discriminate and were segregated and I can recall an incident where we were all playing one day—and I'm probably the only black in the group—and suddenly someone said, "Let's go to the movies." And everybody's all charged up to go to the movies. And suddenly there was a remembrance that we couldn't all go to the movies, because Ev, as they called me, could not go to the movies with them. So the trip to the movie was cancelled.

But what we did do often was to go to Evansville, [Indiana] across the river, where we could all go to the movies. We could all sit side by side and enjoy the movie. I often think back today at how not only some of those youngsters did this, but their parents also insisted that, "Hey, we're all going to go together as a group and Everett's going to be a part of the group." In addition to going to Evansville, having grown up perhaps two doors from the golf course had an influence on my life also, because it allowed me to see how the other half lived—the values, how the more affluent people in the community lived.

My father was a butcher; he was a chief sausage maker. We were not upper middle class people, but my father made it possible for any of us who wanted to go to school to further our education both through high school and into college. I didn't work when I went to college because of their generosity toward me, their concern that I did get a quality education. Getting back to the golf course, I observed how persons were encouraging their youngsters to seek a higher education. Some of those persons that I caddied for would inquire, "Everett, what are you going to do with your future?" and "Why aren't you making some plans?" And I think they probably had as much of an impact upon me eventually going onto an institution of higher education as did my parents and my instructors in high school.

Do you feel that going to a segregated school system was a detriment to you or did it have some positive effects?

When I got into the fifth grade, I started to go to the city elementary school. I met up with a group of students where we formed a scholastic rivalry. We weren't satisfied to get a "B+" when someone else got an "A" or "A-." We would challenge the teachers to explain why one of us got a slightly higher grade than the other. There was this dedication that we were going to be as good as the other person. But there were a number of instructors who certainly influenced our desire to be competitive. We had a chemistry teacher and a biology teacher in particular, who spent lots of time with us after school allowing us to conduct experiments that were beyond the scope of where we should have been in our education and encouraging us to become better students and talking about the worth of getting a college education.

Did you have any particular mission behind your college education?

There was a challenge there for me as a student, who came from an all-black environment, to be able to demonstrate that I could compete on an equal level with a majority of students. I think that that started with my home where both of my parents instilled in us as siblings that we were as good as anyone else and we could do as much as we wanted to do if we took advantage of those opportunities.

So where did you go after you left Evansville?

I went into teaching at a small school in Morganfield, Kentucky, an all-black school, and I taught sociology and history as well as being the basketball coach and the track coach. I'm a natural sports lover and I had great experiences there.

While in Kentucky, did you take any part in civil rights activities?

Oh, yes. Being a part of the NAACP [National Association for the Advancement of Colored People], we had protests at some of the local fast-food services, in about the mid-50s, about '56, while I was at Evansville. That's when we were determined that we weren't going to continue to have to suffer such injustices. We were very involved in protest marches as well as some counter-sitting.

I gather this antedates the sit-ins that started in Greensboro.

Certainly our involvement in trying to control what was happening in our area of the community started before the civil rights movement of the early 60s.

Where did you go from Morganfield?

From Morganfield, [in 1960] I went to North American Aviation, in the city of Anaheim. I could not get into an office type of position when I first started there.

I was very lucky in getting a job at Rockwell, and I say "lucky" because of the events that occurred. I had been trying to get employment and they were hiring people like mad at this particular time in Anaheim because it was just opening up. I visited the personnel office, I believe in Downey, and I had a conversation with someone there and he said, "Well, we don't have anything in Anaheim but they're going to start hiring people." So when I came to Anaheim I asked about opportunities for employment and they said they didn't have any. I said, "Well, Mr. So-and-So said that if I came here I could probably get a job." And he said, "He said that?" I said, "Yes." He said, "Well, sit down for a few minutes."

They arranged for me to go in and meet with an interviewer. His first words were that they didn't have any jobs at that time, but why didn't I sit there and give some background. He read through my application and we sat there and were talking and he happened to look at the fact that I had gone to the University of Evansville. He said, "You know 'The Big O,'" meaning Oscar Robertson, who had graduated from Indianapolis and had gone on to the University of Cincinnati. His son had been at University of Cincinnati at the same time as Oscar. We sat there for about an hour and 15 minutes talking about basketball and he looked around and says, "Look, let me just check something." He looked behind him and there was a stack of requisitions and he says, "I can't get you into a project administration position just now, but look, I've got a job over here as a shipping-receiving crater," or something like that, and he said, "You know if you take this job, there's a possibility that within a short time you might be able to get a chance to get transferred into something that would be more desirable for you. Will you take it?" And I said, "Yes, because I'm desperate for a job," and I took that job.

Within a few days, I got notification from the company that that they weren't hiring people in my field, at that time. But within a period of about four and one-half weeks I had met one of the guys from the project area and had given him a resume. He took it back to his boss, and he got me a transfer out of that shipping area into that administrative area that I was trying to get into. I recall after I had been in that job for probably two or three months, I got another note from the Personnel Office saying that they were not hiring people in that [project area].

Another interesting facet is that when I was trying to get into that area, they told me that they were only hiring people with business administration [degrees]. When I got into the unit, I found that there were other historians, there was a guy with a degree in forestry, and there was a mortician. Most of the people who were working there were either working on their AA from a community college or only had community college, except those people that I've named. That was a very disappointing thing for me to find out; because it meant that where I had believed that California was this land of milk and honey, it wasn't all that it was cut out to be.

I stayed at Rockwell for four and one-half years and had moved up the ladder, again being the only black in that particular unit and having some very good experiences there. But I was always the last person on the totem pole and Rockwell was going from having some 32,000 people at this location down to something like 12,000 people, so they were consequently laying people off. Every month someone would panic who was on the list above me and quit. I finally got tired of that and went to Aeronutronic Ford and applied for a position and was hired.

While at Rockwell, I became involved in the NAACP. We were trying to find ways to get the company to hire more black people, and my predecessor as president of the Orange County Chapter of the NAACP was a person by the name of Wyatt Frieson. Wyatt Frieson had initiated some contact with several major employers about opportunities for blacks to get into those companies and he called this an NAACP industry committee. I then became president of the NAACP and Wyatt became chair of that particular group, which has become known as the Orange County Equal Opportunity Employers Association where employers are providing opportunities for not only blacks, but Hispanics, women, etc., today, and are still a functioning group.[2] This was about 1964-65 when Wyatt actually started that NAACP industry group. You, Larry, will also recall that, because you and I were members of the NAACP.

Eventually, when I started working at Aeronutronic Ford, a very interesting thing occurred. During this period of time, the so-called Detroit riots and Watts riots were in progress and Mr. Ford supposedly was watching the city of Detroit burn when he decided that he and other business people in that city should take more of an interest in the community that surrounded them. So he put out an edict to all of his plant locations and subsidiaries throughout the United States and demanded that they become involved and knowledgeable about their local community. And I'm working at Aeronutronic Ford and the company apparently had no awareness that I was also the president of the Orange County Chapter of NAACP, because they sent me a letter asking me to meet with the executive vice president and the directors.

I accepted their invitation and the topic they had asked me to speak about was "What Problems Do Minorities Face in Orange County?" An interesting thing happened that particular day. I went to the executive dining hall and I'm sitting there and my director, who I report to, is coming to this meeting and he stops and he sees me there and he says, "Everett, what are you doing at this meeting? Why are you here?"

I said I'd been invited by Mr. Lawson, who is the executive vice president, to meet with him today. And he [my boss] wants to know why. He thinks it's because of some job-related problem. And I said, "Well, I think that will be explained when I get inside." He was a little irate about why I was being so evasive but I had a chance to go in there and I introduced myself as the president of the Orange County Chapter of the National Association for Colored People. I gave my presentation about the problems that minority-group persons were having in the county and I said, "My director, who happens to be sitting over there, is such and such and he is probably the only person here who realizes that I'm an employee of this company."

[2] All of the county's major employers like Rockwell, Hughes, Hunt Foods, Collins Radio, and Ford Aeronutronic became members of this organization, which served the dual purpose of affirmative action and combating discrimination within their own company.

At that time, we were talking about problems that minority persons were facing in Orange County, and by far the two major problems were employment and housing. In Orange County, blacks could basically only reside in two communities, in a small area of Fullerton and in Santa Ana. When black professionals or any other black employees were moving into this county, they were shuttled into either Fullerton or Santa Ana and shown property there. My theme for several years in Orange County was that Orange County in its embryo stage had an opportunity to do something that more settled and advanced cities did not have an opportunity to do. That is, that they had a chance to resolve the housing problems, the employment problems, etc., and should not have permitted any barrios and/or ghettos to exist or to start in this county, because we had a chance to prevent such things.

I would say, looking back, that while we did see some changes made in the housing patterns and such—and today we don't see those same kinds of problems—that a barrio and ghetto did develop and remnants of those remain today. We see that still today [1982]—Santa Ana, in my opinion, would be Orange County's only urban city in the sense that they have this diverse population of blacks, Hispanics, senior citizens, and a majority community.

When you came out with your wife in '60, you moved into Santa Ana. Did you immediately join the NAACP?

I almost immediately joined the NAACP, partially because of the difficulty I first experienced in trying to find housing. The then-president of the NAACP probably was Vincent Mark.[3] Because we were visiting him as our physician, he encouraged us to belong and participate and join with him in the NAACP.

What was your perception of Santa Ana and particularly the black community of Santa Ana when you first came here?

It was, in my opinion, a rather passive community of black people. It had its older element of very established black families, some having been here for generations and others having moved here during World War II with the military and having cemented their roots in this area. But again, it was not, in my opinion, a very progressive community in that it did not seem to be involved with the totality of the county or even the Santa Ana community, and we were at that time seeing areas of Santa Ana that were changing block by block to all-black enclaves.

Was the church or the NAACP widely regarded as a leading organization?

I would suggest that it was the churches that were the center for the activity of the black community and probably were the most influential in the black community at that particular time. Although, as the years came and went, I think we did see the NAACP becoming a very important focal point of the entire community and during the '60s was in a very prominent leadership role not just within Santa Ana, but wherever black people were involved in the county.

---

[3] Vincent Mark was president in 1961 and 1962, Walter Collymore in 1963, Wyatt Frieson in 1964, and Everett Winters in 1965 and 1966.

You mentioned difficulty when you first came out attaining housing.

When I first came to Orange County and to Santa Ana, I was being shown small two-bedroom homes where people were asking escalated prices for those homes that probably were built for $8,000, and they were trying to sell those homes to blacks for as much as $20,000. I was forced to buy a new home because of that. I saw them tearing down an orange grove and eventually that's where I purchased my home. But, those homes were not constructed for black people.

It just happened that the first person who bought a home there was a marine whose name was Rudy Francis, and apparently, when Rudy moved into that home and was the first to buy, the builder must have changed his mind and decided that he wasn't going to be able to sell those homes to an integrated group. That whole group of some thirty homes eventually was occupied by only black people.

On top of my house, Larry, the house that I lived in for some sixteen years, was something I would never change or do anything with. Sometimes I would go up there to look, and on occasion, take some of my friends up there. On the chimney of my house, it said "black nigger house" written in what do you call that, tar, or whatever they use to put on the roofs. It was on the very top of the chimney and the cement would be there on the top of the chimney and it was some building tradesperson's way of noting that these were homes that only black people were in. Even when I sold that home, I took somebody up on the roof and I said I hoped that as long as you're here, that you never change that because it has some significance with the black community.

Is that tract still an all-black tract?

It is not now an all-black tract. It is probably one-third Hispanic now. We are seeing a mixture of people; we're seeing younger white families now moving into that area along with Hispanics, so it's a conglomeration of blacks, Hispanics, and whites. At one time, below First Street, there were no blacks, then below McFadden, then it was past Edinger, and then further on south. But this has happened throughout the county. It's gratifying. When I drive around the county and I look at Mission Viejo and various other areas and see a black kid playing on the street, I get a lot of pride out of that, knowing that this county has made some change.

About that time we decided to set up a human relations group.

At that particular time, there were a number of young black families that had moved into the county—Jess Berry and myself and I know that we were active in the NAACP; Irv Smith along with the Scotty Biddle and people like that, who were old-time people. I do know that during that time, that I and some other persons were frequently being invited into various homes in Fullerton and Santa Ana and I think Costa Mesa, to talk about housing opportunities. And they were trying to form what would have been a predecessor to the Orange County Fair Housing Council.

By 1964 we also had Proposition 14. Do you feel that brought more interaction between interested whites and the black community?

Very definitely. I saw very much interaction there, lots of positive interaction there, on the parts of both the white and the black community.

Of course out of this came, by '65, the Orange County Fair Housing Council. Did you play any role in that?

I was on the board of the Orange County Fair Housing Council. I was not a super active member of that group because at that time when that was being organized, I was still president of the Orange County NAACP and we were putting out fires with housing and employment. The NAACP was always contacted when a person was unable to get a home by helping to file a lawsuit or actually going there to talk to the owner or assist that family in finding other housing so that they would be able to have some shelter.

You made the comment that to many blacks in Santa Ana, north Orange County, particularly the area of Cal State Fullerton, almost seemed forbidden territory.

In 1972, just prior to the time that I left Aeronutronic Ford to come to the university, we conducted a survey of the city of Anaheim. At that time, I can't recall what Anaheim's total population was, but I can tell you that Anaheim had more industry and they were the county's largest concentration of employers. And Anaheim had more blacks working in that city than any other city in the county, but there were less than fifty black families living in the total city of Anaheim. So until after the '70s, we did not see great movements of black people into north Orange County even though we had people in Fullerton who were working with us with fair housing committees. It seemed as though there was just no activity on the part of the northern part of the county to do anything with respect to integrating that community and to really be concerned in general about the problems that black people may have had.

Were there also any feelings that police would harass blacks who came up here?

Oftentimes, black persons who would be traveling through the city, in the evening in particular, would be coming from their places of employment, taking the same route almost each night, and would be stopped on a weekly or monthly basis and the police would fill out a little white card; it was a form of identification card as they called it. And it was a form of harassment because they knew that many of these people were traveling there each night to and from Santa Ana.

Was this in any particular city—Anaheim, Fullerton?

Anaheim, Fullerton, and even in Santa Ana that was occurring. Persons who would be traveling up State College, which was a major boulevard at that time, would be stopped regularly, sometimes twice between the time they left their employment here in Anaheim and the time that they arrived in Santa Ana. They would use these cards to note the identification of the person and the type of vehicle, and yet you'd be stopped in the next two weeks or another month. We were convinced that it was a form of harassment.

You may recall that when the NAACP met, at the Santa Ana City Library, it was not unusual to find the police out there taking license plate numbers. They would wait until the library had basically cleared out because most of the people who were then remaining would have been at that meeting for the NAACP.

Do you recall a person by the name of Jim Hillman [Chair of the OC Fair Housing Council in 1967] whose [wife] was in real estate and was at Rockwell for a number of years? One morning, Jim Hillman arranged for me to meet him at his home and he had a guest there who was a member of the Orange County Sheriff's Department who wanted to share some information with me, and he proceeded to show that he knew that there was a file on me. He proceeded to tell me the type of cars that my family owned, the locations that my car could be found, even when I was bowling, or what friends I would have been going to. They could tell me each night of the week; he could tell me where I was at what kind of meetings. I know that all of my activities were being followed by the local police and oftentimes the FBI. I changed jobs. I went from Rockwell to Aeronutronic Ford. Left Rockwell on a Friday—May 6, I think—and Monday, May 9th, I started to work at Aeronutronic Ford and a member of the local FBI team called me at my job at Aeronutronic Ford and said, "Welcome to Aeronutronic Ford. We hope you enjoy it."

Was he being facetious?

No, he wasn't being facetious. I think the intent was to let me know that the FBI was aware of my movement. When you go into Aeronutronic Ford, there is a secured area because of the types of contracts that it has. They cleared my paperwork in less than a week when in most cases employees don't get cleared for a month or sometimes two months with all the background checks they have to make. My paperwork cleared within a week. It just goes to state that the FBI and many of the city officials were well aware of my movements and the movement of other persons who were actively involved.

Do you feel this is because of your involvement in the NAACP?

It was because of my involvement in the NAACP. There were times when we would be attempting to intercede on the behalf of other persons. I recall once that I was in a place called "Jim's Place" on First Street in Santa Ana and I just happened to go by there and I saw several police units. I walked in and was trying to find out what was going on. They had passed a guy and they spoke to him and he didn't return their greeting. Several people witnessed that he did not return their greeting. And as a result, they then went to their police unit, phoned back in, got a report on him, came back, and were about to place him under arrest.

By this time, tempers are flaring on both sides. I asked if I could talk to the officers, and they refused to talk with me. Things were beginning to boil over and I got on the phone, called the chief of police, and he got it at home and called the police department. Those police officers left that area within five minutes. No one was arrested.

I think there was cooperation in some ways between the police, the FBI, the NAACP, and the other people in the community, particularly when there was the unfortunate incident of the officer who was shot there. Terrible things happened as a result of that, but through the NAACP's efforts and the police chief [Allen] at that time and the FBI, I think that cooler heads prevailed and caused that whole situation to be curtailed in a much more rapid time than before.

When did you start with Ford?

Actually, I started as their Affirmative Action Officer about 1968-69. At that time, I was a personnel relations specialist and my primary functions there were working with supervisors in putting on training programs for supervisors that were in the area of human relations, and particularly with respect to working with multi-cultured groups.

Were you the first affirmative action officer that they had?

Yes, I was the first and we adopted one of the first affirmative action plans that industry had here in the Orange County area. At Aeronutronic, we were spending considerable sums of money to recruit, transfer persons from the East and the Midwest to the West Coast. We're talking about blacks in particular who were engineers and scientists and we were attempting to find housing for those persons in the Newport Beach area and encountering considerable difficulties in getting those persons housed.

That same kind of a problem we did not have at Cal State Fullerton because by that time, the housing patterns were beginning to change and it became our problem finding housing that persons could afford. It was a financial thing rather than a discriminatory kind of situation.

There were some similar situations in the sense that at Cal State Fullerton, when I arrived here in October 1972, as the university's first affirmative action coordinator or officer, we did not have an affirmative action plan and it was necessary to start that plan from scratch.

Thank you very much, Everett.

DOROTHY MULKEY[1]

Dorothy Mulkey came to Orange County in 1962, following a tour of duty with the US Navy. Soon after coming to the county, she and her husband, Lincoln, filed a housing discrimination lawsuit, Mulkey v. Reitman, *which eventually was heard by the US Supreme Court. She was the first African American employee at Pacific Telephone's main office in Orange County. Ms. Mulkey lives in Santa Ana and is active in her Second Baptist Church and in community service organizations. Photo 1966.*

Where you were born? And tell us about your family.

I was born in Western Kentucky; it's the coal mining area and my daddy was a coal miner. He was a little tiny guy—guess that's why I'm kind of small. He worked in that mine for forty-some years. Once I left home, women were actually allowed to go into the mine and work. Can you believe that? They made big bucks, but they didn't have enough money in China for me to go into the coal mines, because you get your fingernails dirty. I couldn't do that even though we had a lot of soap. I couldn't wait to leave because back in the winter when it snowed, it was like six feet. I'm only five feet tall, so you know that didn't leave me much leeway. Now, I didn't like going to the car to unlock it, and you have to use the hair dryer to unlock the lock. I didn't know what else was out there, but I knew I wanted more than that.

Where'd you go to school?

I went to school in Kentucky in a little place called Earlington. And it's funny that you ask that because every three years, we have a high school reunion, but the reunion is not for the people that graduated when I did; it's for everyone that ever graduated from that school. The reason for that is because if they just invited my class, there'd be less than twenty people.

---

[1] Oral History No. 3508. Interview date: March 2005, at an office of the Orange County Human Relations Commission, in Santa Ana, California. Interviewers: Eli Reyna and Yvette Cabrera.

So where did you meet your husband?

I met my husband when I was in the military. I went into the US Navy two months before I was nineteen years old and I was stationed at Newport, Rhode Island. I met him after a year and a half of my service.

When did you get married?

Well, actually, I think he must have been pregnant because he wanted to marry me immediately, but I said, "No, I can't do that. I don't know you from Jack the Ripper." And so we actually went to this little Baptist church in Newport, where I sang in the choir, and we went to the minister for counseling. And he couldn't understand why my husband was in such a big rush to marry me. He said to me, "Is somebody pregnant?" And I'm going, "If it is, it must be him because it couldn't be me." Anyway, we agreed to a six-month courtship, which we did because my time was almost up and he still had about almost a year left. So I think he knew I was going to leave because I actually had a scholarship to Kentucky State College and I was going to use it, but obviously I didn't, because he got in the way.

Well, what happened? When did you move to California?

We moved to California in December 1962. He came from a broken home where the mother lived in Texas and the father lived in California. So we came to Santa Ana, because that's where his dad was, and I was seven months pregnant at the time. When we came to Santa Ana, we moved in with my husband's parents; they had a big house over on Townsend Street. There were just the two of them, and because I was very pregnant, I let them wait on me, because that's what they wanted to do, and I'd never shied away from attention. And so they actually acted as not only parents, but as baby sitters, et cetera. They were marvelous.

My father-in-law was a tall man, just like my husband, and was very loving; he's a hands-on kind of guy, just my kind of man. So after my first baby, Michelle, was born, February of 1963 is when we began to look for a place of our own. Because as loving as people are, there's only one woman in each house, and even though I look like a little girl, I didn't act like one. That's when we began looking for an apartment. I had been used to certain standards of living and the apartments that were available to us at the time were not what I was used to.

Though not having come from a luxury background, I came from a very clean background. The plumbing was good and the kitchen looked like a kitchen and it smelled good. It was adequate. The houses that were available to us [in Santa Ana] were not adequate. We knew there was more because my husband worked for the post office. He was a letter carrier. So he knew the new apartment buildings that were vacant, because he delivered mail there daily. And that was the beginning of what later became the case.

What happened?

Well, here's what happened. I was at the beauty shop on Fifth and Bristol, Cut and Curl. There were only maybe two main beauty shops for blacks in Santa Ana at the time. And I'm sitting there getting my hair done and this lady in the chair next to me—everybody knew my father-in-law because he's a deacon in the church and he's known all around town. She goes, "Oh yeah, you're Mulkey's daughter-in-law. How are things going?" And I'm going, "Things would be better if I could find a place to stay; you know we've kind of outgrown our welcome at this house." And she goes, "Well, I know of some apartments," and I go, "Yeah, we've been there but we don't want them in Little Texas," or whatever they called it. And I told her about these new ones that were completely vacant. The lady I was talking to, her name was Scottie Biddle—I didn't know at the time that she was an advocate for the NAACP. She was one of the VIP people in the NAACP, so she said to me, "If you really want some help, I think my organization can help you." I go, "What does that mean to me?"

And so the next week, they had a little call meeting, which my husband and I both attended. And they actually outlined a strategy plan and it was very simple, something that I had seen on TV but had never experienced firsthand. And it was that Lincoln and I would go to the apartment, talk to the manager. We had already clipped the newspaper, so we knew there were vacancies. He knew, because he delivered mail to the ones that were vacant. Then behind us, a Caucasian couple would come for the same rental. And so we did that at three apartments. And if I had a recorder I could have said, just punch this button, because they told us the same thing. "I'm so sorry, if you had only been here maybe an hour earlier,"—two said an hour earlier, one said a day earlier—"but let me take your name and we'll call you." Whereas, the two Caucasian couples were offered the place on the spot and they came after us. So, we took the information back to Scottie Biddle. They had this big NAACP meeting and she called in the ACLU [American Civil Liberties Union], because most of the organizations at that time worked together, and so she said to me that we will find you a place where you can live temporarily. But by this time, my father-in-law and my mother-in-law were so protective, because I had this young child, and they didn't want me any other place other than their house, especially since what we wanted was not available. And so that was the beginning of the case.

How did you know that they wouldn't rent to you?

My husband had talked to one of the tenants at the apartment building on West Brook Street where two were empty and two were taken. He wanted to verify that, which they did. So we knew that the places we wanted were available. We didn't know that they wouldn't rent to us, because we thought the color of our money was the same as anybody else's, having come from the military, where you can't do that. We did not expect that we could not have the place that we could afford to rent. We had no idea that would happen.

Was it the NAACP that sensed that you might get discriminated against when you went out looking for apartments?

Absolutely, because it had happened before. The NAACP was very aware that in Santa Ana or that in Orange County, period, that blacks had their places and the other people had theirs, so they had experienced this type of behavior previously.

You found that out after those two white couples went after you. How did you feel?

How did that make me feel? Angry. I felt very angry. How dare they do that? If they were not going to rent to me because of my habits—maybe I didn't keep my house clean, or maybe I was rowdy, maybe I played loud music—I could have dealt with that. But, they were renting to people just like them, which I was not, except if you cut me, my blood will run as red as theirs. So they had no right to refuse rental to us based upon the fact that we were a different color. They had no right to do that. So I was very—No, I'm not going to say I was angry; I was mad.

But, I had given the military three years of my life and my husband had given them five. So, I guess I had a problem with a country that would allow you, a young girl, to go in at eighteen and a half to serve in the military, and yet when I came out, I can't find a suitable place to live. I had a real problem with that.

Once the white folks asked for [the apartment], did you go back and talk to the managers or people you had talked to?[2]

After the Caucasian couple had been offered the three apartments that my husband and I had sought, we did not go back to redo it again, because I guess maybe it was pride that wouldn't allow me to go back, because they had already closed the door in our faces once and I was not about to give them that satisfaction of doing it again.

Did you realize that you were making history at that point?

Actually, the realization of making history was not even on the backburner of my mind at the time. My objective was: I had this young child and I knew I was going to have other kids because we had talked about that and I wanted to bring them up in a way that they wouldn't be fearful of coming home, and I wouldn't be fearful of having substandard living. And so making history was not in my vocabulary. That was not why we initiated the suit.

Did the thought ever cross your mind that maybe living here wasn't a good thing?

Apparently not, because when you're twenty-three years old, you don't have a clear vision of the whole picture. All you're concerned with is your little piece of it, and the piece that I was concerned with was the here and now, not the here, now, and then later. So, no, I wasn't fearful of that. But I knew that if there had to be a start, why shouldn't it start with me?

---

[2] Because of the complexity of the Mulkey lawsuits, we have, for the sake of clarity, rearranged some of the paragraphs in Dorothy Mulkey's oral testimony.

When we came to Orange County, we knew where we were coming to. We knew we weren't coming to a little city in Kentucky where the blacks are on one side of town and the whites are on the other; but I felt that I had nothing to lose. You've already closed the door. If I don't open it, it's my fault; it's not yours. Because you see, when you tell me, "No!" today, that's good for today and I'll accept it for today, but tomorrow, that "No!" is not there anymore. I'm back in your face again. So we took this with the understanding that we knew it was going to be a long struggle, and I jokingly said, "Michelle will probably be a teenager and we won't want to live in those apartments by the time this case is closed." What actually happened, that a lot of people didn't know, is that Neal Reitman called our house and he said to my husband, "If you drop the case, I'll let you have that apartment. What do you think?" And I said, "No. You've already slapped me on the right side [and now] you want me to turn it so you can slap me on the left, too? You had your chance; now you take it." The man cried on the phone, "Do you know I could lose everything I've got?" And you know what I said to him? "You've already taken most of what I've got."

So what happened as you were going through this Proposition 14—it passes in California?

Proposition 14 was a law before we tested it.[3]

Okay, so you were challenging a law in this case.

Oh, we absolutely knew that we were challenging a law in this case. I also know that you have a right to challenge a law in any state and that just because Californians had rejected our plea, it was not the end of the story.

The NAACP, the ACLU, and there was another organization [American Jewish Congress], which I can't remember, took on the case. We had like a townhall meeting with the organizations, a bunch of interested citizens in Santa Ana, and my husband and I. We talked about what would happen with this case to test the validity of Proposition 14.[4] My father-in-law was working for Tom Keys, who at the time was a prominent realtor, and my father-in-law actually maintained Tom Keys' model homes. And he was told that if he knew what was good for him, he would get his son and daughter-in-law to back off. He had some very powerful friends and they were not happy with the publicity that we were getting.

So people started calling you.

Every time we came home, they were there. They were sometimes waiting at the post office for my husband to get off. [Television] Channel 7, Channel 4, Channel

---

[3] The test Mulkey refers to relates to the dismissal of their 1963 *Mulkey v. Reitman Unruh* case, which was thrown out (dismissed) in December 1964, after Proposition 14 passed. In other words, the Mulkeys were appealing the dismissal.

Proposition 14 was an initiative which had the same effect as a law, but as an initiative, it prohibited all fair housing laws, present and future. This is opposed to a repeal, which would have simply struck down the specific Unruh and Rumford Acts and may not have been deemed unconstitutional.

[4] In January 1965, the Mulkey case was appealed to the California Supreme Court.

2, everybody was all over it, because they knew we were going to test the validity of Proposition 14. At the time, Second Baptist Church was on Second and Baker and was a little corner church. There were maybe fifty members, and they were all extremely supportive.

How was the coverage of the media?

I think that the media at the time was far different than the media is right now. They weren't flashing bulbs without asking your permission, and I really didn't mind because I knew the changes were right around the corner, and I also knew that someone had to initiate those changes, that in Orange County, which is a Republican county even now, things weren't going to happen unless somebody pushed the right buttons. So why shouldn't it be me?

Can you describe the atmosphere in Orange County at the time with regards to the treatment of minorities?

I had always been kind of radical because my mom had always told me go for what you want, never compromise unless you have to. And so after I had my baby, Michelle, I decided I wanted to go to work for a bank and my father-in-law told me that black people didn't work at banks in Orange County. And I said, "Okay," so I went right down to Bank of America and I applied. And the guy, the operations manager, said, "Okay, what would you like to do?" And I said, "Well, I never worked in a bank before, but I'm a fast learner. Anything you can teach somebody else you can teach me and I'll probably learn quicker and be better at it."

So I got the job. I was the only black employee in the bank, so that when anyone came in—this was 1964—I stuck out like a birthday cake at a quiet dark party, and that was fine. I think I stayed with Bank of America maybe a year and a half and I decided the baby sitter was making more take-home than I was. So I went right across the street to United California Bank. Once again, I talked with the operations—well, obviously by this time, I had a year and a half experience, so he hired me on the spot. And I stayed with them maybe two or three years and I

Mulkey v. Reitman

The lawsuit filed by Dorothy and Lincoln Mulkey in 1963 against Santa Ana apartment house owner Neil Reitman went to the California Supreme Court in January 1965. At stake in the case was the constitutional viability of Proposition 14, the anti-fair housing initiative. The Mulkeys retained an attorney, David Cadwell, and added well-known ACLU attorneys A. L. Wirin, Fred Okrand, and Herman Selvin. The court's decision, in May 1966, was that Proposition 14 denied the Mulkeys their rights under the Fourteenth Amendment to the US Constitution.

This decision was immediately appealed to the US Supreme Court, but on May 29, 1967, Proposition 14 was voided by the Court in a 5-4 decision. Chief Justice Earl Warren cast the deciding vote. The court argued that Proposition 14 established the right to discriminate as a basic state policy that violates the Equal Protection Clause of the Fourteenth Amendment. This decision restored fair housing laws in California and was a factor in the passage of Title 8 of the Civil Rights Act of 1968, which outlawed housing discrimination throughout the United States.

decided enough of this banking stuff. I don't want to do this anymore. I just quit and I went to work for a temporary office service.

One day at lunch time, I went to the Union Bank building to cash my check and I noticed that Pacific Telephone had an employment office right in the bank, so I went in there on my lunch hour and I filled out an application. They're always interested in you when you've got military background. And so the lady took me upstairs to the business office of Pacific Telephone, and she said, "I don't know what you'd like to do but you fit right in here." And I had seen a desk and it said "WATS" on it, and I said to her, "I thought WATS was in Los Angeles; I didn't know WATS was here." And she thought that was so funny and I didn't get the joke and I found out later that WATS stood for Wide Area Telephone Service, not the WATTS that was in Los Angeles.

Were you the first African American?

Absolutely. I was the first African American to set foot in the business office in Orange County. That office was in the Union Bank building in Orange. We occupied seven of the twelve floors there and it was a wonderful experience. The telephone company has a variety of jobs based upon where you want to go and what your goals are. So, I had been with them about nine months when one of the managers said, "People like you if you're talkative, if you're pleasant, and if you have a goal." That seems to be the hot button. She told me that I should apply for the Disneyland position from the telephone company, because people from all over the world go to that exhibit and the exposure and the atmosphere would be something that would last a lifetime. And so, obviously I didn't know anything about the telephone company at Disneyland even though I had seen the 360-degree circle theater that they had. I applied for the job. I was out there the next week in my little short skirt and my little halter top and stuff. So that's an exceptional experience, which told me something right then and there, that you have to ask for what you want and you have to conduct yourself in such a way that people know you deserve it, and you'll get it.

Tell me about the day when you heard the [US Supreme Court] decision. Where were you; what happened?

Actually, I was at work and I had gotten a call from one of the TV stations, before the NAACP could tell me, and I tried really hard not to react, but I had to share with the manager that something gigantic had happened and I really did have to go home and he understood. When I got home, I think everybody that had a camera or magazine was there waiting for us. It was like a breath of fresh air had come in, and a lot of people said, "Well, how much money did you get?" But that was not the objective. Personally, we didn't keep one penny, because it wasn't about the money. I felt elated. I felt like why couldn't we have done this without all the hoopla? Why did it take four years to go from point A to point B? But you know what? In my family, we're a bunch of long livers; some of the women have lived till they're ninety years old. So, I figured I had time; I was still in my twenties.

What was the settlement?

I don't remember what the money was. But whatever it was, it went back into the NAACP and the ACLU. Sometimes you have to have values that are not about the almighty dollar.

Did you ever talk to your children about what happened? Are they very aware of this story?

My children are very much aware of the story, and if they're not, someone else will make them aware of it, because you can go online and you can click Mulkey versus Reitman, Reitman versus Mulkey, Proposition 14, and get a lot of information. So yes, my children, their children, are very much aware of how this all started. I have three girls.

So the case made it all the way to the Supreme Court?

It went to the California Supreme Court and then it went to the US Supreme Court.

Did your case have an impact nationwide then?

I would imagine it did, given all the text books it has gone into since then. Yes, I would say that it probably had a national impact.

The day the decision came down from the Supreme Court, what were people around you saying? What was the general attitude?

The people that I worked with probably had no knowledge of the case, that I was the Mulkey in the *Mulkey v. Reitman* case, because we didn't talk about it and we were advised not to talk about it. So at the time the decision came down, I was elated. But we knew we were going to win the case. There was never any question in our mind that we weren't.going to win the case when it went to the US Supreme Court.

Do you remember the votes?

No! I do not remember how many votes. [Five to four, with Chief Justice Earl Warren casting his vote in favor of the Mulkeys]

Over time, has the impact of what you did sink in a little more about the difference it made in other people's lives by taking the case to court?

Yes, as a matter of fact it has, and it's really ironic because as people uncover the facts and they call me and they bug me and e-mail me and so-forth, I guess I really didn't realize the impact it made, even on the college kids. And I get a lot of calls even within this church house from people that are very much interested, when all they have to do is go online and get the facts. So yeah, I guess if I had known back then, I'm sure I would have done the same thing. I don't know anything I would have done differently. Sometimes you make more of an impact when you don't know what the end result is going to be.

Did you have any other experiences with housing discrimination after the case was settled?

Actually, no. I wanted to buy. When I bought the house that we're in right now, that was absolutely no problem. This was 1970 and I found a realtor that got us in really quick because we got the house from an older couple. And there was some kind of tragedy back in Texas and they had to leave immediately and they paid the closing costs and we moved in. But, at the time we moved in, the neighborhood was primarily black; and now, I think, there are three black families on the block. The rest are Spanish and other ethnic people. So, changing times. But, you know what, I love that house. I have no mortgage, it's free and clear. I have spent more in refurbishing the place than I actually paid for it. Can you believe that? It's what I want. You know, I'll pass it on.

What kind of things are you doing now?

Well, I spend about half my time at this church. I've been on the trustee board on and off for about the past twenty-five years. In addition to that, I do the other half of the volunteer work with the SBC Telecom Pioneers. That's a national organization where we do local community service work. I especially work with elderly citizens, blind kids, troubled teenagers; that's my calling. And so I do that maybe three days a week. I organize and we have tremendous projects.

That's a very good story. Thank you.

GLADYS SMITH[1]

Gladys Smith was born in a small country town, Hawkins, Texas, in 1941. Her father was in the US Army and they moved to Denver, Colorado, where Gladys started school. Eventually, they moved back to Texas, and stayed until she was eleven or twelve years old. Her school in Texas was all-black, and even though some of her neighbors in the area where they lived were white, they did not associate with one another. During her time back in Texas, her mother obtained a divorce and they moved to Seattle, Washington. Mrs. Smith lives in the city of Irvine with her husband Ervin. Photo, 1964

So you ended up in Seattle and you lived in the city proper?

Yeah, we lived in the city. Not like the suburban area here. I went to elementary school through college in Seattle. Our neighborhood was multicultural. Elementary school was mixed: white and black and Japanese, very few Mexicans. The social life was very different, because even though we went to school in an integrated situation and the churches were mixed and all that different kind of thing, socialization in terms of parties and things like that, surprising enough, were very, very segregated. It was amazing. The different parties, whether they be a house party or a party at maybe the YWCA, it was noticeable there was segregation. I think my graduating class was like a third black. Blacks were not in the majority, but they were a big number.

Did you have any role models at that time?

I had a teacher—in fact, I had a couple of teachers that were very, very instrumental in terms of me going on to school. Both teachers were Caucasian. One was a science teacher that really encouraged me to continue on and go to college. At the

[1] Oral History No. 3396. Interview date: September 29, 2004, at the home of Gladys and Ervin Smith in Irvine, California. Interviewer: Robert Johnson.

time, I didn't think I would be able to because we were poor. Then I had a Latin teacher who was very instrumental in terms of me going on to college.

I decided I was going to go to college [Seattle University], so then I had to work to go to school. I worked full-time and went to nursing school full-time, so I didn't have very much time for socializing as such. I would get off work at eleven o'clock, and if there was a party going on, I would have somebody come by and pick me up and then I'd go to the party for a little while, and then I'd come home and have to study

So then you graduated, and where'd you meet your husband?

He was going to graduate school at Seattle University. Actually, he had dated a good friend of mine, and after they broke up, I didn't see him for a couple years. Then I ran into him when I was in college. He didn't remember me, but I remembered him. He was fascinated by the fact that I knew who he was. Seattle had four waves of engineers that were brought into Seattle because the Boeing Company was doing quite well with the space program. He was one of the first waves that came in. As I say, it was good pickings for the young ladies. When I met him, he was *Ebony*'s Most Eligible Bachelor in 1960.

Being from Wyoming, his early life must have been different from yours.

A *lot* different. There was a black community in Casper, Wyoming—a small one. But segregation was quite noted there, too. He went all of his school years through junior college in Casper. He went to the University of Colorado in Boulder. He wanted to go into the prestigious [US] Air Force Academy. But he didn't make it. His brother had been a Tuskegee Airman, so he wanted to join. So when he got out he headed for Washington. But he was always on his way to California. He told me that the whole time we were dating. "I'm on my way to California."

What brought you two from Seattle?

Erv had worked—I don't remember—five years at Boeing. The Dyna Soar missile was discontinued so he was due to be laid off. He interviewed at Philco-Ford, which is in Newport Beach, and that's where he landed.

That was an experience, because we knew nothing about Orange County or living in Orange County. They shipped all of our belongings, including our car. This was like the end of '63. He landed the job in December, and I didn't want to leave Seattle before the holidays were over. So he came a couple weeks before I did.

I think when he first came, he was going to do it on his own. We thought we were going to live in Newport Beach. Well, he went looking for a place, and surprising enough, every time he found a place the people told him, "You realize during the summer the prices double." So he thought, well, what do I do now? The lady told him, "Why don't you just drive on back up to Santa Ana. You'll probably find some place." He drove back into Santa Ana, and I think somebody directed him to the black neighborhood, which was between McFadden and First Street in Santa Ana on Raitt and McFadden. I think it was called the Raitt Apartments.

We were trying to find this place, and I think at the time this apartment was being sued by Lincoln Mulkey because this gentleman did not want to rent to blacks. My husband said, "My furniture is coming. I need a place." He said, "I don't care if you're a doctor, lawyer, Indian chief, I'm not renting to blacks." He said, "You can go on down the street. They might rent to you." I think after about four days he finally got the apartment on Myrtle Street. So I hopped on a plane and arrived here. That's when our adventure started.

He traveled a lot. The first weekend he was gone, I heard somebody was knifed down the street, and I was scared to leave the apartment. Then I think the next month he was gone somebody got shot. So when he came home, I said, "We gotta move, we gotta get out of here!" We had to battle with the man to get our deposits and stuff back, but they did give us our deposits back. He found, just about four blocks away from where we were, another apartment. It was a duplex. It was better.

You mentioned the Mulkeys. Was that first set of apartments the ones owned by Neil Reitman [of the famous *Mulkey v. Reitman* case]?

I think it was the first one, and I think it was still in litigation when we were trying to get in, and the guy said, "I don't care. They can sue the pants off me." People in the neighborhood sort of gave us a bad time because my husband went to work every day in a suit. We just stayed to ourselves and didn't do a lot. I started associating with Johnson Chapel Church, and a few friends around. We'd meet and play bridge and things like that. We were just looking to move out of the area. I had a baby, so I was wondering what the schools had to offer. Also, I guess Ervin had met Dick Petherbridge, and he was knee-deep in fair housing.

I don't know if you're aware that Orange County was very heavily Birch Society. Well, my husband, with his political agenda, went to long meetings and wound up realizing that it was a Birch community and to the point that he felt that somebody was thinking about doing away with him. He never had any threats, except a couple of times he was stopped by the police and had to spread-eagle on his car and all these other kinds of things.

Why do you think they did that?

Well, he had a fancy looking Bonneville convertible. It was a very flashy-looking car. I think that was one of the tickets and the fact that also he was dressed in a suit. It was in a neighborhood where you didn't see people that dressed like that. So because of the rental situation, and the police stopping us several times before the Watts riots, that's why he got involved in fair housing. Because also, we had these grandiose ideas that we were going to buy a house right away, until we realized the price was so much different than Washington. We had to save for a couple more years before we were able to buy a house.

You said he met Dick Petherbridge. Was that during the time of the battle over Proposition 14, the repeal of fair housing laws?

Yeah. They were fairly good friends. My husband, in Seattle, he was involved with CORE [Congress on Racial Equality] and also he was instrumental in Seattle in terms of the black movement, in terms of the marches on the stores that a lot of blacks were boycotting. He did a lot of those marches. In fact, he hosted—I think Martin Luther King came to speak at a community rally, and also Harry Belafonte. My husband also did a radio show in Seattle in terms of current black issues that were going on and stuff like that. He's always been very, very active in the black movement.

And also, you two were friends with the Bortzes [who co-founded the Orange County Fair Housing Council with Petherbridge].

Yes. Paul and Judy Bortz were good friends. Not only did Ervin work with Paul at Philco-Ford, but he also was involved with the Fair Housing Council. There were several teams of people that actually would test out how unfair people were being treated. Like a white couple would go to see if an apartment was for rent, and vice versa. A black would go in and they'd say it's not for rent. Then the white couple would follow behind them. The only thing I did was phone calling, because I had a baby. They needed someone to do phone calls—contact people whether there was a rental available—so that the group could go out or calling people for meetings and stuff. [2]

You lived in Santa Ana, but you always had in mind moving out.

I think we moved out in '66, '67. Yeah. We moved to Tustin. They were nice apartments. There were very few blacks, probably .5 percent. But, there were a lot of military families in Tustin in those apartments. Surprising enough, we didn't have any problems getting the apartment. I think we only stayed maybe not quite two years. Our house was completed in '69.

What are your children's names?

Anthony is the oldest, and Sherry's the youngest, the girl. They're five years apart. Both of them are Californianites. He was ready for school when we moved here. He actually started to school in Tustin. He was in kindergarten.

Was that one of the reasons for moving out of Santa Ana?

Yeah. I had a couple of schoolteacher friends saying that the school district wasn't very good, and there were a lot of problems. So I wanted to get out of the area. Well, needless to say, Tustin wasn't much better for us at the time because the teacher kept sending notes home saying that she had problems with my son. But then, my son knew his colors, he knew his numbers, everything. He was in an

---

[2] The Orange County Fair Housing Council was founded in early 1965. The founders and early members were people of all races who had fought to defeat Proposition 14. One of the founders was Richard Petherbridge, who had worked for A. L. Wirin (Wirin represented the Mulkeys in the famous *Reitman v. Mulkey* US Supreme Court case) and chaired the organization for two years. He was followed by James Hillman, a black administrator at Autonetics, who lived in Orange, and James Allen, a black marine officer who lived with his family on the El Toro marine base.

afternoon class, and he was fresh and ready to go. He was giving the teacher a fit. I went over to visit her one day, and she said, "He needs to be put on Ritalin." I said, "Mm-mm." So I went to my pediatrician and talked to him, and he said, "No, let the school district do it. Let them test him to see what's going on." He did have dyslexia but he tested two years above his age. That was the only issue that I had, but I stayed on top of it. I said I wasn't going to let anything give us a bad time. I had my doctor to help us out. I just didn't let Ervin get involved in it because he was a little bit more aggressive about it. I said, "Let's work through it."

Were you working at the time?

No. I worked when we were in Santa Ana. Santa Ana Hospital hired me, and they told me I would only have one weekend a month off. I thought that's a little strange. So I left there, and I thought, I'm not going to fight any battles just to get a job. I went down the street, and I saw a sign in the Bank of America one day saying they were hiring, so I went in and they hired me. I worked three days a week. Then I had another baby, so I didn't work for a couple of years. Then I went back to school. Then I went back to nursing.

Did you have any problems moving into a house in Irvine?

Yes, we did. I think all the years from '67 to '69 we were looking everywhere. Every time we'd go to a realtor they would take us right back into Santa Ana; I guess you want to call it the ghetto. Finally, we just decided we'd start doing it on our own. We would get in our car and just drive one direction. I think we went to the groundbreaking for UCI [University of California, Irvine], and we were looking all around. We went to see the models, and either the security guard or somebody would not let us see them. So my husband decided he was going to talk to Dick [Petherbridge], or some other lawyer, and say, "Can I sue 'em?" Dick or someone, said, "They can't do that. You gotta go back." So we went back another time, and it was different security and they let us through all of them. We decided on living in this area.

When we first moved in, it was a mixed group and they were very lovely people. But I must tell you that every time I was out doing the yard, watering, people almost run up on the curb looking, because I was black. Or I would be out in the park with my kids and people would ask me, "Oh, your husband must be white." And I said, "No. He's not white, he's black." "Well, he must be either in the military." And I said, "No, he's never been in the military." And they said, "Well, is he a doctor?" I said, "No." I never would tell them what he was, but it was like they made all these assumptions because I lived in the neighborhood. And I'm still one of the original owners. I think every house around me is on the second or third owner, but we stayed put in the same place.

Were there any other black families around here?

There were a couple, but they weren't solely black. There was like the husband was black and he was married to an Anglo lady. That's what we saw at the beginning in terms of neighbors. Probably after we were here for about a couple years, we started seeing a few black families move in. When I shopped for groceries, or we went to church, or any socialization, we went out of the community because there were no activities in the community as such.

Did you continue going to Johnson Chapel?

Yeah, I went to Johnson Chapel for a long time, until I started working at night. My kids started to grow up and I was having one just going to be entering college, and another one was going to be following shortly thereafter, so I had to figure out some way that we wouldn't be poor, so I was working two jobs. I worked for Orange County Head Start, and then I started to work for Saddleback Hospital. I worked at night, a couple nights a week. I think it was in 1970 we moved into the house. I went to work for Head Start, because it was an easy job. It was six hours. I didn't have to worry about long day childcare and all that kind of jazz. It was a nice situation.

When you moved to Irvine, did Erv have any trouble with the police? Was he still driving his fancy sports car?

No. We'd gotten rid of it. We'd gotten a little Mustang. We did not have any trouble here. We did in Tustin a couple of times. It wasn't because of our car. I had several Anglo friends, and they would baby-sit for me. We'd get stopped at night. In fact, one night I was stopped taking the baby-sitter home. They claimed that they had noticed us going into the area and then coming back immediately. I said, "Well, I'm taking my baby-sitter home." The only time [in Irvine] that there was any problems is when my son started driving. He had the most God-awful color Volkswagen. It was sort of a fuchsia, a pink. And it was low. He got stopped a couple of times, because they thought he was a gang member or something.

When we first moved in, we had a nice-knit group of friends. We all moved in at the same time, like this whole cul-de-sac. Everybody knew everybody and sort of watched each other's kids, and we baby-sat for each other, went to the movies together. The only problem that I had when I went back to work was childcare. So I called a baby-sitting service and this lady—the color drained out of her face when she opened the door and saw I was black. I mean, I think if she could have fainted, she would have fainted. I really had a hard time leaving my kids with her after that, but I had to go to work. I went to work and I came back, and I thought, I hope when I come home my kids will not be dead or something or other. That experience was sort of unnerving.

How did things go for you at work with regard to being black?

When I went to work at Saddleback [Hospital, in the south county], there were very few black nurses. Working at night, I have a tendency to be cold, so I would wear a sweater. My name badge would always be underneath, so people didn't see it. I worked in the pediatric department, so whenever I would get a patient—the RN had to go down and pick up the patients from the emergency room.

This one night, they called me and said I had a patient in the emergency room, so I went to the emergency room, and I stood around and stood around. I kept wondering, Where's my patient? What's going on? So I went over finally and said, "I'm here to get the pediatric patient." They said, "We're waiting for the RN." I said, "Waiting for the RN? Didn't you call the peds floor, and you know that the only person on the floor is an RN?" And they said, "No, we didn't." I said, "I'm the RN." (laughs) I think there were only a couple other black RNs working in the hospital, and most of the [other] blacks that worked there were either in housekeeping or in the cafeteria.

Did you continue going to Johnson Chapel after you moved here?

I went. Erv wasn't a churchgoer, so therefore, whenever something was going on, he would go with me. Since we were out here, I stopped going as much. I would go every once in a while. Since my mother has been here now, I go to another church. I don't belong to the church, but I go to another church on a regular basis. It's in Santa Ana. It's in the same area. The black churches are there. I mean, we've gone to the Methodist—there's a Lutheran church around the corner and stuff like this, but not on a regular basis. We've gone to University Church. But most of the time we go over to Santa Ana to the black church [St. James Missionary Baptist Church]. I sing in the gospel choir over there and all that kind of stuff.

Did you get involved in parent groups—PTA or PTO?

Yes, I did. I made sure I went to every back-to-school night. I was involved with the PTA, the Boy Scouts, Girl Scouts, and Indian Guides. I was a calendar mom for the Girl Scouts. You name it, we did it.

How about the civil rights things?

Ervin was more involved. He was still involved with—not so much fair housing anymore—but he was involved with the Black Business Alliance organization they developed. The NAACP, he was involved with.

What schools did your son and daughter go to?

My son went to Irvine High School, and my daughter went to Woodbridge High School, because we were right on the border. You could go to either school. My son went to Cal State Fullerton; my daughter went to the University of Arizona.

Let's talk about them growing up in Irvine. What was their social life like?

I thought at the time it was good, but evidently, from my son, it wasn't. He always had buddies. It was always like—I want to say like Mutt and Jeff. It was usually my son, the black kid, a Japanese kid, and an Anglo kid, and you could see all three of them. They found more mischief and stuff to get into. I mean, they rode bikes and fell in holes. They were still building all around us, and they would find all these places to climb fences and all kinds of stuff. So they were the three musketeers. They were friends up until high school. He did the high school stuff, but my son didn't do a lot of dating. He's still single. Both my kids are still single. They're in their middle to late thirties. My daughter was good in sports. She was the state champion. She went to school on a scholarship in cross country and track. She ran the eight-hundred and the mile. She played basketball also. And my son wrestled.

Did they do any other extracurricular things?

My son was on the debate team, and he won an award for the debate team. They both were quite active in school in terms of being in everything they could be in. They went right out of high school into college—mother was busy pushing. Both of them were in honors classes. Our daughter was courted by the University of Arizona for her cross country and for her track. And she also was a good student. She went on full scholarship for five years. She did well. She graduated with her degree in marketing management. She lives in Las Vegas.

Our son's degree is in criminal justice. He sort of floundered around different places. He, at present, is manager for an Aaron Brothers store down in Dana Point, but he's worked in security, all kinds of security. His passion was to be a policeman or something like that, but I guess he waited too late to really push it. He's not finished law school, but he's still working on it. He lives in Orange now.

Do you think that living in Orange County was a positive experience for the children or a negative experience?

I think it was a little bit of both. As parents, you're so busy trying to get the best for your kids, so I think a lot of the cultural background got lost, especially for my son. My daughter, I tried to make up for it because we belonged to Jack and Jill. It was developed for black professionals. Jack and Jill, it's a coed type of club—doctors, lawyers, and professional people bringing their kids to a social gathering. They did all kinds of social things with different families throughout the Orange County area. We'd meet either at my house, or we'd go to Fullerton, or we'd go to Big Canyon. And the fact that she was into track and all those kinds of things—she benefited a lot better than my son.

What were your feelings towards Orange County politics?

When I started realizing that we were in Birch country, and as heavily and strong as Ervin was in politics, I was a little fearful. I really was a little fearful. We had a divided house. I think he was a Democrat when we first came. Then he became a Republican, and I'm a Democrat. He even went to [US President Ronald] Reagan's first inaugural, I think—or was it the second? Anyway, he was invited because of his political affiliations. He was really active in politics and very much an activist.

So here's a guy that's heavily involved in civil rights, but yet chose to be part of the mainstream of Orange County, which was to be a Republican. Why did he become a Republican?

I think he believed the Republican philosophy. I think also part of it was it was not the mainstream for blacks to be a Republican, so he always sort of went against the grain in terms of those things.

You mentioned earlier about the Birch Society and the newspapers.

It was sort of scary, because Ervin had top security clearance, and a lot of times when he went out of town I didn't know where he was. He would call me and say he was okay and whatever, and he would be home a certain day. So his affiliations with the Republican Party and with all the movements that were going on—it was really sort of scary. Then when you'd hear about certain things happening in the area, and considering blacks were being stomped and jailed sometimes, but he never was jailed for anything. I just told him be careful. I said, "We still need you."

Having to do with the positives and the negatives of living in Orange County and how these relate to your life—could you discuss these?

Erv and I have talked about this. Our life has been full. We liked the way we lived. I think if I had to change anything at all, I think we'd be involved more in some of the black activities, mainly for the kids. I think they know who they are and they have a strong feeling about that, but socially, I don't think they're able to mix with blacks very well. For example, my son—this is sort of funny—he was chosen for *Love Connection* [TV program] one year. He was on the show. He chose a date. This girl was flabbergasted by him.

She was black. I think what happens to a lot of black kids, if they're not steeped in their culture, if you don't have the hip-hop and you don't talk the hip and all this other kind of thing, they call you an Oreo. I think this is what he ran face into, and he wasn't able to talk the way she talked. I think she was from Long Beach. It was interesting. But she was fascinated with him. I said, "If you want to get married, it sounds as if—he said, 'Mom, I'm not ready to get married.'"

I think my daughter had a well-rounded social background. We pushed. I think I should have done the same thing with my son. I think he would have probably been a lot better off. Even though he had a good growing up and a good relationship, I don't think he had as much relationship in his own race and culture.

And the schools have been okay, the job market?

We fought for the schools pretty hard. As I said, the way I worked, I was always at the PTA meetings, at any kind of meeting. If we had any problems, I made sure I'd meet with their teachers. I talked with the counselors. I made sure I helped them with picking the classes they needed to be in. If they were having problems, they got tutors, or I tutored them. I was happy with the school situation. The schools were pretty good, I think.

Everett Winters told me that he wished there was a black middle-class community in Orange County.

Yes. I think all of us did, because we all sort of — Everett Winters, [Wyatt] Frieson, [Johnny] Williams, I think it was Clarence Lee, Burton — they were teachers. There were all kinds of people that were teachers and we associated together, and we all moved out to different areas. We all met in Santa Ana, but we lived in different parts of Santa Ana and sort of banded together with the fair housing and all these different activities going on. We socialized together, we were in bridge clubs, the wives did bridge clubs, and we did picnics and social stuff together.

But it didn't happen, so there's no Inglewood, View Park [in L.A. County], in Orange County. The community is scattered.

That's what happened: a few here, a few here, a few here, a few here. I think at one point with Leon Berry down in Mission Viejo, there was a small group sort of collecting there because quite a few black families moved down in that area. There is a church down there, but they just called it the Neighborhood, and it was just neighborhood people that knew each other, and they sort of collected. I think a lot of people came from other areas to visit. They'd go down when they had affairs and things like that. But we never did have an Inglewood.

Do you have any favorite stories that you'd like to tell about being a black person in an almost all-white Orange County?

When we first moved here, all of us were great friends and we got so that we had dinner together, we had picnics together, and we'd go to movies. It was like a person would come in my house to have dinner, I'd go in their house and have dinner, they would watch my kids, and I would watch their kids. It didn't seem to matter that I was black. It seemed like the outside world had a problem with us being black, but we really—maybe that was just a glowing moment. When the kids were young, it was like twelve houses of us. We would have block parties and stuff in the park. Halloween—dress up. We'd decorate our houses and that kind of thing. Since we've been in our house, we haven't had any major, major problems with being black.

The one place I've had problems is when I go to like the church or working for Head Start or wherever, people ask you, "Where do you live?" And I say, "I live in Irvine." They say, "Oh, you live in Irvine, that ritzy place?" And I say, "Wait a minute. I work every day, and my husband works every day. So what does that say? We're working people." He said, "Well, Irvine is that ritzy place."

Thank you very much, Gladys Smith, for letting me interview you.

JOHNNY WILLIAMS[1]

Johnny Williams was born in Shreveport, Louisiana, in 1938, and is very proud to be a graduate of Grambling State University. His father and mother were sharecroppers in Caspania, Louisiana. He came to Orange County because work was available. He worked as a teacher, counselor, and administrator in Santa Ana at the junior and senior high school and community college levels and has been very active with youth at his Second Baptist Church. He and his wife live in Costa Mesa. Photo ca. 1960.

Did you come with your family to Orange County?

I'm the only one in Orange County; the rest of them live in Los Angeles County or San Bernardino County. My sisters came in 1956. Joann came here in 1959. I visited Los Angeles in 1962 between my junior and senior year at Grambling State University. I worked summers at Sears Roebuck and Company in order to get additional funds for college. Went back for a year and finished my education at Grambling State University. I moved to California in February 1964. I originally went to Chicago to work, but it was so cold there I packed up and came to California. I've been in California ever since.

The reason I left in the first place was because the salaries for teachers were so low in Louisiana. And both places offered better salaries and benefits for teaching. So I came to California. The first two years I worked as a workshop director for the Orange County Association for Retarded Children. In the meantime, I was going to school at Cal[ifornia] State [University,] Fullerton, to complete my credential work. In August 1966, I signed a contract with Santa Ana Unified School District. There I remained until 2002 when I retired.

When did you get married?

[1] Oral History No. 3056. Interview date: August, 2003, at the Second Baptist Church, in Santa Ana, California. Interviewer: Robert Johnson.

I got married in September of '64. I was already engaged when I left Louisiana, to my sweetheart from Grambling State University. She was from Rayville, Louisiana.

What impressions did you have of Orange County before you came?

Most of my friends lived in L.A. County, and they had a very negative feeling towards Orange County. Because, number one, [there were] very few blacks in Orange County; number two, it reminded them, especially in the early sixties, of the South as far as getting housing, and segregation. I encountered the same problem when I came to Orange County.

I ended up getting an apartment house through a marine fellow that I did not know. At that time, he lived on Minnie Street—Minnie and McFadden; mostly marines [were] living there. So I applied for an apartment. The first time, they said it was completely rented out. The marine said, "This is my friend, he's looking for a house." That's how I got a house, the marine fellow. I stayed in the apartment house for one year. Then I moved from there to the corner of Myrtle and Raitt in Santa Ana, and I remained there from '65 until 1972. In '72 I relocated to Costa Mesa, California, where I reside at the present time.

Did you say that your family moved to L.A.?

My brother, my sisters. I had a lot of my classmates, also from Grambling, in Los Angeles. And they had a feeling that Orange County wasn't very welcome to blacks in 1960, so they remained in L.A. When I came to Orange County, they were very surprised.

Then why did you make that decision?

I had a major in social science with a minor in Special Ed. There was a job in Orange County for an assistant director of the Orange County Association for Retarded Children. I applied for a job, and I got the job. I worked there from '64 to '66.

Were you surprised that you got the job, from what you had heard from the other people?

Yes. I was the first and only black hired by the association. But my employer was very great. I get some of the feeling that there are some people, especially Caucasians, that are not all negative. We have some good ones. I met quite a few through the association.

Were there any other black people that lived on Minnie Street?

I was the only one for a while. Later, another black marine moved in the apartment house across the way from me. So we had two black couples there.

Did you have any trouble moving on to Myrtle and Raitt?

No, because, see, when I came here to Orange County in 1964, most of your blacks were located from Eighth Street to McFadden, from Bristol to the river bed, all in one pocket, known at that time as "Little Texas."

Why did they call it Little Texas?

Because, I guess, most of the blacks lived there; a lot of them moved from Texas there. So that's why we referred to it as Little Texas.

I know Connie Jones called it that, too. And her family actually *was* from Texas.

When I came to California, Connie Jones's family was already here. Actually, her grandmother, Annie Mae Tripp, was one of the very prominent members of the Second Baptist Church. When I came here, I joined the Second Baptist Church.

You told the *Orange County Register* that you tried to buy a home in Costa Mesa, and then when you showed up, suddenly the price jumped up.

I went down myself to view the house. When I got there, they said it was sold. After I came back to the high school I was working at, a white friend of ours said, "I'll get it for you." He went down and acquired the house, and I went down immediately after him and put a $500 deposit on the house. That way, they couldn't say the house wasn't available. The house I bought was middle ways in the tract. What happened—later on they offered me a corner house. I guess they felt that with a black being there, it would be hard to sell a house in the middle of the block, so I got a corner house, which was a better deal.

At the same tract, a friend of mine put a deposit on a house right behind my house. They cashed his check, gave him a receipt, and then later, they told him the house was not available. In those days, J. R. Gibson Real Estate Company sold most of the houses. They would show you houses in certain areas only. At one time, we had about sixteen black teachers all located in the same area.

Barbara Hill in '63 became the first black public school teacher in Santa Ana.

Barbara Hill was first, and Mrs. Ollie Whittaker was the second one. When I came here in 1966 and was hired, they had a quota, per se. They were hiring two blacks per year. They hired me, but they wouldn't hire my wife. My wife, Rosette, went to apply for a job and got a job in the Garden Grove district. She worked at La Quinta High School; she was the first and only black at that high school for a long, long time.

Santa Ana was still only hiring so many blacks per year, and most of the blacks were assigned to schools located west of Bristol, mainly Monte Vista and Lincoln Elementary Schools, Smedley Junior High, and Valley High School. I was the first black teacher assigned to McFadden Intermediate School. I did my first three years at McFadden. Then I went from teaching to a counselor. I was the first black counselor in Orange County, and I went to [Santa Ana] Valley High School.

I stayed at Valley High School from 1969 through 1996. I worked as a teacher, a counselor, assistant principal.

Jessie Allen said you had a great influence on getting black teachers into the Santa Ana school system.

What happened—I would tell friends of mine, "Come and apply in Santa Ana." At that time, I had a pretty good connection with the superintendent. I'd go and say, "I've got some good candidates." At that time, they would hire the candidates. I would really go out and just recruit people just to come to Santa Ana, because you had quite a few black students coming into Santa Ana then but no black instructors. So I began a one-man recruiting. And the same was true of Santa Ana College. There were very few. When I first started working at Santa Ana College in 1970 as a part-time instructor, you had maybe one or two black teachers. I eventually got a friend of mine, Gloria Bailey, who's here at Santa Ana College right now, who commutes from L.A. every day. They had a very negative feeling toward living in Santa Ana. They would rather commute than live here.

Connie Jones, who, like you, is a member of the Second Baptist Church, told me that 70 to 75 percent of the young people at the church now graduate from college.

At the present time, we send quite a few of our students back to historical black colleges—for example, Grambling, Prairie View, Texas Southern, Southern University, Alabama A&M, Howard University, Fisk University, Tennessee State. Because a lot of us came from those schools; therefore, we encourage our kids to go back there. For example, I'm from Grambling, my wife finished Grambling, my daughter finished Grambling, my nephew finished Grambling, and three nieces finished Grambling. So a lot of kids from this church went to Grambling. We really push the kids to go back, because it's a great experience, especially if they're born and raised in California.

It gives them an opportunity to have a social life, which is difficult in Orange County, a social life with other black young people.

Right. Fraternity life back there, sorority life back there, and just plain meeting people from different areas that you never met before. Like I say, coming to Orange County, the most blacks you can find is on Sunday morning in a church. After that, they spread out all over the community. The friendship and the fellowship are found in the black church on Sunday morning. Most of our members at this church now live countywide. Very few live in Santa Ana.

Do you see that as a negative or a positive, or just a fact of life?

I think it's very positive and a fact of life too. People go away to afford to live, so they begin to spread out. A lot of people moved out to Corona, a lot of people live in Riverside, some other people live in South County, Huntington Beach,

Fountain Valley, and Garden Grove—everywhere now. I would say 95 percent of our members of the church come from other cities back to Santa Ana.

Do you have any favorite school stories relating to the fact that you're black in this mostly non-black county?

I work very hard to get my students to go to college, regardless of race, creed, or color. I work very close with community colleges. I tell students, if you can't afford to leave the state of California, go to a community college the first two years and transfer. We tell kids we have Cal Grants available. We have scholarships available at Santa Ana College for minority kids, or any of them. Most all your colleges now have programs for minority kids. I tell them, "There's no reason for not going to college these days." I say, "If you want to get a good job, make a decent salary, have a lifestyle that you enjoy, go to college. Get the degree. Most companies will train you to meet their needs, but the bottom line is you need a degree." I stress that in my school, my church, my home. Wherever I go, I follow education. That's the way up.

Do you have children?

I have one daughter. I have three grandkids and one on the way, [which] makes four. I have a set of twins. My oldest granddaughter is now at Dr. Martin Luther King School. She's eight. She's in the English-Spanish immersion program.

So your daughter lives in—

Santa Ana, also. At one time, she taught school in Santa Ana. My son-in-law is the pastor at the New Covenant Church in Santa Ana. I was his counselor in high school. We only had a few black kids in school, and my goal was to make sure, whether you were black or not, you go to school, you go to college, you get an education.

You had the opportunity to observe your son-in-law even before—

I didn't even know it then. What happened—his father was the chairman of the board at the New Spirit Baptist Church. At that time, I was chairman of the board of the Second Baptist Church. We used to exchange between Second Baptist and the New Spirit Church. He was an Orange County kid. He was born in Orange County. My daughter was born in Orange County, too—October 20, 1965.

I had questions relating to positives and negatives of living in Orange County.

I've enjoyed living in Orange County. To me, it wasn't any big deal. I found a place I enjoy. And the key thing about my location is that when I bought the home in Costa Mesa, I was close to my school, my wife's school, my church, and my babysitter. They were all in the same area. My babysitter lived on the corner of Civic Center and Fairlawn. You probably remember Isaac Curtis.

Oh, yeah, the football player.

His mother was our babysitter. All the way up I knew Isaac Curtis. His brother's name is Malcolm Curtis, and his sister's name is Lois Curtis—three of them in the family. Isaac lives in Cincinnati now.

He played football with the Bengals.

He played football for eighteen years, and he's a very successful businessman back in Cincinnati right now. He went to Santa Ana High School. Then he went to the [University of California] Berkeley and San Diego State and finished down there.

Tell us a little more about social life. I know social life centers around the church, but not for everybody in the black community.

Well, at one time they had a club there in Santa Ana on the corner of Fourth and Bristol, and the club was owned by a friend of mine, Ed Cole, who passed away last year. At that time, I know another member of my church, Deacon Lincoln Mulkey Sr., was deacon at that time. His son owned the club. He used to play an instrument in the nightclub there. But, really, my soul goes to my church and Grambling College, Grambling University. I enjoy that. I enjoyed going to school. I enjoy my school functions. I'm not a party type person. I don't need to party. Socializing is okay. I really don't need nightclubs. That's not my style.

Things like crime—any problems living in Santa Ana?

The only problem I had in Santa Ana, during the Watts Riots in 1965—my car was destroyed on Minnie Street. I don't know whether they knew I was black or not, but that's the only car on Minnie Street that was destroyed, that I know of, during the Watts Riots, my car. Otherwise, no. Another thing that's really kind of puzzling, when I first moved to Costa Mesa, one Saturday when I was coming from Costa Mesa to church, and I was stopped by an officer, I asked him, "Why'd you stop me? I'm just leaving home." He said, "Well, I see you with a plate." I guess since I was the only black in the area, he stopped me. So one time, in all that time.

I get different stories from different people, but a lot seems to depend on their age, the car that they're driving, and location.

I drove a traditional car, nothing fancy. Like I say, most times when you see me going someplace, I'm either going to school, to church, or to the babysitter's house. I do go to a meeting once a month in Los Angeles known as the Grambling Alumni Meeting. We have a very large chapter in Los Angeles, so most of the people who live in Orange County that are from Grambling attend the meetings in L.A.

Do you have a story with regard to living here in Orange County?

We've had a very successful life in Orange County, a very enjoyable life here. We've made quite a few friends—all races, creed, and color. So it's been very rewarding to live in Orange County. We have friends that live in different counties around here. One sister lives in San Bernardino County; we got a couple in Riverside County, Los Angeles County. We're all around. The good thing about our family, each year on Mother's Day, we go to one person's home; Father's Day, another home; Thanksgiving, another home. We rotate like that.

How did they used to feel about coming to Orange County to visit?

It didn't bother them at all—did not. We always were a close-knit family. We enjoy going from home to home.

Did they ever talk to you about, or ask you about the Ku Klux Klan or the John Birch Society or things like that?

Yes. But, I had no problem. Coming from Louisiana, you're used to the Klansmen, people being prejudiced like that. So you learn to adjust to those things in life and move on. I don't care where you go, you're going to find racism, whether you're in Orange County or L.A. County, whether you're in Santa Ana or Newport Beach; you're going to find it there and deal with it. I came to Santa Ana, I met some friends here at church, I enjoyed the community, I got a job here, I enjoyed my job here, enjoyed my staff here, so I had no reason to move anywhere else. I enjoyed Orange County. It wasn't a problem here at all.

So you came here because you had a job here.

In my family, wherever you find a job, that's where you stay. It doesn't matter whether it's Orange County or Riverside County. If you get something you enjoy, you stay there and make the best of it. We have friends all over California in different locations. We have to make the best of where we live and try to enjoy ourselves. I don't care where you go; you aren't going to find a perfect community nowhere, so why try to find one? People need to understand that black people weren't hung up on integration. All you wanted was equal opportunities. That was our goal. And if we got that, it was okay.

Anything else you would like to say?

Like I say, we built our brand new church. We left McFadden and Raitt over there. Now we have a larger church location, larger membership, and the good thing about it, we're getting a lot of mixed couples now in our new church. We seat now about a thousand people. We're very proud of our church; we're proud of our members, and proud of our progress here.

Thank you very much, Mr. Johnny Williams, for this interview. It was a pleasure doing this.

SADIE REID BENHAM[1]

Sadie Reid Benham was born in 1930 in Townsend, a small rural town outside of Savannah, Georgia, where she spent most of her childhood years. This interview took place in Compton, near Los Angeles, so when Ms. Benham uses the term "there," she is speaking of Santa Ana or Orange County. In the mid-1960s, she was involved with the first Head Start Programs in Orange County, as well as founding and directing a day care center. Ms. Benham was Santa Ana's first black school board member. She now lives in Farrell, Pennsylvania, and is on the Farrell school board. Photo, 1972.

When did you first come to Orange County, and where did you live?

I think it was on Myrtle Street in the Myrtle apartments when I first moved to Santa Ana. And it was either early 1964 or '65, because in 1965 I became involved in trying to organize Head Start.

Who came with you?

Ezrom, my husband; in fact, the reason we moved to Santa Ana—Ezrom was transferred from L.A. to Orange County to a plant called Telemetrics. It was not that we had relatives there because we didn't know anyone there. And so it was Ezrom and my two girls at the time, Roslyn and Gwendolyn. Jacquelyn was still in Farrell, Pennsylvania, with her aunt.

I came to California in 1959 to become a disk jockey in Los Angeles and when I arrived in Los Angeles, I did not have the money to join the union. I was a disk jockey. I had a show in Farrell called Candy's Rock and Roll. And when I came to Los Angeles, not knowing that I would have to become a part of the union, it fell through; and so shortly, I married Ezrom, in 1964, and we moved to Orange County.

[1] Oral History No. 2902b. Interview date: February 22, 2006, at her daughter Gwen's home in Compton, Los Angeles County, California. Interviewer: Robert Johnson.

So did you have any trouble finding housing?

In Los Angeles we didn't have a problem, but when we decided to move we moved to Santa Ana into the Myrtle apartments, and then we tried to buy a house on Fifth Street in Santa Ana. Someone called and said that he was showing black people this house on Fifth Street and there was a big rigmarole. The realtor lost his license or had to move. I'm not sure how that scenario went, but I know we weren't allowed to buy this particular house at that time. It was across Harbor Boulevard.

So it was pretty far west of what people called the ghetto.

Yeah, from the Myrtle apartments, and I think we were trying to move out a little bit and that wasn't the proper thing to do. I was very outspoken, but really not knowing the makeup of Orange County. I found out very quickly, though, that Santa Ana was almost worse than the South. It was really an eye-opener. I guess they had just passed a proposition where you couldn't buy housing. Was it Proposition 14?

Yes, exactly. [Proposition 14 allowed home owners to discriminate.]

Okay. So, but we were totally unaware of the politics of what was going on in that area. And so that was not a good experience. Ezrom was working at Telemetrics and then he had a second job as a custodian at city hall. And I think as a result of us trying to buy this house that that got wiped out, too. There was a lot of politics behind that.

You had said, either in your book or in your [previous] interview, that Lieutenant Loran Norton lived near.[2]

Yeah. I guess he was on the Santa Ana Police Department at that time. And whoever it was who called him, told this realtor that black people were looking at this house near his house or something. But it was not a good thing.

He was a member of the Birch Society and also had fights with the police chief, Edward Allen.

Well, I had never heard of the John Birch Society till I moved to Orange County. Didn't know who they were, did not know anything about them, so therefore, we were just outspoken.

You looked for a house, but did you buy a house or what?

After the incident with the house on Fifth Street, it seems to me that it became public. We were there for a while but we never felt comfortable. In fact, at the time, I was involved in Head Start. I was still on Fifth Street because the way I got involved in Head Start was that one of the gentlemen came to Goodwill, where I was working, and asked me to be involved in Head Start, and I said to him, "Well, I'm not a teacher and I don't have any credentials." This was '65. Yeah, he says

[2] The self-published book is titled, *From Welfare to the White House* (2002), and the interview by Danelle Moon is OH 2902a, in 1994.

what they were doing was a pilot program that I guess President Johnson had and was just recruiting people from churches. If you were a Sunday school teacher, that's what they used, and so that's how I became involved in Head Start. So I did live on Fifth Street for a while, between Harbor and Euclid.

Oh, so you actually did rent the place that you tried to buy.

Somehow we were able. I think Norton didn't want the publicity, or whatever it was, so we were able to stay there for a while. The kids never did feel comfortable and I'm not sure whether we were there for six or seven months. After the whole incident cleared up and this guy lost his job and saying we weren't supposed to be in that area, we didn't feel comfortable there. Then we moved to 1401 Richland.

But Richland was mostly white, too, right?

Yeah, that block was mostly white, but there were Hispanics on each side of us and I think there was one other black person on that block. It was beginning to be integrated at that time, if I can remember.

So how long did you live there?

I lived on Richland, I guess, ten or fifteen years. I lived on Richland until Ezrom and I divorced and, I believe, that was in, oh, '80. We lived there a long time. Our children, they didn't like it too well. They didn't like Santa Ana really, period.

And why was that?

Number one, we had moved from Los Angeles there and Gwen was doing an essay at Santa Ana High. I'm not sure what she was doing this essay on, but one of the teachers was very rude to her about the book she had pulled out. She'd have to tell you the story, but anyway, she wanted to come back to L.A. She didn't like going to school in Santa Ana at all and it was not a happy time. In fact, Gwen got married really early because she did not like Santa Ana.

I did not realize how prejudiced Orange County was. Coming from Georgia and I'm saying, "God, this place is worse than the South," when we first moved there. Then I was being kind of vocal and what really kind of made me vocal was the fact that I got in Head Start. When we went to the city council to try to get them to be supportive of Head Start, it was just anti-government. They didn't want federal funds. And the headlines of the paper would come out and, I think, I was called an Angela Davis [who was a self-proclaimed Communist]. I think it was Mayor [John] Garthe who called me and he was saying that I was coming in from L.A. being an agitator trying to stir up because I was trying to get Head Start. I wasn't even the one trying to get the Head Start program.

Whose idea was it to have Head Start? Was it Reverend Cooks's?

Reverend [Walter] Cooks and Reverend [S. Z.] Henderson. I'm really new to the area so I really didn't know. I imagine Reverend Henderson, because we met at Second Baptist. It was actually one of the oldest churches and it was a black church.

Henderson was the pastor and Reverend Cooks was the pastor of Greater Light Baptist?

Yeah, I believe so. They were the ones that were really trying to put the program together, and how I got involved is they came to me, working at Goodwill as a cashier, and asked me to get involved. In fact, at times, Ezrom just really wanted to pick our family up and leave Orange County and go back to L.A. because it was always some kind of harassment going on. There was a lot: the Black Panthers, all of this uprising, Angela Davis, all this black power and all that stuff was going on. And I was not a confrontational person. I mean, I was supportive of blacks rising up, but I got pulled in saying that I was still a part of whatever was going on and that was not good.

At the time, there was no training. So what they did— his was a pilot program for the summer of '65—they took people who were Sunday school teachers and used them and tried to follow the pamphlets the government sent out. So that's how I became involved through Reverend Henderson, Reverend Cooks, and Reverend [Thomas] Shipp [of Calvary Baptist], where I was a Sunday school teacher. I think those were the three black churches, and also, I think, Johnson Chapel. Reverend Cooks was really the spearhead of the program, and that was a summer program. And then, after the summer pilot program, we wrote another proposal to continue the program, Head Start, and that's what made me become involved in Orange County. That's what made me political, because then you had to fight to keep the program.

I attended a meeting. It seems like it was upstairs at some church. You were at the podium talking and all the people there—other than Charlie and me, two white guys—were black women.

What we wanted to do was about empowering women. So we talked about poor women and tried to get them to organize and to have a non-profit organization. That's why we were reaching out to try to get an organization to form this Parent Involvement Council and that's what I was trying to spearhead at that time. And I guess the fact was that you all came and you got the message. And somehow we got [the attention of] Lester Van Tatenhove, [Orange County Superior Court judge]. He heard about us and I don't know how he got the message, but that's what I was trying to do. And the young lady, Lily Alexander, that was working with me, she was a little bit more knowledgeable. She was a typist and we tried to put together [a non-profit organization].

Alta Manning [present Head Start Director] thinks you started it, but you previously said, "No, I didn't start the whole thing."

Well, I was involved in the first one in 1965 and I think I was vocal. But we didn't have the sophistication, so the Community Action Council came in and there were three little black organizations that they kind of swallowed up. I think that's when

I just tried to do the Creative Day Care Center, because one of the things they [day care centers] would try to do was make women independent. I thought, oh, I know women who don't want to be on welfare but I said there is no way for them to work and no nursery schools taking black children. Instead of being involved in Head Start, I started the Parent Involvement Council and [it's connected to the] Creative Day Care Center, there at 1202 First Street, that opened October 14, 1968.

This is a good time then to talk about the Creative Day Care Center.

Well, the thing that motivated me to try to start the Day Care Center was to empower parents. And what I found was that even among the black women, many of them wanted to go to work. Okay, so there was this one day care center that would not take black children and what were we going do with the children? So they're saying, we don't want you on welfare, we want you to work, but who's going to keep the children? So this motivated me to start the day care center. In order to even be a parent in the day care center, you had to either be working or going to school. I would say, "You know it's not for you to stay home and watch soap operas, it's for you to either go to school or go to work." And we would be open twelve hours a day, five days a week. Again, we had no money, no plan; I just had an idea. I just wanted to do this and so I'm not sure how Lester Van Tatenhove got a hold of me, but he learned about the idea I wanted to do and they had the first War on Poverty Program at UCI [University of California, Irvine].

Lester came to me. He says, "Well, if you want to do this, you're going to need help," and he says, "I have asked them to put you on the program to speak and tell your story." And I said, "You did what?" I said, "I'm not a public speaker, I'm from the South." I said, "I know you did not do that." So he said, "Well, it's just going to be a small group," and he says, "You know, people can't talk about poverty in Orange County." The city was saying, "There are no poor people." That summer alone we had recruited three hundred kids. In order for your family to qualify to be at Head Start, your income had to be below $3,500 [per year] for a family of four. So I guess Lester was considered a liberal person. He knew there was a problem, but the city was saying there wasn't a problem. So somehow this had to be brought to light. There was Dan Aldrich, [County] Supervisor [David] Baker, and myself. Dan Aldrich was the chancellor of UCI. I don't know who else was on there and I was scared to death. So Lester just kept saying—he was like the coach—he says, "Say you would like to open a day care center and you need help and you want people who are interested in the poverty program."

And people did come. I don't know what I said that day; I did not have a written speech. I didn't write because I was scared to death, but somehow was able to motivate enough people to come and help us at the first meeting we had at the church.

And what church was this?

This was Calvary; this was at Calvary Baptist Church. And we went from there and then we formed the board. There was some attorney that came forth; and you must have been very interested—you and Jim Clark [pastor at Trinity Presbyterian

Church]—because I remembered you all giving us the refrigerator. I can remember the first refrigerator, but somehow you were the spearhead in getting Trinity involved after that conference. And so it went from there, and the day care center lasted about twelve or thirteen years. And then after the day care center, I ran for the [Santa Ana] school board. The day care center really made me politically involved, because there were very few black teachers in the school system. Remember the big confrontation where we had the big lawsuit right before Mary Prior got elected to the school board? They didn't want to service the Hispanic community and the Hispanic children were growing and growing, and so that's what happened—made me political.

Other than Head Start, did your church or any of the other black churches get involved in these issues?

Nobody but Reverend Cooks. Reverend Cooks seemed to be the one that was leading; he became the spokesperson for the black community. Reverend Henderson started but Reverend Henderson left shortly after I came to Santa Ana, so I don't know about any other one. Even my own minister, Reverend Shipp, was not. His church was in Santa Ana but he lived in Long Beach, so he was doing some activist stuff, but it was in Long Beach so he was very low key. He didn't even push for Head Start as much because he did not live here and he didn't want to be criticized for not living in the area. So Reverend Cooks took the good and the bad. The community was very excited about having the Head Start program and the kids being involved, but he got highly criticized. The *Register* was just anti-Head Start, was anti-government, was anti-black. I don't think they even had a black janitor working for them at that time. Yet, the community was happy on one side, but the press was tearing it apart, and I kept saying, "Where are we living, what kind of place is this we are in." Ezrom would be uneasy. He'd say, "You're going to make me lose my job and you can't be vocal, and you can't be saying [things to the press.]" And if you would say something to the press, when you read it, it was something else; it was just very negative. And then the young people in the community were hollering, "Black Power," and there was some Black Panthers rising up.

How about the relationship between the community and the police?

We didn't have any confrontation. I never had any confrontation with the police. In fact, when [Martin Luther] King died, Chief Allen had written a poem that I took to the funeral and somehow, we always had kind of a relationship, Chief Allen and I did. It wasn't real visible. This man seemed to want to do some good things, but again he was the chief in this real conservative environment.

Tell me about some of the people that were in power at that time—for instance, you and Everett Winters.

We were both part of the NAACP and our issues were different because I was a strong advocate of children with disabilities and welfare mothers. I was really for the poor and he was more for the elite black and so that's where we would kind of come together. Jess Berry was the first black person who was elected to the school board. Jess and Everett were very good friends. And then there was a Hispanic young lady. Those were the people that were in power. There were times we'd support one another and other times the opposite . . .

How about Annie Mae Tripp?

Yeah, Annie Mae and her sister [Scotty Biddle] and I, we had all come basically from the same community. Also, she was more for the underdog; she was more for the poor people, people that didn't have a lot. So usually, we would end up kind of like on the same side, whether it be speaking out for people who wasn't as vocal and didn't have as much even in housing, for better housing, and a place to stay in. I was very supportive and Annie Mae was very supportive of me. Like if she met somebody at Trinity or some other resources, she'd say, "Oh Sadie, so and so, I told them about you." And in fact I think I met Betty Thompson through Annie Mae, because Betty was doing Vacation Bible School. Annie Mae told her about the day care center and Betty would come get kids from the day care center, take them to Bible school. And I remember one time—I could see her right now—Betty was responsible for them all having little Bibles and they talk about it today when I see them. They would say Miss Betty gave all of us Bibles. So Annie Mae was very supportive.

How about some of the other people, the white folks that had a lot of power then, like the Grisets and Ogden Markel?

Markel, he said I was a radical. When I first came on the scene, or as we started with Head Start, the older man, Griset, seemed like he wanted to do it, but Orange County had this image.

An image of not wanting federal funds?

At times he would say things like, "Well, if you go to my church and speak." And I remember one time we were somewhere and he slipped me a note and told me to speak to one of the groups at the church. He didn't want to come out publicly in support of black people or poor people, but yet in his heart he knew there were poor people in the Santa Ana community, but [what he was communicating was,] "I'm not going be the one to take the forefront, because of my colleagues."

Old man Griset and Chief Allen, I think they could envision that in ten or fifteen years that the city was going to change and that these people did exist, but they weren't going to take the lead. Remember, I'm working with poor people, so I had to confront Grandville Peoples, chief of welfare. That's their job and so they weren't going to rock the boat, and they would say they didn't have the power. Mayor Griset and Granny Peoples, here were some people who weren't critical in the press. And I used to sit in the evening after dinner and say, "You know, the city's going to change," and I didn't think it was going to change like it has, but I couldn't imagine their thinking, and I'm saying this is the sixties and seventies. I expected them to be more progressive, but they weren't. But it was almost like, "I'm not going to lose my job over this."

How about Griset's son?

Dan. Well, by the time Dan came on the city council, it was a whole new generation. I worked very well with Dan, because when Dan was mayor I was on the school board. I mean, he was much more progressive, and by that time we were into building schools and being very supportive, so you know it was a whole different level.[3]

Why have you had this interest in education?

Well, I think part of the motivation was the fact that when I left the South, I was given a Stanford-Binet test once and I fell below the sixty percentile, and when they tried to explain it to my dad, he didn't understand what they were talking about. He sent me back south to go to school. I could have very well ended up in special-ed classes and been labeled mentally retarded. And so when the suit happened with the Santa Ana school district, it was almost like a flashback. They were saying that the Hispanic kids could not learn. And so, to this date, I take a special interest in children with disabilities or special education to make sure the kids are tested or put in the right classes and that they're given whatever they need and that we follow through.

Do you think Orange County prepared you?

When I look at my life and where I am today, Bob, in many ways, I would not take back the experience I've had in Orange County. I learned so many different things, even to the fact that when I arrived on Santa Ana's school board, Jim Richards, who sat right next to me, sat with his back to me for almost two years, but by the time I left, we had really become friends. One of the things that happened was that when I became president, I said to him, "If I'm going to be president of the school board, I cannot function if I don't have the support of all the members, and what I would like to do is for you and me to get to know each other." I invited him to lunch, and we sat, I imagine, for three to four hours, and talked to each other. When he got to tell me about his background and his history, it was just heart rending, and from that day, we became friends. And, what I learned from that experience is that we really don't know each other. I mean, things had been told to him about black people and he'd been raised in an area where there weren't a lot of black people, and we had to make an effort to get to know each other.

---

[3] In 1954, the US Supreme Court judgment in the *Brown v. the Board of Education* suit required the desegregation of America's schools. This had been preceded by the *Mendez v. Westminster* lawsuit in 1947 requiring California schools to desegregate. But, in the days before the *Mendez* and *Brown* decisions, segregation of black children, unlike Mexican American children, was not an issue; there were too few black students anywhere in Orange County for white school boards to segregate them. Later, when housing segregation led to a few predominately black schools in Santa Ana in the 1960s and 1970s and lines were moved to keep black students in black schools, there were teachers, parents, and elected black school board members like Jessie Berry and Sadie Reid (Benham) who worked to reduce segregation and the effects that came with segregated schools.

The two people who opposed me the most, Richards and Mary [Prior], by the time I left that board, they became my friends. They were very disappointed when I didn't get elected the second time and they think the fact that I married John Benham [who was white] in Orange County . . . And they said that if there's ever a time when you can get appointed to this board or something, we will make sure that you get back on. I ran for office [county supervisor] knowing I wasn't going to win, but I wanted to talk about welfare. I learned the strategies. If you have an issue, you need to be able to talk about it. I made lots of friends. I love Orange County. I wouldn't take it back.

Didn't you move out of Orange County for a short time and then came back and moved to Brea?

I moved out of Orange County, yes, and I lived in Brea for a while, and then I moved to Huntington Beach. When I came to Farrell, I moved from Huntington Beach. I moved to Huntington Beach after John [Benham] had passed away in '89. And I thought Huntington Beach was where I was going to be forever, and then my mom got sick with cancer and I just couldn't afford to keep coming back and forth. Mom lives in Detroit, but I never did like big cities, and so that's the reason I chose to go to Farrell where my children were. And it's only three hours from Detroit, so I could just go there at any time.

Tell me about churches that you went to here. Did you go to one church or did you go to a number of churches?

I just went to Calvary. That was the one church. Now, whenever there were programs, I would associate with Second Baptist and all the various churches, but Calvary was my home church—Calvary of Reverend Shipp.

What were the positives and negatives of living in Orange County?

I think the most negative thing to me when I first arrived in Orange County was the fact that you could not purchase a house anywhere and how prejudiced it was. We had moved out from Detroit to Los Angeles and I just could not believe that there existed another place on earth that was as prejudiced—the attitudes that I would hear and some of the thinking of some of the people in power. That was the negative. It took me a while to really kind of just absorb the attitudes of the people in Orange County; but then I met people like Lester [Van Tatenhove] and you and [Pastor] Jim Clark and Betty [Thompson].

And then you see this other side of people reaching out; you kind of wonder. It did help you to balance, because, like I said, my husband right away said, "Oh, we need to get out of here. It's not good and the kids are complaining." And yet there were some good elements and so you just keep hoping for the best. I think that was the positive and I say that's the positive side even today. When I go back East and they'll say, "Where did you live," and I say, "I lived in Santa Ana and Huntington Beach." "Where?" "Orange County." And they'll say, "You [really] lived in Orange County?" So Orange County's image really is nationally known now, and I think that was the negative part. But, the positive was that when John and I got married, the whole city shut down, practically, and was at our wedding. When I look at those films and those pictures of people who were at our wedding, and even to this day when I come in to Orange County, I have friends like you and Bob [Pietsch] that I go see. Those are things that you can't take away. Those are the positive things.

Do you have a favorite story about Orange County? About being a black person in Orange County?

I think my favorite story is how I met John [Benham], because John was the controller for the Compton Unified School District. He was invited to a party one of the judges was giving in Newport Beach, and I was invited to the same party. It was predominately Republican people, and I told this guy, "Eddie, I would go with you providing that nobody takes my picture here because I'm vice-president of the Democratic Party and here I am at a Republican birthday party, a party that's predominantly Republican." And I said, "Please don't let anybody take my picture." I said, "This cannot get out." And so that was the night I met John Benham. And John was a very conservative Republican, and when John and I got married, it was just a miracle. It was an unbelievable situation for him to be a strong Republican, as he was, and I was a liberal Democrat. But yet we had a good marriage with the kids, and so that's my favorite story.

That's a wonderful story. It's a super ending and thank you very much, Sadie Reid Benham.

HELEN SHIPP[1]

Helen Shipp was born in the small rural town of Alamo, close to both Atlanta and Macon, Georgia. Her father was a mechanic and her mother was a housewife. When she was four years old, they moved to Detroit, Michigan. Her mother and father divorced, and when her mother died, she went to live with her birth father in Miami, Florida. She was nineteen when she married Felton Shipp in 1954. They came to Santa Ana in 1965. Mrs. Shipp lives in Santa Ana and is active with the Orange County Black History Commission, which she helped found.

Tell us about Michigan. Were the areas you lived in integrated?

It was about half and half. You were allowed to go into many stores and didn't have to go to the back. We moved from Detroit to Wayne, Michigan, in 1946, when I was eleven. We were mixed there, and neighbors got along with each other. So it wasn't too bad. Even in Miami [Florida] it wasn't too bad.

What were the worst things?

The worst thing is there were some places in Miami at one time, in [1952], you could not go and eat. So that was just like Georgia. But then by 1955, you were able to do those things. But there was this thing—you couldn't drink the water, the water fountain thing. "Colored over here," would be the sign, and "whites over here"—that would be the sign.

How did that make you feel when you were a kid?

Oh, well, you know, at first I couldn't understand that because we were used to just being children and talking to any race children. And in Michigan, our neighbor was a white family. And so we didn't know anything about the color barrier, because everybody that lives on Russell Street was just one family. If my mom ran out of

[1] Oral History No. 2387. Interview date: April 9, 1994, at the home of Mrs. Shipp in Santa Ana, California. Interviewer: Wendy Barker.

flour, she could go next door to Miss Sylvia. And then as the years passed and you began to get older and you begin to go to school, you've got to go here and they go there, and that type of thing. I'm just grateful I didn't come up in the slavery time because I don't know if I could have made it.

When your mother died, you moved back to Florida in 1952. And what was it like then, in terms of segregation?

It was still segregation. Civil rights hadn't kicked in. And even after it kicked in, it was still prevalent. Today there's still some; it's just not as bad. I can remember the time when my sister was in the hospital and they didn't allow you to come in; you had to go through a certain door. I remember that one. I have relatives that look just as fair-complexioned as you, and so (chuckling) we sent her in. Because when I went in, they wouldn't give me any information on my sister. They were just talking and not paying attention to me. So my cousin, she went in. She could put on that talk, and she had her hair fixed just like the whites did. She just went right on in and asked where my sister was. She told them that she was from out of town and that she needed to see her, and they let her in. Well, when they let her in, she came to the side and let us in.

We used to send her in places, instead of going to the back. A lot of times when you go to those back places, it is so dirty and nasty, you don't even want the food to come out. We would send her in the front door to get the food, and she would bring it out. And then sometimes we would meet her, and they would be just looking, my God, you know. It was really bad traveling.

I would think it would be hard to not get really angry.

You see, if you really got angry, it would cause a problem. I have been in some places where I hear them calling my father "nigger." And my father had a hot temper. So my mother would always say, "Pray, because your daddy's going to get loose." And she always said, "No matter what they call you, you know who you are." That was my mom's philosophy. "You know who you are, so don't even answer." She said, "When they call you 'nigger,' just keep walking. Don't act like you know what they're talking about." She was that type of person that you couldn't walk on her, don't rouse her, but she always had a lot of wisdom. She would say, "I don't care what they say. You know who you are. I named you Helen; I didn't name you nigger, so you keep walking."

You have to be really strong inside.

Yeah, you've got to be. You got to have a strong temperament, yeah, yeah, yeah. Because I know my kids—sometimes we would tell them about some of the things that come back to your memory and my kids will say, "I don't know how you made it." I say, "Well, I always thought about what my mom said." And she was the type that always talked to me like I was an adult. That morning she died, she said, "Now you watch over your brother and your sisters." She says, "I don't care what happens; I don't want you guys separated. I want you with your father, and you're the mother like you've been for a long time." Because like the last four months before she passed, she was really telling me everything about life and living, what to do, how to do this and how to do that. And so I guess that's why I'm able to make it today, because of that strong wisdom that my mom put into me. And she always said, "Whatever you do, don't forget God, because that's your road map." So I'm sure that that's what keeps me going, because you can't do anything without the Master.

How did you come to move to Orange County?

My husband Felton—there's twelve boys and six girls in his family. His oldest sister lived in Long Beach. She and her husband had been there a long time, and she had talked her mom and them into moving from Miami to California. So Felton just came to see if he could find himself a job, and he found a job right away at Delco Batteries in Anaheim, where he's at now. He's been there ever since 1965.

His brother was pastor of the Calvary Baptist Church, which he still is pastor of, here in Santa Ana. One of the members there knew the fellow that used to live in this house and knew he had a house for rent. My husband wanted us to come, and so he rented the house from this person, Jim Bates.

And you've lived in this house the whole time?

Yeah. Yeah, I haven't moved. (chuckling) He rented the house because he didn't want to live up in Long Beach. I just didn't like the atmosphere for some reason. So we moved to Santa Ana and we haven't gone out of Santa Ana.

A lot of blacks apparently had a hard time finding housing.

It wasn't hard for us to find housing, because, see, it was a black man that owned this house. And so we moved into the house with the assumption that if you want to buy it—and so when he got ready to sell, we were the first one he offered it to. And so wasn't any sense in us trying to find another house, because you've got to have so much for a down payment. When I moved here in '65, I was pregnant. I was carrying Eric at that time. And then Byron was born in '67, and Dwayne was born in '75. I have ten children.

When you first moved here, what did you do?

I said I'm not going to work. (chuckling) I got involved with the church, and one of our members was the president of a Head Start, and they were beginning to have a problem. She was looking for a secretary, and my brother-in-law, Reverend Shipp, he said, "Oh, you guys need to get Helen." And I said, "Why did he say something like that, because I don't intend to work." And so I started helping them until they got a secretary; the wrong thing I should [have] ever done. That's how I got involved with the Head Start Program. I started in '68.

Were there any incidences with prejudice or anything like that?

You could see it all around. But see, I wasn't too involved with anything then. But you could very well see that Orange County had prejudice. But then, sometimes it all depends on how you carry yourself, too. Sometimes you go into the store and they don't want to wait on you right away. They're going to get the next person if he's white, and then, "Oh, may I help you?" That type of stuff.

What do you think is the biggest change in the black community in the time that you've lived here?

Oh, the biggest change in the black community, I think, is more blacks are getting into homes than they were when I first came. And more blacks are definitely getting more into the county and the city positions than when I first came, because I didn't see anybody before.

Was there a time when you saw a turning point?

I think the first thing that I saw was when Robert Bobb was the city manager and he was a black fellow. Allen Doby is still with the Parks and Recreation, and they said that had never been. And now we have them all over the county, and in good positions. Usually, they want to hire you to clean the bathroom and do the floors, work in the kitchen, that type of stuff. But we have blacks in the planning department now at the City of Santa Ana, and not only Santa Ana, but in Orange County. But I think that Santa Ana has the most blacks in higher positions than these other places. It could be because they started out earlier here.

Let's talk about Head Start. You said that you got started from—

Volunteering as a secretary, which I still am. I'm not classified as a secretary, but it's still doing the same thing. So I've been working with them since '68. Head Start started in '65. At that time, they were at our church, which was Calvary. I started off part-time, and as they began to get more children, then they put the secretary on full time.

So, when it started, what was the predominant race?

At that particular time, the predominant race it served was blacks, because we were right over here. And then later on more Hispanics moved in. Where I am now, we have predominant Vietnamese. We have a very low percentage of black and Caucasian. Our site has moved. But we get predominant whatever is in that area.

Well, let's move to history. You were instrumental in setting up the Orange County Black Historical Commission.

In Miami, we used to have what we called The Classics, and The Classics would be a gathering of blacks. And we would have a parade and then the two schools, Florida A&M and Grambling, would play a football game. It was like a celebration of black history. So when I came to California, they weren't doing anything. One day—I think I was talking to Carolyn Jimerson—I was saying it would be nice to have a Black History Parade commemorating Black History Month. "What do you do in Santa Ana for Black History Month?" And somebody said, "We don't do anything." "You don't do anything?" I said, "We've got to keep this thing going, you know? They have to know that we can get together and do something besides fighting and causing problems and all this other stuff that they say." So that's how it really started, and that was in '79. So it was a group of us. Then we had Reverend Richard Kessee, Jr., Charlie Shaw, and Margaret Ramsey. Anyway, we tried to start a parade.

You all knew each other through church, then, or through the community organization?

Through the community and church. And see, when you're working in the public, you meet a lot of people. So it was like city employees, church people. Carolyn Jimerson and I have been friends ever since I've been in Santa Ana. You know how you'd just be casually sitting around talking, and it came up. So they said, "Well, why don't you put it together?" I go, "Jesus." So we started talking about it, and we tried to do little things, and we find out that we had to have a petition with twenty-five names on it stating that you wanted a parade and blah, blah, blah . . . So we did our homework. Margaret Ramsey and I knew Ed Frieson. His wife was a teacher at Lincoln. She taught my kids, but he was a lawyer. Margaret and I took our information to him and said, "Ed, we want to start an organization, and this is what we want to do. We don't have a name, Ed." He said, "Okay, so this is what you want to do." So he named us, he wrote our bylaws. He did everything for us. So that's how it started. By 1980 we had it put together, and we had our first parade. Then in '81, the City [of Santa Ana] came in and started financially helping us.

The first year, I knew the chief of police real well, (chuckling) and I went and talked to him and was able to get paperwork done, and they'd tell me what to do, and I would go talk to certain people. We only had like eight entries. We had more than that, but the week ahead of that when we was going to have it, it rained. So people had to go other places, so we only had eight. And everybody was saying—even the chief of police said—"Shipp, you are crazy." And I go, "Well, you know, you got to crawl before you walk. And if you keep putting it off and keep putting it off and you never do it, you never will get started." And he said, "All I can say is that you're

Black History Parade

The first annual February Black History Parade was held in downtown Santa Ana in 1980, when the population of that city's black community was near its peak. The next year, the parade was held in west Santa Ana, in "the neighborhood," and passed by many of the homes of black residents. That year's event included a fair (now called the Cultural Faire) at the nearby Jerome Center grounds. By adding the fair, people were brought together in one place. Later, as many in Santa Ana's black community moved to the suburbs, the fair gave folks from various churches, organizations, and cities an opportunity to come to town, for at least a day, to be a community again.

In 2004, the name of the parade was changed to "Multicultural Parade and Faire" to obtain greater financial support by reflecting the ethnic diversity of the city. Many in the black community believed that by broadening the theme, the contributions of African Americans to the city was being diluted. The following year, the parade and fair were renamed the "Orange County Black History Multicultural Parade and Faire."

crazy." I go, "Okay, just as long as you're just going to bare the streets and let me go." (chuckling) So it was one of those things. But it was the start.

How do you think blacks are treated in Orange County?

Some of the blacks in Orange County are treated terribly. See, I haven't run into a whole lot of it, but I've known people that have, and some of my kids have, with the police. I know that if they stop you, they stop you with a different method. I know Hispanics and blacks; they are really nasty with them. You *know* what I'm saying? And then you have some stores that you still go into, that if you're Hispanic or black, sometimes they hesitate about waiting on you. Because they always try to put that thing up, they're afraid of you. You're violent or something on that order. And don't let a group of black kids go in. Because I have been in stores and they followed me all around the store. I told one person, "You know what? If I didn't come in here to buy something, I wouldn't be in here. You don't have to walk behind me because I'm not going to pick up anything." I said, "And why are you watching me? Your own race is stealing like hell from you." He looked at me, and I just turned around. I said, "I don't even want anything out of this store," and walked on out the door.

It must be hard, though, emotionally to have to deal with that.

Yeah, yeah. Well, you see, I can deal with it. My kids are the ones can't deal with it. They're all grown now. I just tell them, "Hey, you know what? Sometime it's better to use your head and your mind and your wisdom to get around people."

What was your reaction with the whole Rodney King incident?[2]

Oh, God. What was my reaction? They finally got caught. I just pray all the time, "Lord, just let them get caught. Do something." Because it's time. Blacks are being tired of being pushed. That's why a lot of time I think that the violence comes up. You get tired of being pushed. And when they show *Roots?* I would always have to be praying that my kids didn't get into a fight when they went to school. Because the first white boy that says something to them, that was it, you know? And kids are kids. I don't care how old they are, they're still kids. And then I always tell mine, it'll depend how they was raised in their home. "You guys were raised that you respect everybody that respect you." You know what I'm saying? And color means nothing. Because we all hurt, we all get sick, we all stink if we don't take a bath, and if you don't brush your teeth, you're in trouble. My philosophy is that I was left in the oven longer than you. (laughter) You know what I'm saying? Because we're all human beings.

I know one night my son was just across the street, and he was coming home, and the cops turned the corner with the bright lights on, and because he was running, they thought he was stealing. They got out of their car and they chased him around

[2] In 1992, Los Angeles police were caught beating a black man, Rodney King. The beating was videotaped and the police were charged with using excessive force. The police were acquitted by a mostly-white, non-black jury, leading to an outcry in the black community. On the evening of the verdict, "riots" began. More than fifty people died.

the house. And one of my other sons was in the room and he heard the running, so he looked out the window. And he said, "Mom, I think you need to go outside. They're chasing Eli." And I went outside and this cop wanted to get smart with me. See, I used to belong to the COP [Community Oriented Policing], working with the police.

And so he was getting smart and I was getting smart. So I said, "You know what? I don't even have to talk to you." And I looked over at his badge, "All I need is your number. Let me call Lieutenant Slurger. That's all I need." And when I said, "Lieutenant Slurger," whoa, he backed down. And then I said, "Elijah, come on." I said, "What are they chasing you for?" So the cop told me, he said, "There was a robbery up the street, and he fit the description." Elijah said, "I haven't been up the street. I only walked from my yard to that house right there. I have not been up the street." He said, "Well, you were running." Elijah said, "I ran across the street and was running into the house because it's cool." And, oh, he just went on. But when I said, "Lieutenant," then he calmed down, "Ma'am, we're sorry, but he fit the description." I said, "You're full of junk. He hasn't been up the street, so how can he fit the description? You saw a black boy run from across the street, you saw him running, and you didn't know where he was running to. And when he came through that little slot right there in my fence, you didn't know. But what you should have done is not get out and point your gun and chase him." I told him, "What happens if you accidentally stumble and the gun goes off? What happens? You got problems." I think that's harassment. If they harass you, well, it'd make you angry. I'm glad of the pictures that they caught with Rodney, but I just don't even understand how Rodney is still living because of a beating like that.

What do you think about the black-Latino relations in Santa Ana?

I think that children will get along if adults stay out of it. My boys used to go with Mexican girls. Many of them right now see me, act like I'm their mama, because they've eaten so many times over here and they've been so many places with my boys. When our motor home was running and my boys was in football, we were just all one family. The older families that are here, they're used to getting along with people that are here. But a new generation coming in, I think it's a mind thing. If you've been taught you don't play with blacks, you do this to blacks, they're a slave, they're this, and they're that, well, then as soon as you see a black, that's going to be your reaction.

Were there other blacks in Orange County involved in civil rights?

Oh, yeah—Sadie Reid and the different organizations. Harriet Tyler, she's been here a while too.

Why have you seen black children as an essential area to work?

Because once you get that education, nobody—white man, black man, Mexican, Chinese, whatever—nobody can take it away from you. And I think education is where it's at for not only the black race, but for any race. But especially the black race, because they always say that blacks are dumb, they don't know how to do nothing, and that sort of thing. So I'm always a pusher.

There are things like drugs working against Head Start and the church. Where does the blame lie?

I don't believe it's blacks. I honestly believe that it's some person that got money. Blacks don't have money. You got more Caucasians that have money. And I'm saying that they could curtail that thing, because how many people are able to buy this stuff? And that's why the blacks are robbing and going on. They got a taste of it from somebody, so now they figure they got to have it. So what do I do? I take my mama's stuff, I take my sister's stuff, anybody's house I can get into, just to get their stuff. Don't make any sense to me. But, the government and the law, if they were doing their job, I think it could be cut.

How do you evaluate black families in Orange County today [1994]?

They're improving their education, their way of life. They're really finding out what's going on and trying to get an education. You can't get a job if you don't know how to do it. You know what I'm saying? So, if you get that education, then you're able to get a professor's job, you're able to be a teacher, you're able to be an executive board director, or that sort of thing. And it just doesn't happen because you're black. You've got to get the basics, so you've got to get that education. And most of all, my belief is that if you've got Jesus, then He'll teach you how to do. Because God is love. He teaches you how to love everybody. So your whole thing is right there in God's word, bringing yourself up.

This was a great interview. Thank you very much.

Part Two

My First Orange County Home Was in the Suburbs

Introduction

It was about 1920 when Mary Owens's grandmother, mother, and uncle arrived at the Fullerton train station. Mary's mother, Jessie, and uncle were babies who had come with their mother from Alabama, at the request and with the financial help of her mother's older brother, Neff Cox. He was working in Brea, but living on Truslow Avenue, just south of the Fullerton train station. In time, Mary had various aunts and uncles who were living on Truslow, two of their homes having been built by uncle Neff. Neff Cox was a bootblack in Brea and was well liked by the citizens there, but he, like all other blacks, had to leave Brea by sundown. Brea was a "sundown town."[1]

Not only were black people prevented from living in "sundown towns" like Brea and Orange, and prevented from purchasing property in areas that had racial covenants like the land that Richard Nixon's father bought in Yorba Linda, but it was almost impossible to find any apartment to rent or property to buy outside of the Truslow area. But that was the rest of the city's and county's loss. In the 1930s, on the same Truslow Avenue where Mary Owens grew up, lived the Owens family and the Berkley family.[2]

Fortunately, we have an oral history of the Owens family as told by Mary Owens. Along with her own family history, she tells about Penny, the activist and loving aunt, and Penny's nephews, the seven Owens boys, all of whom but the youngest, were outstanding athletes in Fullerton High School and college. Brig, for example, played thirteen years with the Washington Redskins, and later, as an attorney, was the National Football League players' representative. Penny's youngest nephew didn't like sports as much as books, so he also became an attorney and practiced in Fullerton. Although the Berkleys, who also lived on Truslow, have all passed away and we do not have their oral histories, they need to be mentioned.

The Berkley family, mentioned in the general introduction to this volume, came from down-state Illinois, the father having been a coal miner and union activist. Son Tom played basketball and ran track for Fullerton High School and Fullerton Junior College. And in the late 1930s, he ran track for UCLA on the same

[1] See CSUF Oral Histories OH 1720 and OH 1726 for comments regarding Neff Cox. Sundown laws and ordinances with regard to a person's place of residence were declared illegal on the basis of the Fourteenth Amendment, by the US Supreme Court in 1917. No city of Brea ordinance or resolution regarding a black person having to be out of town after sundown has been found, and if it had been enacted, it probably would not have been legally enforceable; but this did not stop enforcement of supposed ordinances by police or citizens throughout the United States. Brea was not the only sundown town. The city of Orange also had that deserved reputation. In 1925, the city had one black family living at the location where the father shined shoes. By 1940, of the 8,000 residents, there were no black persons living in Orange.

[2] The land in Yorba Linda upon which sits the home where President Nixon was born and raised—now the site of his presidential library—was once restricted by a racial covenant. This covenant in the Nixon family's 1914 deed of ownership reads as follows: "That no part of said premises, or the improvements thereof, shall ever be sold or leased to any individual other than of the Caucasian race."

team as former L.A. Mayor Thomas Bradley. After he left Southern California, he went to Boalt and Hastings law schools of the University of California. He then established what became a major law firm in Oakland, and eventually purchased and ran the *Oakland Post* newspaper. Other than Dr. Martin Luther King, he was the only black person to have an Oakland street named after him; this naming resulted from his many contributions to the city. His sister, Ruby Berkley Goodwin, became famous as an author of poetry, an autobiography, and a newspaper column; an actor; and the secretary for the actress Hattie McDaniel. For many years, she was active in city and cultural affairs.

How could there be two such extraordinary families in a town that only had eighteen black people living there in 1920, forty-one in 1930, and still only fifty-seven in 1940? Was it because the parents of these children wanted something they believed their children would not get if they lived in underachieving areas and because they were willing to face the pressure of being the only blacks in an almost all-white city? Was this true in other county suburbs?

The total black population of Orange County, outside of the city of Santa Ana, stayed at about 120 people over the two decades from 1920 to 1940. This was in spite of the increase in the Fullerton population from eighteen people to fifty-seven. Other than Laguna Beach, most other cities' black populations remained close to zero or decreased during the Depression years. By 1950, Fullerton was still considered the other city where black people lived and remained living, mostly on or near Truslow Avenue. This reputation remained in spite of the fact that Fullerton still only had seventy-seven black residents in 1950.

The 1950 US Census showed that the county's black population, outside of Santa Ana, had increased to 456 residents, mostly in Anaheim and Newport Beach (the latter probably due to an increased number of live-in maids and their children), and the marine bases in Tustin and El Toro. Other than these, there was little change in the status of blacks outside of Santa Ana by 1950. From the federal census, we find the number of blacks (adults plus children) in the cities with over 3,000 residents outside of Santa Ana, Fullerton, Laguna Beach, Newport Beach, and Anaheim were as follows: Brea (2), Buena Park (3), Costa Mesa (9), Garden Grove (4), Huntington Beach (3), La Habra (0), Orange (3), Seal Beach (2), and Westminster (1). Author James W. Loewen would consider these cities "sundown towns" because he would, for good reason, argue that it is not by accident or solely the choice of black home seekers, but it was due to housing discrimination that these numbers are close to only one family unit per city.[3]

Although the total county population was increasing at a rapid rate, there was little momentum in changing the status quo regarding segregated housing in the early 1950s. Two appalling incidents involving the Lee and Harris families, though not recorded as oral histories, highlight both the difficulties in obtaining housing outside of Santa Ana and the changes that were beginning to take place in the mid- to late-1950s.

In 1954, Dr. Sammy Lee, a Korean American who was the first American of Asian descent to win a gold medal at the Olympic Games, tried to buy a home

[3] James Loewen, *Sundown Towns* (New York: The New Press, 2005), 213-215.

in Garden Grove. In spite of the fact that he had served in the army and was the State Department's Sports Ambassador to Southeast Asia to show the world what America stood for, he was denied purchasing a home in a Garden Grove housing tract. In a taped interview by a reporter from the *San Francisco Chronicle*, the developer stated that "we don't sell to yellow bellies" in his tract and that he would not sell to Lee. This became news across the nation, and suddenly, Orange County realtors and others were saying that they don't discriminate.[4] Though in most cases this was not true, it was a starting point in breaking down residential segregation in the county. In 1956, housing in the city of Placentia opened to blacks.

In August 1956, the Harris and Joseph families bought homes in a blue-collar housing tract at the junctions of Iowa with Kansas and Missouri Streets, just south of Orangethorpe Avenue. The tract included what is now a section of the 57 Freeway. Before the Harris family were able to move into their home, their house was heavily vandalized. White neighbors provided support for the family, but near the end of the first week, the house was firebombed. In the middle of the night, a Molotov cocktail was thrown through their two young daughters' bedroom window, catching the curtains on fire and singeing the bed. Although the children were not burned, the event was traumatic for both families; nevertheless, both families remained living in the tract.[5] Following the Lee and Harris incidents, an organization named "Orange County Council for Equal Opportunity" was formed to combat housing and other forms of discrimination. Also, as in the Sammy Lee case, many people came to the support of the two families and word spread that in Placentia there was another place where black people could live. By 1960, there were 176 black people living in the Placentia area; a majority of them living in the two-block tract. Included in the tract was Charles Ray, who chose to live in Placentia because of its proximity to his work at the new Autonetics plant in Anaheim.

It was work that drew black people to the county, and work there was. The1950s and 1960s brought major corporations involved in electronics and aerospace to the Orange County suburbs. In 1958, Hughes Aircraft opened a division by the Fullerton Airport. In January 1960, North American Aviation purchased eighty acres of land in Anaheim for its Autonetics Division, which was to eventually employ 35,000 workers by the mid-1960s. In the south county, in 1958, Aeronutronic began the development of their facility in Newport Beach, and this was followed in 1960 by Collins Radio Company's plant construction in the same city. These were major corporations that provided jobs for skilled and unskilled workers alike. And they needed housing.

By 1961, the Rays, the Cheetams, [See the Rays and Cheetams annotated biographies in Appendix 1] and the Smiths had all moved into the Kansas-Missouri

---

[4] Molly Frick Wampler, *Not Without Honor, The Story of Sammy Lee* (Santa Barbara: The Fithian Press, 1987).

[5] The fire bombing was reported by newspapers in Santa Ana, Fullerton, Anaheim, and Orange, as well as the *Los Angeles Times*, and the African American community newspapers: the *California Eagle* (published in Los Angeles) and the *Los Angeles Sentinel.* The headline in *The Register* (Santa Ana) of August 21, 1956, read, "Fire Bomb Hurled into Placentia Negro's Home; Children Periled." The subtitle read, "Midnight Attack Sets Fire in Bedroom Where Two Youngsters Slept."

tract. By this time, most of the white folks had moved out and the neighborhood was mostly composed of blacks as well as a few Latino families. The homes were not expensive and it was an opportunity to live in a suburban setting adjacent to large groves of oranges, for which the city was noted. As mentioned earlier, for Charles Ray, this meant living close to his work at fast growing Autonetics. John Smith knew that other Marine Corps families lived there and Earnie Cheetam simply wanted to live in Orange County, in spite of the fact that people said that black people couldn't live there. Starting with the Rays, eventually all three families moved to larger and better housing. The Rays and Smiths moved to lovely all-white middle-class neighborhoods in Placentia, and Earnie Cheetam moved to Anaheim. But, for the Rays in 1966, the move out of the ghetto was difficult; they had to win a discrimination suit in order to purchase their new home. It was difficult for others as well. Placentia's black population increase in the decade of the 1960s was only ten!

Unlike Placentia in the 1960s, the black population in the city of Orange increased from 9 to 213. A considerable portion of this increase was due to black families moving into three tracts, in different parts of the city that were developed by Joseph Eichler. Eichler, who started out as a developer in the Bay Area, had a policy of not discriminating in the sale of his housing. His homes had an avant-garde style, each with an atrium that allowed light to permeate the entire house. That open style was a turn-off to some potential buyers, but the fact that his tracts were integrated appealed to some white families. So when black families moved in, the white families stayed and the tracts remained integrated. The Jo and Ken Caines family moved into one of the homes in 1963 and although Ken is deceased, Jo was still living there in 2008.

By the time of the 1970 census, there were no longer any "sundown towns". As jobs opened up and fair housing laws came into being and were enforced in the courts, black families moved into homes and apartments throughout the county. This development occurred in spite of the fact that discrimination in buying and renting was still the rule and not the exception. Those African Americans who wanted to live in the Orange County suburbs could find housing if they had the patience and the resources to keep trying and did not give up when lied to or told that they were not wanted. Often, the move also required the support of black people as well as white people such as Ralph and Natalie Kennedy and attorney Bob Ward, as well as the help of fair-housing organizations. In Joshua White's case, in 1961, this also required the courage to remain in his Anaheim neighborhood in spite of a bullet ripping through his apartment when he first moved in. As the decade of the 1960s came to an end, it became considerably less difficult to find housing in the suburbs, as the Clemons family, who moved into Orange in 1971, found out. And like them, more black people were living in all-white neighborhoods.[6]

The middle-class lifestyles of black people in the Orange County suburbs generally were similar to those of their white neighbors; this was particularly true of the children who grew up in the suburbs. Blacks, who came as adults in the 1960s and 1970s, came with their own accents and maybe church or Masonic affiliations,

---

[6] Robert Ward, former mayor of Fullerton: CSUF Oral History 3289.

but soon settled into the lifestyle of the majority community. That is not to say that they did not have to deal with discrimination or racial profiling or were not conscious of the fact that they were black. Time has not erased that condition. A black person living in Anaheim in 1924 was extremely conscious of his or her race when viewing Klu Klux Klan members driving down the road in their hoods and robes. And blacks, even now, are conscious of their race when seeing a police car when they themselves are on the road. But, through the 1970s and 1980s, the lines dividing blacks and whites became increasingly blurred. Life styles and ideas regarding fashions, movies, sports, and music were melding and black and white young adults in Orange County were speaking with the same accents and were not only hanging out and dating, but were marrying as well.

Chapter 4
North Orange County African American Neighborhoods

Mrs. Cox, Mrs. Berkley, and Mrs. T. F. Fitzgerald spent Sunday p.m. with Mr. and Mrs. J. W. Carroll.—Mrs. Cox has returned to her home this week after spending a week with her brother in Los Angeles.—Mr. and Mrs. Berkley at 229 ½ Easy Truslow gave a fish fry—Mr. and Mrs. T. Walker were the guests of Mrs. Rascoe on Thursday night.—by request of the president of the Handicraft Club Mrs. G. E. Rascoe—entertained with a whist and 500 party guests—Rascoe motored to Elsinore and Riverside.[1]

The column "FULLERTON," in the *California Eagle* newspaper, provides a glimpse of African American life in Orange County in 1926. This was the year that the later-famous Berkley family moved to Fullerton and quickly became a part of its social life, a social life that included Mary Owens' relatives, the Cox family. Because there were so few black families in Fullerton at that time (only nine in 1930), their social relationships with family and friends extended to Santa Ana and Anaheim as well as Los Angeles County. Mary Owens was only a young child when she came to Fullerton from Los Angeles in 1940. Life as she describes it was probably not much different in Fullerton's black community in the 1940s from what it was in the 1920s. The African American population had only increased from eighteen people in 1920 to seventy-seven by 1950.

Following a stint in the army during World War II, Warren Bussey came to Fullerton and moved in with his brother. He had no difficulty in finding work and started his own maintenance company. In 1951, he married Maime Ebla. The house they rented on Truslow Avenue burned down in 1953, so he and his wife moved to Santa Ana. A year before the Busseys moved out of Fullerton, Natalie and Ralph Kennedy had moved into the city. The Kennedys were a white couple who became active in civil rights in the early 1960s in areas such as fair housing and justice for farm workers. Ralph became the moving force in creating and providing leadership to the Fullerton Fair Housing Council in 1965. It took the efforts of fair housing people like Bob Ward (OH 3289) to help the Reverend James Carrington obtain housing in Fullerton in 1968. And it had been Penny Owens, Mary Owens's aunt by marriage, who had originally encouraged the reverend to start a church in Fullerton.

In nearby Placentia, housing opened for blacks in 1956 when two families—the Harrises and Josephs—moved, under frightening circumstances, into what became the city's ghetto. Four years later, Charles Ray's family and marine sergeant John Smith's family moved there, but without incident.

[1] The *California Eagle*, various snippets from May 21, 1926 to August 27, 1926. The *Eagle*, a prominent weekly "race" (African American) newspaper published in Los Angeles, would print a column titled "FULLERTON" every few weeks. This column provided news from Orange County's black community in Fullerton and Santa Ana.

Also without incident was Wacira Gethaiga's 1961 move from Kenya into a private home in Anaheim, from where he spent a senior year at Anaheim High School. But that was not the case when Josh White moved into Anaheim in that same year. In 1960, the census showed forty-eight black residents living in Anaheim, a number down from seventy-four residents in 1950, in spite of the fact that the city's population had increased seven-fold to 104,184. In 1961, the white community continued to dig in its heels with regard to more blacks moving into the city. So after Josh White moved into his apartment, he was harassed and received many threats. One night, he was fired on and bullets came into his bedroom. Josh White's welcoming was a far cry from the idyllic image of Orange County painted by reports in the *California Eagle* thirty-five years before.

MARY OWENS[1]

Mary Burch Owens moved from Los Angeles to Fullerton, in Orange County, in the early 1940s, when she was a small child. Therefore, most of her recollections of school and her neighborhood begin in the mid-1940s. She married into the famous Owens family of athletes and talks about their family, as well as her own. Her husband, Leon Owens, passed away in 1993. In his memory, Mary founded the Leon Owens Foundation to support high school and college students. She still lives in the Fullerton home she and Leon purchased in 1962. Photo, 1966.

Please tell us about your parents.

My dad—well, he was from Louisiana. His parents moved here when he was young. When I say "here," I mean California. They resided in Los Angeles. My grandparents resided there until they died. My mother, Jessie, was born in Alabama. My grandmother decided she wanted to come to California. She had a son, and his name was Neff Cox. He had his family here in Fullerton, and he was working in Brea. So he told her he would give her train fare and she can come to Fullerton. So she came to Fullerton with her baby children, a son and a daughter. At that time, my grandmother knew no one here except her son's family.

So my grandmother moved with my mother, who was a baby, and my uncle, who was a baby. Those were her last two children. It was a large family. In fact, when my mother was born, she had sisters and brothers who already had families. But, see, my grandmother kept having kids. These were to be the last two, from what I understand.

Where did your family come to live? Was it in Fullerton?

The first thing they did was they came straight to Fullerton, just like he [Neff Cox] told them to. He met them at the station. He was living on Truslow—he had

[1] Oral History 3288. Interview date: July 14, 2004, conducted in Mary Owens's home in Fullerton, California. Interviewer: Robert Johnson.

started his family—and they moved right across the street. I'm not sure how it was financed, but they bought the home there and later built another home for my uncle and his family. His name is James Wesley Cox, but he was the baby, so they called him Babe.

Then my mom lived with her sister, who lived on Harvard. Then she got a house on the corner of Harvard and Truslow, which was a very large home at that time, for us. That's where we started living in Fullerton, and like I say, I can remember from about two to three years old, when we started living there.

I had my uncle Neff that lived here, I had my uncle Theo who lived here. My Uncle Babe, who was the baby that came with my grandmother, lived here. We had, at various times, different people. My aunt, who had moved to Chicago from Alabama, came and resided in Fullerton. Her home was right next door to my grandmother's, and it was much larger than my grandmother's house.

And she was on your mother's side?

Yes. She married a Filipino. Her name was Torion. My uncle, he worked for the cannery down in San Pedro and he'd bring back fish, and he would sun dry fish. That was the first time I'd ever had it, and it was the best fish. He had these high poles, and he put a screen box up there, and it would just dry. He'd leave it out there for several days. It was like—we eat beef jerky now. Well, we had that fish jerky that he would prepare for us, and we really enjoyed it.

So, tell me about your neighborhood growing up.

My neighborhood growing up was fantastic. We all went to Maple School, which was just a beautiful school at the time. The street was Maple Avenue, and it was lined with maple trees. We couldn't wait till the fall to see the colors that changed with the maples. Then there were leaves all out in the street, and we'd be playing in the leaves. Now, across the street from us the Owens family lived.

My cousins, who were Coxes, lived down in the middle of the block. Across the street, my grandmother lived, and her daughter lived. My grandma had had a stroke, so my aunt moved from Los Angeles to take care of her, and she had a son who also went to Maple. Then my Uncle Babe, who came with my grandmother to California, lived in the new house that they had built in the back. He had two daughters and they now live over on Pine Street. My uncle died some years ago, but his wife, who is now eighty-one or eighty-two, still lives there, and both of her children live there.

There were other black families.

There was the Morris family, Walter Morris. He's the third house from me. We are neighbors now, but he used to live on Truslow. He's just a tremendous guy, nice family, and one of my schoolmates at Maple.

Did you play sports and games and all in the street, or at the park?

Naturally, we played in the streets. We played kickball, and we played tag. There weren't a lot of cars when we grew up. Maybe you'd see three cars parked on the street, and that was about it. Everybody always either went on the train, or we had taxicabs in Fullerton at the time, and they would just come and pick up people who had to go to work. It was a safe place to be for the kids, for all of us. We really enjoyed it. And of course, the park at Maple School was a wonderful place. We played all kind of ball: football, basketball. And, of course, we had to play tetherball. That was so much fun.

The teachers were just great. When you were in class, everybody was on their best behavior because they would report you. They would call your parents or send a note home by one of your siblings, because they didn't want you to tear up the note. The parents would come. They were very serious about education, so we didn't get into too much trouble. We had different principals coming in. They always seemed to fit in with Maple School. It was a wonderful experience at Maple.

Was there a pool in town?

During the summer it was great, because the high school opened the plunge to the whole community. We had to get our money from our moms and dads. It was very minimal, the amount of money that we had to pay. And if you came and you said, "Well, I want to come here but I don't have any money today." "There's a towel. Go jump in the plunge." During the summer, we lived there. We really enjoyed it.

Did you go downtown?

We were downtown at least on the weekends, because that's when we went to the movies. There was the Wilshire Theater and the Fox Theater. On Saturdays, we went to the Wilshire Theater. [We] just had a fantastic time there. We got money, and it was like a quarter from your parents to go to the show. What was left over, you could buy candy, or you could buy a drink. I mean, all for a quarter. Then on Sundays, we would go to the Fox. Oh, it was a beautiful place to be, and it always had the latest movies. The difference when we would go on Saturdays at the Wilshire, it was always cowboy pictures that we loved. We'd go to the Fox, we'd see musicals and we'd see dramas, and we'd get scared and everything. It was a lot of fun.

You didn't have to sit in the balcony or that kind of thing?

No. In fact, we loved it downstairs. All of us. I mean, the kids, no matter what schools they were coming from. You get to know everybody by going to the park. Amerige Park, or sometimes we'd go to Wilshire and play, because it wasn't fenced in or anything. It was open. So we got to meet people from all over, and we'd just go and have fun.

So in Fullerton, are you saying that there really weren't any places that black kids couldn't go to?

As far as school and playing with your friends, no problem. The problem with Fullerton was housing. That was the problem.

Finding housing outside of this area.

Exactly. That was a real problem.

So, it was a good place to be as a teenager.

Well, I lived here until after junior high school. After junior high we moved to Los Angeles. I went to a private school. That's why we moved. My dad wanted me to go to a Christian school. It was just marvelous. It was so different from what I had been accustomed to.

The young man that lived across the street from me in Fullerton, he was older than I. He was in the navy. When he came home, he was asking about where did we move, my sisters and myself. So he came to visit us. We just talked. We had so much in common. I asked him all about his family, about Al, and about what's David doing now, and his sister Laurence. So I started seeing my husband-to-be; he'd come by maybe once every other week.

Had you known him, though, in the neighborhood?

He was one of the older ones. I never played with him because he was older, but he was real friendly. He delivered papers every Sunday to us. He had a little wagon, and he'd go all through Fullerton with the Sunday papers. He was just a real good friend. My mom says, "You know, I really like Leon, but I think he's getting serious about you." I said, "Serious? We just go to football games and afterwards out to eat or something." That was about it. He'd call maybe once during the week to see if there was any activity I wanted to do, if I wanted to go to Knott's Berry Farm, or anything. I'd tell him, "That sounds like fun."

Then after that—this was maybe six or seven months later. It was Christmas, and he came with gifts for my mom and my sisters. He was very kind, and he gave me—he said, "I have something special," and he had a ring. I said, "Oh, I can't take this." I showed my mom, "Mom, isn't this beautiful?" She said, "Oh, he wants to give you a ring." I said, "Oh." I had no intention of getting married. At that time I was going to Los Angeles City College. It was just like a new atmosphere for me, just going from a private school to a public school. And being free.

Probably the best thing for me in life was the fact that my dad said, "I want to put you in private school. I think you'll enjoy it." That's because I loved going to church. I went to the Foursquare Church right on Amerige and Lawrence, here in Fullerton.

Oh, you went to the Foursquare Church.

Oh, my, yes. In Fullerton, when we were little kids, we always went to the Foursquare Church. I mean, everybody went to church when you were little. When we were growing up you had to go to church. All of us, we'd go to church on Sunday mornings and have a good time. Mexicans went, blacks went, and we just went to the Foursquare Church because we enjoyed it.

Did the Owens family go, too, to the Foursquare Church?

Oh, the kids. Oh, yeah. Laurence and Sonny and Al, all of them. Sister Tepple was the pastor, and she lived right across the street. It was just an amazing place to go to on Sundays. And we couldn't wait. We would work in our workbooks, and when we came on Sunday, we had everything filled out. She'd go through them, she'd check them, and give us an assignment for the next week. We'd have programs on Thursday night. We would go, and maybe we'd sing, or just listen to a message or something. We really enjoyed the Foursquare Church.

When you went to elementary school, when it came to eating lunch, do you remember who you sat and ate with?

We got to eat twice a week in the cafeteria, but usually we would go home. So what would happen, my mom would go to work in the afternoon. She'd have lunch and everything ready for us and send us back to school, and then she'd call the cab and she'd go to work. She worked for the Jewett family. They did a lot of development of homes, because it was a lot of orange trees and everything out here, and they did a lot of building. We had our lunch, and we'd go back and play till the bell rang.

With whomever you're sitting next to, in other words.

And whoever your friends were. There were just a few of the black kids. At that time, we had a *bracero* program and we had a lot of Hispanics who would come into the area. But they would leave; they'd come to school part of the time and then they'd go back to Mexico. It's not that way anymore. Everybody stays here now. Then we had, just down the street, black people, white people, Mexicans, like that.

I don't even remember being segregated in Fullerton, except when you got older. It was different then. But when you were in grade school and junior high school, there was no problem. Not at all, from what I can understand, because my uncle graduated from Fullerton High School, and he never had a problem. He said you just fit in with everybody. Well, it was different then. Everybody tried to be polite to each other.

Did your family also go to church?

That's interesting, because my grandmother was super religious. I mean, she loved the Lord. Relatives would come from L.A., from Long Beach, from all over, and out in San Bernardino. There'd always be something on the weekend happening at my grandma's house; and my aunts were that way too. They loved church. They would have dinner and then Sundays were real special, because they would have services for my grandma. My grandma was paralyzed, and she was either in a wheelchair or she was in bed. My aunts went to the Foursquare Church and later they started going to Los Angeles to the larger churches there.

But the afternoons were for my grandma. Like I said, her brothers would come. She had cousins that moved from Alabama to Los Angeles too. My grandmother had plenty of company on the weekends, but she was quite a bit by herself during the week. We'd go over after school and make sure she was okay. My mom always said, "Go see about your grandmother." Grandma was wonderful. She'd sing to us. My uncle would come with his autoharp. My other aunt would play the piano and we'd start singing. Sundays were wonderful.

Tell me about your husband's family. The Owens family is famous because of athletics. I think the oldest brother was named Jewell.[2]

Jewell was really an outstanding ballplayer. Now, that's the one that I can say maybe—when you asked me a question about not being accepted as a black person. Everything went fine in high school. Then he started playing semi-pro ball. We'd go all over with him. He'd be down in San Diego. He'd be all over the place. But he never got to rise to the level that he should have. He always said it was because he was black. But I think what he did was open the way for the younger ones. It was very hard for him.

Now, you said your husband, Leon, was in the service.

He was in the navy. It was in the fifties. We'd go down to see him, and at that time, we did it because we were coerced by his family to see him. He came back home. He started working for the Bridgfords [of Bridgford Foods]. He'd be making deliveries for them, and sometimes on his way back from deliveries, he'd stop by when we were living in Long Beach, just to say hi and how are you doing.

We started seeing each other more and more. Leon was a very likable guy, all kinds of friends. And the Bridgfords really liked him, especially Mr. Bridgford. In fact, after we got married—he'd see Leon all day, right? But on Fridays, he would always call him. He just wanted to make sure he got home okay, is everything all right, and I'll see you Monday. Mr. Bridgford was a good guy. And Leon really liked him. He worked for him until Leon died in 1993. As a result of that, we had a huge, huge funeral that was unbelievable. The people were wonderful. After all this had happened, a friend of mine—her name is Carol Singleton, she lives in Santa Ana now—she said, "Mary, you gotta do something in memory of Leon." So we did. We started a foundation. Wonderful Dick Ackerman helped me with just everything. No charges, everything pro bono. I'll never forget that.

Was Leon the first of the Owens brothers to pass away?

Leon was the second. Jewell, the one that I told you about that was just a tremendous athlete, died early. He was in his thirties when he died. But Leon was—that was something. His brother had been ill for some time. He was in the hospital for a long time. But with Leon it was so sudden, and it was such a shock.

---

[2] The Owens boys all played sports at Fullerton High School. Jewell, the oldest, was a senior in 1950; Marvin, the second youngest, was a senior in 1968; and Jessie, the youngest, ran the distances in track that same year.

How about other brothers?

David [Sonny] is the one that lives two blocks over from me. Just a tremendous athlete. He was a hurdler at Fullerton High School. I know he was a state record holder. And he really enjoyed what he was doing. He went into the service and came home and married a very nice young lady from Haiti, just super. He's been very helpful, just very helpful to the family, to my family and to the foundation. Who was the next one?

Oh, Alfred. (laughs) Alfred is the kind of guy he was in high school. He's still that way. He lives here in Fullerton. He is the gang leader. Everybody's at his home. They love downtown Fullerton. You'll see them anywhere there with his group. Al is just fantastic with people. He's got his friends from grade school all the way up (laughs). Everybody knows Al, and everybody loves Al. He's a great guy.

Somebody wrote that he played for the White Sox.

He went down to Florida, and his dad was so thrilled. He wanted him to be a baseball player. This guy was just a natural born athlete, just great. His picture was in the local paper and everything that he had gone to Florida, and it wasn't long and Al was back home. He says, "I want to play ball, but I can't stand Florida." He was accustomed to the friends that he hung out with here. He said, "I don't like it. It's segregated. I can't stand it." His dad was terribly upset. The scouts were really high on him, but he said, "Not for me." If he could have just jumped into the majors. At that time, there were a lot of black athletes really sacrificing themselves, because it was very segregated.

Then there was Brig. He must have been a pretty smart guy, because of all the things that he's done as an attorney.

Brig was always a determined guy. He was great at Fullerton High School, at Fullerton College. Brig was just a very likable, very talented guy. He graduated from Fullerton College, and he went to the University of Cincinnati and he met great people there. He met his wife there. Patty came from a very nice family. In fact, Patty and Brig got married before he left to go to Texas, because he was drafted by the Dallas Cowboys. That was so great for us.

They would play [in pre-season training] at California Lutheran [in Thousand Oaks, Ventura County] and we'd take a trip out there to see him. We'd eat with them and watch them when they'd go through all their little routines. My kids were little then. Karen, I guess, must have been about three or four, and Darren maybe was in second grade or so. They loved going because Tony Dorsett was out there. Anybody that they had seen on TV, on the Cowboys, were so pleasant. They'd come over and they'd start talking. They'd chase the kids around.

So you had Darren and Karen and—

Sharen. We would just pack up the car, and we'd spend the day there, at California Lutheran. When he [Brig] was sent to Washington, D.C., we didn't see him much.

He'd come back home though, he'd always come home. Little did we know that he'd end up in the top seventy of the greatest Redskins. I mean, God, this is fantastic. When I saw that, I called him. I said, "Brig!" He said, "You saw it in the paper?" I said, "Yes." He said, "I knew you guys would be calling."

He had other responsibilities. Was he a players' representative?[3]

Yeah. He was a player rep. He's the type of guy who really likes being involved. And he's helped so many of the kids go to college. He's just the kind of guy you're proud of. I know his dad was really proud, and his mom, too.

And his parents, what were their names?

Alfred Owens, Senior, and then Roxy Lee Owens. Mom to everybody. They're Texans. They came here because their dad had found work here. Roxy Lee was probably the most loved. She cooked every weekend. No matter who came to her home, you were welcome. On Sundays, they'd sit on the fence, out from the sidewalk to the house, just sitting and talking and waiting for dinner. She never felt like she was overworked or anything. She'd have everything for them, and they'd better come. She was a wonderful lady.

She started dinner about two o'clock every single day, because she cooked everything from scratch. Everything was ready for when her husband came in. She was a marvelous woman. On the weekends, relatives would come from L.A., from Wilmington, from all over. Because they all came from Texas. It was a good experience.

Well, after Brig Owens was Teddy Owens.

Oh, Ted was wonderful. He loves working with kids. He really enjoyed his job working for Fullerton, and he enjoys his job now. He's got three children. One was outstanding playing softball here in Fullerton. She got a scholarship to Cal State Bakersfield. He was very proud of her. She's a super young lady. He has a wonderful wife.

Did all of the brothers and sisters marry black people?

Everyone. That's very interesting that you asked that question, because they were very popular in high school in dating, so when they were dating, it was different.

They felt free enough in the 1950s to have interracial dating?

They had friends, uh-huh. They were always over at the Owens home, too, and always felt welcome. When I say friends: male, female, all. Mexican, white, more blacks, Filipinos. Whatever they were, they would be there. One sister dated a Caucasian guy for quite a while. A real nice guy, and we really liked him. They made just a great couple. A nice family, and his family liked Shirley, and our family liked Michael.

---

[3] Brig Owens was the Redskins players' representative for seven years and later became the number two man in the National Football League Players Association.

There's Marv Owens. He played for the Cardinals and the Vikings.

Great, great athlete and great personality. He's probably one of the nicest people you'll ever meet. I say that about every one of them. (both laugh) Their mom did a great job teaching them how to behave. They had to mind their mom, because when they were little, if they didn't mind their mom, she'd get the strap out and that was all. That would just bring them to know that she wasn't going to play. So they really respected her. Marvin was just a lovable, smart guy. His son just graduated at the university. His daughter graduated. I think she wants to go into the movie business. Anyway, she's doing post-grad work at USC [University of Southern California] right now. They both went to schools in the South.

Then there's one more brother. His name is Jesse.

He was very atypical of the Owens boys, very much so. He used to come over. He loved music. He loved people. But he didn't care for sports. I mean, he had no inclination. (laughs)

He became an attorney. A brother said, "Oh, he was really smart."

Jesse was smart. Jesse's been dead for some time now. Got sick. My daughter would go by to see Jesse. He had recuperated, we thought, from his illness, and she'd always go check on Jesse. She called us, and she said that he had died, and we could not believe it. It was terrible for the whole family. But to lose the baby is very, very difficult.

He was younger than his sisters. Now, are there three sisters?

Laurence. She was a wonderful—she was a teacher here in Fullerton. She would teach elementary school. I know she was at Acacia, and she was here at Maple. She was ill and we lost Laurence.

Shirley has a super family. She has three beautiful daughters. She's just involved with so many things. She's really into school activities, anything that she can do to help her girls. Her husband's a fantastic dad. She made a great choice. (laughs) Shirley, she's a good mom, and she's a good sister-in-law.

Dorothy works for Fullerton College. She's in charge of purchasing there for the Fullerton district. She's got tremendous kids also. Her daughter went to Howard. Her son, I think, went to Chico State. She's been with the school district, oh, gosh, most of her adult life. She has a great position and a lot of responsibility. Her husband works for the school district also. Rufus Whitehurst. He's a nice guy, very supportive.

How were they in terms of athletics?

I think they were good in what they did, but they didn't have the aspiration that their brothers had to really push on and go into sports the way that *they* did. They did it in a way that (chuckles)—they had all the zeal, and they were determined. Yeah, they were good athletes, but they weren't—

There weren't that many opportunities for girls.

Uh-huh, the way it was for them. They were, and they still are, tremendous young ladies.

You married Leon. What year was that?

In 1960. I lived in Long Beach, and then we moved here in '62. After I got married we were always in Fullerton, every weekend. Leon was here every single day, in Fullerton. And he'd always go see his mom. He was working here, so he was here every single day. And weekends he wanted to be here. It was just that kind of a thing. Everybody came to their mom's house on the weekend.

Where did you first live when you got married?

In Long Beach. That's where my mom was. We lived there for two years. We were looking for places. The only place we ever looked for a home was Fullerton. We *had* to live in Fullerton. That's how Leon thought. He worked here, his family was here, and he wanted to live here. At first, we had gone to look at apartments, and they would not rent to us. Leon said, "You know, we're going to have to buy a house here." That's what happened. We bought a house, this house.

I can say that the best thing that we did was to move to Fullerton. Leon was fine. He made good decisions about people and situations, and he was very sensitive to the kids, and very demanding of them, too. Very demanding. When Darren played sports in high school, he lettered for four years. He played all sports like his dad: basketball and baseball and football. He just loved it. Like I said, that was when he came home and said, "Dad, look what I have." "Oh, I knew you'd get this. It's a talent. You're an Owens. You have the talent. And you're my son." My son has done well. He lives in New Mexico.

Are all three of the children married?

My daughters are not married, have no desire to marry. Karen is the elder daughter, and she works for Horizon Media in Los Angeles, which is a fantastic job for her. She travels a lot. She's just into entertainment because of her job. Anywhere I want to go, she'll take me. Sometimes she'll surprise me and say, "Mom. I've got to be in Europe next month. I'm taking you with me." Things like that.

Sharen works for the District Attorney's office here in Orange County. She does her job, she enjoys her job. She's very good. She's always been very studious. She did a double major at USC, and she did everything within the parameters of time. That was just probably the best place we could put her, because she got to be with so many different people and do things that she really enjoyed doing. And she loves USC.

The president of USC wanted to support your family.

Oh, he was marvelous. We were going into this conference, and he was standing there just greeting everybody. He wanted to know, "Do you have a son or daughter here?" I said, "We have two daughters here." And he said, "*You* have two daughters here?" My husband kind of looked at me and smiled. He says, "Yes." He was really amazed and sort of taken aback. That's when he offered us—if we needed any help from him, the university will just pitch in and make sure—"You've got two kids here? They're going to graduate." Leon being the man that he is, said, "No, we've got it all under control. We've been planning this for years." He's like that. He looks into the future. We started getting letters from the president telling us that he was very proud of us and he said, "But don't hesitate if you need us to help you." It worked out well. My daughter started out with a great job and has done well. We went to all the SC games.

Tell me about Penny Owens. She worked for Fair Housing.

There's nothing like her, nobody. Any little thing that she didn't like, she would vocalize it. I mean, vehemently she would vocalize.

And this is Leon's aunt, right?

Yeah. It's his dad's sister. Penny Owens. Penny didn't have children, but she loved her "grands," as she called them. She says, "Those are my grands." I said, "Okay." And from the time I can remember, because they lived across the street from us, she never forgot them. They had new pistols and holsters, or a bow and arrow, whatever was going on then. She would buy them Roy Rogers, Gene Autry, anything. She'd buy them boots. When Christmas came, or a birthday came, boy, she was there with the presents. And she was free with her money. She worked hard, but she loved her nieces and nephews, and she shared with them. She was wonderful.

She was the first one on our block that had a TV set, small TV set, and she would let us come over and watch wrestling. We used to love watching wrestling and roller derby. I mean, we just ate it up. Then she said, "You guys have to go. I've gotta go to work in the morning." "Oh, it's Saturday. Can't we stay? We know you're not going to work." She said, "Well, if it's Saturday, then I'm going to church in the morning." And she would. She'd get up early and go in to Los Angeles to church. She's the most giving person I've ever seen.

Rev. [James] Carrington said she talked to her pastor in Los Angeles and said, "We need a Baptist church in Orange County."[4]

The thing about that is that Penny would do anything to have a church. On Saturdays she'd be out at the park selling barbecues. She'd get out there and she'd start cooking, and people would stop by. She'd say, "Well, what do you stop by and say hi for. You better buy something." You know how Penny was, very forceful.

She said, "This is going to a good cause." People said, "Okay. I'll get this from you and I'll come back and get some more." And they would. They'd come back and say, "Oh, give me two more of those plates. That was good barbecue." She'd do chicken and she'd do ribs. Penny was marvelous. All the police knew her, because sometimes they'd have to go over to her house and kind of calm her

[4] The Rev. Carrington's interview is the final interview in this chapter.

down. But guess what, Penny always loved what she did, and she did change her lifestyle. She got herself under control. I really miss her.

I know, with regard to Fair Housing, she filed some lawsuits because of discrimination. Was she also on the back of the police force, too?

I have an uncle who was very much like Penny—very forceful, determined to get his way, and he'd want it resolved. It was so funny; someone had taken something from my mom, and she told him. He said, "What? Well, you're going to get it back. I'm going to go down to the police department, and I'm going to tell them what happened, and I think I know who did it and they better bring it back." So he goes down to the police department and immediately got results.

That's here in Fullerton. Some of the police he was very friendly with, and he respected them; others he didn't respect. Penny, she had problems because she liked to drink on the weekends, and she'd get noisy and a little out of hand. But like I say, that didn't last forever. She just changed her lifestyle and just was somebody I loved. I always loved her because she was good to the neighborhood kids—I mean, *all* the neighborhood kids. If she had something, if it was just fruit, "You come over to my house. I've got something for you." And that's what it would be. She'll just say "We're going to make hamburgers today." And she'd start cooking. She was good for the neighborhood.

Did you or anybody in the family get involved politically?

The only thing that really got me involved was the closing of the [Maple] school in the sixties. That was devastating to the area. That was the only time that we really took time to go to meetings, go down to the district office, really get involved with the superintendent, and let them know exactly what our feelings were about closing the school. I realize now that we were right on target. It really didn't help. I'm not going to say it didn't help anybody. It may have helped some, but not the majority.

And the issue was integration, so therefore we're going to close the school. Then all those students would go to the other schools. And then they would be integrated.

The kids were getting a good education. They mixed well. But they closed down the school. Busing here and there. Oh, it's amazing. It is just amazing how much money they spent on this particular plan, and then come back.

Was it popular with the community?

When you say "popular," getting up early, getting the kids on the bus. If they miss the bus, then what? It was foolishness. But for some kids, it wasn't, because actually they did make good friends, and they did see another side of Fullerton, rather than just the Maple area. So I can't say it was 100 percent bad because it wasn't. They made friends, and my kids still have friends.

Maybe you have a favorite story about living here.

Oh, gosh. I couldn't say enough about people that I live around. I've got marvelous neighbors, and most of them have been the same neighbors since I moved here. A few houses go up for sale, and as soon as they do, somebody's relative buys them. They tell them, "Okay, this house is available. Come move here." We've got all kind of neighbors here, and we enjoy each other. It's our little community.

Are you glad you stayed in Orange County?

You know what? I thank God every day for this place. I know the stereotypes for Orange County. When we go visit relatives, "Oh, you're still in Orange County? Oh! That place is so racist." But what happens? Those same people move to Orange County, get good jobs, find churches that they like, and they say, "It's not as bad as I thought. I kind of like it here." Then what do you know, in a few more years, it's, "Oh, I wouldn't go back to L.A." Orange County is not perfect, but it's a great place to live.

Well, thank you very much, Mary Owens. This was a wonderful interview.

WARREN BUSSEY[1]

Warren Bussey describes in detail what it was like growing up in a very small Texas town. After serving in World War II, he came to Fullerton, in north Orange County, where he and a friend started a maintenance business. His wife, Maime Ebla, worked with him and also worked as a maid. They also owned a café, saved their money, and bought property. His wife has passed away, but Mr. Bussey still lives in Santa Ana. Photo, 1962.

Can you describe what it was like living in Texas?

There's a little place, which they call Bobo, out in the country, about four miles from Tenaha, Texas. I tell everybody that I'm from Tenaha, but really I'm from Bobo. We got our mail out on a rock. I was born there in 1923, brought up, raised up, and went to school in Bobo.

Growing up, how many siblings did you have?

Eight boys and four girls and we were all growing up together there in Bobo, Texas. And my father passed in '32. My oldest brother had left home; I guess I must have been about eighteen, so I was the man of the house there. So I had to do all the providing and everything for my momma and my baby brothers and sisters. Right after he passed away, momma went down to the social worker and they asked her how old a boy did she have. She said, "I have one eighteen years old." "Well, we can give him a job on the WPA [Works Progress Administration] and try to help you out." So I worked on the WPA for about two years and then the WPA work played out. Then I went to work at Tenaha at the Caught Cotton Compress and that was only done in the fall. Then after the compress closed down, I left Bobo and went to Beaumont, Texas, and I got a job at a ladies' dress shop and I worked there for better than two years.

---

[1] Oral History 3878. Interview date: June 22, 2007, at Willard Allen Kimbrough Masonic Lodge # 91, in Santa Ana California. Interviewer: Monte Starks.

What were your father's and mother's name?

My father was named Sam Milton Bussey. My mother was named Lonnie Bussey. My father married her when she was only sixteen years old and he was about twenty-nine years old. All their lives, that's all they done, worked on the farm. We had our own farm, our own place; we weren't sharecropping or whatnot.

How was the neighborhood in which you lived?

It was a nice neighborhood. I guess maybe about five hundred families in that neighborhood and everybody was real close. If your house needed covering, all of the neighborhood would get together and cover that house. The men would do the work and the ladies would all come and cook. And when anybody got sick during the farming time, they would pitch in and go and work the man's crop. And you could leave your house, leave every door wide open, and you didn't have to worry about anybody going in and taking anything. Our neighborhood was all blacks. The whites, I guess, were maybe about three miles up in their area. We and the whites got along real good. In Tenaha, we had a white-owned drug store and when I come in, "There comes my cousin, Sam." So everybody was real lovely there.

Now, how often do the Busseys get together for a family reunion?

Not too often, but every nineteenth of June the community would get together and have something. It was when my father and my uncle were there on the farm.[2]

JUNETEENTH

It wasn't until June 19, 1865, two months after Lee's surrender at Appomattox, that blacks in Texas received the news that they were freed. This became a day of celebration that continues today. This event is celebrated, not only in Texas with an official state holiday, but throughout the USA. The celebration is named "Juneteenth." Because many in the black community of Santa Ana have strong Texas roots and because of the wide popularity of this celebration, in 1994 the Orange County NAACP and the city of Santa Ana sponsored the first of the annual local Juneteenth Celebrations.

Can you tell me what style of clothes you wore back in that time?

Khakis, overalls. I put on overalls and my white starched shirt and my old brogan [ankle high] shoes shined and we really thought we were dressed up. And we didn't have many clothes, so a lot of times my momma had to put us to bed, wash our clothes, and iron them for us to go to school the next day.

Can you describe what it was like during the Great Depression?

Yes, yes, I can describe it because I know my mom was a hustler. She would go out in the field and get watermelons, cucumbers, squash, cabbage, all different kinds of veggies, peaches and pears, figs, and we would put them in a wagon, and

[2] The 19th of June is a holiday called Juneteenth, a celebration of the end of the Civil War in Texas. This is still celebrated in Santa Ana each year.

she would take them to Tenaha, to the white folks, and sell them. And she wasn't getting too much on them, but we did survive through that.

What did your brothers and sisters do to help around the house?

Well, at that time, the boys had to do the girls' work and the girls had to do the boys' work. So it was a rotating thing. My mom said, "You might grow up and get married, your wife gets sick, then you'll know how to cook and how to clean house." And she would tell the girls, "If your husband gets sick, you know how to go out and feed the hogs and feed the horses, milk the cows and get out in the woods and cut wood, all of that." So we had to do each others' chores.

And how did your father feel about that?

Oh, he went along with it, 'cause one of my sisters, Addie Dee, had to get out there and plow right beside me everyday, just like I was doing. And they had to get out there in the woods and cut wood, saw. We had a wood stove and a wood fireplace, all that. So they had to get out there and help us do that, too.

Do you recall any family members going off to fight?

I went in September 1942. I finished my basic training and I was a pretty good marksman, on rifles, so they put me out there for rifle instructor. And it was so cold, my hand and my feet froze. So when they got ready to ship out, they shipped me to Victorville, California. I stayed there until 1944. And they sent me from Victorville to Palm Springs, California, trying to get my hands and feet well. And that's where I got discharged, in '46.

After I got out, then I really wasn't able to perform or hold a job down, and I wished I had stayed in, because Uncle Sam was taking care of me then. My brother lived in Fullerton, California, so I come on in and was staying there with my brother, and then I met a guy, Charles Abernathy. He just had got out and his health was bad. Then we got together and said we were going to open up a maintenance service. That was in 1948. So part of our business was in Fullerton and part of it was in Huntington Beach. He had the car, but I didn't. So he said, "Well, I'll take the work down by the beach and you take the work in Fullerton." I said, "Well, I don't have no other choice because you have the car, but I can walk back and forth to the work here in Fullerton." I told him, "That's a deal."

What was the name of your business?

Bussey Maintenance. There was a Studebaker dealer in Fullerton. I went there and talked to the man about doing his maintenance work, so he gave me the job. He had an old 1939 Studebaker, four-door, so he said, "That old Studebaker out there, if you can get it to going, take that and use that until you'll be able to get your truck." I drove to work in it every day. He gave it to me for free. And on Sundays I wanted to get up and go riding around in it and every time it would break down on me, but all during the week, every week, it would take me back and forth to work.

And I used that old car until 1951. Then I bought me a new, brand new, Champion Studebaker, from him.

And then I met a little ol' girl named Maime Ebla and then she and I, we got married. I met her in '50. We didn't get married until '51. We had a very, very good life. I guess with being single so long I had some maybe evil ways (chuckle), but she put up with me. And we never did separate. And she worked right along with me. And in '52, I bought me a brand new van, a Chevy van, and we were still living [on Truslow] in Fullerton.[3] And in '53 we went to a show and when we came back, the house we were renting burnt down. We had worked and saved up a little money and we came over to Santa Ana, looked around, and we bought this house on 1450 West First Street in Santa Ana.

And then you moved to Santa Ana. Why did you choose Santa Ana?

Orange County was prejudiced, and Fullerton was more prejudiced than Santa Ana. And there were more colored living in Santa Ana than there was in Fullerton, but there were just very few. I knew practically everybody living in Fullerton or Santa Ana at that time, colored.

Going back to Fullerton in the 1950s, how would you describe the relationship with your neighbors and the community?

We [blacks] were only living in two blocks. Everybody knew each other and we got along real good. We didn't have to worry about locking no doors at that time. So we got along real good.

Were you the only African Americans living in your neighborhood?

No, there was whites and Mexicans. It was all races. Living in California at that time, it was more prejudiced than it was in Texas. I'd go to work, and after I get there, I could go all through the house, but when I go there in the morning, I had to go through the back door. This was in California. And that went on until up in the 60s, the late 60s.

And talking about work, at that time you could get seventy-five cents to a dollar an hour. That was what I could afford to pay my help and for me to make a little profit. And I guess that went on for about four or five years. My wife, she was doing maid work. She would get seventy-five cents an hour and then I was doing pretty good with my maintenance work. So she said, "Well, I'm going to ask for a dollar an hour and if I can't get that, well, I'll just quit and start helping you." So she asked for a dollar an hour. She got it. And all the rest of the women heard about it and they got mad with her because the people she was working for were liking her and they give her a dollar an hour, but the other people where the ladies were working, they went and asked the people for a dollar an hour and they refused to give it to them. My wife worked for them for so long and then we opened up a

---

[3] This was the street and area where most of the black families lived in Fullerton in the years after WWII. The Owens and Neff Cox families lived on Truslow.

café in Santa Ana on Fourth and Hesperia, right there on the corner. Jimmy's Café. That was in '55 to '60.

And what did you serve in the café?

Soul food: chitlins, corn bread, ham hock, neck bone, all that. Business was good. It was slower during the week, but on the weekend it was real good. They wasn't making too much money. So they would take their families out then to eat on the weekend.

Now, were you the only café in the neighborhood selling soul food?

No, there was another café about a half a block from where I was located. We didn't sell beer in our café, but at that other café they were serving beer. So I continued with my maintenance service until my wife was taken sick. She was sick better than two years, and then they tell me I was going to have to put her in a rest home. That was in '82. And I told her I'd give up my business and come home and take care of her. She worked hard to help me accumulate what we have. So, I felt like I could spend the rest of her days there with her, be at the house there with her. So I did. I stayed there with her until she passed away.

You were one of the original members of the Kimbrough Masonic Lodge in Santa Ana. How did you become a Mason?

Well, my father and my oldest brother were Masons in Bobo and I always wanted to know what they were doing and why I couldn't go. But I guess I was too young. And then after I moved, I met about four guys; they were going to Los Angeles. Finally, one of the men who already was a master Mason, he talked to the past master about coming down here to see if he could get a bunch of us together.

You had to have twenty-five people or more before we could have a lodge down here. And we worked on that and worked on that until we was able to get that many men who said they would join. And then they finally let us join, come and be a proud Mason. So '57, I think it was in September, we went up to St. John Number 5 in L.A. We got three degrees in one day and the next thing we did, we rented a hall on east Fourth Street [in Santa Ana], and we stayed there. It must have been about five years. And that building caught on fire next door to what we were renting and that whole block got burned down. That was between '62 and '65, somewhere near there. And then we moved from there to Bristol and Myrtle in a house.

I understand that there was a white California Masonic Lodge off of Sycamore. Did you have any relationship with them?

I didn't have any relationship with them, but I knew about it because I would do maintenance in the building right next to it. Now that was on Fifth and Sycamore. They didn't stay there too long. After they moved, one or two of the brothers visited their lodge. I think they must have had a dance or something. And at the time they did this, our brothers got in trouble for visiting, because we wasn't supposed to affiliate with them.

I'd like to ask you about when you bought this house in Santa Ana. How difficult was it for you to buy a house in 1953?

The problem wasn't here. I guess that's the reason why I bought here. But in Fullerton, I was working for a general contractor. They were building houses all in Fullerton and Villa Park and Garden Grove. And Villa Park, I want to buy one out there, but they wouldn't sell to a black out there. There were three brothers who were big contractors and after they wouldn't sell there, they told me to come to Santa Ana. He thinks I might be able to buy a house. And I came over to Santa Ana and talked to a real estate agent and they showed my wife and I this house and when they showed it to her, "Oh, yeah, I want this. I want this." And we had $2,500 we put down on the house and our house payment was $58 a month.

I was working and she was working and we doubled up, over doubled up on the house payment. And we had twenty-five years to pay for it, and in less than six years we had the house paid for. We didn't do nothing but work, go to work, go to church, and back home.

What church did you attend?

My brother was going to Second Baptist Church. I would visit him all the time at Second Baptist. But Calvary Baptist, it was small and they were trying to get started there, and I knew the pastor at that time. I decided I'd join and help him out.

You mentioned several times that your brother was out here. So how many of your family members moved to California?

I have two sisters still in L.A. and my brother that passed away, he was living in Anaheim. And I had two other brothers who came out here and lived out here for a little while. They worked at the shipyard. The other one, he got out of the service and he stayed here for a while, but they went back to Dallas, Texas, and started a trucking business.

Do you have anything else you'd like to add?

No, the only thing I'm saying is, they are no longer segregating students, but down through the years I have had real good luck. And so many different times I had so many good offers, but I always said, "If I had known and had the education, I guess I could have been a multi-millionaire." In fact, all these houses in Laguna and all that, I was working for a rich white lady and she offered to let me have all that ground down there if I just paid the tax on it. And at that time, taxes weren't nothing much, but we weren't making that kind of money so I couldn't afford it. Over here, where Disneyland is, a guy offered to let me have an orange grove there for little or nothing. Property was so cheap there then.

That was way before Disneyland opened. Disney wasn't thinking about coming in there then. And while I had a piece of property up in Perris [Riverside County], I got that for a hundred and fifty-five dollars, an acre and a quarter, and could have bought the whole of it. There was an old turkey ranch up there and could have bought the whole thing for little or nothing, but I never thought the dang thing would be worth anything. I still have it.

Then I bought a big house in Lake Elsinore, [Riverside County].[4] I think I paid twelve hundred dollars for that. And I sold that for forty-five thousand. I bought another on Third and Baker here in Santa Ana. I bought that for three thousand and I still own that. So I got two rental houses there, and so I'm getting good rent out of that.

Well, I must say you have done well for yourself.

Thank you, very kindly. But I had a good lady on my side. My wife was really good and we worked together.

---

[4] Lake Elsinore was one of the few recreation places in southern California where blacks could buy, rent, and simply visit without limitations.

RALPH and NATALIE KENNEDY[1]

Ralph and Natalie Kennedy grew up in New England. They are both white. Ralph graduated from the US Naval Academy and went on active duty in 1947. That same year, he and Natalie were married. In 1950, he was called back in the navy during the Korean War. In 1952, while Ralph was still in the navy, the couple came to Fullerton to live. Ralph worked at North American Aviation, was campus minister at Cal State Fullerton, worked for the Orange County Fair Housing Council, and was editor of the Fullerton Observer *newspaper. Ralph is deceased and Natalie, having retired from teaching, still lives in Fullerton. Photo, 1977.*

Ralph, how did you first get involved in social issues?

Ralph: I would say it was in the early sixties, when I became associated with the Presbyterian Church here in Fullerton. And then at a meeting of the National Presbyterian Church, I became heavily involved and aware of social issues that were of importance across the country.

Natalie: I think that I was always aware on a person-to-person level and not really very active in any large movement. But in little things, like in school, when they wanted to do something that I didn't like or when I was PTA [Parent Teacher Association] president, I made some statements about God in the salute to the flag.

That got me into a little trouble, and I became suddenly more active for a while. They checked Ralph's standing at North American Rockwell because they were saying that I was a Communist. There was a whole big movement with the John Birch Society, and they looked into this, and they called all our friends and

[1] Oral History 3459. Approximate interview date: Fall 1997, at an office of the Orange County Human Relations Commission, in Santa Ana, California. Interviewers: Eli Reyna and Rusty Kennedy (the son of Ralph and Natalie Kennedy).

the minister and the city and everybody. They went to North American Rockwell and got a lawyer and checked into Ralph's background, because he had a special—

Ralph: A top secret clearance. Fortunately, we had such a good reputation here in Fullerton that nothing came of all of this.

Natalie: We got out of that. But that's more the level where I was involved. Also, when Ralph got something going, everybody that was around us got involved in picketing and having people on our street sign petitions, things like that. I also took people in to the FEPC [Fair Employment Practices Commission] and stuff like that, for black people who were trying to get into housing.

Ralph: The open housing petition was one of the first manifestations of civil rights activities that we were both involved in. This occurred back during the civil rights revolution throughout the country, and there was a lot of discrimination going on in housing in this area. There were not many black people in Fullerton, not many people of any color in Fullerton. It was a pretty lily-white community. Yet, suddenly people were becoming aware of this as a potential problem, because in the East it was so important because of the extreme oppression and everything that black people faced.

In this area, we decided that one way to show that we were a community which was not like that was an open-housing petition. We went around to the different churches and tried to get them involved. The concept was for people to sign these open-housing petitions, and then the sum of all of their names would appear under the petition as a full page thing in the local *Daily News Tribune*. We finally were able to pull that off. All I remember is there were hundreds of people who signed it, enough to fill the page.

Natalie: I remember a smaller one that we did on our own block when there was a Chinese family trying to move in about six houses from us. There was a deed restriction that we didn't even know enough about to notice when we signed in there that made it so minorities would not be welcome.[2] I'm not sure how it said it. So we got a petition going all around our neighborhood. Everybody signed it, and they got in. That was very early. That was in the fifties.

Ralph: The state passed the Rumford Fair Housing Act [in November 1963], which made it illegal to discriminate in the area of housing against ethnic minorities or races. The large coalition of banks and property owners and realtors throughout California got an initiative on the ballot, which was Proposition 14. It was designed to repeal the Rumford Fair Housing Act, which had been in operation for about a year and also to make it illegal—and this was their big mistake—to make it illegal for such an act to ever be enacted again. Unfortunately, even after all of the work that we did in the community, debating people all over the place, in Orange County,

---

[2] These deed restrictions were not enforceable after 1948 because of the US Supreme Court decision in 1948's *Shelly v. Kramer*, and in 1952's *Barrows v. Jackson*, but they remained on the deeds. The deeds generally included a phrase to the effect that the property can only be sold to people of the Caucasian race.

Proposition 14 passed three to one, and statewide two to one. But they had this thing saying the legislature's hands were tied even if they wanted to pass such an act in the future. That's what made it unconstitutional, so it was thrown out. That was the beginning, by the way, of the whole fair housing ethic throughout the state. Here in Fullerton, we were one of the first in Orange County to have a fair housing council, the Fullerton Fair Housing Council. Later on, that became a part of the Orange County Fair Housing Council.[3]

We used to try to help families of ethnic minorities, mostly African American families, find housing in the area. One of the early people that we tried to help was the family of Jim and Ann Hillman. We showed them around and finally were successful in helping them find a place in the city of Orange. Later, Jim became the chair of the Orange County Fair Housing Council and he remained a leader in that effort until he finally moved out of the area.

Natalie: When Ann and Jim Hillman were looking for housing in Orange County, they came up against all kinds of discrimination. Ralph and I went house hunting with them. They finally found one in Orange, and they moved into that house. The first night, somebody came up and threw eggs and potatoes at their house. Sometimes when they'd go away people would write on their door like, "Negro go home." A few times I think they even had a cross put on the porch, but I don't think it was burned, just stuck there. That wore itself out in the first couple of months, I think. After that, I don't think they had any problems. They basically were happy in Orange County.

Ralph: The Fair Housing Council then, which Jim was one of the early leaders, grew and expanded and became more effective throughout the county, working mostly in the area that he had originally been helped in, trying to help people find housing. And prove, in some cases, when they were being discriminated against, that such discrimination had taken place, and they could sue them. After years of proceeding in that way and hundreds of thousands of dollars won in suits, the word got around to the landlords and the apartment owners and they became more clever, more subtle in the way they would discriminate.

One of the more insidious effects of that was that they got the idea that maybe we can't overtly refuse to rent to somebody or refuse to sell to somebody, but we can make sure that they don't build any housing in Orange County that's affordable to relatively poor people, many of whom are going to be ethnic minorities. So in this indirect manner, the society in general was able to continue this discriminatory effect. However, again there were efforts in the county, citizen efforts that were aimed at creating affordable housing throughout the county.

I actually was one of the starters of the Fullerton Fair Housing Council, and years later, after I graduated from USC [University of Southern California] with a

[3] The Fullerton Fair Housing Council may have preceded the county-wide Orange County Fair Housing Council, which was formed soon after Proposition 14 passed in November 1964. The first chair of the OC Council was Richard Petherbridge, a white attorney, who also worked with ACLU and had helped lead the county fight against Proposition 14. Petherbridge, like Ralph Kennedy, was involved with justice issues in both the black community and with farm workers. See the Marjorie Petherbridge Oral History 3030.

Ph.D in urban studies, I went to work for the Orange County Fair Housing Council as an affordable housing specialist. We developed in the county—with some other people from the Human Relations Commission, League of Women Voters, the ACLU, and other groups throughout the county—a housing coalition. We also helped to found an Orange County Community Housing Corporation, with Allen Baldwin as our first executive director. Now, some fifteen or twenty years later, he's still holding forth, and the Community Housing Corporation has built hundreds of units spread throughout the county, which are for mostly larger families, and all totally affordable forever.

Natalie: I think added to that it might be worth mentioning that in the early years of fair housing, they spent a lot of time with people who had been discriminated against. We would send one person in. I used to do that a lot. You'd go in and see if the apartment was open. Then you'd go out and send in the black person, and they would tell them that the house was not available, that it was already rented. Then we'd go in together, and I'd say that we had come because we wanted to get this housing for this person. Once they wouldn't do it, we would take the person in to the FEPC in L.A., and they would make an application and they [the FEPC] would handle it. Several cases we won. One of the problems we had, for instance, a black person that lived with us, when I took him in—he wanted to get an apartment early on—he went through the beginning of the stuff, and then he couldn't hold out. It was a big pain in the neck. So a lot of the black people who were involved in that didn't want to spend all their life going in and out of this kind of a problem.

Ralph: Later, the Fair Housing Council made it possible to do that all right here in Orange County. One of the interesting things we did with the Fair Housing Council at that time is they decided it would be great to have some kind of a training film for all of our, as we call them, checkers. Those would be the people that would go with the African American or ethnic minority family to try to rent an apartment. Since I was the only old white guy working for the Fair Housing Council, I got the part of the landlord, and I had to look real ugly and mean. The people there always kidded me about that.

The church we were involved in happened to be the Presbyterian Church. They had established an organization called PIC, Presbyterian Interracial Council. It was made up of laymen and ministers, clergy from all around the greater Los Angeles area. The first president of that was a black minister by the name of Jim Jones, who had a church there in South Central L.A. The second president was myself. So I did a lot of work with PIC in this area. One of the efforts we supported was not only the effort on housing discrimination and school discrimination, but also the farm worker movement.

Home Visit was another one of the early efforts here in Orange County. The idea of the home visit was to try to get a lot of people of different ethnic and religious and racial backgrounds to sign up willing to come to a host's home. The person who was getting the names of all the people willing to participate would divide all the names up and make sure there was some African American representation, some Latino, some Jewish, some Catholic, et cetera. Then they would come into the home, and the host would have a discussion planned and get them involved in knowing and meeting each other.

Natalie: I went to a meeting at Maple School, which is located in the southern part of Fullerton. There were mostly Mexican American students who were going to that school, but there were a few black students, too. Dr. [Russell] Parks, who was the superintendent of schools in Fullerton at the time, a year before the big movement to have everything integrated, got the idea that we should try to do something creative in Fullerton. I went to this meeting, and they discussed how to integrate and had all these different ideas. They had a few people from L.A. who came out and talked. We talked for a long time about what to do.

Well, the person who sat next to me was this man from L.A., and his name was Jim Carrington.[4] It turned out he was a minister. He was very young—he was maybe twenty-five. He wanted to have a church here. He was kind of nosing around to find out how to do that, and he discovered he couldn't even find a place to live, never mind find a place for his church. Right away, I told him about fair housing Ralph was involved in and the things we had done. We got together with them and tried to help through the years. We visited the church, Friendship Baptist, which he finally got started over in the Maple School area.

Ralph: One of the funny things, too, every year they'd have a city program in Wilshire Auditorium here in Fullerton. They'd be talking about different city problems. Jim Carrington and I were pretty good friends by then, and we would always go and sit in the front row. Nobody would ever mention the problem of race or racism or anything like that, so we would sort of flip a coin to see which one of us was going to be the one to raise the question right near the end of the program. (chuckles) Just to stir things up a little bit and make sure that they knew that there *was* such a problem here in Fullerton.

Natalie: The whole Maple area thing became a big deal. There were committees all the time going on all about Maple School, and Ralph got on the next committee that was involved with that. The school board and the superintendent ignored all the committee's plans, including the one recommended, and established their own plan, which became known as Plan E. Plan E was you shut down Maple School and bus out all the students.

Ralph: So they made a community center out of the Maple School and they got some preschool things in there that were pretty good. But the school, as a neighborhood school, was shut down, and those parents for the next fifteen or twenty years had to have their children bused out into other areas.

The United Farm Workers was another program we became involved in through the church, through the Presbyterian Interracial Council, and through a member of the council whom I had interviewed regarding the *bracero* program, the Rev. Chris Hartmire, who was the then-director of the California Migrant Ministry. That was the early sixties. Chris and I became good friends, so he would often

---

[4] See the James Carrington oral history, OH 2366b, and the Robert Ward oral history, OH 3289, for more on Reverend Carrington's attempts to find housing.

have his secretary call me and send me all over the greater Los Angeles area with a couple of films he had on farm workers, and I would speak to different groups.

For example, I remember speaking to the Italian American Cultural Society in Los Angeles. This is a bunch of old union guys. Some of them spoke broken English. But, boy, they really had their hearts in the right place, and after I showed them the film and gave them the pitch about the farm workers needed to unionize so they could share power with the growers over their lives, I didn't have to say it twice to these guys. They passed the hat and gave me a collection of money before I even left the hall.

Natalie: It was around that time, too, that Ralph started the Friends of the Farm Workers in Orange County, which really became the central movement. They interviewed managers of stores, they boycotted, we picketed, we leafleted, and we did everything I can think of to try to raise money so we could send it to the movement. When [Bobby] Kennedy came to Delano [Kern County], for instance, we went up there and we brought other people from Orange County.

Ralph: One of the calls I got from Chris Hartmire was to come to Delano in the middle of the night, along with a bunch of other people, and we met at the Skycrest Motel in Delano, I believe, and they woke us up at about four-thirty and talked to us and told us what had to be done. They needed to challenge a declaration which the sheriff said was that none of the farm workers could holler at the people in the fields. If they did, they would be arrested. So we would be at the end of the field yelling, "*Huelga*!, *Huelga*! [*Strike*!, *Strike*!]," to let the people in the fields know, at least those who spoke Spanish, that there was a strike, because many of them would not have worked there if they'd known there was a strike, but they were not told that.

They divided us into groups that could go and yell *huelga,* and those that could stay in jail, and those that had to get out in a day, and those who couldn't go at all. I was working as an engineer for North American Aviation at the time, so I had to get out and get back to work the next day, so I stayed just a half day. They arrested us and took us to Sacramento because we hollered *huelga.* One of the interesting things, my friend Chris Hartmire was supposedly not going to be arrested because he was going to arrange for getting us bail and getting us out and telling our families and everything. So as they put us in the paddy wagon and closed the back door, which had a window in it, I looked out the window and there was an officer grabbing Chris Hartmire and shoving him in the car. He ended up in jail with us. (laughs)

Natalie: We saw the picture of this happening on the TV. Our kids came and said they saw their daddy on the TV. Shortly after that, another attorney from PIC called up and volunteered to go up there and he would get Ralph out. I told him it was prearranged, but I didn't really know the details. I didn't know he was going to stay in jail.

Ralph: We were challenging the constitutionality of that ordinance. It drug on for a couple years and eventually the ordinance was thrown out of court because it was clearly unconstitutional. The reason that I do this, and Natalie would probably have a similar reason, because it comes out of our faith, faith in the idea of love and the idea that love is best evidenced by serving your fellow man in whatever kind of difficulty they may be in. Clearly, it was our association with the church and our emulation of Christ, who gave the commandment to love God and love man as yourself. Certainly this is the way to love God—is by loving men in all of their different difficulties.

Our family was involved in a lot of these things, too. For example, I can remember taking the whole family up on the March to Sacramento when Cesar Chavez and his farm worker supporters marched from Delano to Sacramento. We joined them just the last couple of days before they got to Sacramento. Our whole family went up in our station wagon and marched into Sacramento with them. So there were opportunities that we tried to make available and include our children in, so that they got a flavor of all this.

Remember the program through the church, through the Presbyterian Interracial Council, where we brought students from Hattiesburg, Mississippi? This was in the early sixties, too. A lot of the black students in that area couldn't get into any of the colleges; they were all-white colleges. So the church got the idea that we'll take some of those students and give them scholarships. In Fullerton, for example, they set them up with families. A student by the name of Walter Early joined us and went to Fullerton Community College and eventually graduated. I guess he graduated from Cal State Fullerton, too.

Natalie: Also, an interesting thing about Walter is, the first time he came, we were actually going to Long Beach to see Joan Baez, and we thought he would be happily coming along. Well, he didn't really particularly want to come, but he did end up coming. The other thing was, he wouldn't take his shoes off, and we were all a very barefoot-type family. He would be sitting perfectly straight and with his shoes on at all times. Of course, that went away after a few years of living with us, but in the early years, he had been trained to always look a certain way. He walked downtown in Fullerton, and he was smiling. Everybody was smiling back at us all the time, and we realized it was because he walked along smiling at everybody. He was really quite interesting. He's remained a friend of our whole family ever since then. He now has a family of his own and lives in Orange, very happily. He's doing very well. Father's Day he came up and told Ralph that Ralph was the only father he had ever really known. It was very exciting. He hadn't really said anything like that to us before.

We've latched onto the theme from, I think, the United Nations. It's, "Live simply that others may simply live," which is Ralph's philosophy.

Thank you very much, Ralph and Natalie.

JOHN FRANK SMITH[1]

Born in Nashville, Tennessee, John Smith, from six years of age, was raised in Louisville, Kentucky. He was one of the first six hundred or so black people in the US Marine Corps and served in WWII, Korea, and Vietnam. He studied at the Temple University Law School and the US Naval School of Justice. He and his wife came to Orange County in 1960 and moved into the Placentia "ghetto." He and his wife, Jacqueline, still live in Placentia, in a lovely neighborhood.

Growing up in Louisville, did you have contact with white people?

The only contact I had with white people was when we would go shopping, which we called downtown, and it was segregated. We couldn't sit down and eat an ice cream cone or have a hamburger or anything. We couldn't even go inside the stores and try on a pair of shoes. We had to know our size. Couldn't try on any suits, jackets, sweaters, or shirts; you had to know your size, and that's the only time we had contact with them, until the police came around.

What did you do after high school?

I went to Kentucky State College [for a year], which is an all-black college in Frankfurt, Kentucky. Then I enlisted in the US Marine Corps on December the 10, 1942.

Were there many black marines at the time?

Not too many. The first original black marines enlisted in the Marine Corps on June 15, 1942. At that time, we had our training in Camp Lejeune, North Carolina, and it must have been maybe six hundred, from all over the United States. Camp Lejeune was segregated, all-black marines. We went overseas as black marines.

[1] Oral History 3458. Interview date: February 16, 2005, at the home of Mr. Smith in Placentia, California. Interviewer: Robert Johnson.

When did you first come to Orange County?

I received orders to report to Marine Air Corps Air Station, El Toro, in 1960. In the process, we had to have a place to live, my wife and I. I talked to some of the white marines, and they said, "I live in Santa Ana," and some said, "I live in Placentia." I said, "Okay. I'd like to live there, then." So we decided that we would live in the city of Placentia, if we could find a house. But every place we went, they wouldn't sell to us, until we went over here on Kansas Avenue.[2]

Now, these were realtors?

Oh, yes. They said, "We cannot sell to Negroes, colored people." But, there was one tract over there that had all Negroes, colored people, and we moved there April 1, 1960. That's when the Marine Corps moved all of my furniture into that place over there on Kansas Avenue.

Did you have any thoughts about Orange County before that?

No. But when I came here, I knew it was very prejudiced, very prejudiced. Because then I had to drive my car from Placentia out to El Toro. I was married, had a wife, the one I'm married to now.

Did you have children by the first wife?

Oh, yes. We had a daughter by the name of Frankie LaVerne Smith. The second marriage was to Peggy Laws Smith. With her, two daughters: Francesca, like Mother Francesca, and daughter number two was Teresa Ann. And then there's a third daughter; her name's Renee.

So when you moved here, you had—

I was married to Jac, to my wife I'm married to today. Her name is Jacqueline, middle initial A, Smith. We got married January 18, 1959. But we met each other in 1952. Because I was going overseas, we couldn't get married. I said I won't get married until I get at least twenty-five or more years in the service, because I was going overseas all the time, in a lot of combat. We had two children. We had daughter number five, which is Josilyn. Then we had a son, John Frank Smith II, no junior. (chuckles) So that's five daughters and one son, three marriages.

So you first came to live in Placentia. You had no problem because there were other black people there?

---

[2] In 1960, roughly one-sixth of all African Americans in Orange County lived on the El Toro and Tustin Marine Corps bases, while many other marines lived in Santa Ana and nearby towns. Improved opportunities in the US Marine Corps in the 1950s and 1960s for African Americans led to a high achieving group of blacks joining and making the marines a career. Best known of the El Toro marines was Frank E. Petersen. In his autobiography, he tells about his Orange County experiences in the 1950s, starting with being the only black pilot and officer at the El Toro base. Marines, like J. J. King and Rudy Francis, upon retirement, became active in the Santa Ana community.

There were other black people there. There were no white people living over there in that tract. All black. You met Charles Ray [COPH Oral History 3457]; I think he worked at Autonetics. We had Frank Cisco over there. He was the chief custodian over here at El Dorado High School. Most of them that lived on Kansas Avenue worked at Autonetics, most of the people, except those that were in the military. Let's see—about five black marines lived over there, and the rest of the people worked for Autonetics and worked for the Unified School District as custodians.

Was the neighborhood 50 percent black?

One hundred percent black. There were no white people living over there. That's the only place they had black people living here in Placentia. As we moved out, then the Latinos moved in. I sold my house over there on Kansas Avenue to a white. While I was living over there on Kansas Avenue, I retired from the Marine Corps, and that's when I went to work for the County of Orange in the superior court.

Are there any stories that you have about that neighborhood?

There was a fire, right across the street from my house, over there on Kansas. I went in the house, I went inside this fire, and I brought two kids out, two children out. The only people that knew about it were the people over there on Kansas. The fire department was talking to me about it, and the police officers. Joe O'Doherty—he was Latino—and he says, "You know, you're a brave person. Why don't you come on and join the Placentia Police Department? We could use a man like you." That's when I started with the Placentia P.D.—1964, '65, one of those years.

While your family lived on Kansas and you were still in the marines, your job was—

Legal chief and personnel sergeant major, until I retired in 1968.

Did your family have any problems in the sixties not being served in restaurants or being denied access to anything?

They would go to other tables first, and they would finally come to us. But they didn't act pretty nasty or nothing like that. I didn't have any problems. One of the waitresses, she came and she spilled some coffee on me. I said, "Ma'am, you know you should be a little careful like that. You didn't burn me, but I'm a little upset about it. So please don't do that again." I said, "Now, send me another waitress over here before I get angry." That's the only problem we had.

Now, you did know one ex-marine, and he was known for his work in far-right-wing organizations. His name was Johnny Johnson.

I know Johnny Johnson. Oh yes, I do. When he was in the marine corps, he was with the stewards branch. They served the officers. That's how he was recommended for warrant officer, and they accepted him over John Frank Smith. I was recommended for a commissioned officer's rank eleven times, and I've got the paperwork to show you. They passed me over. He got it, being the first black warrant officer, because he was the officers' steward.

Were you aware of his ties with the John Birch Society?

Oh, yes. He became an insurance salesman, and that's the last I heard of him. As a matter of fact, he sold some insurance to one of my daughters and one of her sons. So that's the last I heard of him.

So you retired from the Marine Corps. Did you go to work for the Placentia Police Department?

I went to work for the Placentia Police Department as an active reserve police officer in 1965. I worked every Monday, Wednesday, Friday, and Saturday. I got paid for that. From 3:30 in the afternoon until 11:30, that shift. And on Sundays, I used to direct the traffic over there at the Catholic Church on Bradford.

Did you have any problems with the citizens of Placentia when you would do your police duties?

When I first started. I would stop them if they would run a stop sign or stop light, for illegal parking, or something like that. I would say, "Sir, may I see your driver's license?" Or, "Ma'am, may I see your driver's license, please?" They were very nasty. They said, "I'm not going to show no nigger my driver's license. You're not a police officer." I'd say, "Well, I'm in uniform and my badge says Officer J. Smith, and if you don't show me your driver's license in the next five minutes, I'm going to lock you up. And if you really irritate me, I'm going to take care of you." I had a couple of ladies who spit in my face, but I didn't have any trouble with the men. My partner was Joe O'Doherty; he was Chicano. They were pretty nasty to us, for a while.

Was that the case all through your time in the police force?

At the beginning. Once they knew of me and my partner Joe O'Doherty, everything was pretty well under control. We had a curfew here in Placentia for under eighteen years of age for all the children. We used to go to the Bargain Basket, which was over there on Chapman, about ten minutes to twelve at night. We'd say, "Okay, you guys, it's almost midnight. It's time for you to leave and go home. We'll be back in three minutes and one minute is gone." That's what I would say.

Tell us the story of this house and what you went through getting it.

We were driving around just looking because we wanted to move from Kansas Avenue. We saw this [white] lady; she was passing out cards. She was a realtor; her name was Lorena Hodges. She said, "I'll see if I can find something nice for you." She found this place for us.

Would other realtors do that same thing?

No. She did. That's how Charles Ray got his house, and Ted Davis, and all these other black people that lived over here in northern Placentia. We got our homes through her. She became very, very popular and very, very famous, and she made a lot of money.

Then what happened? You moved into this house.

When we moved in, the people were looking, standing all out in the street. They saw these big moving trucks. The wife was a little shaky. I wasn't. After we unloaded our furniture, one of my daughters back in Philadelphia got married, so we went back to her wedding. When we came back here, people began to throw rocks at our windows and things like that. They broke out a window. So we were pretty well upset. My wife says, "Maybe we should move." I said, "No. We've got to have someplace to live, and we're going to live here, regardless." So I was putting the grass seed in out in the parkway and about eight men came, and they said, "We don't want no niggers living here. When niggers and colored people move into a white neighborhood, they make our property value go down. You got two weeks to get out of here." I said, "Sir, I have to have someplace to live." Somebody had told me that morning, "Why don't you just put your off-duty weapon in your back pocket?" I was still with the Placentia Police Department. I was standing out there, and this one guy poked me and says, "You're leaving now."

I said, "Sir, please don't do that. Please get your hands off me." "You don't tell me." So he slapped me in the face. And I pulled my pistol out of my back pocket. And I hit him upside his head, and the blood fell from his head. I turned to the rest of them and said, "All of you get off of my property right now. I'll kill all of you. Don't you never ever come around here bothering me again unless you're ready to kill me, because if you come here, I'm going to kill you." That's true now. I said, "I'll kill you, kill your wife, all your children, and your dog." My wife was standing there, "Daddy, please. Daddy, please." You should have seen those guys run.

Then after that, the next week, then they broke windows out again. So I got myself together and called some of my marine buddies, and about thirty of them came out here with a marine corps pickup truck—white and black marines from El Toro. We canvassed the neighborhood, like door to door. They said, "You don't want to mess with our little Gunnery Sergeant Smith. If you do and if he tells us about it, we're going to come take care of you." That was in 1968.

Things were pretty quiet, pretty quiet after that. I had a few run-ins with the people. Then one of the things that really hurt me real bad was, when my son John got old enough to go to school, the teacher refused to teach him. He was the first black [student] in her classroom, and she says, "I'm not teaching black children. They're not supposed to be as smart as white children." I didn't know this until one of his little classmates came by and told me one day, this little white girl. So I took off from work, and I went over there. I saw this for myself. They had John sitting over in the corner, facing the corner, the teacher did. And she was writing on the board talking to the other students. I went in the classroom and said, "Ma'am, what does this mean?" She said, "Who are you?" I said, "That's my son.

My name is John F. Smith, and that's my son." "Well, I refuse to teach him. Why don't you put him in another school? He doesn't belong here anyway."

So I went straight to the office to see the principal. I told him about it, [that was] after I talked with his office person. She says, "He doesn't want to see you." I said, "You tell him that Mr. Smith, Officer Smith, is out here right now, and if he's not out here in the next five minutes, I'm going to come and get him, and four minutes are gone." (chuckles) He came out. So I took him to the classroom, and I showed him. My son was still sitting there in the chair. I said, "You need to talk to this teacher, and I'm going to the Unified School District." Which I did. I went to the Unified School District here in Placentia and reported it. So the next week, they had another principal and another teacher. That really hurt me real bad. Her problem was she was from the South. She said she was from Mississippi. She talked like it. She had the accent and whatever.

At that time, my wife and I, we attended the [mostly white] Presbyterian church over there on Bradford. That's where we met Josh White [COPH Oral History 2141]. My wife, she sang in the choir, and I was an usher in the church. We started going to Friendship Baptist Church when I heard about it through some friends of ours that lived in Fullerton. That was in '65. [I was] one of the original deacons, assistant deacon in the church. We were ordained deacons at Friendship Baptist Church. Reverend James C. Carrington [COPH Oral History 2366b]—he was a very young man at that time, very young man.

You became a Superior Court clerk. Tell us what that means.

Superior Court clerk was an assistant to the judge. The main job of the clerk was to answer the telephone, assist the judge with all the legal documents and papers, and whatnot. No one could go in to speak or talk to the judge unless they talked to the clerk first—me, Mr. Smith; me, not the bailiff, not the man that was in uniform. I was in civilian clothing. You had to speak to me. Even his wife, if she called on the phone, she had to let me know who she was. All the lawyers that came into the courtroom, they had to see me before they saw the judge.

So that was what you had gone to Temple [Law School] to learn. Then you spent those years in the Marine Corps legal department.

That's why I got that job in Orange County. And they were very prejudiced against me down there. When I went to apply for the job, I was talking to this lawyer, an officer in the Marine Corps, a friend of mine. He says, "John, why don't you try Superior Court in Orange County? They don't have any colored, Negroes, down there. You'd be one of the first, and that'd be right down your line. Why don't you go down there and shake them up?" He said, "When you go down there, be yourself," and I did. They submitted the application to me, and they had an opening for one Superior Court clerk. When I got the application it said "race." I looked at it and I put quotation—capital J—unquote. And I filled out the application with my military background, my college experience, and whatever, all that on there. They called me up, so I went in for the interview. They asked me, "What does this J stand for?" I said, "That's what I am." They said, "What does it mean?" I said,

"It means Justian, J-u-s-t-i-a-n, Justian." One of the interviewers, he said, "What does Justian mean?" I said, "Just anything I want to be and not what you want to proclaim me to be." "Okay, Mr. Smith, you may leave. We'll let you hear from us."

And you got the job.

Nope. So they called me back, and they administered the test to me, and I scored a ninety-three on the test. They said, "We'll let you hear from us." So about four weeks went by, and they called me up. They said, "Well, we're going to have to retest you again. Did you have any help with this?" I said, "No." So they retested me, and when I took the test a second time, I scored a ninety-seven. They said, "Okay, okay, okay. We'll let you hear from us." Two weeks went by, and I received this phone call on a Friday. Bob Carrillo—he was Hispanic, assistant county clerk—he said, "This is Bob Carrillo. John Smith, how are you today?" I said, "I'm fine. Did you call to tell me I didn't get the job?" He said, "No, on the contrary. Mr. Smith, can you be here at work at eight o'clock Monday morning?" I said, "Ooh, yes, sir." I told my wife. I was so happy.

So I reported to work at eight o'clock that morning. And when I walked in there, they looked at me, they threw all the papers at me. They didn't know I'd had legal background and legal experience in the military. They said, "Where'd you learn all this?" I told them, "In the military." I went through the training program. I excelled in everything because, as I said, the things that they figured I couldn't do, I had to pray hard on that, and my mind told me I could do it. That's how I am. That must be my blessing and my gift from the Master above. My soul belongs to Almighty God, the Lord Jesus Christ, and I believe that. And I know that.

After that, they said, "We're going to send you over here to work with this judge." So, they sent me to work for Judge Lester Van Tatenhove. He was the first judge I worked with and he accepted me and was so glad to see me. He hugged me and talked to me and took me under his wing and taught me a lot of things. He said, "Well, you've already got legal background. I'm so glad to get somebody like you." I was with that judge for fifteen years.

Well, he was a pretty famous guy.

Lester Van Tatenhove. I know his whole family. He was Presbyterian. I went to his church and he went to my church when we were Presbyterians. We were just good friends. His wife and my wife and I, the four of us, we went on vacations. Then when he retired, I went to work for another judge by the name of Judge John Smith. He was a corporal in the Marine Corps when I was a sergeant. He was a white guy. I worked with him for another five years, and after that, I worked for another judge, a third judge, which was white. His name is James Cook. He still sits pro tem judge now. So Judge Van Tatenhove passed away, and then Judge Smith passed away, and Judge Cook is still living. I'm older than all of them and out-lived them. I'm eighty-two years old this year. But in that courtroom, everybody knew John F. Smith, the clerk of the court. Yes, sir.

Did your family's life revolve around the church?

[Yes], around the church. My wife is a mother of the church to this day. My son, he sings right now. He's got a voice. He sings in the choir at the church. My daughter goes to church—she sings—all my daughters, they all go to church.

So you didn't spend much time with marine corps things and social life or clubs and organizations.

Oh, yes. I'm a 33rd-degree Mason. I was an Elk; then I became a Mason, a 33rd-degree Mason. That's the highest degree that you can achieve in Masonry. I was twenty-one. That's sixty-one years, right?

Was it integrated?

No, this is an all-black organization. We had a chapter here in Orange County. Now the chapter I belong to is in Los Angeles County, but we still have a black chapter of Masons here in Orange County. Now, the only time that we associated or affiliated with the white Masons was when I went to Santa Ana and they invited me over to their lodge, which is right over there on Eighth and Broadway. I was the first black Mason to go to their lodge.

Do you think the Masons are dying out now?

No, they are still a part of the black community—very, very strong.

What was it like for your children with regard to their social life?

Well, my daughter was very active. My wife, she had her in little dance groups and different clubs and stuff like that. My son John, he was very active. He can sing. He's very talented. He was a wrestler at El Dorado. He was the first black high school wrestling champion in the state of California. He's very artistic. He plays the organ, the synthesizer; he plays the bongo/conga drums, which I taught him how to play. And my daughter, she's a dancer, quite a dancer. Jocilyn was born in 1959. John was born in 1963.

Did she date? Mostly white kids, black kids?

Both. My son never dated a black girl. (chuckles) He's married now to a white girl. There weren't too many black boys around here, either, for my daughter. She dated—I never taught my children to segregate—mostly white. She married a black person.

What did your children do after high school?

They went to college. John went to Cal State Fullerton, and Francesca, she went to Fullerton JC. He majored in criminal justice, police science. When he got out, he was a police officer. Now he's an entertainer. He has his own band. He's into real estate now. And my young daughter Josilyn, she just got her master's degree last year, Mother's Day. She teaches in Orange County—elementary school.

What have been the positives and negatives of living in Orange County? Like crime?

Well, as far as the crime is concerned in Orange County, it's minimal. This is a very quiet county as far as crime is concerned, in my opinion. Especially the city of Placentia here—gosh, it's a pretty nice place to live—very, very quiet.

How about the fact that the black community dispersed? There's no black middle-class area.

That's true, because the black people over here were professional people. That's why we moved, to get out of that ghetto. A lot of them have moved from here. They live in Anaheim Hills now; they've moved to Riverside, they've moved to Pasadena. And we still keep in touch with each other; we're very good friends. As far as I'm concerned, Orange County is a beautiful place to live. I don't have any problem here with the people. I go to Stater Bros, Albertsons, Vons [all supermarkets]. I go all around here. They call me the mayor, black mayor. (chuckles) Black mayor of Placentia. (laughs)

So Orange County hasn't been a problem with regard to social life and friendships.

Not for me. I know a lot of people in Orange County. As I told you, I retired three superior court judges. I know [Mike] Carona; he's the sheriff. He used to be one of the bailiffs in my courtroom. I know a lot of judges that are sitting now. A lot of ministers, I know the police officers, I know the firemen. This is my city. I love Orange County. Life is good to me. I go to church. I'm on the usher board now, after I retired as being a deacon. I'm the oldest usher on the usher board at Friendship Baptist Church. We have over 130 ushers. We have small kids ushering, from the age of six years old to eighty-two, boys and girls.

Have you had any problems with neighbors in the last few years?

Oh, yeah. They threw eggs on my wife's Jaguar. They threw eggs on my Rolls Royce.

I noticed the top was cut.

We were getting ready to go to church just before Christmas in *her* car, the Jaguar, [and discovered that] someone had cut the head and one arm off a dead cat and threw them right out there on the lawn.

So racism doesn't die easy, is that right?

No, it doesn't die easy. I told you, they threw eggs on the side of her car, on the other side of my Rolls Royce, cut my top. People are crazy.

The positives, though, outweigh the negatives?

Oh, sure. I just hope I don't catch anyone, because if I do, you know they're going to go to jail. And I hope I'm not angry at the time because I'd have to take care of them. Gunny Smith will take care of them marine corps-wise. That's what I'm saying. If I'm on tape, I'm on tape.

I've known many marines, and you are—I won't say typical, no. You're even more than typical (chuckles) of the marines. Thank you, Gunny Smith.

JOSHUA WHITE[1]

Joshua White's parents were from rural Georgia and migrated to Oklahoma. Through high school, Josh White received his education in predominantly black, and sometimes all-black, Oklahoma schools. Although he received most of his education in segregated schools, he was also involved with people in the white community. He picked cotton in the fall and worked in a chain grocery store throughout high school and college, working his way up from plucking chickens to assistant merchandising manager. During the years in and following high school, he became involved in his county's branch of the National Association for the Advancement of Colored People, and in 1951, in Atlanta, was elected to its National Youth Committee. He now lives in Plano, Texas.

Tell us about your involvement in integrating El Reno Junior College, in your hometown of El Reno, following the famous *Brown v. the Board of Education* decision.

I decided then to be one of the test cases for the NAACP and I was the first test case in Oklahoma on that US Supreme Court decision, 1954. It upset everybody in my hometown. I was the guy everybody looked to, including my religious employer. He was the vice-mayor of El Reno and had been on the city council for years. The dean of the junior college was a customer of this store, right across the street, and I'd pack groceries for him at the check-out counter. And then all of a sudden all hell broke loose; this black guy wants to go into the school. I got into the school there and was the first black to graduate from the junior college.

I had started out at a black college and then quit and stayed out for a while. Now, I was not going back to the segregated school, Langston University [in Langston, Oklahoma]. After having fought to break down the barriers there [at the junior college] it would've been defeating my purpose. I went on to Oklahoma

[1] Oral History 2141. Interview date: October 31, 1974 at Mr. White's Orange County office. Interviewers: Lillie King and Chris Kirby.

State University [in Stillwater, Oklahoma] and I became quite active. While I was there, I got active in umpteen things: Young Democrat club and SAMS, Society for the Advancement of Management. I also was invited to become a member of the international fraternity, Delta Sigma Phi, an honorary business fraternity. And again I guess I broke the color barrier at Oklahoma State University in that fraternity. I ran for state president of the Young Democratic clubs of Oklahoma—and that was in 1960—but I was not successful in that quest. Still, we put up a pretty good race.

I graduated from Oklahoma State University with a BS in Business Management, May 29, 1960. It was during that last year my mother took ill right at the mid-semester of my senior year. I asked her how she was feeling. She said, "How did you make out on your tests?" One other thing that she said was, "You surprise me. You didn't go along with all of your other classmates in high school. You happened to choose the field of business and you ought to be a math teacher or some kind of teacher because those jobs are available for you there in teaching—a coach, or something like that. But let me tell you that I hope and pray that you'll be able to get something in your field when you get out of school and get a job in business. And someday, [maybe you will] just have your own business." Those were her words. So we were quite close.

She died February 3 [1960] and was buried on the sixth [of February], 1960. And then May 29 was my graduation. My father was there and I was showing him around the library and I just picked up this book and the title of the book was *Creative Leadership.* I had left my mother's picture in it, and lo and behold, when I picked up that book, here she is. (laughter) And so you just have a mental picture; there she was on my graduation. So, I guess she disappeared, and she said I'll be with you on May 29.

What happened after you graduated from college?

All of my classmates were white. I was the first black to graduate from the College of Business, Oklahoma State University. But everybody who got the degree, they interviewed. All of my classmates knew where they were going when they graduated on May 29, except me. I had no job offer at that time. So being active in politics, I was approached by a Congressman candidate to work his campaign—take care of the minority communities. I actively campaigned down in the Sixth Congressional District of Oklahoma and got him elected. And he wouldn't have gotten elected without Josh White, I can assure you, because I got the black votes and the minority votes in that area.

I decided that I would not go into civil service work, to work for government, or anything like that. I always had been involved with the private sector; [I] worked from my upbringing in the Independent Grocer's Alliance, the retail store. I was active and interested in government. I liked to have something to say about who's going to be the power structure. So, I've always been active in that decision-making process and I still am and still going to have something to say about it.

I was wondering about when you joined that youth committee. Did you go to Atlanta, Georgia?

Oh, yes, I was the delegate from Oklahoma. The Youth Work Committee was a committee set up to work to have more involvement of the youth in the NAACP. That was the springboard, the beginning of a youth division of the NAACP back in 1951. And I was on that first committee. I think I have a photograph somewhere of me and Dr. Ralph J. Bunch, who was the keynote speaker at that convention at Atlanta, and I'll never forget that.

How much importance did you play in that particular movement?

Let me tell you, the youth were the ones that played a significant role, because I think it was back in 1958 when the first sit-ins really started. And these guys might give Dr. Martin Luther King a lot of credit for a lot of things, but I can assure you that those first sit-ins started in Oklahoma City. And my twin brother [John] was heading it.[2] I personally was not that active in it as my brother was. He was the state youth leader of the NAACP. You see, I was active earlier and it seems like when I start things and then I go onto something else, my brother picks up where I left off. So he happened to pick up from there. Of course, I was in the background giving a little counsel and advice whenever it was needed, because I had the experience with the NAACP.

Josh, how did you get to California, and in particular, how did you get to Orange County?

I drove a black and white Mercury, and I went from San Fernando Valley to San Diego, all over, interviewing employers to no avail. So after I got through all of that, I decided that what I should do is, since I was brought up in the church, I would turn to the church for some help.

At first I came to Los Angeles and I set up and did my own little thing of tax returns in the spring to keep food on the table. I ended up having to spend all of my savings and I had to strip my insurance policy of cash value. So following that period, after a year or so, these ministers wrote a letter to all the churches in Southern California. That letter went all over and it fell upon pretty good soil. And the soil happened to have been Orange County. One evening, I received a telephone call from a man in personnel at Autonetics and his minister had made the big plea that particular Sunday. So it came from the pulpit and he went up and got the letter. And so I landed in Anaheim. Of course I had a rough time then.

You mean you had a rough time finding adequate living facilities in Orange County?

Oh, yes. Well, my car was worn out; I had no car to speak of. There was no way I could have commuted through that heavy metropolitan Los Angeles traffic to and from Orange County. I didn't want any excuses, so I said, "Well, let me move to Orange County."

---

[2] The sit-ins in Oklahoma City followed the first sit-ins in Wichita, Kansas, that were a few weeks before. This was 1958, about a year and a half before the most famous sit-ins in Greensboro, North Carolina. His brother is John White and is quoted in the book *Dissent in Wichita,* written by Gretchen Cassel Eick (2001).

I decided to go around looking at apartments. Doors were closed. After I couldn't find any I wanted, I approached the Presbyterian minister and asked him to help me find an apartment. They went around with me, accompanying me, to try and find an apartment. Doors closed in their faces. We couldn't do anything. So they said, "Well, there's a single fellow who works at Autonetics over there with you who is a deacon in the church, Anaheim First Presbyterian Church. We will talk to him and see if he would entertain you with a roommate."

So he did; and he accepted. He happened to be from Pennsylvania, so I was all right. He got in trouble with his landlord for taking me in; they insisted that I got out. So he said, "Well, he is my guest. He is not permanently living here." So one day I found an apartment in the area. This guy said it was a new apartment and he and his brother just moved in. So outside of his family, I was his first tenant. But he said, "I would not have rented to you if you had come by about three weeks ago when we first moved in. I rented to you even though I know the economics wouldn't be good for me. But two weeks ago I had just become a Christian, and had it not been that I had just become a Christian, I wouldn't have rented to you and it was just the love of Christ in my heart." So that's why he rented to me.

The whole block of neighbors raised hell—that black guy—they didn't say "black," they said "nigger." Moving in this neighborhood, everything just broke loose. And then there was a big splash in the papers. And so when they heard about it, the mayor of Anaheim called me. He came by the house. And so I stayed there and I got threatened and telephone calls. I got all kinds of threats. I was fired upon—shots, one night, came right through the bedroom. I don't know how close. I kept the bullet there for a long time. So that was about fourteen years ago [1961].

Did you have any assistance from any other group of people like the NAACP of Orange County?

No, no. Everything that I did was on my own, and the only avenue I had was through the church. And I know there weren't any organizations that were active around here then.

You must have been motivated by something in order to endure such treatment. What was it?

Well, I guess this super power within me and my earlier experiences in Oklahoma and having gone through those things, that I guess I had tough skin. I always, again, go back to my Christian heritage or my religious background of having faith and that there's a power greater than myself and I know that I can make it through. And so Martin Luther King said, "We shall overcome." I just felt strongly that way, that I was going to make it and I was going to do it at all cost.

After I got situated and got in my apartment, I said I'm now a citizen of Anaheim. I'm not going to let this continue. I'm going to bring it to their attention, now that I've done it quietly. So I went before the city council and made a speech. During that period, I was invited by the Greater Anaheim Kiwanis Club and I made a speech. And we also formed an Anaheim Human Relations Council. I was involved in that back there in those days by working on Proposition 14 for fair housing. I've always believed and have been there helping the causes of the underprivileged, the minorities, and so forth in Orange County.

Were there other blacks working in Autonetics then who were active in the community in any way?

No, no. Most of the blacks wanted to get on back to L.A. and to Compton [Los Angeles County].

Did you get to know any other blacks then in Orange County?

Oh, yes. I got acquainted with Everett Winters (See Chapter 3) and I got acquainted with Jess Berry back in those days and we met eventually. I guess it was almost a year before we met after I got here.

You were invited to join the JCs.

The Anaheim Junior Chamber of Commerce. I was the author and developer of a training course, leadership development course. And I felt that this was an area in which I had strong suits and I wanted to offer that to the group. One day I received a telephone call from the mayor of Anaheim inviting me to serve on the Anaheim Citizen's Charter Study Committee. And had it not been for the JCs, I know I never would have been invited. So I was appointed and I helped write the charter for the City of Anaheim. I helped write the charter in a city where I was refused housing, in a city where I didn't know that I was going to have employment, and in a city where my life was threatened. Anaheim, it had been in existence for over a hundred years, and here comes this person from Oklahoma that had a big hand in the Anaheim community where the Klu Klux Klan was, where they had white sheets a few years before I got there. That's a fact.

In what capacity did you function at Autonetics?

Well, I was in the department of education and training, which is a part of personnel. I was the staff person to the manager of education and training. I got a promotion, thank God, in a year's time, transferred over to the administration department. I left Autonetics in the fall of 1965. Watts broke out in August of 1965. I received a telephone call from the personnel manager of Autonetics saying that North American would like to nominate me as a candidate for ICBO, Interracial Council for Business Opportunities of Los Angeles, a private funded organization funded by Ford and Rockefeller Foundation. There were twenty-three candidates and out of the twenty-three, they narrowed it down to four and I was in there. They finally selected me and then I asked for a leave of absence from Autonetics and they granted my leave of absence, which allowed me to continue my fringe benefits. I went up on my mission and had some real experiences in Watts.

Could you tell us about some of those experiences?

Well, during that time I was able to, for the first time, bring the financial community together: the insurance companies and the banks. I had a meeting with all of the bankers because blacks down there were not getting financial help or loans down there for their businesses. There were a lot of frustrations that really brought Watts on. For all my efforts down there I received the Hollywood JC's Distinguished Service award. I shared it with Gary Owens. Steve Allen was the keynote speaker that night in Hollywood. Of course, Mayor [Sam] Yorty at that time called me up to his office. So I got some plaudits—I got some plaques to show what I did in Los Angeles for the one-year stint.

Josh, please elaborate on your return to Orange County.

In the spring of 1966, I returned at a time when two things happened. One, was that the job I left was not there for me when I got back. So thank God it was a leave of absence, so I couldn't be out of a job. (laughter) So I got a different job, a better job I think: master of planning and programming, and then later a contracts administrator.

Before I left, I had moved into Placentia from Anaheim. What happened was I was internal vice-president of the Anaheim JCs and, of course, I ran for president. They weren't ready for me to be president over there and so I was defeated. I decided Placentia needs a JC chapter. I got, by a one-vote margin, to organize a JC chapter in Placentia. So I was chairman; I was the founder. That year, as I was called away to go up to Los Angeles, I had to resign. And so when I returned back in the spring, what happened was that the Placentia JCs were just getting ready to hold their elections. I threw my hat in the ring. The other guys had been campaigning for three months or four months and there were several members who were new in the organization. There were charges and countercharges: "He's a carpetbagger!" (laughter) Have you ever seen a JC carpetbagger? So Josh White had the label on him as a carpetbagger. I won the election on the third ballot.

I was named outstanding local president of the whole district of North Orange County that year, the year I was president. I had a good chapter; I had everything going. Of course, I had people quit on me and I got rid of some because they had to produce: shape up or ship out. I think there were several blacks in the organization—three or four blacks in the organization.

I decided to run for national director of the California JCs. And I became national director of JCs, by campaigning all over the state. And I was in charge of signing the portfolio of community development. And after that year as national director, there was an opening for state vice-president. So I decided because of my time, age of thirty-five, to run for vice-president. So I ran for vice-president of the California JCs and got elected in Sacramento. It was for an incomplete and unexpired term.

Then I decided I want to go ahead and do my thing and go all the way to the top and run for president of the California State JCs. And I did. I had the backing of my local Placentia JCs—they backed me all the way—and even had Anaheim backing and all the people in this area of Orange County. And so we did the campaigning properly. People got things together and we rented a private airplane.

And I flew from one end of the state to the other. I'll never forget that little, old, private four-seat plane. Campaigning all over the state…

I was unsuccessful. I "lost my heart in San Francisco"—that's where the convention was, in San Francisco. But it was quite an experience. So I said, "Okay, my year's up and I'm retiring as vice-president of California JCs." I got one of the five outstanding national director's awards, so I figured, let me get into life insurance, and so I went to work for Equitable Life and became one of the outstanding agents. I won all the contests, got a free trip to New York.

After having gone through the life insurance business, I decided that I would branch out on my own. I gave myself a hard look at the total picture, the big picture as to what I am doing here. What can I really do to bring together all of these experiences in my lifetime? And where am I going and where do I want to be ten years from now? What is it that I can do to serve the most people? I decided that I would go into management consulting because this is an area that at least would make me feel comfortable. I know this was one of the dreams of my mother and one of the things I hoped for. And so as I explored, we decided to call it Josh White Associates, JWA.

Josh, tell me about your first political campaign.

I served as manager of Jess Berry for the school board for the city of Santa Ana. There was a time when I thought there had to be a real political awakening within the black community of Orange County. And with Santa Ana being the hub of the black population, this was a natural starting place with my experience in politics and in political campaigns as described earlier in a congressional campaign.

I never told you about my departure and going back to Oklahoma for five or six weeks and how I got actively involved in my twin brother's campaign, who ran for state legislature and became the first black elected legislator in the House of Representatives in the state of Oklahoma. So I went back and ran his campaign and it was successful.

So with that background and that experience, I really got active and organized and managed Jess Berry's campaign. And we put it together here in Orange County, in Santa Ana. We were quite proud to elect our first black man to public office in Orange County and Jess Berry was that man. Education is quite important in the black community because the only way black folks ever got ahead is through education: knowledge is power. And so by having a black person up there, of course, it brought about bringing the first black man in a big top administrative position in Orange County as a principal.

Since you've been here, have you noticed a change in the people of Orange County, as far as their attitudes towards minorities?

Most definitely. I have noticed a significant change in attitude in the people in this area. I think that blacks and browns and other minorities are being more openly accepted here in Orange County. As it relates to racial prejudice, this still exists in some business and industry and governmental agencies. But there has been some beginning to eradicate these prejudices. I think that there are more opportunities for minorities to run for public office. I don't think that in the future, race is going to be a factor in being successful in an election in Orange County. I feel that I will succeed in some elections in the future.

Josh, if you were to seek office, would you stay in Placentia or would you seek a base, maybe in Santa Ana, where you might have more grassroots support?

They said, "Josh, why don't you move to Santa Ana?" And a number of young ladies that I dated said, "Move up to Santa Ana. Why are you in Placentia? Why are you up north?" And I said, "I like it up here. I like it in the Anaheim area." I will not be going to Santa Ana where there is a large black population, where there is a cluster of other minorities, where that community of Santa Ana has approximately 50 percent minorities. I feel that I can remain in north Orange County, and I have every confidence in the electorate of north Orange County in the Placentia-Anaheim-Fullerton area—will elect Josh White to public office.

I know that you have been involved in some tremendous organizations here in Orange County.

One was the Orange County Human Relations Council Committee.[3] When I was at a UCI [University of California, Irvine] public seminar, we got involved in saying whether or not we wanted to have a human relations council in Orange County. At the meeting in Santa Barbara, a group of human relations people—our new congressman-elect Jerry Patterson was there, and Fullerton Mayor Frances Wood, and former mayor, Ray Veer, was there. And so I was the guy that said, "Let's go. Let's do something. Stop talking about it. Let's form an organization. Let's get something viable that's really going to get at the heart and crux of these problems in Orange County."

And so I was chairing a steering committee of this group of people in attendance on the weekend up to Santa Barbara. And there was a tie vote whether or not we should form a human relations council and get a committee going and get moving. And Ray Veer constantly reminds me, "If it weren't for your vote, Josh, we would never have had a human relations commission in Orange County." And so I was the chair and it was a tie vote and of course everybody should have known which way I was going to vote. So we decided we'd form a human relations council.

And then we got into the organization of different groups. Let's go into the barrios and let's go in and really find what the citizens' input would be. We often neglect the grassroots people who are most affected by these things. We tend to sit in our ivory tower and have no empathy for that little man down here. This is one of the reasons I have to admire Manny Mendez, you know, because he gets right on down to it.

We had people like Dave Collins, my landlord here, who was very active with the Human Relations Council of Orange County. Manny Mendez succeeded

[3] The Orange County Human Relations Council was a non-profit corporation, which is not to be confused with the Orange County Human Relations Commission, a later-organized county government organization that was to follow and is still active.

me as president and he did a good job in terms of trying to carry on the policies and philosophy.[4] So thank God we have a human relations commission in Orange County. Bob Batten was chairman of the board of supervisors at the time the Human Relations Commission was formed. I can recall two spokesmen from the black population of Orange County—those were Jess Berry and myself—that spoke before the Board of Supervisors that day urging the establishment of the Human Relations Commission here. The Human Relations Council of Orange County no longer exists because our task was over once the county said, yes, we'll form a human relations commission.

Now, let's move into the Orange County Black Business and Professional Men's Association. Here again, this organization started because there was a need within the county for black men to get together. The Orange County Black Business and Professional Men's Association was started in 1970. It was my understanding that there were attempts before, two or three times, to start this organization. We met several times down in Santa Ana. Of course, everything centers in Santa Ana in terms of the majority of blacks in Orange County. I hadn't even entertained the idea of considering running for anything. And so the gentleman who insisted on my running and who got up and made the nomination speech was J. J. King. So I assumed the presidency of the association, the first president of the association. We said unemployment is a problem in Orange County. Blacks need training and we have to bring in an organization that will train people. And so we said we were going to sponsor the OIC, Opportunities Industrialization Center.[5] And that's what we did: launched it, we organized it, and we were responsible for nurturing, babying that organization. And today it's a viable organization in our community of Orange County, having a budget of about $350,000.

OIC was one of the accomplishments of the association during my year as president. Also, we had *The Second Edition*, a black newspaper which started and led to what it is today, a Chicano newspaper in Santa Ana, because the Chicanos never had a newspaper for themselves. I have to say that blacks started a lot of things in Orange County; we lead things, Chicanos follow. But you can't be a leader unless you follow. And so after the Chicanos did a little following, they are now becoming leaders and blacks are becoming followers.

But you know in Orange County, it's a beautiful thing where there was some animosity and friction between the blacks and browns. Now I see there is a coalition of togetherness and harmony that's appearing here on the scene between the two ethnic groups. There are still a few around that will be anti-black and anti-brown, but for the most part, that relationship is good.

---

[4] Dave Collins was a white Anaheim realtor who had the courage to oppose Proposition 14 and was involved in the early days of the Orange County Fair Housing Council. Manny Mendez, besides his involvement in the Human Relations Council, was one of the founders of the Orange County Community Housing Corporation.

[5] OIC is founder Leon Sullivan's famous minority training organization out of Philadelphia. Jim Hillman, who worked at Autonetics and chaired the Orange County Fair Housing Council, left Orange County to work for Sullivan.

Josh, is there anything else you would like to tell us about your early background?

My early background is an indication of coming up in a good Christian environment where it says, "Train up a child in the way that he should go and when he is old he shall not depart from it." And I don't find myself departing from a lot of these Christian principles because I'm active in the church now. I'm an elder in the Placentia Presbyterian Church and I'm a commissioner at the Presbytery level, representing my church.

Thank you very much, Josh White.

JAMES CARRINGTON[1]

The Reverend James Carrington is the senior pastor of the large Friendship Baptist Church in Yorba Linda, California. Rev. Carrington was born in Pittsburgh, Pennsylvania, on September 25, 1933. He tells about the obstacles he faced in starting the church, which was first located in Fullerton, and the help he received from the religious community in overcoming these obstacles. He also tells about his involvement in housing discrimination issues. Photo ca. 1970.

Rev. Carrington, where did you receive your religious training?

Well, my story's a little different than normal. I dropped out of the high school in the eleventh grade and joined the navy at seventeen. I got out of the navy in 1954, and in 1957 I went to church at Paradise Baptist Church in Los Angeles as the guest of a friend of mine who had invited me and some of my buddies. Shortly after that, I reunited with God in my life, making Him first place.

Then about a year after that, in 1958—July to be specific—I was called to the ministry and God spoke to me. Then I went back to night school at Jefferson High School in Los Angeles; I got my high school diploma from there. Then went on to Reed College of Religion in 1960 and graduated there with my bachelor in theology. Then in 1964, I was called to Friendship Baptist Church in Fullerton to be its first and founding pastor. I was married at the time. I got married in 1960, and I had one child, a daughter, when we started the church. We were living in L.A., and then we moved to Fullerton in 1968.

Did you have any trouble finding housing in Fullerton?

Well, it took us a year to actually come up with a house that I was finally given permission to buy. I had to go and sit down and confront the vice-president of the

---

[1] Oral History 2366b. Interview date: October 29, 2003, at Pastor Carrington's office in Yorba Linda, California. Interviewer: Robert Johnson.

loan department [at Lincoln Savings and Loan] for approval, because in 1967, the first house that we tried to purchase, I was denied. It was a house in Placentia. After that, we ended up being on like a roller coaster for every house that we submitted an application to purchase. For one reason or another, I was always being denied. Racism was very rampant during those years, especially in the area of housing. I later found out, through my experience, that the loaning institutions were the godfathers of the communities, because most of the houses were being built and owned by tract—certain institutions. And in that way, they could keep minorities out.

I owned a house in Los Angeles, so we weren't that anxious to get out of that house until we bought a house in Fullerton. What happened was, one of my members met one of the professors at Cal State Fullerton and told him that my wife and I were trying to buy a house in Fullerton. Where he lived, in the northeast part of Fullerton, there were two houses coming up for foreclosure, and he knew the dates, the time, and all of that. He told me if I had X number of dollars and if I had a particular house I wanted to buy, I could go to the foreclosing place that morning that it first came on the market and lay down that X number thousands of dollars, and then I would get the deed to the house. Then all I had to do was negotiate with whoever held the first. That's what I did.

However, I did not know that Lincoln Savings and Loan was the one, *again*, who was going to be holding the first on that, but I took my attorney with me, Bob Ward, and we went down and confronted him in Los Angeles. We worked things out and they finally gave me the opportunity to buy the house. I could take over the first.

Regarding your church, in whose homes were you meeting and was it an all-black church?

It was all black from the beginning; then we had a few whites join later. We did that Wednesday night, and then they said, "Can we meet on Sundays?" So we started meeting on Sundays and having worship service. We did that and every time we would close out a service, we'd say, "Okay. Who's going to invite us to their home next week, and where are we going to meet?" Sometimes we met in the living room and dining room. That became our sanctuary. Sometimes we met in people's backyards, and so forth, when the weather was nice. But we didn't do it for too long of a period because we were able to rent an industrial building and we stayed there for a number of years.

Why did you pick Fullerton?

What happened was, my pastor's brother-in-law was a pastor in Watts. Reverend K. D. Flynn was his name and we were very close friends. One Sunday morning, I was led to go visit him. I didn't really know why, but the spirit was on me, so I told my wife, "I'm going to go worship with K. D. today." And she said, "Okay. I'll see you when you get home." So I went out there, and when I was walking into his office, he said, "Carrington! Man, I'm so glad to see you. I've been planning to call you, but I've been so busy I didn't get around to it. I have a member in my church who lives in Fullerton." I didn't even know where Fullerton was at the time. He said, "And she's been wanting to start a work." That was the language we used back in those days for starting a new church. He said, "Would you be interested?" I said, "Yeah, I'd be interested." So he said, "Well, I'll introduce you to her when she comes to church today, and we'll set up something."

Sure enough, he did introduce me to her. Sister Penny Owens was her name.[2] Afterward, he said, "What I'll do, I'll get Penny to call the people together, and then I'll go down to Fullerton, meet with them, and see if they are sincere about getting the church going. If they are, then I will bring you down and introduce you to the people." So that's how it worked out. I brought my wife down on a Wednesday evening, met with the people, and they were very enthusiastic. They seemed very sincere that they really wanted to start a church. There were enough people to really make a go of it, so we just stepped out on faith and believed in the Lord. I liked the area. The few blacks that were in Fullerton at that time, they all did not live primarily in a ghetto, per se. They were scattered out. But that was another challenge later on.

What were your impressions of Orange County before coming here?

All I knew on the surface—Orange County was very racist. They had a reputation for that. After getting here and finding out how things really were, we worked through a lot of that. Of course, I met a number of people, especially after Dr. Martin Luther King was assassinated, and we decided, okay, enough is enough, and we need to start making some changes come about in the community. I figured that we were the only predominantly black church north of Santa Ana, so all these various cities were out there. Blacks were being recruited from the South and from some of our colleges and universities. So when these people would arrive, they were having a hard time finding housing. The companies were giving them a job, but now finding housing was the thing.

A number of us whites and blacks got together and we started doing some intervention work trying to open up that area. That's how the fair housing came into action, because some of us so-called liberal people, black and white together, worked together to make that happen. Then, later on, we also helped establish the Human Relations Commission in Fullerton, which was the first one ever in Orange County, and that is still going even to this day.

What did you and your wife do in fair housing?

We used to go around knocking on doors, especially in housing situations and apartment complexes, and even in some houses that were up for sale. It was done more in the housing for rent, because we had a number of black students that were enrolled in Cal State Fullerton University; they were accepted but they couldn't find housing. We used to target that. The wife and I would go to the apartment and talk to the managers and getting prices and see what they'd tell us about open vacancies, and so forth. Then behind us, a white couple would come and get a

---

[2] See the Mary Owens Oral History 3288 in this chapter.

different opinion, different sense. But that's how we worked that to find out what we could do.

Because of our work—your work, my work—black people were able to find the housing of their choice here in Orange County, eventually. This resulted in a wide dispersion of black people. There is no ghetto. If we had not worried about fair housing, would that have been the right thing?

I think, in the long run, it would have been worse, and it would not have been in the better interest for all of mankind by letting the old area of Fullerton become the ghetto. I have to admit, initially, when we purchased our first piece of property on Lemon Street back in the year 1969, I remember standing out on the lawn one day and visualizing, once we get a building on this piece of property. Traditionally, when whites moved out, blacks moved in. So I'm saying, that being the case, our church is strategically located in the place that blacks are going to come, and this is the area, and we'll be right there to receive them, and it's going to be great.

However, it did not happen. The number one reason why it did not happen is because the area where blacks were expected to come was in the lower-income housing bracket. However, the blacks who were coming to north Orange County specifically—and not so much into Fullerton itself but the other cities—were being hired by industries, and they were being recruited from universities and colleges, so they were getting a fairly decent wage. They weren't looking to buy homes of that caliber [low-income area housing] at that time, so they moved outside. So that enabled them to scatter throughout all these various cities and buy better homes. That prevented a black ghetto in north Orange County, so many of us today are saying that was for our good. Even though we went through some hell in living in areas where we were maybe the only black—like where I ended up moving. My daughter was the only black child in the whole school. So there were some issues and concerns that we had to go through earlier on because of that. But it gave white people who had never lived around blacks an opportunity to find out that we all are equal, and we all have something to give to humanity. And all of this other stuff that they were throwing up, they found out wasn't necessarily true. It turned out good.

Do you think there was a positive relationship between your work in civil rights and human relations and the growth of your church?

When Dr. Martin Luther King was assassinated, I was holding down a full-time job at Aeroneutronic Ford. The day after he was killed, I received a call from the campus minister of Cal State Fullerton University. He said, "Can you get off your job and come and participate with us in a memorial service here on campus? Dr. [William] Langsdorf is president of the university, and he would like to have you come, because you're the only black pastor in the area. We want you to do a prayer or read a scripture, or whatever." And I said, "Fine." I'm going prepared for that, but when I arrived, the black student union president, he said to me, "Pastor Carrington, Dr. Langsdorf wants you to address the professors and the students as well." I said, "Oh, my God. What do I do now?"

I prayed quickly, and the Lord answered and directed me to the first chapter of the Book of Joshua, where Joshua takes over for Moses and is given the charge to do so. So I spoke from that passage of Scripture, and I was trying to inspire the people that all of us need to embrace the lifestyle that Martin Luther King had, ending up giving his life to build a better community worldwide. We won't necessarily be asked to go to other states and all of that, but right here where we live. Wherever we live, let's try to work together and do some things together to break down this racism that exists now.

I think that out of that a lot of things began to happen. I do know that some people that worked for various companies in the employment department, they knew me, and I got to meet a number of them. What they would do when they would hire blacks into their company—one of the first things they would do on the side, very casually—they would say, "There is a church here in the community, Friendship Baptist Church, a predominantly black church, and you can call over there and talk to the pastor. That's where a lot of your people hang out." We got that type of support, so that brought a lot of people in. We weren't advertising in the newspaper and all of that. You wouldn't even know we existed because we were not on the main street in an accessible place where a sign could be put up, Friendship Baptist Church. We were at a dead-end street at the very dead end of the cul-de-sac in an industrial building.

Were those people like Bernice Hurd at Hunt Foods?

Right, yeah. Bernice was one of my main people that used to feed people into—and everything, yeah. We ended up getting the reputation early on that we were a middle-class congregation, upper-middle-class congregation, and some people who have small minds, and so forth, said, "I don't want to be a part of that because I don't want to identify with that." But we did carry that type of reputation for a while. It has its good points and it has its bad within the family.

Did most of your members live in Fullerton?

Our congregation, from the beginning, was a commuting congregation. As we started growing, they were really coming from other cities. That's one of the things that made it difficult for us, because there wasn't one area that we could send out flyers or knock on doors. They were really spread out, and even to this day, we're still spread out. We have them coming all the way from Moreno Valley [Riverside County], we've got them coming from Los Angeles, we have them coming from Long Beach, we have them come in from all the cities by the ocean, down Capistrano, and around.

You used the term "predominantly black."

I don't believe we were even a year old before we had the first white person join our church. So as a result of that, down through the years, we've always had someone of these different nationalities joining our church. They joined it not because of the exterior, but they joined it because of the interior and my preaching and teaching to all people. So they feel comfortable with that.

How has the dispersion of the black community throughout Orange County affected the social life and friendships of black people?

We've gotten along pretty good for the most part. As I look back over a span of thirty-nine years, most of them have ended up marrying within their own race, per se. There's some, just a few, who have married the opposite races or different nationality, but that's just a handful. So, everybody found their own niche, still finds their own niche. It was a problem for some, more in the area of high school type things, for prom times and all of that. But most of them got through it. My daughter got through that as well.

You have one child?

No, I have two. My son was born in 1969, so there's eight years' difference in my son and my daughter. But he was born here in Fullerton. He encountered more problems in school than my daughter. I think that was because his personality was very strong, and you would have thought that he was raised in Los Angeles and then came out here with his hard-core conviction of being black. He'd let you know real quick, "I'm black, I'm proud, and I don't just take anything." He's a very, very intelligent and very gifted young man. He ran into some problems with teachers because he'd be bored in class because they weren't moving fast enough for him. He'd be doing nothing, and when they'd get a test, he'd ace a test, and they can't figure out, "How can you ace a test? I've observed you in class, and you were like you were in another world somewhere and you weren't in class, but still you ace the test."

He was just bored, and the teachers in school had not confronted a black young man like that, and they didn't know how to handle him and caused controversy for him. I remember having a last meeting with the principal over here at the high school, and I said, "Enough is enough." So I just took him out and put him in the extension educational system here in the Placentia-Yorba Linda area and let him just go on up and get his high school diploma that way. He went through that in a few weeks and did all the work that was required of him. How in the world do you take all these tests and pass them so quick? So that's what he did.

So do you feel it's been a positive experience for the children, or negative, living here in Orange County? Did they go to college?

My son didn't go, but my daughter went to Fullerton Junior College for a while. She went about a year or so, and then she ended up getting married. My son didn't get into college or university. He is a musician by trade. When he was a youngster, preteen really, he started playing the drums. We took him and got him some lessons in music. That turned out to be his career. He now has a small band, and they play professionally. And also he plays for the church. Both of them are married. But that's where his love is and his creativity comes out. He's able to work with all, because even the band, the band is integrated. A white fellow started it, and they've been together now for some years.

My daughter, who works in stores, selling and all that kind of stuff, she's very able and gifted to work with all types of people. They both turned out good in that respect. They got their own identity. The wife and I, years ago, we used to laugh at my daughter because when she was on the drill team in high school, sometimes we heard her on the phone. She had one way of talking when she was with us and at the church. Then when she was talking with her classmates in school, it was a different way she spoke. And we could distinguish right away who she's talking to just the way she talked about things. It was very funny and very interesting. You would hear her voice, and if you were in another room, you would think all-white girls are in there, because she just blended herself in, articulating in the white style. When she was with the black kids and young people at church, then there was a switch.

Do you find that being raised mostly around whites provides some sort of advantage in life—finding jobs, and things like that?

If they learn quickly how to play the game. By living in this environment, they're more exposed than a lot of persons who come strictly out of the ghetto, and therefore, have a certain degree advantage over their counterparts in that regard. Like I say, they would know how whites normally react to some things, and they wouldn't be so prone to push the button and get all excited about that. They'd put it off and say that's just typically white, so just keep on going.

Do you feel that members of your congregation feel isolated from the white community around it?

I don't feel that they're isolated. I think, by and large, there has not been all of that openness, and just being who you are still exists. So when we leave our setting here and our involvement in the church, a number of our members belong to different fraternities, sororities, and other types of organizations, predominantly black organizations. They do their socialization in those particular arenas. There are a few that are in businesses that cause them to be in integrated situations outside of the church, and they seem to like that, enjoy that, and they keep going.

Do you have any favorite story, or stories, relating to you being a black person and living in almost all-white Orange County?

Well, I think one incident comes to mind that was earlier on in my pastorate. I was asked to come and preach at the First Presbyterian Church in Placentia. Knowing whites as I did, I knew I was going into a different environment—even though it was a religious environment—than what I was accustomed to. I was trying to figure out, okay, how am I going to handle this situation? How can I break this coldness in the sanctuary? What I did after I was introduced to the congregation, before my message and everything—I got up and I did my formal acknowledgments. Then, "If everyone would please say, 'Amen.'" They said, "Amen," but when they started saying, "Amen," they started laughing because they knew where I was coming from. It was a very touching moment when that happened because it kind of broke the ice. Then they knew that I knew a little bit about who they are and how they worship and all of that. I'm from a high-powered, very enthusiastic, very supportive, loud environment when it comes to worshipping God, and they are very laid back. So that helped break the ice.

Later on in my message that I ended up bringing that day—I forget exactly the title of the sermon and all that but I did recall that I caught their attention—that in creation when God made man, God made man from the dust of the earth, and then he blew into a man and became a living soul. I said, "Now, I haven't seen any white dust, never have." Oh, that got them to thinking, working a little bit. We got along that day. I shall never forget that experience.

Well, the last question: Are you glad you came to Orange County?

Very much so. Because I would have missed out on a lot of blessings, and especially divine intervention in my personal life and in the lives of others that I've witnessed. So I just praise God for what he has allowed me to do, because being here, as opposed to being in L.A., I really had to call on God for a lot of things. We did not have the resources like if we would have been in Los Angeles. So, in order to get where we were, we had to totally depend on God. And God opened up some rivers for us, like the Red Sea. God provided us with our first permanent church building that was placed on our property. God touched the hearts and minds of the Presbyterian, the Unitarian, the Baptist, the Catholic, the Lutheran, the Jewish synagogue in Fullerton back in the early sixties when we purchased the property. Bob [Ward] again was involved with that. They gave us over $7,000 that we needed to pay for the down payment of buying the land. They did it without me having to talk to the pastor or go to their church, or whatever. They just gave it to Bob and said, "Here. We want to help you."

Some churches invited me so the congregation could actually meet me. One of them was the Episcopal Church. I went there to preach on Sunday morning, and after the service was over and I'm going to my car. A young lady, who had a couple small kids, she said, "Pastor Carrington, excuse me. I want to help you guys get a church, but I'm going in the hospital tomorrow, in fact. I've got to have some surgery done. And I don't have any money with me outside of this thirty-seven cents. Would you be offended if you'd take this thirty-seven cents that I have?" Before I could get to my car, another woman came to me, and she said, "Pastor Carrington, you got a minute? I want to make a contribution to your church fund so you guys can get your property." I said, "Okay." So she reached in her purse, she gave me five new $20 bills. So I get thirty-seven cents from one and then get a hundred dollars.

Thank you, Pastor Carrington, for letting me interview you.

Chapter 5
Migration into South Orange County

In this book, the term "South Orange County" refers to communities generally south of where African Americans lived in the beginning of the 1960s. These were cities located south of Anaheim and south-east of Santa Ana, where there were virtually no black residents, except for the two important exceptions of the marine air facilities at El Toro and Tustin.

South of east Anaheim is the city of Orange. The first oral history in this chapter is that of Wacira Gethaiga, who grew up in Kenya and who provides a foreign person's view of what it is like being black in Orange County. Although he first lived with a family in Anaheim, the major part of his interview involves his experiences when he attended Chapman College in the city of Orange.

In 1960, there were only nine black residents in Orange. By 1970, there were 213. This increase was, in part, due to the opening in the early 1960s of three housing developments called Eichler homes, named after the builder. These three were scattered from the south to the north of the city, and each was integrated in the sense that residing in each development was a small number of black families. In 1963, the Jo and Ken Caines family, including their six-year old son, Chris, purchased a home in the second Eichler development, in the north part of Orange. Except for having to deal with a presumed neighborhood stabilization issue, their move went smoothly. Seven years later, the Clemons family also moved, with no problems, into an all-white neighborhood of Orange, which was only a few blocks west of where the first Eichler tract was built in the south part of the city. The Caines's oldest son, Chris, and the Clemons's son, Robert, each became student-body presidents of their large, non-black Villa Park and El Modena high schools.

James McKay, his wife, and his son had been living only a short time in Watts when that area of Los Angeles exploded. This was in the summer of 1965. When the revolt/riot was over, they got Jim's "uncle" in Laguna Beach to take them into his home. They stayed there for about a year, and Jim found work at a local carwash. In 1969, under more relaxed conditions, Barbara Youngblood, a physical therapist, and her engineer husband, Fred, came down from northern California. He having a job waiting for him at Autonetics in Anaheim. They first rented a house, and then purchased that same rental house in Westminster and later found out that they were the only black family to own a home in that city of 55,000. Another "first" came later when Barbara Youngblood went on to law school and became the first black female attorney in Orange County.

WACIRA GETHAIGA[1]

Professor Wacira Gethaiga was born in a small village in the central part of Kenya. He tells about his family and schooling in Africa and his coming to America. His story points out differences in being raised an African, as opposed to experiences of most African Americans. In spite of his background, he still had to deal with some of the same problems faced by American black people, such as housing discrimination and racial profiling. Professor Gethaiga lives with his wife Waithera in a home near Cal State Fullerton University where he chairs and teaches in the Department of Afro-Ethnic Studies. Photo, ca. 1970.

Please tell us about your life in Africa.

I was the youngest in a family of six. I had a sister before me and a brother, and then four other sisters. My third sister, her name was Wairimo, had become a teacher, like all the other members of my family, except my mother. My father was the first teacher. He didn't have much education, but the missionaries were reaching out. Anybody who could read and write was a teacher. He established schools, he established churches, he did all of those kinds of things. That was his life goal.

Since all the members of my family were teachers, I think I benefited from their being older than I was. When they came home from school, I would pester them to see what it is they were doing. My eldest sister was already a teacher, so she would help me. She would take me with her to class, because I was still not old enough to go to school. They'd give me a slate, and I learned how to write before I was four, or something like that. There was always a quest for knowledge, and I wanted to do that.

---

[1] Oral History 2151b. Interview date: January 14, 2005, at the Afro-American Resource Center at California State University, Fullerton. Interviewer: Robert Johnson.

An African at that time, educated, had two choices. One was to work for the government, if he got that far, or to teach. So there was always the possibility that I was going to become a teacher. But I didn't want to. However, my many travels from one part of the country to the other, living with the people and learning new things, also increased my knowledge and my desire to learn.

Sometimes I would lose a year of school here because I was not there the year before, and I did not belong to that particular ethnicity. In the process, I learned about three or four different local languages. My sister, the third one, left teaching. She went into journalism, and she met an American woman who was traveling, who sponsored her to come to the United States. Now, that became a goal. I kept on saying, "Maybe down the line I'll get a chance to go outside." That started about the late 1950s, not even knowing that it would ever happen. Through a combination of things—my sister, her friend, and some friends that she had met in the United States were able to get support from a family in Anaheim: Charles and Elaine Bradd. They were my family here.

So in 1961, after a long process, I got admitted to Occidental College [in Los Angeles County], on a partial scholarship. So I came to Orange County in September 1961, for starting school at Occidental College. Instead, I spent the next year at Anaheim High School, which was wonderful because not only did I get to polish my language skills, but also learned something about American culture. I was one of the first foreign students from Africa at Anaheim High School. From there, in 1962, I went to Occidental College. Luckily enough, my sister was also a student there, and she was in her senior year. So at least I was not like a fish out of water. At that time, there were four black students at Occidental College. It was a small college, but there was not a single African American in that campus. All four were from Africa.

When you first started going to school in Anaheim, what was it like dealing mostly with white people?

In Africa, we really did not deal with the Europeans. Their system of education was a three-tier system. There were the African, the Asian, and the European schools. The European schools were A-class, class one; the Asian schools were number two; the African schools were [not even three, but] number four. Basically, the classes were taught in English. We had been trained from fifth grade to speak nothing but English in class at school. It really wasn't like something that I hadn't had.

Most Kenyans had never really seen a white man face to face when I was growing up. The only reason why I had come in contact with them was because of the fact that we were a member of the Church Missionary Society, which became PCEA [Presbyterian Church of East Africa]. Every so often, the minister that had been sent over there would come into our rural areas just to visit, to see how the church is going. We would listen to them in their broken Swahili and Kykuyu and forgive them for all of that, but at least they were there. There was no relationship between an African and a white person, other than one of master and servant. My father refused to ever work for one after carrying one in a rickshaw back in the latter part of the nineteenth century. It was just like slavery.

I had had the opportunity, by chance or by design, to move from one ethnic group to another during my growing up period, seeking education, trying to save myself during the Mau-Mau. So I was used to movement. When I came to Anaheim, the family was wonderful with me.

You stayed at their home?

I stayed at their home. The school was a few blocks away, so I used to walk there. A woman from Germany, who was also a foreign student, was staying with a family two streets away, so we used to walk together. This was 1962. As far as when I went into class and whatever, there is that initial thing. You are interacting with all of these people. You don't know who they are, they don't know who you are; but nobody's attacking me, so I really didn't feel threatened.

Were there any other black children in the school?

In Anaheim High School, there were none at that time. There were a few Mexicans. One of them is a professor at Fullerton Junior College, and we've been friends ever since. Actually, they kind of allowed me to be in their group. I was also being sponsored by the church that the Bradds belonged to, the Methodist Church. So I used to go to church at that time, and I was a member of the young people's association.

That relationship in and of itself had a very lasting effect on me, because being the only black in the place, I never really felt out of place. I could take care of myself; I couldn't argue with anybody. So it was not the kind of antagonism that people are talking about. I even didn't know that there was much of a problem. And the reason is this: that for us as Africans, we knew nothing about the, quote, slavery existence of black people in the United States. Our [American] history, as far as the British were concerned, went until 1776. When they lost the colonies, what they taught us about history ended there.

Did the family in Anaheim take any flak because of you being there?

Not that I know of. And this was the reason: Mr. Bradd had gone to the Congo in 1960, during the crisis in the Congo. He was there trying to build a church. They had to be evacuated. Then their daughter, the oldest one who was my sister's friend, was very interested in international students. She had gone to Chile, and she had brought a Chilean woman to stay with them. They had a family that had a very proactive daughter, who was befriending everybody, and they all came to the house. When I was living with them, it was like a small United Nations. So often we had people from New York, like from the Bronx; there were people from Ghana; there were people from Nigeria; we had my sister from Kenya.

I would say the family in Anaheim and the Methodist Church in Anaheim were very, very proactive in terms of trying to bring about racial awareness in the United States. So if there was any flak, it would have been outside of that particular family. Even with the grandparents in that house, we became very good friends. Their youngest son was about fourteen at that time; we were sharing a room. I always felt like I was part of that family. When I left the family, they were able to also sponsor a relative of mine from my other village. He came and stayed with them for several years, eventually going to Westmont College and is now back in Kenya. That [racial] part of it never really became a problem.

Most of what I remember about the Civil Rights Movement, initially, was because of sitting with a woman from London to New York. She was talking about Malcolm X and how awful this individual is, and I'm saying, "Malcolm X? I don't even know who this person is, and why is she so afraid of Malcolm X?" [This was in 1961.] Why is she so afraid of this person? She said, "Well, the Black Muslims, this or whatever." She talked my ear off all the way through the flight. So I made a point to get to know who Malcolm X was, who Elijah Mohammed was, who Martin Luther King was.

In Anaheim, where I was going to school with Hispanics and whites and other people, there were no problems. Actually, I spent most of the summer of 1962 as a YMCA counselor, and there were no problems with the kids, no problems with parents. The people in Anaheim, I think, are very exceptional, in almost every case. I remember those years very well.

So when I went to Occidental College, like I told you, there were only four of us Africans. But the next year, the Rockefeller Foundation provided some money to bring in African Americans. At that time, elite institutions were including African students into their campuses, but not African American students because of their issues on discrimination and segregation and all of that. So the Africans that came to the United States in the early sixties had a better chance, if they were qualified, to get into these elite and semi-elite schools that African Americans could not get into. So there has always been that kind of little tension, for some of the people really didn't know what was happening. And even at that time, we didn't know. We, the Africans, were just looking for a chance at an education. We really did not know what was going on here; our history was really deficient.

I graduated in '66 from Oxy [Occidental], and I came to Chapman College [in the city of Orange] at the end of that year. One of my former faculty members at Occidental College had become the dean at Chapman College, so I got into Chapman. I stayed there for a year, and then went to UC Berkeley, and I came back down here. So Orange County has been very much of a base.

Where did you live during that year at Chapman?

Chapman at that time had three Kenyan students, and the same year, in 1966, they brought in ten Africans from the French colonies. They were being housed on the campus. Myself and another Kenyan, we were graduate students, and we are not eligible for housing, at least there. So we tried to find apartments on the outside, and we couldn't. Eventually, the campus allowed us to stay in the married students' quarters. David and myself got one of the rooms over there, so we shared that. Then we were trying to get an apartment outside. We were calling any time we saw an apartment because we wanted to move out. We wanted to cook for ourselves and maybe find girlfriends.

That is where I met you, [Bob Johnson], because I was trying to get an apartment, and it was advertised, and we had called. We were told it was there.

We got there, and we were told it was rented a week before. It was still in the paper, and when somebody called back, it was still available. Then you helped us.

In particular, my wife, Lois.

She tried to help us get into that apartment, paid the deposit, and whatever. Then they saw that we were these black folks, and they would not let us have the apartment. When I lived here, it was really very much like a cocoon. I really didn't meet that many black people when I was in Orange. But we could not fail to notice what was going on across the country with the sit-ins, with the beatings, and things like that. So we got involved in many ways, individually and collectively. And of course, being a foreign student and a visa person, there are so many restrictions about the things I could do and could not do. I could not be arrested demonstrating. In any case, nobody was demonstrating in Orange. But wherever I was, at Occidental College and then at Chapman, I was involved with groups that were pushing the Civil Rights Movement. I got into some marches when I went to the East Coast in 1963, '64, '65, but always being very careful not to get arrested.

You had told me about your relationship with the city of Orange police and what happened there with regard to identifying you.

I had this jalopy I guess you call it—an old car, 1948 Ford. It was like a two-seater with an extended back. I paid a hundred dollars for it, and I could go anywhere I wanted. (laughs) When I came to Orange, back to the campus, I would pick up a tail, a police tail and got stopped many times. I would tell them, "I'm going to Chapman College, I'm a graduate student at Chapman College." Now, since there was really nothing that was wrong with the car, old as it was, they would let me go, but they would follow me all the way to the married students' quarters.

I was working in Anaheim, as a stock boy at the Broadway store in Anaheim. So when I got in my car and I'm going back to Orange in the early evening, I would be followed. Got stopped many times. Now, things didn't really get worse until the school started, and now there are three or four people in my car. And the police would follow me, same thing. I kept on complaining that we were being stopped for nothing. We are not speeding. We have not broken any law.

Well, we started complaining to the administration at Chapman College. The president of the campus said, "Well, we shall see what we can do." Now, remember, there are no black Americans in this place, so it's not like it was technically a civil rights issue. I mean, we didn't think so. We thought that we are just being harassed because we don't belong in the area.

You're saying there were no African Americans at Chapman College, only Africans.

Only the Africans. Of course, I didn't know everybody at Chapman College. I just knew that there are hardly any other black people there. There were about thirteen of us on campus. Not all of them were driving with me, but every time we got stopped, we would complain. Eventually, the president said, "Well, we can talk to the police and see what we can do." And they did. The first thing the police said,

"Well, we really don't have anything against your African students, or anything like that, but we need to know who they are so we can know that they are not coming from someplace else." Their plan was for us to go to the police station to get our pictures taken, and then when they see us, then they would let us go.

Whose idea was that?

That was the police; that was their response. When we talked to the president of the campus, we said, "No. We are not criminals, and we don't have to carry an identity pass." It was the idea that the police are going to use our pictures to identify us from other blacks. Hence, we become special, and that is also another form of harassment in and of itself. Okay, here is a select group of people. Those ones you don't touch, but you can beat the crap out of everybody else. So we refused. And I don't think that we were being very political, that we were being pro-civil rights or anything like that. It was just the feeling of being separated just because we come from Africa.

There were not that many blacks residing in Orange. Orange is the most lily-white city, basically, and they were keeping everybody out who was not. I do remember that black people coming from Santa Ana—by the time they get to where the 22 Freeway is now, they would either pick up a police tail or they would be stopped.

Their solution was to get our pictures and distribute them to the police, so when they see us, they know these are safe people. Safe from what? We are not here trying to be that. It was really kind of a basic principle of human rights. I felt at that time that we were being denied that human right, just like it had been denied to African Americans and everybody else. I would not say that we were really standing on principles, but I felt that we needed to let them know that first and foremost, we are human beings. We just happened to be black.

The college was supportive. I really can't say enough about Chapman College. I think Chapman College took responsibility for the foreign students to the max; they wanted to make sure that they had a good experience in the United States, in Orange, and that they did learn something. So I can't fault the administration there. They were doing the best they could. Even when we were working with Mrs. Bob Johnson, I think she actually helped us get to understand the United States a lot better than we could have with anybody else.

One of the students, a friend of yours, Bob Choto, was able to eventually find housing off of the campus. I can remember that you would sometimes walk with him to his house, and you would have to pass the John Birch Society meeting place.

We would be walking [on Glassell Avenue] from the Orange Circle towards the freeway, and I kept on saying we really need to stop at this John Birch Society and find out what it is. Somehow, the windows would be open, and somebody would see us coming, and they would just head for the door. Then all the curtains would come on closed and the door is closed. We'd knock there, and nobody would answer the door, and nobody even would peek out on the other side. So we figured that there was a reason why they were hiding from us, and I think you taught me about the John Birch Society. I didn't even know what it was.

It was that kind of place where discrimination was not out in the open except in certain areas. Because there were so very few of us in Orange, in Anaheim, people did not feel uncomfortable until there was a critical mass, and we didn't have that. So we can't say that we were really an irritant that much. People who saw us, they just saw us and they maybe would ask, what are they doing here? But we were not accosted.

It was in Orange where I'm walking on Glassell, going the other way [from the freeway], and this young boy saw me, and then he was looking at my hands and said, "Don't you wash your hands? They seem like they are dirty." I said, "No, that is my color. Just like you have white color, that's just mine. That doesn't wash off." And the mother was so upset, "Don't you dare do that again." I said, "Don't worry about it. If he has never really experienced a different kind of individual, when is he going to learn?"

Later on, of course, we'd find that getting an apartment in Orange was a problem not only because we were students, but even when we were teachers. When my friend came to Orange, his wife was white; he was teaching at Chapman College. He had a job in San Bernardino, but he could not get an apartment in Orange. So when she went looking for an apartment, she went with a white man and got the apartment, then brought her husband. It was a big to-do, and the manager was upset. But they had already signed a lease, so they stayed. (laughs) Sometimes you had to do things like that.

You went to UC Berkeley. Then you came back here.

I came back here to teach at Cal State Fullerton. Your wife had introduced us to Beth Voien. She would invite me to her house, and I got to be friends with her and her family. I was the one who was encouraging her to go back to school. I found her to be very creative, to be very open to ideas. I said, "Well, you can just go back to college, and maybe you'll finish something. Maybe just learn something." Because she was interested in Africa—she was interested in all kinds of things. When I left Orange in 1967 to go to UC Berkeley, she had started taking classes at Cal State Fullerton.

In 1970, [Professor] Larry de Graaf was involved with the group that set up a program to bring in minority students—Hispanics, blacks, Indians—to Cal State Fullerton. Up to that point, there had been no active recruitment of any of these groups. That started because there were all of these sit-ins and these demands, non-negotiable demands, on most of the other campuses. So they were aware that it was going to get here also, and they were forward-looking enough to want to stem that tide. They had also brought a black person, who was working with Beth Voien, and they had been charged with recruiting the faculty who would be able to teach Chicano Studies and Afro Studies. The guy we brought here started looking at people in graduate schools. Berkeley, of course, was famous because of the riots—the People's Park. I was there.

Beth notified me that they were looking for a person in that area. So when I learned that there is a possibility that they're hiring some people, I put myself on the market, was invited to come down, got interviewed. At that time, I did not have any hope of getting the job anyway. But I was ABD [All But Dissertation] and they were looking for somebody that at least would be able to start something. I was really just looking for something to do. Then I was back into Orange County.

When did you meet your wife, Waithera?

I had met her about the time that I came to Chapman in '66, '67. We started dating sometime in the seventies. She was going to Chaffey Junior College [San Bernardino County], and later on she went to Cal Poly [Pomona, in Los Angeles County]. When I came down, we got serious, and that's when we got married, about 1971, after my second year here.

What had you been doing here? Teaching?

The beginning of the Ethnic Studies program here in 1969 was really just an idea. There were two Hispanics and two blacks. They were looking for Ph.D. program people so that they did not have to pay out all that much. I got the idea we were not staying here very long. We were able to work together collectively to develop a curriculum that was really Ethnic Studies. We were able, in the very first year, to get the program through the faculty council and the academic senate so that we got a degree program instead of just a program, which would have been wiped out as soon as the money ran out.

How do you attribute the fact that you survived?

Well, I think it's because nobody really expected us to be here for very long. We, at least the original four of us, concentrated on academics. We wanted to develop quality programs. Some of the curriculum at that time was not worth anything. But here in Fullerton, we could not get away with that. We did not have the student base to support that kind of thing, and we had to also sell ourselves to the institution in terms of the relevancy of the kind of studies that we were planning to do here. Not only that, all four of us were students. When I realized that I may be here for longer than a year, I decided to enroll in Claremont Graduate School [Los Angeles County]. I would have gone to UCI, but being a foreign student at that time, it was going to be more expensive, or just as expensive, as going to Claremont. And Claremont was much more supportive.

In the early seventies, one of the students, James Pugh, was interviewed for *Harvest*.[2] He had very strong language—"black nationalist" language. How did you get along with a student like this?

---

[2] *Harvest*, Editors: Priscilla Oaks and Wacira Gethaiga. Published by the Oral History Program, California State University, Fullerton, 1975. Oral History 2139, interview dates: October, 8, 10, 18, 1974. Interviewers: Jody Wallick and Murphy Holmes.

Our classes were not necessarily political. We were not here to develop militants. The issue was to educate them, or to get information to them about what they hadn't learned and how to negotiate the system. You can call people names, but if you really don't have any business to back them up, it does not make your case any better.

I've been very lucky, in an African American Studies program, in the sense that I come from a totally different perspective from where they come from. In the sense that I have never not known that I am black, that I'm a human being, and that I have a reason for being where I am, that I have a right to be there. I never did live in a farm with a white man so that he can jump on all my ideals. I actually would have been a militant Mau-Mau sympathizer had I been old enough.

So yes, we had some very outspoken black students in the classes. We had the Black Panthers, and I invited them to come to my class, because I wanted the students—white, Asians—to know that these black activists, if you want to call them that, were not necessarily bad people. They are people who are just trying to open people's eyes. I was not going to hide anything. I was not going to say that a white man is bad or good. The issue is, are your rights being trampled upon by others? So from that perspective, I have never really been in fights with my students. In disagreements, yes, but never in fights.

I know UCI got in trouble in the sixties for inviting certain people to UCI. How was this different at Cal State Fullerton?

Because we were so very small, we were not going to create much in terms of unnecessary turmoil. We had at one time some very militant Black Student Union leaders that would not let a black woman be seen with a white man. Yet, they themselves had white women that would be part of their groupies. People should really have a right to associate. We don't have any entitlement. This is an academic institution, and we have to deal with the institution from an academic perspective. I have never really believed that just yelling and yelling is going to do it. It did have a purpose in 1968, '69, and '70, but after that, other things took precedence. The war in Vietnam became more intense; Chicano Studies became bigger; Asian Americans started to feel their oats.

In the process of doing all of this, we managed to develop a curriculum for people trying to find out about Africa, about African Americans, about civil rights. Since Orange County was never really that much involved with the Civil Rights Movement, like in the South, they had to learn it in school. So we made sure that they learned it. I think it was 1972 or '73 we brought Ralph Abernathy here.[3] Orange County has this image of being anti-black, but that's not really the case. I have lived here long enough to know that most of the people do not go to sleep every night saying, "How are we going to get rid of them."

Then you and Waithera had children; and when were they born?

[3] Ralph Abernathy followed Dr. Martin Luther King as the head of the Southern Christian Leadership Conference (SCLC) after King's death.

One was born in 1970, and the other one was born in 1977, both girls. The first one is Wanjiro, and the second one is Wakanyi.

Do they feel at all African? Do they feel African American?

I don't really think that the issue really comes up that often. The only time it does come up is when my older daughter would say, "You should have taught me how to speak Kikuyu and Swahili." The people they were interacting with were white children in the neighborhood, and it's very difficult to teach people or kids a language that they're not going to be hearing on a constant basis.

I have tried as much as possible to take the kids back to Kenya to meet their relatives. They were able to meet their grandparents before they passed away. But they still have that language thing. Now, the older one, her grandfather on her mother's side, spoke English. He owned a little store, and he and she would spend the whole day together, because he loved to hear her speak in English. I think they have adjusted pretty well. They do not worry too much about whether they are Africans or blacks. They are human beings, and they are Americans in their way of thinking. They do have the two heritages, and each one of them will choose where they want to be.

The kids went to church when they were young. Mostly they went to a Christian church right across from the campus where most of the people in the community went. I did give them the opportunity to go to church, to go to Sunday school, and all of that, but I was not going to push that on them. I'm not anti-religious. I'm actually very religious, but not necessarily in the Christian way, because as I grew up and as I explored more, I found that there are lots of things that could have been done differently to make Christianity or religion really a meaningful experience for us. I think I have laid the moral foundation for them to follow, and they are doing that. We participated in ceremonies and rites of passage in other areas, but the family was always central.

Socially, what did the family do?

Actually, what happened through the 1970s and early '80s, was that in the African communities, there was at least a gathering going on at somebody's house every other weekend. Everybody came. They would bring their beer, we would barbecue, dance, and those kinds of things. So there was never a lack of contact. So as far as our socializing, we did that almost invariably among the Africans. We'd invite some black Americans that we had become friends with, like the ones I was working with here, but it never extended all that far to where we ended up like in Santa Ana or inner city Los Angeles.

So there was a large enough African community in Orange County.

Not in Orange County, mostly Pomona and Los Angeles. But as Africans, I think we all have that foreigner's kind of thing. We are so few that we could identify with each other and feel like we had something much more in common right here. We were driving all over the place. We'd go to Riverside, we'll go to Pomona, we'd go to L.A.

So your children experienced that, but where was their social life?

Their social life was mostly with the white kids in Orange County. They both went to Cal State Fullerton after Troy High School [in Fullerton]. Then the first one finished and went to New York University and has a master's in social work, and the other one finished her B.A. here. The older one worked for several years as a social worker in New York, and then worked in the bank. Kind of got tired of that and decided to apply to the Peace Corps. Ended up in Samoa and spent two years there. Now she is back in New York. The other one is still here.

Do you have much of a relationship, other than through the university, with the African American community?

There is really no black community in Fullerton in and of itself. There are really not that many things that we do outside of the university that involve us. I guess there is that feeling of being an outsider in some cases. I wouldn't really call myself a center of African American activity. Most of my social relationships are with Africans. Now Africans live in Orange County too, lots of them. I mean, there are large groups. When you consider the 1970s and '60s, we were very few. But today, I don't really have to go very far. Because of that, the critical mass in terms of Africans here is large enough that I could do all my socializing within that community.

What would you like to tell us at the end here?

I would say that on one hand, my living in Orange County was little more a blessing than something else, in the sense that Orange County being what it was and then my coming in a time when people really didn't know what to do with me as an African or as a black person, and really having the loving relationship with my American family, and then meeting people like Lois Johnson and Beth Voien and their families, I've never really felt like an outsider in this place. And the more I interact with the students, even though today the majority of them are Anglos, I feel that I'm really just part and parcel of Orange County.

[Regarding practicing what I teach,] I used to be a checker when we would be denied housing over here at Cal State Fullerton—the apartments around here. Black students, not very many, would go to try and get an apartment, and they are told there is no apartment. So the president's office would call me and say, "We have had some students saying that they are being discriminated. Would you go in there as a checker?" I have done this many times. We teach a class on the history of racism. The students fight against it, they say it doesn't exist, but they do like to come in and at least discuss those issues of the day and see how the present and the past are interrelated. And that has become possibly one of our better classes on campus.

Thank you very much, my friend.

JOSEPHINE CAINES[1]

This interview of Jo Caines and the following interview with her son, Chris Caines, provide a multigenerational view of an Orange County African American family. At great length, in the unedited oral history, Jo Caines discusses husband Ken's and her family backgrounds and their own history before and after marriage. This edited version provides highlights of that material. Jo Caines is an extraordinary individual who has been deeply involved in many organizations and causes ranging from the Cub Scouts to civil rights to working as a program manager at Orange County television station KOCE and being vice-president of the California Association of Public Broadcasting. Although Ken passed away in 1998, Jo continued to live in the Eichler home that she and Ken had purchased in 1963. Jo passed away January 3, 2009. Photo ca. 2000.

Tell us about your parents and your racial or ethnic background.

I'm kind of a mutt. My dad was Isaac Otto Robinson, and his father was a mixture of American Indian and black. His mother was white, and she was Jewish. My mother's dad was Walter Nat Turner, and his great-grandfather was the famous slave Nat Turner. They said he was a genius, but he was a little crazy. My grandmother, I didn't know. Her name was Isabel and I understand she was half French and half black. So that's as far as I've gone. I understand that there are a lot of other things in my background. As a matter of fact, my cousin from Philadelphia tells me that we are also the ancestors of Thomas Jefferson; as so many others have claimed. Thomas was very busy.

Tell us about the kind of neighborhoods you grew up in.

I lived in Philadelphia until we moved to Atlantic City, [New Jersey], in 1941. The schools in Philadelphia were partially integrated. Then from there we went to

[1] Oral History 3052. Interview date: April 17, 2003, at the home of Josephine Caines in Orange, California. Interviewer: Robert Johnson.

Atlantic City, where the schools were not integrated. It was an all-black school and I had a bit of a hard time.

How did you view your family?

Well, I guess we were middle-class, because my grandfather did go to college; however, he chose not to be the teacher, for which he got his training. He became the person in a fancy restaurant? The concierge or something like that. And he was always very, very distinguished, with his white collars and vests. He sent my mother and all four of his children to school. She went to training for a teacher. Didn't care for teaching. Then she went to training for a secretary. Didn't care for being a secretary and ended up being a fantastic chef. She taught my father to be a chef.

During the Depression, they were doing pretty good until the late thirties because he helped build bridges, and she was cooking. So we never were poor at that time. From the time I was born until I was nine or ten, things went fairly well for our family. Some of us lived together with relatives and supported one another. But in the late thirties, things became very difficult, and that's why we moved to Atlantic City, for my dad to seek work, because building bridges was over. For a year, living in Atlantic City, we were very poor. We lived in a one-room boarding house, the three of us. I was an only child.

[In high school] I was a fairly good student. I wasn't the very top of my class, but I was a high achiever and worked hard and I had some talents. I was very, very popular in high school. I loved high school. I sang; I was athletic. It was just a wonderful experience for me. I was a good writer and I was a good debater and I was a good performer and a good athlete. I didn't know what I wanted to do with my life, except that I did enjoy writing more than anything. I applied to New York University [NYU]. I was accepted, but most of my black friends went to schools in the South.

Where did you meet your husband Ken?

Well, I met Ken at NYU. His background was very interesting. He was first generation West Indian. His mother and dad were both born in the West Indies: St. Kitts and Montserrat. His mother had a French accent and his dad had an English accent. They were very, very wonderful people. They weren't crazy about me at the beginning. My father-in-law-to-be did like me, but my mother-in-law didn't. You know, it was her son. Interesting enough, back in those days, in the late forties and fifties, black folks had their own thing. I was a little dark for my mother-in-law, dark complexioned. I think she envisioned her first son having a black young woman of fair complexion, and I didn't turn out to be that. But I won her over. By the time we got well into our marriage, I loved my mother-in-law and she loved me dearly.

I remember Ken telling me that he was in the service during the Second World War.

Well, Ken went to Tuskegee, and as you know, the air force at that time was segregated, and the army as well. I remember Ken saying that he did want to fly, but he didn't quite make it to be a pilot. I don't know the reason why, because he was bright enough, but I know he did fly for a while but he didn't make it. I remember people asking him, "Did you go overseas?" And Ken said, "Oh, yes, I went overseas: Mississippi, Alabama." (laughs) He was angry about that. He was angry about the fact that he didn't [get his wings], because Ken always wanted to accomplish what he went after.

At that time, the railroad was also segregated. The black troops had to sit in the cars right behind the engine, and the white troops had to sit in the back where there wasn't as much soot. And Ken and his friend, who were more fair-complexioned, were told to go sit in the back. Then he said, "Well, we're black." And they said, "Well, you're not black enough." (chuckles) He had a lot of anger about those things.

You married while you were still in college?

When I got married, I didn't have a job but I finally found one—a temporary job at a black newspaper for about four or five months. Then I got a job at Standard Oil of New Jersey, which is now called Exxon. It was called Creole Petroleum. I was the first black person hired at Creole Petroleum; I was a messenger and I passed the mail around. But I was very cheerful, and I was very outgoing, and people would say, "Do you like being a messenger, do you like being a mail girl?" And I would say, "No, [but it is alright] as long as I don't stay this way." Sure enough, in about six months, I was promoted to the personnel department. Then *I* started hiring people, particularly the minority folks who came to look for work.

Why did you leave New York, and where did you go next?

We always said if we had children, we would like to leave New York and venture out West, someplace where there were more open spaces. We both agreed to that. We took trips across country to see where we wanted to live. We stopped off in Denver, Colorado. It was everything that we had hoped for. Our son, Chris, was born in May of 1957 and Ken said, "I'm going to run back out to Denver to see what the job opportunities are." When he went there, it seemed pretty good. So he said, "Yep, let's do it." Chris and I left in September of '57.

We almost starved to death in Denver, because by that time there were no jobs. The 1957 recession had set in. It was the first time that I'd ever seen my husband cry, because he felt he couldn't take care of his family. He was either overqualified, they would say, or not experienced enough. He tried to be a taxicab driver. He tried to be a box boy at the grocery stores and a cashier. I must have typed maybe five hundred letters for him looking for a job. He was called for quite a few interviews, but when they saw him and saw that he was black, they turned him down.

Then he saw a job loading boxcars. You knew my husband; you never could picture him loading boxcars. (chuckles) He would have to be at work by five in the morning. I used to make a box lunch for him, and I'd always put a note in there to tell him how much I loved him, to cheer him up, to make his day better, hopefully, because he was so miserable. He had that job for about six or seven months.

And then, finally, there was a job opening——I think it was at Martin——a job opening for a human-factors scientist, which was a new phrase to us. So he applied, and lo and behold, he was hired. In the meantime, we opened up and took over a cleaning establishment, and we were in the cleaning business, cleaning clothes for a while. I was babysitting the neighborhood kids. And we were doing all kinds of things to try and make our life better.

Denver's where we really began to get involved in civil rights and all of those things that were important to the quality of life for people. Ken worked very hard in the NAACP. He worked very hard in the Housing Authority and fair housing. I don't think they called it fair housing then. But one of the jobs was to try to make people realize they didn't have to live where they were. They could move anywhere.

Then Martin closed down. They promised to transfer their employees, and so we moved to Lompoc [about 150 miles north of Los Angeles in Santa Barbara County]. Then Ken got a job with McDonnell Douglas. We moved down to L.A. and we lived on a street off of what is now Martin Luther King Boulevard.

We stayed there until we moved to Orange County in February 1963. We heard about the Eichler homes[2] long before that. We always dreamed that maybe one day we would find one, but we never thought they would be here in Orange County. We had seen them in Palo Alto, we'd see them in Walnut Creek, but we never thought there would be Eichler homes here in Orange County.

What were your views of Orange County, from an L.A. perspective?

Well, from my perspective, first of all, it was a little tainted, or someone tried to taint it. The sorority that I belong to, the Delta Sigma Theta sorority, had a chapter in L.A. There was a choir, and I felt I would get involved that way, singing. And I did. There was a woman who was in the choir with me, who lived down here in Orange County. She was a black woman. After rehearsal, I introduced myself and told her that we were thinking about moving to Orange County and [asked] if she could tell me something about it, and she was extremely negative. She herself was a math teacher at McPherson Junior High [in the city of Orange], and her husband was the first black pharmaceutical director of the Orange County Medical Center. It's now UC Irvine. So they were well educated folks, but she was very, very negative about it. She said people looked at her funny, she said they looked at her boys funny, that she still came up to L.A. to do all her buying. She came up to L.A. to go to her church and for her doctor. She didn't do anything in Orange County except live in the house and teach.

[2] Joseph Eichler was a home builder from the San Francisco Bay area. He was well known for both the open style of his homes and his non-discriminatory policies. In the early 1960s, he built three tracts of housing in the city of Orange; the Caines family moved into the first of these. This was in a city that in earlier days did not allow blacks to be present after dark, and as late as 1950, had only three black residents out of a population of ten thousand.

She lived right across the street [from where we eventually moved]. And she told me about Eichler in our conversation, and I said, "We're thinking about moving to an Eichler."

And you knew that Joseph Eichler was non-discriminatory?

Yes. We knew his philosophy; we also knew the features and styles of the house that we loved, the very modern glass approach. We didn't think about being discriminated against here, because of Eichler's philosophy. So after meeting with her and her husband, who was not negative, and her boys, who were about my boys' age, we kind of thought, hey, we're going to live across from each other, and at least we'll have each other.

That was in December, and then in early January, we received a phone call from the realtor, who also lived here. He said, "Jo, I would like for you and Ken to come down for a meeting, because there are some neighbors who are a little concerned about you moving into the house." My heart just jumped down to the bottom of my stomach. I said, "But why?" He said, "Well, they just have some questions about you living on this block. But I want them to meet you and see what kind of folks you are."

We had another couple, another white couple, and a guy named Jim Goff, who Ken used to work with. He was buying a house on the next block. So here we are, the two of us, we're sort of doing the same things. Good friends moving, he was moving on that block, we were moving on this block. When I told Ken about the phone call, he told Jim, and Jim said, "Well, we're going to go with you." He said, "If they are going to give you a hard time, we're not buying either." So the four of us went to the realtor's home. The front door was slightly open into the atrium, and we could see in his house. There must have been forty to forty-five people there. So it made you a little nervous about coming in. Didn't even get to tell you about some of the times when we were going across country that I had to hide in the bottom of the car so that Ken could rent us a motel room. Because of his complexion [he would rent the room]. Or we would go at night so they wouldn't see too much, rent a motel at night.

This particular day when we came here, we went into the house and we told them that we understood how they felt. What they wanted us to do was move around the corner. They wanted us to move around the corner because there was already a black family on this block and a Chinese family.

When you say "they," you mean the group as a whole.

Well, that was a surprise. Of all the people there, there might have been only eight or ten people who felt that way. The other people came in our behalf, never having met us. They came with their books about white flight and the fairness of this, the fairness of housing, and everybody has a right, and they came in our behalf. That was a pleasant thing. So Ken came from the practical point of view that we wanted to live in the middle of the tract, a small block where our kids could play safely. I came from the philosophical—I understand how you feel, but I bleed like you bleed, I love like you love. Some of our neighbors used to tease me about saying that. (chuckles) We left there really feeling uplifted because there was only a handful of the people that wanted us to move, and they mostly were on this block. So we felt good about moving in.

However, when we got to our home in L.A. that night, about quarter to twelve, before midnight, my mom, who was living with us at the time, said some lady had called, and I was to call her no matter what time I got home, and that she was from Orange County. Well, it happened to be the black woman across the way. She was upset because she hadn't been invited to the meeting, and she said, "Well, why do you want to move on this block?" I said, "Because we chose this house." So she said, "Well, I guess your husband's stubborn like mine." I said, "No. We both decided on this, for good reasons." So she said, "Well, you wouldn't consider moving around the corner?" I said, "No." She said, "Well, all right." That was like Tuesday. On Wednesday, she calls me again and said, "Have you reconsidered? Wouldn't you go around the block?" I said, "No."

So then on Friday of that same week, about six o'clock, a young woman named Judy Rickey, who lived in the house on the other side, called and said they happened to be in L.A. She and her husband would like to come over and talk. I said, "He's bowling. This is Friday bowling and he won't be home until nine." "Well, that's just fine. If you don't mind, we'll shop until nine and we'll come by." They came by at nine o'clock that night. They were a young couple. They looked scared. They said, "We were asked to come to offer you and Ken five hundred dollars." I said, "For what?" "If you would move around the corner." I said, "We don't want to move around the corner. We like the house." "Well, we didn't agree to it, but they knew we were coming up, so they asked us to offer you the money." She never said who "they" were. Ken looked at her and said, "Well, let me see. How about twenty-five hundred or three thousand? That way I can put in my lawn, I can get some drapes for my house." Their eyes got real big. Then Ken said, "Look. Forget it. I am just kidding. Just have a glass of wine or a cup of coffee because we're not moving around the corner, and you're not going to offer us five hundred dollars." Those two people sat down and they didn't go home until almost one o'clock. We became such good friends in three hours. And they felt so relieved. They went back, and I guess they must have given them the word that we were going to move there, regardless.

So we moved in. Actually, we had very good neighbors. This neighbor next to me was sort of standoffish. The neighbor across from me was very friendly. They had four kids. On the corner was the only house right here that the man wouldn't even talk to us. Clark was just three years old, and his little head only came to the doorknob. He'd say, "Hi, Man." And the man would not talk to him. The wife was great. We had an open house; we invited the neighborhood. Everybody came except him, and they did move within the year. But then we got these wonderful neighbors who came in, the Nashinos. They moved in and they've been here since Leslie was a year old.

I joined the League of Women Voters in 1963. I think that was about the time—was it '63?—the Rumford Act was being tested, or something, or being passed, or not passed? About fourteen of us met at the Anaheim High School, and I think that was '64. We were making speeches here and there and all over the county. I'm trying to remember who called us to come to that meeting. It might have been Ernestine, I don't know. I met Ernestine Ransom [see Chapter 1], who was a black woman at the League of Women Voters meeting.

In the meantime, I was getting involved. I was the first black—"the first black," one of these days that will go away—the first black Cub Scout leader and we used to meet here. My co-leader, she was a very tall white gal, Diana Smith, and I used to have the meetings here. Chris was involved. He was the Cub Scout.

I remember one day a gentleman rang the doorbell and asked if he could come in to talk to me about the [Orange County] Grand Jury. We talked a long time. He said that they were really trying to recruit more minorities and younger people because grand juries tend to be older people and all white and mostly retired. I've been always interested in politics and legislation and this kind of judicial thing, and I said it seemed very time consuming. I mean, I had three children.

What year was this?

I started in January 1969, so this was '68 that they came to me. Leslie was only like four years old. She was in day care. I was substitute teaching anyway, so I would put her in day care at least three or four days a week and the boys were in school. I talked it over with Ken, and he thought it was a good idea.

So you were a year on the grand jury?

A whole year. That was one of the most exciting experiences that I've ever had. So many things came out of that grand jury that year, the *L.A. Times* wrote an article about us. The mayor of Santa Ana was very conservative, and he was really concerned about people with communistic tendencies. He also did a lot of raiding of people's homes. If there was a crime committed, particularly in the black community or Hispanic community, sometimes they'd pull people out of their homes at one or two o'clock in the morning. The grand jury knew about this. It was something we wanted to look into that we thought was not right.

We interviewed him, and then about that particular time, a young man, who was a juvenile delinquent, was being transferred from a place where they were being accused of stealing soda or something to juvenile hall. He and his friend were in the back of a bus, taunting the police driver and companion. When they arrived at juvenile hall, they let this one young man out, and he escaped. They locked the other guy in, and the two policemen went after this one fellow all around the area of the juvenile hall. It was a hot day. They captured the boy. The reason I say it was a hot day is because the air conditioning was off in the juvenile hall administrative building, so they had their windows open. So they came to the window and saw that the boy was captured and was being beaten, not only by one policeman but by both. So they were accused of beating this boy. He had to go to the hospital.

He was black and the policemen were white. We decided to recommend that the policemen go to trial, because that was our job to decide. We were taunted because you don't go and say policemen have committed anything wrong. So the police chief came to us and more or less reprimanded us. "What's wrong with you?

Why would you do that?" We said, "Because we think they're guilty." He more or less said, "You might be sorry you're doing this." The day after New Year's, we were subpoenaed, our grand jury, to come to court because of what we had done. We said we think they're guilty. I mean, the boy was helpless. He didn't have anything, and people were looking out the window and they saw him being beaten, and we just think it's not fair. Then they took them to court, and we went to the trial. It lasted about three days.

The policemen's attorney was so big and tall and strong, and as I said, they were trying the boy, talked about finding drugs in his hair and all the bad things he had done. And his attorney didn't speak up for the boy and say, "That's not what we're here for." It was a Friday afternoon, and it was like four o'clock, and the judge said he was going to make a decision whether they should continue and finish it that day or come back Monday. I don't know if you know Mary Miller, from Laguna Beach. She was on the grand jury with me. She and Judy Rosner. We went to the potty to take care of things. We were there for maybe fifteen minutes, went back, and the courtroom was empty. We said, "What happened?" "They declared that the policemen were innocent." I had written on paper weeks before that, "They will not be found guilty." And they were not. So that was very disappointing to us.

From the grand jury, after that wonderful experience finding out how this county is run—from the jails to health to education to administration to everything, the detention homes for kids, and all of that—people think you're an expert. So people began to call me about different things. One of my first visits to KOCE [Orange County PBS television station] in 1972 was to come and talk about the grand jury. I started being asked to be on commissions and committees, and what have you. And Josephine kept on saying yes. (laughs) But it was because I enjoyed it so much. Anything that I could get myself involved in that could maybe change things for the better for people.

When I was on the grand jury, the question of a Human Relations Commission came up, and we recommended that the county have a Human Relations Commission. I remember Ken and I debating over that, because he felt that if you have a Human Relations Commission run by the county, they would really control you, and that he wanted one that would be autonomous.

Now, I think there was one. Didn't Josh White start one?

Yes. They tried one and it didn't work out. My feeling was that the county has a responsibility, and that they should be involved, and that should be part of their priority. I remember going to testify to the board of supervisors. They had us testify for it, and we had to do some hard selling. I think we must have gone to I don't know how many meetings for that, and finally, they okayed the Human Relations Commission. But they gave them no money, no office, no nothing. (laughs) So, some of us who were there just said, "Okay, do one thing at a time." I went to the board of supervisors only for those things I really, really felt were important. Because if you went too often, they would ignore you, but when they saw me coming, they usually knew it was pretty important.

I went to seventy-three meetings to try to establish a housing authority in Orange County. We were the only county of this size that didn't have a housing authority. The reason I know I went to those meetings is because Ken made sure I kept track of the mileage. (chuckles) "This can come off on our income tax," he would say. So, I would show up for things that I really felt were important, and they began to respect me. That's why I was asked to be on the Citizens Direction Finding Commission.

It was a commission that the board of supervisors established to look at our county as a whole and to give them advice on the direction the county should go. We called ourselves the commission that dared to dream, because we tried to think of the future. At that time, it was like 1972, '73, and we were trying to think about the year 2000. We tried to think about: What were you going to do in the city of Irvine and anyplace beyond where the homes were very expensive and the neighborhoods were very expensive for the people who were going to service those people? Were they going to have to travel miles in a rickety car from Santa Ana down there? Was there going to be housing available for the people who were going to have to work there? Even teachers, many of them couldn't afford to live down there. However, most of our suggestions, I think, ended up in the supervisors' circular file. (chuckles)

There was a lawsuit eventually against the City of Irvine and they provided some housing for university professors.

If they had just listened to us and planned for it, but they didn't. It's so funny—hindsight.

What do you think motivated you to get involved in these things?

I think it was something way back when I was a youngster, and I think it started in Atlantic City in high school. I felt very comfortable in an integrated school; however, at lunchtime they would have a band play down in the gym so the kids could dance. The black kids were never down there. They were sitting up in the balcony by themselves. And the other kids were having fun dancing. I watched that for some months. Finally, I went up there and I did a little lecturing. I said, "Why are you here?" I said, "That's your right to be down on that floor. This is your school as well as theirs." I started doing that right then. I think of the rights of people, and I think of all of this, the discrimination, the prejudice, the what-have-you, that was going on in our country in those days. And also some of our leaders who were coming along then—President Kennedy, Martin Luther King—all that stirred my soul.

I'm really a passionate person about [being involved], Ken and I both. I mean, we both like to be involved. Denver had its part in it when he was involved with the housing there. It built up until I'm almost a crazy person for it. The more I did it, I became addicted. I got involved with the United Way, the Children's Home Society, and seniors. Remember the War on Poverty at UCI that year, 1969? We had workshops and what have you, yes. It was very exciting. I was on the Social Service Commission for the county.

Why don't we talk about your social life?

Well, there was social life, not as much as it was later on after we became so involved in different things. At first, our black friends used to come and visit us from L.A. And we used to laugh because they used to tease us. They said they had to come down at night so nobody could see them. (chuckles) As our living became more integrated, so our social life became more integrated. We played cards almost every other Friday at somebody's house here. And most of the parties were in this neighborhood right here, or maybe the next block. We didn't do too many things until both of us became involved. Ken got involved with the YMCA. And I got really involved in the schools here and became president of their PTO [Parent Teacher Organization].

It was our feeling that when you have growing children, you have to really center most of your activities around them. And that's what we did. All those people on this block that were there at that meeting, back in 1963, became our best friends. We were always at one or another's home. At one time this block—I think it has twelve houses—had forty-three kids on it. It was a very secure feeling because we were all looking after everybody else's kids.

So almost all your social life was through integrated structures as opposed to black sororities or black churches.

Ken wasn't very much of a church person. First we went to Trinity Episcopal Church when it was that little cute chapel down there off of Chapman Avenue [in Orange], or somewhere around there. Chris was an altar boy. That lasted for about a year. We would go to church intermittently. We didn't do a lot of church stuff, but we were very, very spiritual. The kids prayed, we prayed, we talked to God, and it's always been that way. And I still do. But Ken evidently had a very bad experience when he was a kid with his church, and so he kind of turned it off a little bit.

Even the NAACP and the Urban League—that was something I was really involved in, trying to get an Urban League here from the very beginning. We successfully had a good Urban League here. They had to raise fifty thousand dollars on their own as a non-Urban League organization before they could become an Urban League. And they had to convince United Way to take them on as members. So that was a process that took a couple years. It turned out to not be successful because we ended up having two very bad directors. So it vanished. But it was a good experience while it was going on.

The NAACP has never been what I had hoped it would be. They would only come out on Martin Luther King's birthday and Black History Month. I think they're doing better now, but I'm not sure.

Are you glad you came here?

I am. I think Ken and I were meant to come here. We were meant to meet these kinds of challenges. Everybody has challenges of health and those kinds of things, but we were really meant to have social-issues challenges so that we could try and help make a difference, to make things better for people.

As long as I'm working with people, motivating people, listening to people, helping people, I'm a happy person. I'm a happy, happy person. My life has been very, very successful here in Orange County. Sometimes it's been a struggle. Sometimes you take nine steps backwards before you take one step forward. But sometimes that makes it even more exciting and makes me more determined.

And everywhere you go, no matter how happy you are there are going to be problems, and people problems. When I told you that my neighbor next door was kind of a standoffish person when we first moved here, today she's one of my best friends. Ken was the guy in the neighborhood, because there were about four houses here that were single-women's houses. Either the husbands died or they got divorced. And Ken was sort of the protector. He would check on them. He'd go out for his walk or his bicycle ride. He would take the newspaper and put it at their door. So they loved him. When he was so ill, they just loved Ken and would visit him and cared for him and everything, which brought the women into my life in the neighborhood. He was the one who mowed the lawn. He knew all the neighborhood gossip. (chuckles)

During the time the kids were going to school, the boys were very, very popular, when they got to high school particularly. Chris was a leader in his way. He had so-so grades, but they were okay. Chris was a musician and a leader. As a matter of fact, I really think he should be in politics; he's so good at expressing himself. He and I talk politics all the time here. And Clark was popular also. His personality is outgoing, and he is very, very smart, and he went on to San Diego State and on to UCI. Now he's a wonderful executive. Leslie's extremely smart. But always the youngest in the group, so therefore, her peers were driving cars before she was, going to parties before she was allowed to, so she became very rebellious. But she's turned out to be a wonderful young woman and a wonderful mother.

But they all had their different problems. Although the girls were crazy about Chris and Clark, their parents weren't. Ken and I had to go to a parents' home one night to discuss a relationship that Chris had with the girl. It was very disappointing to me, because the mother and I bowled together and we were friends. We were friends until her daughter and my son liked each other. I have a feeling maybe she was encouraged by her husband to have us come and talk. And we said, "What we suggest is don't push the kids one way or the other because if you push them, you're going to make the situation worse." I said, "They're sixteen years old." Anyway, it slowed down. There used to be notes at the door for both of those boys.

Leslie had a harder time, because you can't miss the fact that the boys are black, but Leslie is fair complexioned and not always did they realize she was a black girl. Sometimes the boys would be attracted to her, and then find out that she was black and it wouldn't go the way she had hoped. So we sent her to the National Conference [of Christians and Jews] camp. We sent her to camp because we both felt she needed to meet different people. And she did. That helped quite a bit. As a matter of fact, she was able to come back and speak at one of the galas about her experiences there.

Did they all marry Anglos?

Chris and Leslie did. And Clark's wife, Julie's mother, is Swiss and her dad is Syrian, so she looks more black than Leslie does. I always have said to them, "The most important thing is love first, whether you're black, red, brown, purple, or whatever." And I've even said about myself, I am not first black. I'm first Jo Caines, and I happen to be Jo Caines that happens to be black

Thank you, Jo Caines.

CHRIS CAINES[1]

Chris Caines, the son of Josephine and Ken Caines, came to Orange County with his family, as an almost six-year-old boy in 1963. He has lived most of his life in predominantly white areas of Orange County. He talks about how he deals with that fact. In his first two years at Villa Park High School, he was the only black student in the school. He was student body president in his senior year. He talks about interracial dating, marriage, and his family. Chris lives in Rancho Santa Margarita in south Orange County. Graduation photo, 1975.

Chris, where were you born?

I came from the Bronx [New York City]. I wasn't there for very long. About six months after I was born, we moved out to Colorado and followed the job trail of my father: after Colorado to Lompoc, California, and then to Los Angeles. I was five, not quite six yet. So that would put us in 1963. We moved right from Los Angeles into Orange County, into this house. I'm pretty sure this was the first house the family ever purchased.

Were there any other black kids in the neighborhood?

There were. Right across the street, we had the Hills, Talbert and Philip Hill. I moved in; I was the youngest, newest kid on the block. They had already established themselves. And actually, I don't even think their parents wanted us to move here. But we came in right across the street. It took some time, but we all became friends.

Were there other kids your age?

Most of them were older, if not much, but I was definitely the youngest, and they treated me such. (chuckles) My brother [Clark] was very young at the time, three;

[1] Oral History 3054. Interview date: May 9, 2003, at the home of his mother, Jo Caines, in Orange, California. Interviewer: Robert Johnson.

nobody bothered him because he was basically a baby. But I was just on the cusp of being a young man, so the kids who were seven and eight saw me as the little runt. I started in kindergarten for a little while, finished the school year, and then went to first grade.

Were you the only black kid in the school, or in the kindergarten?

No. Philip and his brother, who was older. I saw Philip at a distance at school but never hung out really with him at school.

These were the 1960s. Racism, at least among parents, was the norm, not the exception. Did this work its way down to the kids, and if so, how did you deal with it?

Well, certainly there were things to cope with. Going through school, you have your group of friends who get to know you and like you. Then you have the group that doesn't. I remember very distinctly once, it was my birthday, I believe, and we were getting out of school and they were all going to pounce on me after school and give me my birthday whackings. And the teacher gave me about a five-second head start to get out of the class. It was traditional for everybody to go through this, but when it was my turn, it was almost mob-like. I was tackled and kicked and hit, and it was an unpleasant experience.

I mean, there were those times and then there were wonderful times when, because of the social aptitude of my mom and dad, we started trends. And because of their intelligence and their wit and their ability to mingle, we were invited to do lots of things and participated in a lot of events—school events and social events. They were very politically involved. And at a very young age, probably eight, nine, ten, I was out walking precincts, delivering political information door to door. That became a very big part of our lives, being social and being political in this city and the county, and it rubbed off on all of us. We realized that in order to defeat racism and intolerance, you must work from within the system and not from out of the system. The only way to work within is to make contacts, know the system, work within the system, and try to effect change from inside.

Your parents didn't shy away from the subject of race.

No, they didn't shy away from it. They always instilled in us that we treat everybody equally and we should expect to be treated equally. You don't tolerate racism against yourself, but the way you combat it is not violently or rudely, but with intelligence and grace, and that will get you much further than any other means. I remember my mom always saying we have to work twice as hard to get half as far. And that's definitely true. You have to look better, be better, act nicer, and be smarter just to get to the mean level. That being the case, we learned that was the best way to do it. We found out that being combative or arrogant or rude or violent sets you back, because they pigeonhole you that way and then you've got no place else to go.

And still to this day, but certainly then, it was one thing to be invited to a party; it was a whole 'nother thing to date their daughter. You could come and hang out at their house, and it was cool to have a black guy in the house and be one of the buddies. "Hey, one of my friends is a black guy." But when you're talking about dating their daughter and taking her to the movies, that was a whole different world. When we were going through junior high and high school, it was very difficult for some parents to make that jump. Surprisingly, for other parents, it wasn't a difficult thing. I was pretty quick to find that out. You'd show up at the front door and say, "Hi, is Jane here?" And you either got, "Hey, why don't you come on in." Or you got, "Just a minute." (laughs)

Your mother had mentioned your sister being very light skinned and the difficulty she sometimes had when somebody would find out, "Oh, you're black." But you were darker, so you didn't have that.

Actually, I did have that. I had it over the phone. When people would talk to me on the phone, they would make an assumption. Then they would see me in person and say, "Oh." I get that even today. "Oh, *you're* Chris." I get it all the time. I don't know if they don't think that black people are intelligent enough or have the ability to talk without sounding, quote-unquote, "black." But I think that those stereotypes need to be broken down, and slowly are. It hasn't gone away.

You spoke the language of your neighborhood. And your parents, who really didn't have—

They came from good families, and they came up in a social situation that required them to be able to coexist with a lot of different cultures. Especially in high school, people used to call me the chameleon because I could be with any group and be comfortable. I could hang out with the jocks and play football or baseball, I could hang out with the choir people and sing, I could hang out with the drama folks and do productions, I could hang out with the guys in the Key Club, I could hang out with the rockers and hang with them and play music. All those things, all those different groups, I had no problem moving seamlessly between. And that comes from acquiring skills to make people feel comfortable around you and then having them accept you and want to be around you.

Were there many black kids at Villa Park High, or any?

Philip and Talbert, who lived across the street from me, had moved away prior to us going to high school. So when I got there—it was a three-year high school at the time—I was the only one, for two years.

So there was no pressure on you to hang out with black young people because there weren't any others.

It would have been fine had there been. I don't know that I would have considered it pressure, because, again, I could hang out with Hispanic kids, I could hang out with Asian kids, and it didn't make any difference to me. And I tried real hard to not let it make any difference to them. I think I opened some eyes that way with them seeing that he's just a guy. He's not a black guy, he's just *a* guy. And as proud of my culture as I am, I'd much rather be seen as a man first, a father. Then, if you need to go there, okay, yeah, I'm black. But I would like to have people see me the way they see me over the phone, just another guy that's friendly to talk to.

You ended up being the student body president of Villa Park High. Wow! Your mother mentioned you're a very social being.

I was. And the student body president thing was interesting. I had all these groups that I could deal with and intermingle with. And I went up against one of the most popular guys around. He was the blonde surfer, very good looking. From Villa Park, his parents had a lot of money. He was very popular amongst his crowd. But he didn't have the diversity he needed, and I was able to pull it out, I think, mostly through the common man and woman in high school who wasn't blonde and beautiful and rich. And there were a lot of us coming from the other side of the tracks, the other side of the 55 Freeway. (chuckles)

So all of us who lived on the other side of the freeway kind of banded together. I talked common sense when I gave my little speech. I didn't try to be cute and funny. I just said, "Look. I'm here and I'm serious about it. I'll do my best to help you out and be there for you and see what happens." And it turned out well. Yes, I became student body president and that senior year for me was an excellent year socially and growth-wise for me. I had a lot of very wonderful experiences in high school. I got very involved in the music program there, sang in the choir and performed as the bandleader for their vocal ensemble, which was a dance/music group that traveled and did shows and things. I was also very involved in the drama department and was the technical director of a couple of plays and things like that.

You asked me about stories. We were putting on the play *Jesus Christ Superstar*, and I wanted to audition for the part of Jesus Christ. Ironically, one of the other auditioners was the guy that I beat as student body president, the blonde—good-looking, and he had a decent voice. I thought I had a better voice, and I practiced the songs hours and hours and hours for this audition. I announced to the assistant choir director, who was in charge of the auditions, that this was what I wanted to do. He kind of gave me one of these looks like, Are you sure you want to do that particular part? I was like, "Yeah, of course. It's a great part. I've read the book, I've looked at the movie, and I went out and borrowed or bought the soundtrack album and practiced it. I can sing it almost as well as the guy on the thing." And he was like, "Okay. Well, all right. You go ahead and we'll set up an audition for you." And I'm thinking—because in all other aspects of my relationship with this man, I had a good one. It was a good, because I was the bandleader, and I was a decision-maker in the class, and blah, blah, blah.

So I came to my audition, and the guy I was competing against had done his the day before. And they provided a piano player to do the accompaniment with for the audition. Well, when I got there, the accompanist was gone and wasn't available for my audition. So I had to do it a cappella. That was fine. I wasn't very happy about it, but, oh well. I thought I belted it out pretty good. The room was quiet afterwards, and I left. Days later when the decision was made—and I didn't get the part, obviously—I went to him and said, "Why didn't I get the part?"

He says, "Well, you just don't have the look that we're looking for." I said, "What do you mean 'the look'? Did I not sing the part right?" "No, you did fine at the audition." "I know my lines." "Okay. You know your lines. But that's just not what—"And to this day, I don't know if it was him that had the problem with it or whether he got pressure from somebody saying, "You know what? This is Villa Park High School and we cannot have a black Jesus." That's not going to happen for the school play, the big school production. Our productions were big. They were massive as far as their technical and scenery and all that kind of stuff.

I was just naïve. I didn't think that that was going to matter, and I was crushed that it did. I remember coming to a realization. I don't even know if I realized it then as much as maybe walking home or coming home from school and just pondering why it didn't happen. I'm the student body president, I'm a popular guy, everybody likes me, why can't I have this part? And then, oh, my God.

It's very much like come over and be our friend but don't date my daughter. Hey, go ahead and perform, be a performer, but don't represent somebody in a way that we don't think he should be represented.

Did you get any part? Not even Judas or Pilate? (laughter)

No. And I didn't want any other part. That's kind of the way I am. I didn't want to be vice-president of the student body. I wanted to be president. If I couldn't be president, I just wasn't going to do it. And it was the same with this.

How did the dating thing go in high school?

The dating thing was interesting. There are different reasons why girls date you when in high school. One, just because they like you. Two, they're being rebellious against their parents: Let's date the black guy. That'll really piss them off. And, too, sometimes just the curiosity. What is it like to, you know. I think those who dated me for the curiosity thing found that we were pretty normal folks. They'd come over to the house, and my parents were nice and they were very accepting of whomever I brought home, and those who dated for the curiosity found that I'm just a guy and I like the things guys like.

I would say quite a few did it because they were angry at their parents or getting at their parents, or they were just rebellious people. Or they were socially rebellious. I'm going to show the world. They won't tell me who I can—and they were, for the most part, great people. They all had their reasons. Some had agendas other than me, and some liked me for me. It was never too difficult to date, but it was difficult to get serious. That was the tough thing.

Did you go on to college?

After high school, I was working and did several jobs. I worked in music stores. I was quite the musician at the end of my high school years. I had a small group in high school called The Trio. We did a lot of performing. We went on a self-proclaimed tour up to San Francisco and did the after-graduation free and easy craziness for the summer.

Then I got a job working at Ford Aerospace [in Newport Beach] as an apprentice. As great an opportunity as that was—and I was there for a couple of years—philosophically, it was way too different for me. I would walk into work, and there were warheads in the parking lot stacked up, and here I am, a non-violent, non-war person. So I left that program and went to junior college and pursued my business degree and recording engineer degree. I went to Santa Ana, to Fullerton, and I went to Golden West [community colleges].

Your wife is Anglo. What year did you get married?

We got married in '83. She was from Orange County. At the time, she lived in Ontario, but she originally lived just a few blocks away from this house here. She went to Villa Park High as well, but a couple years ahead of me. At the time, I had my own business. I had opened a rehearsal facility for musicians over near Anaheim Stadium. She was in the banking business. But, yeah, I was here being an entrepreneur, running my own business. Then we purchased a house out in Diamond Bar and I changed jobs. I was no longer an entrepreneur. I was working for another company and did that for about three or four years and had our son. Then I had the opportunity to go up to San Francisco to work, and so we moved up there, and we stayed there from '92 to mid-'94, or so. It was about two and a half, three years. Then we came back.

Why did you come back to Orange County?

Financially, it was difficult. Then also everybody we knew and loved was here, and the only way we'd get to see them is if they came to see us, or we had to come down here. So we were constantly doing one or the other. My dad's health was starting to deteriorate a little bit, so it just made sense for us to come back.

Chris, one time your father said to me something like this: "I want my children to be raised in an integrated or predominantly white neighborhood so they can grow up with white people because it's white people in America that run most things. And my children need to be able to deal with them." Now, is that a good idea? Are you glad you were raised in Orange County?

Yes, I think I'm glad I was raised in Orange County. I think it's afforded me opportunities and experiences that I wouldn't have gotten in a lot of other places. I think while that's a good philosophy to have, it's flawed, because of what it didn't allow. Until recently it's been difficult to be as comfortable or to have as much experience with our own culture on a day-to-day basis: being with black people, understanding them as well, and just knowing a little bit more about our culture from that side. Not necessarily saying that I would want to make any changes, because I'd much rather come from this side and learn about our more basic elements than to be a basic element and try to struggle up to get to this side. This way, I think I can get the best of both worlds.

I think to come from the 'hood or the ghetto or wherever you want to say, I think that is such a hard struggle for so many black men and women. I have great admiration for those that make it, and I don't know that I would have that fortitude. That said, if one of us can make it out of there, all of us can make it out of there.

We just have to want to do it bad enough. I don't agree with those who use the excuse, my mom was a crackhead, my dad was a crackhead, and I'm a crackhead, and my kids are going to be crackheads. I understand what they're saying, but I don't accept that as an excuse for allowing the cycle to continue.

I am disappointed in black people, in us as a black people, as a culture, because I think we tend to take advantage of our own more than other cultures. We're not separated by a language barrier, which in the other cultures allows them to be more of a community. Too often we're stealing and hurting and killing each other, as opposed to helping each other. And I think that's a problem that we need to try to correct. I think realization is the first part, and then we need to start taking steps to make that better. I had to find out a lot about black folks on my own, and I love black folks.

So I think there has been some isolation in trying to immerse us in a more integrated culture. Some of that had been at the expense of our own culture and interaction with that culture. I've had to do that since high school and college on my own, all the while knowing that the essence of that statement is true; "When in Rome, you have to do what the Romans do," and we're in Rome. While it's getting better, the struggle continues.

You have one son, and how old is he?

I have one son. His name is Joe. He's fourteen, first year in high school.

Having a black father and a white mother and growing up in this family and in Orange County, how is he affected by race?

When he was younger, I was in a mall with him, and it was just the two of us. He was probably three or four years old at the time. He was getting tired and cranky, and he started goofing around and started doing things he shouldn't be doing, and I kind of got on him about it. "Hey, stop that. Sit down and be quiet." We had stopped at one of the food parks, and I had noticed one of the clerks, or food preparation people, giving me a pretty hard look for quite some time.

This was an Anglo person?

Yes. We were drinking or something, and Joe was being a tired, cranky kid. He spat out—took a big sip of Coke and pfffft all over the place. I grabbed his arm and, "Hey, stop that. You need to behave." Well, this person couldn't really hear what I was saying but came over to me and said, "Why are you with this child? Whose child is this and what are you doing with him?" I said, "Well, this is my child and I was reprimanding him for spitting stuff all over the place." "Well, how do I know he's your child?" So I had to actually get my wallet out and show him pictures of the two of us. While it was hurtful to me, I was appreciative at least that this person cared enough to come. They were just looking out for Joe. But as the rest of the day wore on—and I think that evening I just broke into tears for having to deal—that's something I have to deal with that a lot of parents don't have to deal with.

And your son is very blonde.

Yes, he's very blonde. He's got his mother's coloring. But it was crushing to have to be questioned in that way. And it's happened several times. When I'm with him, people stare. Why are you with him? Why are you hugging that child? What are you doing with that kid? That's hard to deal with. I don't know that he's felt that so much because it mostly happened when he was young, and it doesn't happen much anymore now that he's a big kid. But I know that that was horrible for me to have to experience. I'll never forget the day. I'll never forget when that happened to me the first time.

As far as how *he's* experienced it, I think again that we've made some changes socially in the years. I think it's different now from when he was a little child, now that he's grown up. His friends are—because of the culture we're in and MTV and hip-hop and all that kind of stuff—they're much more into the black culture than a lot of people who are black are into it. They're very into the clothes and the look and the rap and the whole bit. So his friends, I think, actually find it kind of cool that he has a black dad. A lot of people still ask, "Is he your real dad?" And I kind of cringe because I don't want him to have to deal with that question, but deal with it he will.

Another time when I was in a store, and I had Joe on my shoulders, this man I had never met in my life looks at me and goes, "Is that your son?" I said, "Yes, it is." And as loud as he possibly could, he goes, "Oh, my God. That's amazing. He's so light and you're so dark." And I'm just like—I didn't need that in the middle of public and bringing all this attention to my son. I mean, he was almost screaming it. I had to walk away from him. I was rude, but I had to walk away because he was making a scene. Joseph didn't need to deal with that, and I didn't need to deal with it.

Is this an okay place for Joe to grow up in a mixed-race family?

Joe is pretty comfortable. He considers himself black on the inside, and he's said that to me before. I tell him all the time, with regard to school, "Your job is to go to school and do well and to be a good person, and my job is to make a good person who will make a positive contribution to his community and society." That's my job with him. Not a great white person, a great black person, a great man, or a great woman, just a great person who will make a positive contribution. That's all I'm looking for.

Did you have another story that you might want to tell?

I couldn't be more proud of my brother, Clark, and my sister, Leslie. My brother was the middle child, and he dealt with it. At the time, in high school especially, I was pretty high profile. I was Chris Caines, I was the leader of the ensemble, I was student body president, I was a musician, I was playing all over the place in Orange County, all the clubs, I was a pretty popular guy. And he found his own identity and his own character and has the highest educational degree of anybody in our family and is, in his own right, an excellent person, excellent people-person.

That's evident by the way he's gone up the ladder in every situation that he is in, in all the areas of business where it relates to people. In every situation—business-wise, home-wise, family—he's excelled, and he's done very well, and I couldn't be more proud of him.

My sister, I'm very proud of her. She's so intelligent. I don't even want to think about what her IQ might be. But she had a situation where she was the youngest, so she saw her brothers doing all these fun things as older teenagers and stuff, and she couldn't do them because she was young, but she mentally knew what was going on. But she found her own way in sports and in the entertainment field and computer graphics and she's top in her field, too. Now, as a single mom, she's doing that struggle, but she's making it work and she's taking care of business, so I'm very proud of her to do that, too.

Well, thank you very much, Chris, for letting me interview you.

JAMES McKAY[1]

James McKay provides the perspective of an adult, single, African American man in Orange County through the 1970s and into the 1980s, even though he came to California as a married nineteen-year-old in 1965. He was born in New Orleans, Louisiana, and raised in the small town of Smithridge, fifty-seven miles south of New Orleans. He presently lives with his wife in a lovely area of east Tustin, in Orange County.

Tell us about why you came to California.

There was a distant relative that came back home to show his wife where he was born, and she said to me, "You should come to California." I took her up on the offer. The reason is, I was a dreamer, and I could not accomplish what I wanted to accomplish in life in southeast Louisiana. I had a wife and a kid. I was nineteen years old, and I left the wife and the son home with my last paycheck, and I took six dollars and came to California. That last paycheck was eighty-two dollars for two weeks. Five months later, I sent for them, and they joined me in Los Angeles.

I was trying to make my way in Los Angeles, and the Watts riots started in August of 1965. I did not live very far from the Muslim Temple. They had an infamous shootout at that temple. [To avoid being shot] I remember lying on the floor with my wife and my baby on Saturday night. I had this distant uncle; I had a phone number. He lived in Laguna Beach. I called him and asked him to come and get me out. His first response was, "Are you crazy?" (chuckles) "I'm not coming up there." But they declared martial law that Sunday, so he came and picked us up on Sunday.

We drove out of Laguna Canyon and there in front of me was Laguna Beach, the ocean, which I had never seen, and all these people. It seemed so far removed from riot-torn Los Angeles, and I thought to myself, This is the California I saw on television. First it was a cultural shock, but that did not frighten me for whatever

[1] Oral History 33056. Interview date: May 31, 2003, at the home of the interviewer, Robert Johnson, in Tustin, California.

reason, because basically, to me, Los Angeles was in flames. At that time in my life, I was like, I don't understand why they're fighting. I don't understand why the fighting's going on because I had come from the South where things were really bad. In California, you could have a job; I made a hundred dollars a week. By comparison, my paycheck was eighty-two dollars [doing] construction work prior to coming to Los Angeles, for two weeks, working ten hours a day. So to me, life was good. That was my introduction to Orange County.

And your uncle, when did he come to Orange County?

I have no idea. He was a distant relative. From what I understand, he went into the military. That was the only way out back then—you went to the military. And the cousin who had brought me to California and the uncle who I lived with, they both went to the military and remained in the California area.

But he wasn't in the service when you got there?

No, he was not in the service. To be honest, we lived on "Top of the World" in Laguna, on Miramar Street. For the life of me, I could never figure out how we were living up there because he was a gardener. But the uncle also was not afraid to reach out and touch something that was unattainable to him. I think the way he paid for that house was, there were about six of us living there, and we all contributed. He was the only black person in Laguna in that situation. All the other black people that I met lived either on Ocean Avenue, which was where all the blacks were congregated in Laguna at that time, or out in the canyon [Laguna Canyon]. In fact, it had quite a little population, maybe fifteen black people. There was a small car wash in

WATTS, 1965

Watts did not become predominantly black until after the 1940s, as the Second Great Migration brought tens of thousands of migrants from Louisiana, Mississippi, and Texas, who left segregated states in search of better opportunities in California. During World War II, the city built several large housing projects (including Nickerson Gardens, Jordan Downs, and Imperial Courts) for the thousands of new workers in war industries. By the early 1960s, these projects had become nearly 100 percent black, as whites moved on to new suburbs outside the central city. As industrial jobs disappeared from the area, the projects housed many more poor families than they had traditionally.

Longstanding resentment by Los Angeles's working-class black community over discriminatory treatment by police and inadequate public services (especially schools and hospitals) exploded on August 11, 1965, into what were commonly known as the Watts Riots. The Nation of Islam mosque near the McKay's apartment was raided by the police, wounding nineteen men. During the shooting, the McKays decided that Orange County was a safer place to live than South-Central L.A. Gun sales in Orange County jumped during and after the troubles, but other than one large fire, a possible racially related beating, and some Molotov cocktails thrown by both blacks and whites, Orange County remained quite calm.

the canyon at the time, and most of us either worked there or they did gardening, that type of thing.

How did you feel about moving to Laguna Beach, where it's almost all white?

For whatever reason in my life, even with the racism of the South, I never saw myself as being different. So moving to Orange County, to me—that was a lot of white people in one place. My thoughts were not that anyone was going to harm me, because I was in California. Down South, I would have had a problem. California was the way out. I moved into Orange County with that thought, that I had reached the Promised Land, so to speak, for black people, and that white people didn't care. That was the image I had when I went to Laguna.

Where did you work when you were living in Laguna?

At a car wash. There was a car wash in the canyon, a small, tiny car wash. You would really have to be someone from Laguna to know that it was there. That was my first job in Orange County.

How long did you stay in Laguna?

I lived in Laguna probably a year and I moved to Santa Ana. That was because of a job. I took a job with Beckman Instruments as a janitor. I moved to Santa Ana and got my own apartment. At that time in Santa Ana, I would say probably 95 percent of the black people were on Myrtle Street, in the Myrtle Apartments. The Myrtle Apartments was infamous for the race. We were all congregated in that area.

I had begun working two eight-hour jobs trying to buy a house, so I was really not there. Physically or politically, I was not there. The only thing that stood out to me was that, at that time, there was one black police officer in Santa Ana, named Lambert.[2] And anytime something occurred down on Myrtle Street, Lambert came in first. I mean, before any other police unit arrived, Lambert would come in. I always thought it was so stereotypical. We've got to send the black officer in. That stood out to me more than anything else on Myrtle Street at the time.

Did you stay in Orange County?

I went back to Louisiana in 1969 after a divorce. I moved to Louisiana and worked on offshore drilling rigs and returned to California six months later. I had purchased a home on Spruce Street in Santa Ana, Spruce and Myrtle. My wife and children remained in the house, and I moved to Fullerton. Fullerton was pretty much old school. Fullerton was the first real serious racism I encountered in Orange County.

I had this really good friend who was white, so I moved in with him. I was more or less told I could not live there. The discrimination that I encountered was

---

[2] Harlan Lambert, in 1966, was the first black police officer hired in Santa Ana. He was a college-educated army veteran and had been a star basketball player. The fast growing black population of the city, in 1966, was greater than three thousand, resulting in a great deal of pressure placed on the city, by civil rights groups, to hire a black officer.

from the residents that lived there. It was everything from just not speaking to you to complaints, flat tires—silly stuff, nothing physical. Which was one of the things that I really liked about Orange County is that if people did not like the fact that you were black, the discrimination was not physical, it was more verbal. No one would attempt to actually physically harm you, for the most part.

The people who lived in those apartments, they were older. They were not young ruffian types. They were more middle class. Where you had to really worry about the violence was from less educated people. That's the one thing I found in Orange County: the lesser the education, the more propensity for violence, or verbal abuse. That's a general statement, I know, but that's what I saw, that's what I got.

I was working for Beckman Instruments [in Fullerton] at the time, and I began dating one of the girls from the mailroom. That was not taken very well. She was white. That caused quite a stir within Beckman. I was called on the carpet, and eventually, we both ended up quitting Beckman. It was very difficult. Actually, my boss called me on the carpet, and then I went to Human Resources and had him called on the carpet. That's what stopped that. Looking back on it, I'm impressed and I was surprised that the Human Resource Department at Beckman handled it as well as they did, because they did do the right thing. They had a couple of black people—nothing special, janitors—like that. I played on their softball team and I played on their basketball team; they were very big in sports. But I don't think that had any bearing on the fact that they handled the situation correctly. Later on, I tried to reconcile with my wife, and after that ended in '69, I decided to go home. Just, I'm going home. That's when I began working in the oil fields.

In oil fields out in the Gulf?

Yeah, deep-water rigs. I'm deathly afraid of snakes, so I wanted deep-water rigs. There was one black person in the Gulf of Mexico at that time. I was the second person chosen, and I was basically chosen during the interviews—long, extensive interviews that I went through. I was chosen because I had lived in Orange County and I was accustomed to being around white people. They thought that would be a benefit seeing the conditions that I would be under. Again, at that time, I was naïve. On the deep-water rig was thirty-six white folks from Mississippi and Louisiana and myself. To say the least, it was interesting.

It didn't go well?

No. They tried to kill me a couple times, I think. I'm certain. After one accident, which really scared me, I decided, you know what, I'm going back to California, and that's what brought me back to California and back to Orange County. At that time, my mom, Lillie Mae, had migrated to California and she was living on Myrtle Street in Santa Ana, so I moved in with my mother for a short period of time. By that time I had three children. My fourth child came from a brief second marriage. It was a lady that knew my mom. We were introduced, and we hit it off, and we ended up going to Las Vegas, and we were married. The marriage lasted a year. She was a black lady. My children are all African American.

After living with your mom on Myrtle Street, where did you go?

San Juan Capistrano. I rented a condominium in San Juan Capistrano. I had no problems there being black, but I was not there very long. Again, I was working a lot of long, hard hours, so I didn't spend a lot of time at home. Also, at that time, I'd begun trying to educate myself.

Did you take advantage of any of the community colleges?

Mt. SAC, Golden West, Orange Coast.[3] Yes. And that continued forever. As I began to progress in business, I kept taking classes that related to that. Up until ten years ago I still took classes.

So you worked for some Orange County companies that are fairly well known, like Collins Radio [where the interviewer also worked].

Yes. Emerson Electric, Micronics International, Stanford Applied Engineering. Those were some of the larger companies that I worked for. I moved around, because pretty much that was the only way I could progress. Once I was inside of a company without a degree, I could not progress at the levels that I wanted to. But I found that as I accumulated certain knowledge, companies would hire me because they were looking for people who do what I do. With the knowledge that I possess in computer skills, it's pretty much wanted. For the last fifteen or twenty years, people simply wanted someone who could help them, so I think a lot of things were overlooked. I chose my field with that in mind. I knew that there were not a lot of people who did it very well, and I would continue to be employed.

Do you find that it's been a problem for you to be part of a small minority of less than 2 percent of Orange County's population?

I think it's been a challenge more than it's been a problem. Some of the things I've had happen to me would be perceived as problems—I mean, verbal comments or not being able to get apartments. There were housing problems. It's hard to define and say it was racism. I think the more educated people are, the more difficult it is to pin down racism because they're very refined on how they do it. It's done very discreetly.

I remember on one job I had one lady who invited me to her house. I was single then, I might add. But she invited me to her house and actually, being a young, adventurous guy, I thought I was going to get lucky. (laughs) She let me sit in her Cadillac in the garage, and she showed me her satin sheets. I remember thinking, "Okay." But years later, I would look back at that and maybe in her way she was trying to expose me, or whatever. It's just one of those bizarre things that happened.

---

[3] Mt. SAC is Mount San Antonio College, Los Angeles County; Golden West is in Huntington Beach, Orange County; and Orange Coast is in Costa Mesa, Orange County.

One could have perceived that as a problem, of being degraded, and I guess to some degree it was degrading, but again, I've always been one to choose what battles you fight. You just can't cry wolf every time something silly happens. There were police officer friends who actually told me if I got pulled over what to do, what not to do; to paraphrase the comedians, "how not to be an accident." You had to be aware of those things.

Did you run into any problems with the police?

Oh, yes. Yeah. I purchased some condos in Irvine. This was relatively recent. I was walking up to my unit, and two police officers were in the unit. They looked at me and they go, "Are you looking for a police officer?" And I said, "No." I said, "Why?" And one of them said, "Well, you look like you're looking for a police officer." Well, those type things, you just let them go.

I used to drive a little MGA sports car, because I worked part-time for the Sports Car Center in Santa Ana. I remember one year I got pulled over maybe twelve, thirteen times. Not one year. One month. Excuse me. I got pulled over twelve, thirteen times for no other reason. Because I swear I'm a good guy. I really was. I never got in trouble. I did what I was supposed to do.

You didn't get any tickets, though. They just pulled you over.

Oh, no. They would run a want warrant. Never got a ticket, never got arrested. They would run a want warrant, and basically that's it. Irvine Police Department did that quite a bit. I remember getting off the freeway one day, and an officer was at the light. He made a U-turn, pulled me over, ran a want warrant. I knew that you could not win, and you didn't even want to play that game, and I was just not in a good mood. I'd had enough of it. I remember kicking my own car. I remember thinking, "This is the absolute worse possible thing you want to do." But I was so upset. I said, "You know what? You pull me over all the time." I told the officer, "You pull me over all the time. Don't you know I'm here by now?"—because there were no blacks in Irvine at the time, very few. I said, "Don't you know I'm here by now?" You know, I never got pulled over after that. Maybe it was coincidental. I have no idea. But I would be jogging (chuckles) in a jogging suit, I would get pulled over. They would stop me. Things like that used to happen in Irvine.

In Costa Mesa, I was a production superintendent for one company on the swing shift. We would close the plant at midnight every night. Now, there was a guard on duty, but I would be the last one out. My son, John, was working there part-time, as a teenager in the summer months. It was a relatively large company. I had been doing this for a long time. One night I left the plant, and half of the Costa Mesa Police Department pulled me over. One police officer, a lady, had been into the plant looking for a runaway. We're talking shotguns, out of the car. I put the dome light on in the car, which is what one of my friends in Santa Ana told me years earlier. Put your dome light on, keep your hands on the steering wheel—stuff like that. I was telling my son, I said, "You know, don't do anything. Just put your hands on the dashboard." This was a survival tactic. They got us out of the car and did what they do. I saw the one police lady. I go, "You know me. You spoke to me not more than a month ago over at the plant." Because they said when they pulled us over that we had come out of the plant. I said, "Yes, we came out of the plant. I come out of there every night at this time." I remember the helicopter had been above. I said, "All you have to do is take us back around to the plant, and the security guard will verify who I am." We were there forty-five minutes, in the position, for no other reason. To this day, I could not tell you why they did it. Things like that used to happen.

Did you ever have any trouble with the police in Santa Ana?

Actually, when I was pulled over that eleven or twelve or thirteen times, whatever it was, in that one month, it was in Santa Ana. It was in Santa Ana every time. In fact, one time I was just sitting in my car and they stopped me and ran a want warrant. But also in Santa Ana I would get stopped, and I would have a police officer pull over who knew me and tell them to let it go. I knew these police officers from playing ball. Some of these things happened to me when I was young. The twelve or thirteen times I was pulled over with the sports car, I was twenty-two years old and looked like I was like fourteen. But also, after I was divorced, I mix-dated a lot, and I was in a lot of white neighborhoods, so I was profiled. Be it right or be it wrong, it was a lot of that.

What have been some of the positives and negatives about living in Orange County as compared to living in L.A.?

As compared to Los Angeles and Louisiana, there are no comparisons. Orange County was a very positive place for me to live, regardless of the fact that I was pulled over by the police from time to time and the other things that happened. I have a very good lifestyle. Orange County has afforded that to me. I fly airplanes for a hobby. I fly a sailplane. I live in Tustin Ranch now. I lived in Irvine. So obviously, I have been afforded a very good living here in Orange County. All of my friends are from Orange County, and a lot of those friends are white. The people that helped guide me along in my career were white people. So it's not like all white people are out there saying, hey, there's a black guy, we're going to keep him down. That's not true. For every negative thing that happened to me here, there were a lot of positive things that happened to me here. My kids are very well versed and educated. I have to say that living in this town—I would not live anywhere else. Otherwise, I would not be here. I love this place.

You moved out a couple of times and moved back, came back.

Exactly. With Louisiana, there's no comparison. With Los Angeles, Los Angeles was just not conducive to what I wanted from life, from what I was looking for. I did not know how to find it in Los Angeles County, where I understood how to get it in Orange County.

Now, I guess the negative side of it was that you had to give up some pride at some time. There were some very demeaning things that happened at times, but it's how you're willing to deal with it. I could handle it. Some people I know would not have been able to live here. I have relatives—it would have been impossible for them to live in Orange County. I cannot really tell you what it is that allowed me to be able to handle living in Orange County in the sixties and seventies. Eighties and nineties, it's a non-factor.

There were some pretty different things that happened that would be considered negative, but the positive 80 percent outweighed the negative. Housing? Difficult, at times. Trying to rent apartments? Difficult, at times. Being a mixed couple made it relatively easy because I would send the person that I was with in to rent the place, as opposed to my going in first. And that worked. You had to do what you had to do, and I learned to do it well in Orange County to survive. But what it cost me was some dignity. I always said to myself, I will deal with this until I do not have to any longer. At this point in my life, I do not have to, and I do not. But I still choose my battles in which to play, because there are some people you cannot convince of much of anything. There are some people that will probably read this and say, "You know what? That did not happen." (laughter) And I can only smile because I've only touched on it. My main thing was to earn a living, stay safe, and enjoy myself.

After the second marriage, which only lasted a year, you remarried.

Yeah. That's the best thing that happened to me in Orange County. I met my present wife twenty-four years ago at Collins Radio, at Rockwell. Loralee, she was just a kid. I just met this kid and we started talking. We had a few dates, we hit it off well. She lived in Yorba Linda. She was white, so I was concerned that when I go to date this girl that I would run into the problems that I'd run into in the past. That did not happen. And I looked for it. But her mother ended up being one of my best friends, and we're best friends today. It's just a positive thing. My wife is a very lovely and warm and beautiful person. She's just the best thing that happened to me in Orange County.

And she was supportive of you with regard to your children?

Right. In fact, a couple of my children lived with us for a while. My oldest son, James Jr., was raised in Orange County because he lived with me until he joined the service. We lived in Huntington Beach at that time. My daughters, until their teen years, they were raised in Orange County.

[Regarding your daughters] are they married?

They're both divorced. In fact, my youngest daughter, Regina McKay, at thirty-three, she just finished college. I used to call her a professional student when someone asked me what my kids did. My oldest daughter, Judy McKay, she's an office manager for a company in San Bernardino. They're both single moms. My oldest daughter was married to a Hispanic, and my youngest daughter, he was mixed—half white and half black.

And your son, James, back in [Florida]?

His current wife is black. His first wife was white. They met in Germany [while he was in the army] and married. He had problems in Florida being a mixed couple, he told me, because my son pretty much was raised in Huntington Beach.

Do you have some favorite stories relating to you being a black person in Orange County?

I was dating one young lady in Whittier [a city adjacent to west Orange County]. I think Whittier—it's immaterial. I was dating one young lady, and she simply told her mom that she had a date with Jim McKay. I guess her mom assumed that I was a nice Irish guy. When I showed up at the door, she could not hide it. She did a good job of trying. Then she passed out. Her dad came in and revived her mom, and they called the paramedics, because they didn't know what was wrong with her. She wasn't out very long. But I was asked to leave. And she had no clue. When I was mix-dating in Orange County, the first thing I would say—especially when I was younger, when the women were relatively young, if they lived with their parents—"Do your parents know that you—?" It was like, "My parents do not care if you're black." I found that rarely to be true. It's not that everyone fainted, but there's a look in someone's eyes when you first encounter them that is very difficult to hide. Not that I was looking for problems. It was a part of how to live in Orange County. And if you were going to mix-date in Orange County—I'm talking the seventies and the sixties—you had to learn to read the terrain, whether you were welcome or whether you were not welcome. And more often than not, you would get your feelings hurt a lot.

If you really wanted a good laugh, you would drive down Harbor Boulevard in the summertime when the tourists were here. As a mixed couple, you're sitting in the car, and you have whole families at the window staring, just staring at you. You go into a restaurant for a meal, and you're sitting there eating, and there are people discreetly staring because you are a mixed couple. Eventually, it doesn't bother you. You get accustomed, almost, to the limelight, so to speak.

And you feel that a lot less now than you did in the past?

Oh, 95 percent less. People do not even pay any attention to you anymore. But back in the sixties and seventies, it was something. I was at a club in Newport Beach one night shortly after they aired the movie *Roots*. I was a player. I was out there having a good time. This girl came up to me and she was going, "Oh, I saw *Roots*. It was so terrible what was done to you." And I'm sitting there going, "Hmm." It's like I used it for what it was. It was like, okay, if you want to give me this sympathy for the night because you saw *Roots*, that was fine. But to me, it was just terribly comical because I'm sitting there going, "Well, okay."

[There was] a group of people that, in the seventies, they would want to talk to you or be with you because it was cool to be with you. It was cool to be with a black guy or dancing with a black guy at that time. And at one time it was cool in Orange County to be [at] certain clubs, like Off Broadway West in Anaheim and Playgirl Club in Garden Grove; those were the great nightspots where you can mix. There were no issues, there were no problems. You would get a lot of girls in there because it was popular. And you knew that, to some degree, you were being used, but to some degree, you were also just having a good time. You didn't look at it as racial, even though I guess it was.

I do have a question about your mom. She moved to Santa Ana.

She lived in Santa Ana quite a few years. She eventually ended up moving to Los Angeles. She was never comfortable in a white environment. At that time, she moved to Corona [a few miles east of Orange County in Riverside County] with my sister for a while. My sister, my brother, my mother, uncles—everyone migrated here over a period of time. Los Angeles, Santa Ana, in the Orange County area. My brother, Oliver, returned. He remained only for a short period of time and returned to Louisiana, where he prospered there, quite well.

Was he young when he came here?

Yes. He was twenty. A heck of a baseball player, but he went back to Louisiana. For him that was right, because that was good for him at the time. I was adventurous. My mom had an adventurous spirit in her.

Now you've been married twenty-four years.

We've been together for twenty-four; been married for twenty.

With this woman you're in love with. You've been very open, and I appreciate it.

I tried to be candid. I think that the people who would look at this or read this would want to know it's not watered down, it's not diluted.

Thank you, Jim.

BARBARA YOUNGBLOOD[1]

Barbara Youngblood was born in 1940 in Milford, Connecticut. She describes being one of only a few black children both in her neighborhood and at school. Her husband, Fred, came from a small town in Alabama. They met in northern California and moved to Westminster, in Orange County, in 1969, as the result of his obtaining an engineering job at Autonetics in Anaheim. They had no problems in moving to new housing, but Fred experienced police profiling issues throughout their time in Orange County. Barbara was the county's first black female attorney. Barbara Youngblood lives in Huntington Beach. Photo 2008.

Tell me about your parents and the town you were raised in.

Back in the forties and fifties, Milford was a small town, small in area. It's right on Long Island Sound, so it was a summer home for a lot of New Yorkers. Nice, pretty quiet community. One high school in the center of town, a grade school in the center of town, and a grade school on either end. My father had his own business as an interior decorator and reupholstered and made custom furniture. And my mother worked as a housekeeper for one of the doctors in town.

Were there many black children in the school?

In the whole town, there were about fifteen families. My high school, when I started my freshman year, had about three hundred students. And when we graduated four years later, it was about two hundred and seventy-five, and there were three blacks in the graduating class. There were probably about eight or nine in the school.

What was your social life like in high school?

In high school, there wasn't much of a social life in terms of dating, boyfriends, that type of thing. But I was pretty active. I was very involved in sports—played

---

[1] Oral History 3276. Interview date: June 1, 2004, at the home of Barbara Youngblood, in Huntington Beach, California. Interviewer: Robert Johnson.

basketball and softball. Then I had a group of friends, girls; we had a lot of activities. I was in Girl Scouts when I was in grade school and early high school. I never really thought too much about the lack of social life. I was active in school—school plays, the school newspaper, the yearbook, and those types of things. But in terms of boyfriend-girlfriend type relationships, there was none of that at the high school. Social life was okay, though. I didn't have any racial problems in that school.

What was college life like?

I went to Temple University first. I wanted to go away to school. I had a brother, and I think my sister also lived in Philadelphia at the time. So that made it more acceptable to my parents. I lived in the dormitory; I didn't live with them. In the dorm of three hundred girls, there were about five, or maybe seven, black girls, and this was in 1958. The social life there was extensive. There were parties and dances and that kind of thing. There were black students. I don't remember a lot of cultural mix like we have now in all the universities across the country, but I'm talking about 1958, a different time period. There were not a lot of kids from the inner cities coming to the universities living in the dormitories, so it was a pretty select group. I went to Temple for two years, '58-'60. Then I transferred to the University of Connecticut [UConn] in '61.

I don't know whether to call it "sheltered" because it wasn't due to somebody's protection, but the kind of path that I took didn't expose me to an everyday life of racial intolerance, or racial problems. After I started college, I started dating a fellow who was at an army base in my hometown in Connecticut. He was from North Carolina, and that's where I started to learn about a lot of things, in conversation with him.

Where did you meet your husband?

I graduated from UConn in '63, and I got an apartment in Philadelphia. After I spent the winter going to work on the subway, I said, "I'm moving to California." So I moved to California in June of '65, and I met him in December of '65 out here. He was in the air force stationed at Hamilton Air Force Base up in Novato, by Petaluma, Santa Rosa—that area [above San Francisco]. I met him at a party up there.

So you were married when?

February of '66. When he got out of the air force, which would have been October of '66, he went to [Heald] Engineering School in San Francisco, a three-year program. And when he graduated—this would be '69—that was the time aerospace was really having problems. Businesses were closing, people were getting laid off. So he started job hunting, and his job offer was from Rockwell [Autonetics] down here in Anaheim, so we moved down here. We wanted to stay in the Bay Area, but as I said, aerospace jobs were pretty limited, and the Autonetics job came up. That was fall of 1969 that we moved down here.

Tell me about his background. Where did he come from?

He grew up in a little town in Alabama, I think just south of Tuskegee. Of course, he had a lot of negative experiences, but we didn't talk about them much. Things even happened down here that he didn't even tell me about. I'd find out from one of our friends a couple days later.

What did you know about Orange County before you came here?

I'd been living in San Francisco for three-and-a-half years. Everything I knew about Orange County was bad. I remember when we moved down here, I had friends who wouldn't come and visit for the first couple of years and these were white friends. We were active in the Peace and Freedom Party. My husband and I had some conflicts because I marched in some of the anti-war demonstrations and he was in the air force. (laughs) That made for some sore points. Although he supported the position, he couldn't get out and demonstrate.

Most of my friends were long-haired hippie-type musicians and everything. I was working as a physical therapist then, and my last week at work they had a little going-away party for me. They gave me a can of aerosol to spray because the smog was supposed to be so bad. They gave me an American flag to hang from my car window so everybody would know I was a patriot. All kinds of little gag gifts. Going from San Francisco to Orange County was going from one extreme to the other. Particularly San Francisco in the late sixties.

We had some friends who lived in L.A., black friends. They used to make comments about Orange County all the time. We'd go up there to play cards. It would get towards eleven-thirty, twelve o'clock, and we'd be ready to head home because we had a forty-five minute drive. And they'd say, "Oh, that's right. They close the border at midnight. You better get going." (laughs) Those kinds of comments.

Their view was mostly political—John Birch Society, that type of thing. The political activism in San Francisco was *very* much integrated. Carried petitions for lowering the voting age to eighteen and went door-to-door. And those Peace and Freedom Party meetings with black, Chinese, Japanese, Korean, white. Most of the comments and most of the concerns were about the war. I'm talking about 1969. For the twenty-to-thirty age group, that was the focus, the Vietnam War.

Did you have a child at the time you came to Orange County

No, we didn't have children. We adopted our son in 1972.

Where did you move?

We moved from San Francisco to Westminster. We moved from a one-bedroom flat into a three-bedroom house and we felt like we'd moved into a mansion. We moved in November of '69, and in 1970, they did the census that they do every ten years. It may be of interest to you, but I looked it up and for the city of Westminster, the population was fifty-five thousand, and there were two blacks who owned their own home. And that was us.

Did you have any trouble obtaining the house?

No. Actually, we didn't, which kind of surprised me. When it came time for us to move from San Francisco to down here, we knew where we were going to be working. We could look at a map and say, well, this city's too far away to live, and this city's too far away to live. Long Beach sounded like a nice city, because it was on the water and everything, but I talked to some friends there and they said, no, I would not like Long Beach. It's one of those cities that has a ghetto—or a segregated area, and unless you can really spend a lot of money on housing, to get out of that area.

So we just went to a realtor down here, and we rented a house. It was a house owned by an engineer, who had been transferred to Boston, and he had sold it to another engineer. The sale had fallen through. During the course of us leasing it for six months, it went up for sale, so we just went ahead and bought it. Didn't have to move out. We moved in November of '69 and we moved here in August of '76, so that's seven years.

When you moved to this house in Huntington Beach, did you have any trouble?

This house is kind of interesting because it's kind of a different location, with a dirt road and a septic tank, those types of things. It's not the typical home for sale. I wanted some space, and I wanted a two-story house and we had some parameters in terms of where we wanted to live. We were real active in a youth football program. Our son was turning an age to start participating, but we lived out of the area, so we wanted to move into the area where he could play, as well as his dad be a coach and me be involved. We used to go out every Sunday looking around. We looked at a lot of houses. I never got any negative vibes or negative impressions. The concern was the money.

This street, when we first came to see it, was a dirt road. As we came down the street, we saw some people building a house across the street. She was Japanese. We came back and looked at it a couple of times, and it turns out to be kind of a mixed street. There's a couple—he's white and she's Filipino; and there's another couple—he's white and she's Japanese. That's the first time I'd seen that type of integrated street since I'd been in California, so that was kind of interesting.

When we moved in, the Friday that we moved in—we had a lot of friends because of the football program. All the parents really worked together, so we had a lot of friends to help us. A lot of Hispanics. That was a very integrated program in terms of white and Hispanics—not that many black kids playing. So we moved in all in one day. A little kid who lived down the street, who was about fourteen at the time, came over and introduced himself. He told us, "On Friday night, the parents have Happy Hour, so when you get home from work next Friday, come over and my mom and dad are having Happy Hour." I said, "What's Happy Hour?" He said, "Oh, they just have snacks and have a drink and complain about the week." I said, "Okay."

And Sunday morning, I woke up to the sound of somebody walking around in our front yard, and it was the fourteen-year-old and his father. Someone had toilet-papered the house, and they were running around trying to get it cleaned up before we saw it. What they didn't know was, was that our football cheerleaders had toilet-papered our house. We knew it was coming. It was all part of the football program. They thought it was something negative, so they were trying to be real quiet, and they were sneaking around trying to clean up all this toilet paper. I hadn't met the dad yet; I'd met the kid, Dean. I said, "Dean, what are you doing?" He said, "Oh, I'm really sorry. Somebody toilet-papered the house." I said, "Yeah, the cheerleaders did it. We had a game yesterday." He said, "What cheerleaders?" I said, "The football team. Remember I told you?" It was okay.

They thought it was something negative, kind of a negative reaction. I thought it was just really sweet of them to get out there and make that effort. So I explained all that to them, and they were very relieved that it hadn't been one of their neighbors or something negative.

Having lived here many years, did you ever hear about Huntington Beach being a "sundown town"?[2]

I don't know that term "sundown town," but I know—I didn't have many, but my husband had a lot of negative experiences in Westminster and Huntington Beach. He was a jogger, a runner, and he also did a lot of bike riding. I'd say, from '69 to '79, he was probably stopped about twenty times by cops while he was riding his bike. On Sunday morning at eight-thirty, riding to the beach and back. Or jogging. He used to run with one of the moms from football. When we lived in this house, he'd run over to her house—which is a couple blocks over—meet her, then they'd run down to the beach and back.

She was a white mom or a black mom?

A white woman. One time he was running over there, and he just had on shorts and a sweat shirt, because they ran at about five-thirty, six o'clock in the morning before they both went to work. He was headed over to her house one morning, and the cops pulled him over and said that he fit the description of a rapist who had been in the area. So he told them who he was. I don't think he had any ID on him because he was running. So they took him to the house, and the husband, who's a real good friend of ours, opened the door when the cops knocked on the door and said, "Do you know this man?" He said, "No," (both laugh) as a joke. Then he said, "Why? What's going on?" So it was all taken care of. My husband didn't tell me these things. He had lived this kind of life all of his life, and I hadn't. When I heard about something like that, I'd get very angry, and I'd want to do something about it. Plus, by then I was an attorney and said, "We're going to do this," and

[2] In 1940, for instance, there were no black people living in Huntington Beach. And as late as 1960 the U.S. Census showed there were only two African Americans out of 11,000 residents in the city. James Loewen, who authored the book *Sundown Towns* [2005], in conversation with Robert Johnson, considered the city a "sundown town," simply because there were few or no blacks living there.

stuff. He just didn't bother to tell me because it just infuriated me. He had a number of those incidents.

In fact, my son was telling me, about six months ago—my husband and I are divorced, but we're on good terms and see each other occasionally when we have, like, a family thing. And my son was telling me that his dad had taken his car to the car wash, a new black Lexus, and he'd walked across the street, in his suit, to Huntington Center. He'd taken time from lunch at Boeing, and while they were washing his car, he was going over to the Barnes and Noble [book store]. Coming back, he was stopped by the police. I don't know what for. But he was in a business suit; he had his ID on him, and everything. So that kind of stuff is still happening. It just infuriates me.

I went to law school at night. It was finals, and I'd taken the motor home because I'd go early and then some friends and I would study in the motor home. I took the exam, and we went and had the post mortem, where you talked about everything you'd missed. Then I came home. When I got home about eleven o'clock at night, he wasn't home. And when he came in, I said, "Where'd you go?" He said, "Didn't you see me?" I said, "What do you mean?" He said, "Well, when you didn't come home, I got kind of worried so I went out looking for you." He said, "I was following you down Beach Boulevard." But I was in this big motor home and he was in our little sports car, so I never even saw his car. And he got pulled over by the police. I don't know what excuse they gave that time. This was quite a few years ago.

If you don't react properly, it's extremely dangerous. He knows you don't run and you don't react. He had been on a business trip to Boston for Rockwell, flew into LAX, and was walking across the street to the parking lot. And some people started yelling, "Stop! Stop!" And yelling a name, but it wasn't his name, so he kept walking. It turned out it was him that they were after, and they had their guns out and everything. Like I said, he's lived with that all of his life and has maybe reconciled to it. It's just the way of the world. So we didn't discuss it a lot.

You have to deal with it the way that works for you. And he was the one going through it. The incident where he was jogging and was stopped—when he was going over to meet his friend to run—he never told me about that. *They* told me about it. The husband told me about it, because he had made that joke about not knowing him. So when I saw them a couple of days later at football practice, they said, "Did Fred tell you what happened?" I said, "What are you talking about?"

Some people have had no experience like that whatsoever, and some people have had to live with it. He's been one who's had to live with it. When you're riding down Beach Boulevard on a Sunday afternoon on your bicycle and the cops stop you because a bank's been robbed and you're wearing sneaks and a pair of shorts and a tee shirt—not really bank robber garb. Those kinds of things happen regularly.

Why did you switch from physical therapy to law?

When we moved down here, I was in private practice as a physical therapist and enjoyed the job—made really good money for a woman, for a black woman, particularly. Then we had Medicare and Medi-Cal go into effect, and the paperwork got to be so time-consuming. I started getting frustrated and started looking into doing something else.

I'd always been interested in law school, but to do that right out of high school and go to pre-law and everything, my parents couldn't afford that. And I wasn't willing to do the work necessary. Like I said, I was an average student. I was not any great intellect or anything. But then after ten years of physical therapy, I'd finally matured and had a little more discipline, a little responsibility, so I decided to go to law school. And we also had the money, so I could pay for it myself.

And when you graduated from law school, you were the first black female attorney in Orange County. Is that true?

That's true. That's true. I never gave it much significance, because there weren't a whole lot of black attorneys in Orange County, male or female. But that is true. I went to work for Legal Aid in Santa Ana. Working at Legal Aid was when I really started having exposure with other black professionals. There are not a lot of black attorneys. I knew the guys in Orange County. There were three. Milton Grimes [Rodney King's attorney], who's still practicing; a district attorney, Ted Johnson, who's moved out of the area; and Judge Marvin Weeks who has since passed away; and myself. There were just those four of us.

I was an attorney, kind of a general practice. I worked at the main office in Santa Ana; then I switched over to the Westminster office, and I supervised that office doing the same variety of cases. It was interesting. I liked it a lot.

Then you decided to go into private practice.

Well, I thought I wanted to make some money. I liked the work, but you didn't make any money at Legal Aid. I left in '78 and went into private practice, and I did that for about six years.

I liked it, because I liked the work, but most of my clients were friends from football and Little League, or neighbors. I didn't like charging them. I just liked doing the work. I liked the paperwork, the research. I liked the trial work. I liked giving advice and helping. But I needed to get paid. That was the part that I was very poor at. Actually, I hired my nephew, who is an accountant, to do billing for me just so that bills would go out on a regular basis. But I stayed active with Legal Aid. I went on the board of directors for Legal Aid while I was in private practice and stayed active, because I liked that work. I was proud of what they did.

The opportunity came up to open an office in the Compton [Los Angeles County] area. So I left private practice, resigned from the board, and came back [as an employee] to Legal Aid. That was in February 1984. Then we got a grant to start doing something in family law: domestic violence, contested custody, abuse cases. I was developing some experience in family law, and we based it out of the Huntington Beach office, which was ideal for me. So I came down here and set up that program, the family law project.

We had a huge caseload. We did it better and faster because we were used to dealing with poor people and the problems that poor people presented. It was extremely meaningful because it dominated my time, whether I was in the office or out of the office. It was extremely stressful and frustrating to some extent, when you have people who are just barely making it, and they don't have a house to fight over or a car to fight over or a business to fight over, so they fight over the one thing they have, and that's the kids. Particularly in this country, it's devastating to be poor, and it's very hurtful or devastating to be uneducated. But when you combine those two, to be uneducated and poor, it's amazing that you can survive. And a lot of our clients were in that situation.

The abuse cases—the child abuse or spouse abuse cases were just heartbreaking. So, yeah, it did kind of dominate, because I'd be thinking of it at three or four o'clock in the morning, wake up in the middle of the night. So when I say it dominated—in a twenty-four hour day, it probably took twenty-two-and-a-half of the hours. But it always felt good when we accomplished something.

Do you think your being black affected your practice of the law?

I really don't know. I don't think it had any significance in the courtroom, but I can say most courthouses where you do your filing—go and see the clerks and file papers and everything—there's an attorney window, and I could walk up to the attorney window and be told to go wait in line. Then I'd have to say, "I'm an attorney." The only time they knew I was an attorney was if I had my briefcase right in my hand and a suit on or something. That type of thing.

Can you tell me about your social life in Orange County? For instance, was your family involved in a church?

We did have some church involvement when we were in San Francisco, but when we got down here, the black church that I knew of was over in Santa Ana. We were real big football fans. We started watching football at seven o'clock on Sunday mornings, Canadian football. Then we went to the NFL [National Football League]. I hate to admit it, but it didn't leave much room for church. But there were churches available. I did go to the [United] Methodist church right down the street a couple of times. Our social life revolved around our sports activities with the kids.

My son played, my husband coached, and I was either the trainer, because of my physical therapy background, or the athletic director. I was always on the board. For about an eight- or nine-year period, that was our social life. My friends now, the ones that I made twenty, twenty-five years ago in the sports program, now their kids are thirty-five, thirty-six, thirty-seven years old. They're still my good friends. And their parents are my best friends.

Tell me about your son, Tyrone. Where did he go to school?

He was eight when we moved into this house, so he went to the local grade school and Marina High School. He's an athlete, a football player. A very personable young man. Had a lot of friends. Again, at Marina, not a lot of black students.

There was a real mix of Asians, Hispanics, white, and a few blacks, so he had friends from all ethnic groups, all racial groups. He went to four different colleges over about a ten-year period. He's kind of a California surfer kid. (laughs)

Tell me about his high school social life, and dating.

Dating and social life was not a problem for him. His wife is white. He had girlfriends. He had, I think, one black girlfriend for a while. He's a very handsome guy, and he was a really cute kid, so the girls started calling when he was about ten years old. I didn't appreciate it, but—so he's had girlfriends from the time he was about twelve. He got married in 1997. She and I are really, really close. And they have two little girls, beautiful little girls.

So he was involved in sports in high school? Was he involved in any other activities?

In high school it was mostly sports. He was first team All-CIF [California Interscholastic Foundation] in football. He got his A.A. degree from Orange Coast and played football both years there. Then he went to Cal State Fullerton for a year and was on the football team. Then they got a new president [Milton Gordon, an African American, who replaced another African American, Jewel Plummer Cobb], and they canceled football altogether. Sports were really what kept him interested in school, so he left Cal State Fullerton. It's funny, because I'd gone to Italy on a ski trip. When I came back he picked me up, and I said something about football, and he said, "I talked to the president yesterday." I said, "What president?" He said, "The president of Cal State Fullerton."

So he talked to President Gordon?

Because they had dropped football. I was just very impressed that he made an appointment to go talk to the president of a major university about dropping the football program, when he didn't really care about going to school. But anyway, over a ten-year period, he dabbled at the schools and everything. He went to the University of LaVerne, played football again, was All-Conference defensive player of the year his senior year and graduated with a degree in broadcast communications. He worked for Fox Sports West. He interned at ABC, and he really liked it because it combined his sports interests and everything. Then OCN—there used to be an Orange County News channel—they decided to develop a sports division, and they hired him as the director of the sports division, which was perfect. But after three months, they decided not to do that at all. By that time he was married and they wanted to start a family, and he said he needed to settle down. He went into computer sales, did real well at that, and now he's in financing—mortgage loans and stuff, and doing very well.

Does Tyrone see living in Orange County as being a positive experience?

I think he does. He's spent time in L.A. and different areas. But I think for the most part, his experiences were positive. He'd like to come back here. He plans to buy this house when the time comes. Knock it down and put up a *nice* house. (laughs) He likes the beach. He worked all over. He got jobs without any problems. I can drive up Coast Highway and pick out six or seven places that he worked over a three- or four-year period when he was in high school and after he started college. I don't think he had really bad experiences. One, he's a pretty big kid, so I don't think anybody would give him *too* much trouble. And he's a nice kid; he's a personable kid.

I remember when he was about six or seven, my godmother came out to visit from Connecticut, and she was staying with relatives in Watts. She came down and spent the weekend with us, and then I took her home. We drove up to this pretty nice looking house and let my godmother out, talked for a couple seconds, and then got back in the van. My son looked at me and his eyes were kind of big, and he said, "There's a lot of black people around here." I said, "Yeah. This is a black neighborhood." He said, "Oh," and he didn't say anything more. But that was his first exposure. (laughs)

My son's wife is part Hispanic and part Caucasian. They're really lucky because their pediatricians live right across the street, and he and she are Iranian. Their dentist lives two blocks over, and he's Indian. Their little girl's best friend in her kindergarten lives two houses down, and they're Korean. Their best friends are Hispanic. It's great, because my grandchildren are getting this exposure. These are people who are all young, way upwardly mobile young couples. I don't know when they get into the real world what exposure they'll get, but they are meeting a mix of people, which is nice.

Are you glad you stayed in Orange County?

That's hard to answer, because if I hadn't stayed in Orange County, I probably wouldn't have my son and I wouldn't have grandchildren and everything. But I loved the Bay Area. I really did. But I also love this street; my neighbors here are my second family. I wouldn't have that.

Thank you very much, Barbara, for letting me interview you.

ROBERT CLEMONS[1]

Robert Clemons was born in 1939 in a house off of Central Avenue on Tenth Street in Los Angeles. Following a stint in the military, he earned an engineering degree and began working as an engineer at Collins Radio in Newport Beach, in the late sixties, while living in L.A. He tells about making the move to Orange County and what it has been like for him and his family to be part of a small minority living in the city of Orange. Bob and Lois Clemons still live in the home they bought in 1970.

When did you move to Orange County?

I moved to Orange County, the city of Orange, in 1970. The reason I moved out of the Los Angeles area was that my daughter was about ready to go to kindergarten, and I wanted to be situated where she could get into a good school. I wanted to be close to my job, and I knew that I didn't want to stay in the south-central Los Angeles area, where I was born and raised. I got out of the military in June of 1967, and I started working at Collins [Radio Company, in Newport Beach] almost immediately. I guess I'd been working at Collins almost three years.

Did you buy a house, or did you rent?

I bought a house; never considered renting. I purchased a little house when I was in Los Angeles after getting out of the service, then purchased this house when I moved to Orange County. And I'm still in this house.

That's taking a chance to come to Orange County without renting first and seeing how you liked it here.

For some reason, I didn't really have a great fear for personal safety. My main consideration was I wanted to move into an area that already had integrated. I

[1] Oral History 3024. Interview date: February 7, 2003, at the home of Robert Clemons, in Orange, California. Interviewer: Robert Johnson.

talked to you, Bob Johnson, and you pointed me toward a realtor who showed me some places. My criteria was that I didn't want to be the first to integrate any neighborhood. I wanted it to be as smooth as possible. Well, there weren't enough black people out here to really call any neighborhood integrated. (both laugh)

When we moved in, I think I knew maybe one other couple. Then another couple we met. But we knew basically two families at that time. And they weren't that close. One family, they were the Whites. They were about four blocks from us and there were the Hubbards. He was a retired military person. He had two daughters. And they were about four blocks south of us. So those were the two families.

Who came here with you?

My wife, [Lois], two daughters [Sherry and Gina], and my son [Robert]. They were all young. My oldest daughter was about three, my next daughter was about two, and my son, he was about one and a half, something like that.

When you came here, you were an engineer, so you didn't consider your family poor—maybe middle class?

There's a good story behind that. I was the first of my family to graduate from college, and I was very proud of it, and my family was very proud of it. I went into the military and I got out and moved to Watts, back where I lived. I used to get up in the morning and go to Collins Radio Company—white shirt, tie, and everything. Rudy Smith, who was Hispanic, said, "Hey, Bob, I see you get up every morning and you put on a white shirt and tie and go to work. What do you do?" I kind of stuck out my chest, not being arrogant but just being proud. And I said, "I'm an engineer." I said, "What do you do?" He said, "Oh, I'm a sheet metal worker." And I think he was making about twice as much as I was making at the time. I didn't consider myself middle class or poor or any kind of class. I just felt like I had a good job, a career, and that was it.

I remember at the time you said you had a choice of going to work for TRW and living in View Park [in Los Angeles] or staying with Collins and coming here. What made you make that decision?

It was strictly a financial decision. I'm not going to lead you astray. I probably would have wanted to stay there. I would have been around my family, and it wouldn't have been as much of a transition. But financially, the best deals were here. I figured it out to the penny, and what happened was that to buy a house there and to have to commute, it was so marginal financially for me that that commuting cost put it over the top. So I wanted to be closer to my job and also I wanted to be where there were good schools. Now, there were good communities over there. They had a place called Del Amo Woods, which was basically in the Torrance area. You could say that community was being integrated, too, because there weren't many black people in Torrance. But a lot of black people were moving to those homes, and they were *beautiful* homes. Actually, I liked them better than the house

I finally moved into, but the commute kind of eliminated it. So I moved out here. I had no fear about moving out here, though.

Well, you'd been in the service and you'd been used to dealing with white folks?

Oh, yeah.

In college?

Yeah, in college. As a matter of fact, I lived off campus in a house with five guys. We called it International House. I was actually the only resident of California. I went to Cal Poly in Pomona. Of the five guys, we had two Italian guys from New York, one guy who was Czechoslovakian—he was my roommate—then we had a guy from Greece, and a guy from India. (laughs)

Bob, what were your impressions of Orange County before you moved here?

I was very apprehensive about Orange County, even though, as I said earlier, I had no fear physically about anything happening here. I just felt that it was a place that didn't really care for black people that much. Racist, to be quite frank. I always felt that they'd just leave me alone. That was the only thing I was concerned about. I didn't figure anybody would be jumping on me or anything like that. That's the way I felt about it. As a matter of fact, everybody I knew felt the same way. They were always asking me, "Why are you moving to Orange County?" By the time I really considered it, I had had experience out here. I'd worked out here, and at lunchtime we went to the YMCA. I moved around here quite a bit, so it really wasn't as bad as I thought it was.

You said that you found a realtor. Tell me about that.

As I talked to people that I knew, I told them that I was considering moving out here but I didn't want to integrate any neighborhood. I was put in touch with a realtor. The realtor was a black lady [Ann Hillman], and she said she'd show me some places. So I felt comfortable about that. We were shown a number of places, and we finally found one that my wife and I liked. It went smooth with the seller. One reason it went smooth with the seller is he had moved back East and no one was in the home. (laughs) I think he was in a hurry to turn the house over. I don't know how long it had been on the market, but he was ready to sell.

So you haven't moved anywhere else in Orange County.

No, I kind of stick to things. (laughs) I haven't moved anywhere else. I've been here since 1970, so I guess that's about thirty-three years now.

Do you think there was any advantage of you being black and living in Orange County?

I don't see any advantage in being black and living in Orange County. The only advantage I see living in Orange County was I was able to get out of the Los

Angeles area where my kids would have been exposed to things I wouldn't want them exposed to in that environment. That's the reason I moved out here. The advantage of doing that was the lack of that exposure. The disadvantage is that socially they were deprived of being in an environment with black people. They culturally feel that they have suffered. I tell them many times, "Even though you culturally feel you have suffered, you gained in many other ways." One of them is just being out of the physical danger of being in that area. The danger there is not just because the people are black. I think the danger is because of the economically deprived environment. That breeds more crime, and so on.

With regard to your social life, was this area a problem for you?

If I'd have been a real social person, I might have felt deprived. Then again, all I have to do is hop on the freeway to go where I want to go. (chuckles) I don't seek to join groups or be a part of groups. I have my own friends who accept me and I accept them, and I'm satisfied. So I don't strive for anything that really would expose me to feeling socially deprived. That's probably just my nature.

How about Lois? Does she feel the same way?

We're pretty much alike. I think that's why we've been married thirty-nine years. I don't feel she's felt deprived. But I think she probably needs to speak for herself because there might be something hidden there that I don't know about. We go to movies, we go to church, we look at television, we go to the theater. We do things that we won't be discriminated against that much.

Where do you go to church?

I go to church in Compton [Los Angeles County]. Now, that might be a point where you might say that we might have suffered somewhat, because we travel every Sunday to Compton, and that is quite a drive. I do think that if we could have found a suitable church closer, we probably would have—a church where you feel comfortable.

And by comfortable, that has some other black people in it?

Well, yeah. What do they say about the most segregated hour is eleven o'clock on Sunday. But I got to tell you something—it wasn't as bad as I thought it was, because my church started fellowshipping with a church in Orange County, and that was a good relationship. It was in San Juan Capistrano [in south Orange County]. That was in the early to mid-seventies.

There's a little church right behind us. We visited there a few times, and we were well accepted. It started to open my eyes, to tell you the truth, that on a one-on-one basis, you'll find situations where you can be very well accepted. It surprised me, to be quite frank. Right now, my daughter, she lives in Rancho Santa Margarita [in south Orange County], and she goes to church out there. There's a lot of really good acceptance now. So I see a big change there. But your original question was how have I felt deprived socially, and I guess it would be in the area of church. But it was probably my fault as much as Orange County's fault.

So you still go to the Compton church?

Yeah. Like I said, it's a family church. That had a lot to do with it, too. Maybe that had a lot to do with our not venturing out. Maybe our apprehension plus the fact that we were in a family church already just kept us going to the same church.

Some years after you came here, I said, "Why don't you switch to an Orange County church?" And you said to me, "Well, you know, Bob, I'm around white people at work all day long. Then I come back to my neighborhood on the weekend, on Saturdays. Almost all the people here are white. On Sundays, I sort of like to be around some black people." I don't know if that's a very good quote, but I thought maybe it expressed your feelings.

I don't remember saying it that way, Bob. (chuckles) I probably meant culturally I wanted my kids to be able to experience their own culture, so I didn't want to totally isolate them. So every Sunday, they got a dose of their own culture by going back to our church. I hope I put it that way rather than saying I'm tired of being around white people. I don't think I ever said that. (both laugh)

In terms of friendships, do you feel you've made friends in the Orange County community?

Yes. It comes about naturally like it would in any environment, like it would have come about in the environment had I stayed in south central Los Angeles. It just comes from relationships, meeting with people, and you like each other and you decide you want to be friends and be around each other, and it just happens. I made a lot of friends while my kids were in sports around in Orange County playing soccer and my son playing football and baseball. I made friends that way. I made friends on the job. I went from Collins Radio Company as an engineer to Hughes [in Fullerton] as an engineer, and I went from Hughes as an engineer to become a computer salesman with IBM. I made a lot of friends there. It's just that I like people a lot, and we seem to take to each other, and I make friends pretty easily.

With regard to police, have you run into any trouble being stopped?

I've never had a policeman treat me badly. But you've got to remember, I'm sort of a homebody. I'm not out there usually when the players are out there in the streets. I'm just sort of a family guy, and I don't have a lot of encounters. I haven't had a ticket in probably twenty-five, thirty years. I haven't had those encounters. But I know of those encounters. See what I mean?

Now, the only incident that I had—and it wasn't even an unpleasant incident. I used to jog around my block all the time. Here I'm in my stuff jogging around the block, and the guy stopped me. But he was very pleasant. He found out I lived here and there was no problem. But he probably stopped me because I was a black guy running around. He tells me, "You know, there have been a lot of burglaries around here." I told him where I lived, and so on and so forth. He caught on pretty fast. He said, "Have a good evening." So I haven't had those issues. Know of the issues, but I've never had any.

Let's talk a little more about your children growing up here, in terms of their social life, dating, things like that.

You see, my kids had different experiences growing up. As you know, kids are very blunt, and they can be brutal at times. So they had racial incidents—not real physical ones where they were jumped on or beaten up or anything like that, but just verbal. At the time they were happening, somehow it didn't filter down to me. I find out about it now when they start telling me about the things that have happened.

They feel like they wouldn't have had their feelings hurt, had they been growing up in south central Los Angeles in their own culture. And I said, "Wait a minute. You have *never* had your feelings hurt until you've gone to a black school and gotten into it. You can *really* get your feelings hurt there, and you can get more than your feelings hurt." I said, "You think you were deprived, but I think it was really an advantage to you. You learned to live in the environment you're going to have to grow up in to compete in as an adult, and I think it was to your advantage. Yeah, you suffered somewhat, but you got through it all right. It's not as glorious as you think to think that if you'd grown up in another culture, in a black culture, that it would have been perfect, because it wouldn't have been perfect. You'd have the same kind of things but it would have just been black people doing it." (laughs)

They do feel that they were deprived as they were growing up in the area. Dating also. There weren't that many choices around here, in terms of there were not that many black people. They held those color lines more rigidly when the kids were growing up, even more so than now. But I kind of liked it myself because I didn't want them dating that much anyway. (laughs)

Did they have any dates in high school? They all went to what high school?

El Modena [in the city of Orange]. They didn't date much at all. Even when they went to their proms, they went with guys from our church. My son is the one who really broke out, and he had dates. He socially was a lot more active. Both of my older daughters feel that was probably because he was an athlete, and they feel that black males are accepted better. Anyway, everybody liked him. He was student body president, and so on and so forth. He was—what do they call it?—homecoming king. There was a little sibling rivalry and maybe jealousy along that line as they talk about it. They say, "Everybody liked Robert, but we had a hard time."

My next daughter had it easier than the first two. She was the last child. She became a cheerleader, and she was socially active. She didn't date much, though. I think maybe the dating criteria still stood. But it wasn't as difficult as it was for my older daughters. But you've got to remember, there was a time when I had four kids and the oldest was four, so they're packed in there pretty tight. (chuckles)

So your son—was his dating interracial, or whoever he liked?

Whoever he liked. He didn't seem to have any problems. I, to this day, can't figure out why he was so accepted. I was surprised by things in Orange County, especially in the high school. He had a friend who had good insights into things. He was a white young man, nice little guy. He said, "Robert, why don't you run for student body president and I'll be vice, because you can win." I couldn't quite understand that, but the kid knew how popular Robert was. And I had no idea. I don't even know if Robert knew how popular he was. When Robert came back and told me that he was running for student body president, I figured he was riding for a fall, so I was going to prepare him. I said, "Robert, I just want you to know, whether you win or lose, I'm really proud of you." He said, "Okay." They did their posters. He ran. And he won. (laughs) He surprised me.

Then after high school, what did your children do?

After high school, Sherry, my oldest, got a scholarship and she went to Chapman University. She stayed there awhile, and then she decided she wanted to go to UC Riverside. As you know, kids all want to do premed, and you can't talk them out of it. So she went to Riverside. Ultimately, what she did was go to nursing school and became a registered nurse.

My next daughter, Gina, she kind of did like I did. It took me eight years to finish college and get my degree in engineering. Well, my daughter, she started out in pre-med. She went to UC Irvine. Then she started to change her mind, and she went from UC Irvine to Loma Linda and got a degree as a physical therapist assistant. Then she went to Chapman and got her bachelor's and went back to Loma Linda. She ultimately finished up with a master's in physical therapy, and that's what she does now.

My son—once again I'm trying to give him good fatherly advice. He went to [Cal State] Fullerton, graduated in accounting. He told me he wanted to be a lawyer, and I said, "Look, you've got your bachelor's degree in accounting. Why don't you get your CPA, and then you can go back to law." This conservative engineering approach—get something in the hand first. He said, "No, I want to be a lawyer." Finally, he went to law school, and he graduated, and he's practicing law right now.

My last child, Kathy, she didn't know what she wanted to do. She started going to junior college. I thought that was a wise choice. That's the way I started out. She was talking to me one day, and I said, "I think you'd make a good teacher." Lo and behold, I didn't know it, it struck a chord. She started taking teaching courses, and she finally finished. She has her master's degree in education, and she teaches high school in San Juan Capistrano. She teaches at Capo High, and it's the same area where my church was fellowshipping with the other church.

Did your children have any problems dating once they graduated from high school and started into college? And who did they marry? Are their spouses white or black?

They dated who they wanted. My oldest daughter, she dated who she wanted and who I didn't want her to date, as a matter of fact. (laughs) But she got married, and he's a black fellow. She was going to nursing school in Los Angeles when she met him. My second daughter married a Jewish fellow. He's the one who teaches at the black junior high school and helps coach the black Centennial High [Compton, L.A. County] basketball team. He's from back East. He was living in Los Angeles at the time. My son, he married a girl he met in law school. She's Italian and Mexican. They live in Laguna Beach.

Do you have any favorite stories about Orange County having to do with the fact you are black and living in Orange County?

This one occasion, the family and I went to a movie and we came back, and the front door was open. I didn't know what it was. I parked my van, not in front of the house but in front of the next door neighbor's. I told my family, "I'm going to call the police." I went to my neighbor's house and I said, "Bob, I need to use your phone. I think somebody broke into my house." He said, "Sure." They were all sitting there. Bob and his family were sitting around me while I was on the phone. I said, "This is Bob Clemons. I live at [the address]. My door is open; I think somebody may have broken into my house." They said, "Yeah?" And I said, "I want you to know, I'm a black man and I'll be sitting outside in a silver van. I don't want any slip-ups and anybody shooting me." (laughs) Bob never let me live that down. Bob said, "Well, Bob, do you want me to go down there with you?" I said, "No, Bob, they'll shoot us both." I said, "I can go down there." I went to the van and sat down. The police were laughing when they came, and they went in my house. They went all through my house. They said, "There's nobody in there. It doesn't seem there's been a break-in." So they left. But once again they were very nice. To tell you the truth, I feel very comfortable going to the police at any time.

Thank you, Bob.

Afterword

This book is the latest installment in the Weglyn Multicultural Publication Series sponsored by the Center for Oral and Public History (COPH) at California State University, Fullerton (CSUF). Unlike the other books in this series, *A Different Shade of Orange* is focused exclusively on the historical experience of one particular ethnic group within Orange County, California: African Americans. Its authors, Bob Johnson and Charlene Riggins, have selected narrators from COPH's Orange County African American Community Project to recall selected aspects of that group's experience within the half century extending from 1930 through 1980. Their personal reminiscences provide insights into important events, conditions, and accomplishments of their racial-ethnic community, and also reveal its culture, attitudes, and social structure. Collectively, the interviews in this book present a portrait of one of America's largest ethnic groups—African Americans—in an area from which their voices were long absent. It also provides insights into the history of Orange County from a perspective that very few accounts of this area have previously included.

To appreciate fully the historical significance of African Americans in Orange County, however, these interviews need to be placed in broader contexts. First, Orange County at different periods represents two important parts of America. Up until the 1920s, Orange County was not yet a suburb in the common sense of that term: an urbanized, residential community outside the corporate limits of a large central city.[1] It was still largely a rural area, almost entirely agricultural in its economy, with a scattering of what were still small or medium-sized towns. Outside of the South, such areas had seldom been places that welcomed black residents in which blacks leaving the South had sought to live. During the first half of the twentieth century, African Americans did move out of the South in such large numbers that these movements are often called "The Great Migrations." The first, during World War I and the 1920s, was mostly to cities in the North and East. The second, during the Second World War, also came to the West, especially the Los Angeles area. But Orange County, being largely rural and relatively remote from Los Angeles, received only a few hundred blacks during the decade of that war compared to the 143,000 growth in their population in Los Angeles County.[2] Therefore, the stories of blacks in Orange County during these years are the experiences of people living in areas where few blacks lived, and they are most relevant for insights on why so few lived there.

In the years after World War II, the largest population movement within the United States was that to suburban communities outside of major cities. This move was so extensive that by 1980, these communities, often collectively referred to as "Suburbia," had over 40 percent of the nation's population, more than any other

---

[1] Scott Donaldson, *The Suburban Myth* (New York: Columbia University Press, 1969), 47.

[2] Lawrence B. de Graaf, "Negro Migration to Los Angeles, 1930-1950," Ph.D. dissertation, UCLA, 1962, 318.

demographic area. Suburbs had several features that attracted millions to live there. They had a low population density, reflected in the near-universal building of single-family detached houses with substantial yards. These were a refreshing contrast to the row houses or apartments of many cities. Most residents either owned their homes or aspired to do so, and this contributed to a care for property not always found in cities. Suburbs gained a reputation among many scholars and journalists as areas of cultural conformity and aesthetic blandness. But for many Americans, suburban residence was associated with upward mobility and safe, clean living, especially as central cities gained the increasingly negative image of areas of poverty and crime.[3] The main downside of suburban living, long commutes to work, was offset in the 1950s and 60s by the rapid development of freeways in southern California. Finally, suburbs had an unpublicized but widely understood lure to many Americans: almost all the people living there were white. From 1950 on, Orange County was transformed, initially in its northern and central areas, from acres of orange groves into miles of suburban communities. By the 1960s, it was being described as the archetype (in both positive and negative terms) of suburban California. Therefore, these recollections of the lives of African Americans in this county provide many insights into their experiences throughout suburban America.

This growing contrast between the economic conditions in central cities and suburbs, coupled with their increasingly opposite racial populations, became a central issue in the United States during the 1960s. The "urban crisis" was composed of African Americans resuming their wartime exodus from the South, but migrating almost entirely to aging central cities in the North and West. Often poor, with limited education and job skills, they arrived in areas that were experiencing the flight of many of their most educated residents, along with most of their industry and commercial businesses. These whites and their affluence, jobs, and new schools, were mostly moving into neighboring suburbs from which blacks were almost completely excluded.[4] Orange County was a major example of the exclusionary suburb. But the interviews in *A Different Shade of Orange* attest to the fact that blacks, too, aspired to move to suburbs, and in the 1960s some succeeded. Therefore, Orange County serves as a modifier of the gloomy prognosis of the "urban crisis" model. It tells us that the history of blacks in Southern California is not just a story of "chocolate city and vanilla suburbs," as one sociologist put it,[5] but also of their aspirations to share the comforts of suburban living. And against heavy odds, often succeeded in doing so. These experiences, added to those in suburbs around the country, would eventually displace the urban crisis model as the only, or even the predominant, interpretation of African American life in the later twentieth century.

---

[3] Kenneth T. Jackson, *Crabgrass Frontier: The Suburbanization of the United States* (New York: Oxford University Press, 1985), 6-8.

[4] The "urban crisis" model of racial-economic problems in postwar America is much more complex than this brief explanation. See, for example, Edward Banfield, *The Unheavenly City* (Boston: Little, Brown & Co., 1968, rev. 1974) and Thomas J. Sugrue, *The Origins of the Urban Crisis* (Princeton: Princeton University Press, 1996).

[5] Reynolds Farley, "Chocolate City, Vanilla Suburbs: Will the Trend Toward Racially Separate Communities Continue?" *Social Science Research* 7 (1978): 319-44.

For the first two decades after World War II, however, black exclusion was the rule in suburban communities, and Orange County offers many examples of why this was so. At the root was the attitude of residents of the county, which had long been hostile to persons other than Caucasians. This attitude was especially evident in the vote on Proposition 14, the 1964 initiative to nullify all California fair housing laws and allow individual home owners to "decline to sell, lease or rent" property to any person that "he in his absolute discretion chooses." Statewide, this measure passed by a margin slightly under 2-1. In Orange County, it passed by a margin of 3-1, larger than any county except Mono.[6] Such evidences of widespread hostility towards blacks earned Orange County the nickname "the Mississippi of the West," or "John Birch Society country" among blacks during the 1960s. This image remained in the minds of many into the last decade of the century.[7]

While African Americans encountered this hostility in employment, restaurants, and police actions, it was most effective in minimizing the number of blacks living in Orange County and other suburban communities through various practices in housing. Many whites who otherwise admitted no prejudice against African Americans, subscribed to the idea that their entry into a tract would lower property values or would lead to their daughter going out with a black man (an unthinkable association to many whites in the 1950s and 60s). Such feelings were put into practice by various means. In areas like Panorama City, the developer made agreements with local realtors not to sell any houses to blacks. Since the early twentieth century, race-restrictive covenants had been attached to the deeds of many houses, forbidding the sale or lease of that property to anyone not of the Caucasian race. In 1948, the US Supreme Court declared such covenants could not be enforced in court, but realtors stepped in to implement them. Article 34 of the Code of Ethics of the National Association of Real Estate Boards (NAREB) prohibited a realtor from introducing "incongruous elements" into a neighborhood, and African Americans found themselves lumped in with criminals and unclean animals. Landlords used the ploy that they suddenly had no vacancy. Banks and other lending agencies plotted maps of "red-lining" by which areas that blacks moved into were deemed unsafe for loans by financial institutions and government agencies. This practice had been adopted in the 1930s by the Federal Housing Administration, which heavily favored suburban and all-white neighborhoods in guaranteeing home loans. Red-lined areas, on the other hand, were deemed least desirable as mortgage risks. Essentially, this precluded allowing blacks into a neighborhood lest it reduce its mortgage rating.[8]

Orange County in the 1950s and 1960s thus presented the paradox of a dream suburb for whites and the dilemma of exclusion from this dream for blacks. The advance of a freeway out of Los Angeles into Orange County brought a wave of

---

[6] California Constitution, Article I, Section 26; California, *Statement of Vote: General Election, November 3, 1964* (Sacramento: Office of State Printing, 1964), 25.

[7] Interview with Jewel Plummer Cobb by Lawrence B. de Graaf (CSUF Oral History Program, 1990), 166.

[8] Jackson, *Crabgrass Frontier, 197, 208, 215-17;* Lawrence B. de Graaf, "From Virtual Exclusion to Limited Assimilation: Blacks in Orange County, 1940-1980," Paper Delivered at Western Historical Association, October 19, 1990, 10.

residential development to north Orange County in the early 1950s, as its population grew by 225 percent. This was accompanied by an influx of manufacturing plants and jobs, which rose from less than 7,000 in 1950 to over 41,000 ten years later and doubled again between 1958 and 1964. By 1963, the US Bureau of the Census recognized that Orange County had become "a dynamic entity separate from Los Angeles County" by making it a separate Metropolitan Statistical Area.[9] But African Americans comprised only a miniscule portion of this growth, numbering only 3,171 by 1960. While this number would grow four-fold in the 1960s, most of this increase settled in existing black communities, especially Santa Ana.[10] The interviews in this book tell the stories of individual blacks who broke down the barriers in this period and helped form organizations to bring more widespread reform. But through much of the 1960s, as in most other suburban communities, they represented a small silver lining in a dark cloud of African Americans coming to what they thought would be a promised land and finding they were only welcome in crowded and deteriorating ghettos such as south central Los Angeles.

These disparities received little attention from residents or authorities in Orange County until the mid-1960s. As was the case in other regional suburbs, some citizens were so concerned about them that they began to establish fair employment and fair housing councils. But the event that brought widespread notice of both discriminatory practices and African American resentments toward them was the Watts Riot of 1965 and the succession of racial uprisings in cities around the nation in the immediately following years. While Orange County itself had no such violence in the 1960s, many whites became aware that the county had racial problems, and police chiefs, city officials, and company executives sought out influential African Americans to get their ideas on what might be done to resolve them. Local civil rights groups took advantage of this growing awareness, challenging local leaders to make Orange County "a model to the nation," not "a Chicago or Newark tomorrow."[11]

The 1965 upheaval affected blacks in Orange County in another way: it increased the desire of many of their compatriots to leave the dangerous streets of Los Angeles and try to break the noose of exclusionary suburbs that surrounded it. Some of these came east to Orange County, with the result that by 1970, its African American population had grown to over 10,000. But their concentration in Santa Ana or the few other areas of established black housing, led to fears that these might become "institutional ghettos" in which blacks would establish a more complete parallel community to that outside than had already been set up.[12] State laws passed in 1959 and 1963 that allowed persons who were denied the right to buy or lease property because of their race or color to sue the discriminating party, had been only marginally effective up to 1964. Then, they were all rendered

---

[9] Security First National Bank, *Growth and Economic Stature of Orange County: 1961* (Los Angeles: Security First National Bank, 1961), 1-3, 5, 10, 29; *Focus on Orange County* (Los Angeles: Bank of America, 1972), 1.

[10] William Gayk, "The Changing Demography of Orange County," *Journal of Orange County Studies* ¾ (Fall 1989/Spring 1990): 16.

[11] "A New Era in Housing," brochure of Orange County Fair Housing Council, c. 1969.

[12] de Graaf, "From Virtual Exclusion," 17.

unconstitutional by Proposition 14. Two years later, African Americans applauded the irony that a part of California notorious for its racial practices became the site of the court case that declared Proposition 14 unconstitutional. But this victory simply returned the issue of housing discrimination to the costly process of individual civil suits and the tedious requirement of "testing" housing sites, in order to assemble tangible evidence of discrimination. What was needed to open suburban communities to black residence on a large scale was legislation that would make the whole array of exclusionary practices illegal and make local, state, and federal authorities responsible for enforcing them. This measure came with the passage of the Civil Rights Act of 1968. In the wake of its implementation in 1970, most lending institutions, realtors, landlords, and property owners abandoned their overtly discriminatory practices.[13]

Single events, such as enacting a law, do not bring about instant change, and this was precisely the case with the Civil Rights Act of 1968 and Orange County. As several interviews attest, blacks continued to experience discrimination and harassment for years after this act was passed. The newest communities in the southern part of the county were especially slow to accept blacks, leading some observers to declare that a "Mason-Dixon line ran across the county" at Santa Ana—mixed races living north of it and virtually all white to the south. None of the interviews in this volume mentioned this nor singled out 1970 as a year of notable change. Rather, the flow of blacks from Los Angeles and other central cities into suburbs steadily increased, and by the end of the decade, became most notable for the communities into which it was going. Prior to the 1970s, most blacks leaving large cities had gone to older communities immediately adjacent to them, such as Compton, or to a few already established outlying communities, like Santa Ana. Few had been able to enter newer, faster-growing communities, which is where most of the promise of suburbia was located. In 1970, all of these communities in California had only 6,700 African Americans. Ten years later, what were then the newest and fastest-growing suburban cities, had nearly 46,000 black residents. By 1990, they would have nearly 120,000. Orange County was a major part of this change. Not only did its black population grow from over 10,000 to over 25,000 between 1970 and 1980, then to nearly 42,700 by 1990, but this growth was far more dispersed and predominantly located in newer, more affluent areas of the county. The population of Santa Ana grew by little over 1,000 into the 1980s, but the percent of Orange County's blacks living there fell from nearly two-thirds in 1970 to less than one-third by 1980, then absolutely declined by 1990. In Huntington Beach, the black population rose from 99 to 1,218 in the 1970s, and grew similarly in most other fast-growing communities in the 1970s and 1980s.[14]

This integration of African Americans into suburban communities changed the condition of African Americans in several ways. Most evident was their rising employment status and income. In the 1970s, the median income of blacks in

---

[13] Lawrence B. de Graaf, "African American Suburbanization in California, 1960 through 1990," in Lawrence B. de Graaf, Kevin Mulroy, and Quintard Taylor, eds, *Seeking El Dorado: African Americans in California* (Los Angeles: Autry Museum of Western Heritage, 2001), 415.

[14] de Graaf, "From Virtual Exclusion,"44.

fast-growing suburbs nearly tripled and nearly doubled again in the 1980s. This reflected a striking shift from historic employment in blue-collar or menial jobs to over 60 percent of blacks in California having managerial, professional, or other white-color jobs by 1990. In some of the fast-growing suburbs, the proportion of blacks in high status jobs by 1990 almost matched that of whites.[15] During the 1960s, fair employment laws, affirmative action policies, and the formation of collaborative organizations with businesses like Orange County's Partners for Progress, helped to break the ceiling on jobs and allow blacks to attain the level of their capabilities. Many of the interviews in this present volume offer personal experiences of those who were part of an occupational transformation that was even more striking in Orange County than in the state overall. Between 1970 and 1980, the number of black males holding professional jobs in Orange County increased four and a half-times; the number in managerial positions increased ten-fold. Gains among black women were even greater; by 1980, 70 percent of them held professional, managerial, or other white-collar jobs.[16] Epitomizing these gains was the selection of an African American to be city manager of Santa Ana, who summarized the nexus between suburbanization and economic advancement: "Orange County presents a unique opportunity for black professionals and others to become part of the American Dream in terms of living in a location which has tremendous economic growth."[17]

Suburban dispersal also took many blacks out of a condition of de facto segregation in public schools into ones that were racially integrated and usually of higher quality. Again, Orange County blacks typified the experience of other suburban areas. Their concentration in Santa Ana had restricted many of them to a few schools which they shared with Mexican American students. Besides often being inferior to schools in other communities in their physical facilities, these ghetto schools often impressed feelings of inferiority and put down desires to advance in life. One example was the black girl in the 1950s who told her teacher in Santa Ana she wanted to become a secretary. The (white) teacher told her to forget such ambitions; all she could aspire to was to be a maid.[18] As some interviews relate, one avenue of improvement in education was gaining entry into colleges. By the late 1960s, these institutions were recruiting students from diverse ethnic groups, often after pressure from black student groups. From the 1970s into the twenty-first century, "diversity" became a major goal of colleges and universities, and blacks in most suburban communities joined their fellow residents in regarding a post-secondary education as the norm, not an exception. The opening of both education and employment to blacks (and women) in Orange County was evident in the 1980s, when three local institutions of higher education had black female presidents.

Moving out of predominantly black communities in older areas to integrated newer suburban cities also had its drawbacks for some African Americans, and

---

[15] de Graaf, "African American Suburbanization," 427-28, 431.

[16] de Graaf, "From Virtual Exclusion," 20, 30.

[17] *Los Angeles Times,* 13 August 1992.

[18] *Orange County Register,* February 5, 1985, E6.

one of these was the loss of their racial community. Particularly in an area like Orange County, where despite their population growth blacks still constituted less than 2 percent of the population, the dispersal of blacks could bring a sense of isolation, of being disconnected from people and lifestyles they had grown up with. Black students in universities complained that they felt lost "in a sea of white faces." Some parents worried that their children were seeing predominantly black communities only in negative contexts. Some families made regular trips back to inner city communities for church or entertainment. Others sought to regain the "caring attitude" associated with living among other blacks by returning to the South. The latter attitude contributed to a virtual halt in the trend of blacks moving out of the South after 1970, and instead, produced a small reverse migration toward the end of the century.[19]

Another debit side of the movement of African Americans to the suburbs was that they were only a part—albeit a growing part—of the nation's black urban population. Another comprised groups largely left out of Orange County communities or most other newer suburbs. Some were modestly paid workers who aspired to come to the suburbs, but by the late 1970s, found the escalating cost of real estate could be as exclusionary as restrictive covenants. To some observers, the suburban migration left the plight of the inner city even more acute, for it meant the departure of the most educated and affluent blacks—potential leaders and role models for their race. The result was that areas like south central Los Angeles became increasingly afflicted with crime, drugs, and poverty, while middle-class blacks enjoyed a comparatively affluent condition and lifestyle in a safe environment. The frustrations of inner city blacks over their condition gained attention after the 1992 Los Angeles Riots following the beating of Rodney King. Many scholars and observers, by the 1980s, expressed alarm over this growing bifurcation between the middle class and the poor, and it tempered the sense of progress of the black middle class. As one article noted, they "still feel a sense of failure, that in spite of this great [civil rights] movement that achieved some very worthwhile things . . . very little has changed for the mass of black people."[20]

The last decades of the twentieth century saw a change as significant to the future of African Americans in Orange County as the opening of the suburbs: the exploding population of multiple ethnic groups. Once overwhelmingly white, Orange County by 2006 was a mosaic of ethnic colors. Non-Hispanic whites were only 47.4 percent of its population, Hispanics, 32.9 percent. Asian Americans constituted 16.1 percent, while blacks remained slightly below 2 percent. The greatest increases came among recent immigrants—Hispanic and Asian. This demographic development had mixed impacts on blacks in Orange County and suburban communities that underwent similar ethnic diversification. On the one hand, blacks were displaced in some communities, particularly Santa Ana, where former black residents returned to find only a few of their race still

[19] de Graaf, "African American Suburbanization," 432-33.

[20] David M. Grant, Melvin L. Oliver, and Angela D. James, "African Americans: Social and Economic Bifurcation," in Roger Waldinger and Mehdi Bozorgmehr, eds., *Ethnic Los Angeles* (New York: Russell Sage Foundation, 1996), 382.

in the neighborhood. It also displaced some black workers from common and skilled labor jobs. After generations of living as "minorities," it must have been of some interest to see the day coming when this term would become statistically meaningless, as no single group would constitute a majority. But this feeling was offset by the realization that blacks, as well as whites, constituted a shrinking proportion of the population of California, and that all the growth in their numbers in Orange County still left them a miniscule portion of this—and nearly all other—suburban populations. But did this matter? Perhaps not, especially to those like a few interviewees in this book who had formed interracial families and could look to a time when racial identification would be at once more difficult and less relevant. Certainly such a situation had seemed unlikely forty years earlier when three-fourths of its voters had supported a proposition that promised, among other things, to keep their daughters free from any prospect of socializing with black people. So here may lie the ultimate message of a history work like this: that the experiences of any group, like history itself, are in a state of perpetual change, and what seems important to one generation may seem much less so to another.

Lawrence B. de Graaf
Center for Oral and Public History
California State University, Fullerton

Part Three

Appendices

Appendix 1: Additional COPH Interviews on the Orange County Black Experience

With each of the oral histories in Chapters 1-5, the editors tried to maintain as complete a narrative as possible within rigorous space limitations; however, the transcripts have been abridged without the customary ellipses to indicate cuts. A number of Orange County African American oral histories were not included in this book, but some of the interviews are included in the 1974 book *Harvest: A Bicultural Communications Project*, edited by Cal State Fullerton Professors Priscilla Oaks and Wacira Gethaiga. Several interviews were completed in different time periods: 1974, 1994, 2003, and 2004. Included are abstracts of three oral histories—Winters, Benham, and Gethaiga—that were taken at a different time from the oral histories in the main body of this book. Following are abstracts of interviews not used in Chapters 1-5. These oral histories are transcribed and located in the Center for Oral and Public History of California State University, Fullerton.

SHUNTELE ANDREWS

OH No. 2363. Interview date: April 19, 1994. Interviewer: Mae Ussery

Shuntele Andrews was junior high school age when she came to Santa Ana in the early 1960s, after attending Catholic schools in Vicksburg, Mississippi. She was an exceptional student, graduated in 1968, and went to the University of California at Irvine. Her first job was teaching English and social studies in Los Angeles County. She returned [to Orange County] and started teaching at Valley High School in 1976. The second half of the interview stresses her next eighteen years of living and teaching in Santa Ana. Because both Andrews and the interviewer, Mae Ussery, who also taught at Valley High School, are teachers, much of the interview involves the subject of education.

SADIE REID BENHAM

OH No. 2902a. Interview date: May 2, 1994. Interviewer: Danelle Moon.

This oral history covers a great deal more of Sadie Reid Benham's early life outside of Orange County than in Chapter 3 of this book, but less about her life in Orange County. The two oral histories complement one another.

ANNGERAL CARMICHAEL

OH No. 2134. Interview date: October 28, 1974. Interviewers: Arlen Gaynor and Terry Kirker.

Anngeral Carmichael was born in San Antonio, Texas, in 1920. She talks about going into hospital work, starting at the very bottom and working up to head supervisor. Later, she became the chief cook at Fort Sam Houston in San Antonio. She came to California about 1945 and worked as a cook for the movie actor Jean Hersholt. Following his death, she came to Orange County. She moved to Anaheim and "when the neighbors found out it was a black family moving in, all the windows were shot out and the lawn was soaked with gasoline." Because she was black, she had difficulty obtaining a job in the county juvenile hall kitchen, and once she obtained the job, her race continued to be a problem. She went to work at the marine base at El Toro where she had control of the galley, and maintained the hiring and firing of kitchen personnel. Later, she started her own catering business. Like others in this book, she had many wealthy people for whom she catered, and like the others, she had no problems. This oral history can be found in the book *Harvest*.

EARNIE CHEETAM

OH No. 2135. Interview date: October 24, 1974. Interviewers: Darlene Barnes and Ruth Preiss.

Earnie Cheetam was born in the small town of Luken, Texas. She came west with her mother and settled in Oakland. She tells about post high school, becoming a beautician, her marriage, the birth of two daughters, and finally their move in 1959 to Orange County. Their first home in the county was on Kansas Avenue in Placentia—near where the Gunny Smiths, Charles Rays, and many other black families lived. The Cheetams lived there for fourteen years. Earnie sent her three girls to Marywood, a private Catholic school, even though the expense sometimes resulted in the family having only potatoes to eat. She tells about the girls, their education, and how her youngest daughter married Isaac Curtis, the famous professional football player. Her daughters were Girl Scouts and did volunteer work like their mother did throughout much of her life. She tells about the Kansas Avenue neighborhood and the nearby orange groves and the beautiful smell of the blossoms and the train that came by, which they liked to listen to early in the morning and late at night. In time, their neighborhood deteriorated and they moved to Anaheim in 1973. They arrived along with the moving van and their new neighbors helped them move into their home. This oral history can be found in the book *Harvest*.

EARL DEARING

OH No. 3029. Interview date: March 10, 2003. Interviewer: Robert Johnson.

Earl Dearing was born in Washington D.C. in 1934. He joined the marines at the age of seventeen and first came to Orange County in 1955 and lived on the El Toro base. He left and came back two more times before buying a home in Santa Ana. He tells about the major responsibilities he had as a gunnery sergeant in equipment and procurement. Dearing retired from the US Marine Corps in 1971 and decided to go to college, first to Santa Ana College and then to Cal State Fullerton where he earned a degree in business. He tells about social life in Santa Ana and his involvement in the black church, the NAACP, and the Fair Housing Council of Orange County (all three of which organizations he served as treasurer). Dearing had no trouble finding jobs in Orange County and eventually owned a realty business, having received a great deal of help with both job-seeking and his college studies. He states that unlike most black people, he has had no problems with the police.

WACIRA GETHAIGA

OH No. 2151a. Interview date: November 5, 1974. Interviewers: Darlene Barnes and Ruth Preiss.

Professor Wacira Gethaiga, in this interview, goes into considerable detail about life in Kenya, including language and schooling, and contains much less detail about life in Orange County as in the second interview found in Chapter 5. This oral history can be found in the book *Harvest*.

ROBERT HUTSON

OH No. 2367. Interview date: May 31, 1994. Interviewer: Noah Kimbwala.

Robert Hutson grew up in East Los Angeles in the 1940s and 1950s, and like now, it was a predominantly Mexican American area. He had many Latino friends and became fluent in Spanish, something that was helpful in his later work in the justice system. In the first half of this long interview, Hutson tells about both his childhood and his family. His father was an L.A. police officer and retired as a sergeant after twenty years on the force, went to law school, and became an attorney. Robert Hutson served in the military, worked for Western Electric in L.A., and like his father, went to law school and became an attorney. He was told that Orange County was a good place to work, so he went to work in the public defender's office. He tells about helping start the Jefferson Law Society (see Youngblood OH in Chapter 5) and the encouragement he had from attorney Milton Grimes. In 1982, Governor Jerry Brown appointed him to the North Orange County Municipal Court; in 1989, he was appointed to the Orange County Superior Court by Governor Deukmejian; and in 1990, he became the Orange County Juvenile Court Presiding Judge. He tells about how he became a judge in conservative Orange County and also "lectures" on civil rights (Dred Scott, *Plessy v. Ferguson,* and *Brown v. the Board of Education*) and crime and criminal laws (like the Three-Strikes Law).

RUTH MAY

OH No. 2137. Interview date: October 31, 1974. Interviewers: Eddie Gaines and Kathy Ridge.

Ruth May is the daughter of the author Lorenz Graham and the niece of W.E.B. DuBois. She was born in Richmond, Virginia, and grew up in Hampton, Virginia. She went to all-black schools until high school, when the family moved to Flushing, New York, and she went to an integrated school. She received a scholarship to Vassar College, which had four black students in 1953, the year she graduated. She and her husband moved to Los Angeles where she taught reading. While still teaching in L.A. County, she and her family moved to Fullerton so their children would receive a better education. She tells a moving story about an adult, whose life was change by her teaching. She was hired by Cal State Fullerton as a faculty member in the institute for reading, to do research and work with students in the Educational Opportunities Program. Throughout her oral history she interjects her experiences and ideas on language and reading with regard to black and Chicano students. This interview was published in *Harvest.*

TESSIE McALLISTER

OH No. 3225. Interview date: February 18, 2004. Interviewer: Robert Johnson.

Tessie McAllister and her husband came to Orange County from Texas in the mid-to-late 1940s, upon the recommendation of his friend, Percy D. Burton. She and her husband first lived in Dana Point and El Toro and then moved to Santa Ana, where he had taken a job with the city. They first lived in an apartment near downtown and then built a house less than two blocks east of Bristol on 3rd Street. Then they bought a four-unit apartment next to their home. She tells about her church, Johnson Chapel, social life, shopping, her neighbors, and her two children and their families. She also tells about the migration of black people out of Santa Ana and the county.

BOAZ NAMASAKA

OH No. 2153. Interview date: October 31, 1974. Interviewers: Ray Williams and Louise Wainright.

This is an interview of Dr. Boaz Namasaka, a professor at California State University, Fullerton. Namasaka was born and raised, until high school age, in Kenya. He came to Santa Barbara in the late 1950s and lived there with a black family. He tells about the dual African educational system, European and traditional. In this excellent oral history, he goes into detail about the differences in backgrounds between the Afro-American and the African living in America, how they feel about themselves, how whites relate to each of them, and how they relate to each other. He goes on to tell how necessary it is for Afro-Americans and Africans living here to understand each other and how it is necessary to have Africans teaching in black studies programs. Little of this material is specific to Orange County. This interview was published in the book *Harvest.*

TYRONE PERRY

OH No. 2138. Interview date: October 20, 1974. Interviewer: Spring Anderson.

This is a short six-page interview. Tyrone Perry was a financial aid counselor at California State University, Fullerton (CSUF) at the time of the interview. He tells about growing up in Compton in the first half of the interview and then tells about attending CSUF and the academic and social adjustments he needed to make. He then talks about his work. This interview was published in the book *Harvest.*

MARJORIE PETHERBRIDGE

OH No. 3030. Interview date: February 14, 2003. Interviewer: Robert Johnson.

Marjorie Petherbridge is a white person, as was her husband Dick (deceased at the time of the interview). She tells about working in L.A. as a social worker when they were married in 1951, and about losing her job because she would not sign a loyalty oath. Dick was working for the famous ACLU attorney A.L. Wirin at the time. She tells the story of Wirin being kidnapped by Imperial Valley anti-union growers in the late 1930s and the story of Marjorie and Dick's moving to the same area to do civil-rights work in the early 1950s. They came to Santa Ana in 1963 and intentionally moved into an area that was in the process of being integrated. She tells about Dick and Paul Bortz involvement in the "No on Prop 14" campaign,

Dick's chairing the O.C. Fair Housing Council, attorney Dave Cadwell taking on the *Mulkey v. Reitman* case (Chapter 3), and A.L. Wirin following the case through the US Supreme Court. She tells about their children and their families. Author Cary McWilliams told Dick to keep a diary because he may want to write a book. He didn't keep a diary and that is our loss.

JAMES PUGH

OH No. 2139. Interview dates: October 8, 10, and 18, 1974. Interviewers: Jody Wallick and Murphy Holmes.

James Pugh's oral history was published in the book *Harvest.* In the first eleven pages, educational psychologist James Pugh tells about growing up in Harlem, with its drugs, crime, hustling, and fighting, then about going to Wilberforce University, in rural Ohio, where he played basketball. His "in your face" language is very direct as might be expected from a person growing up in the ghetto in the 1960s. In the next twenty pages, he discusses a wide range of topics regarding being black and interfacing (or not) with the white world. He then talks about where he works, the People's Clinic, a child guidance clinic in Santa Ana. It was started in 1971 by black people, Ron and Judy Lunsford and Joe White, all three of whom taught at the University of California, Irvine. He provides both philosophy and concrete details of the programs at the clinic. In roughly the last third of the interview, Pugh again expresses his thoughts regarding the black experience, but with little reference to Orange County.

CHARLES RAY

OH No. 3457. Interview date: November 22, 2004. Interviewer: Robert Johnson.

Charles Ray was born in Texas in 1928 and later came to Los Angeles to live for a short time during his high school years. After serving in the air force, he was hired by North American Aviation and was transferred to Autonetics in Anaheim. In 1960, he purchased a home on Kansas Street in the Placentia "ghetto." In 1966, he and his wife tried to obtain a home in a new up-scale tract, but were denied because of their race, so they sued the builder and won. Ironically, at the time, he was a member of the Placentia planning commission. In 1967, they bought a home near the one denied them and that is where they raised their children. Their children have all done well. His son, Shawn Ray, is a famous body builder, and for a number of years, was one of the top-five in the world. Ray talked about racism as related to difficulties at Autonetics, with a daughter at school (she became an attorney), and racial profiling problems with the police. At the time of the interview, Ray was running his own maintenance business.

SYLVIA TURNER

OH No. 2357. Interview date: April 9, 1994. Interviewer: Lourdez Gonzalez.

Sylvia Turner was born in 1944 into a Washington D.C. middle-class black family and lived there until she went to Antioch College in Ohio. She came with her husband to Orange County in 1970 and had no trouble finding teaching assignments at community colleges and Cal State Fullerton. She taught French, Spanish, and dance. She started dancing at seven years of age, continued through college, and has danced with various ballet companies in Orange County. At the time of the interview, she was teaching dance full-time at Rancho Santiago Community College. Turner explained why there were few blacks in the arts in Orange County when she first came, but that was changing. She was the president of the Orange County Black Actors Theater (see Adleane Hunter, Chapter 2). She talked about coming to Orange County where there were jobs for blacks but few black businesses. She discussed social/service organizations such as Delta Sigma Theta, Links, and Jack and Jill. Also, she discussed affirmative action and the pros and cons of her predominantly black K-12 education.

MARVIN USSERY

OH No. 2365. Interview date: May 22, 1994. Interviewer: Mae Ussery.

Marvin Ussery is interviewed by his wife Mae Ussery. Marvin grew up in Houston, Texas, and because the family was poor, he started working at an early age running errands, cutting yards, cleaning chickens, and shining shoes. He finished high school in Houston, went to City College of San Francisco, and Oregon State on a football scholarship, graduating in 1955. For twelve years he was a commissioned officer in the air force. After leaving the air force, he was hired in 1979 by ITT Cannon to work in the personnel department of their Santa Ana plant. Most of this oral history is about his work at ITT Cannon. He provides many details on the ethnic and gender makeup of the plant, employee complaints, affirmative action, and the effects of many layoffs in the 1990s on people. He explains the difference between equal opportunity and affirmative action, he gives examples, and he expresses his own views as to the need for affirmative action.

CLAY WHITE

OH No. 2386. Interview date: May 16, 1994. Interviewer: Chris Llewellyn.

Clay White was born and raised in Toledo, Ohio, in 1938. He played football for the University of Nebraska, graduated, and taught high school in Lincoln before coming to Santa Ana to teach in the summer of 1965. He tells about his family's lack of choices in finding a place to live and the difficulty in not knowing anyone or about anything in Orange County's small black community. He became one of only a handful of black educators in the school district and they formed a Black Educators' Association to help incoming teachers. He chose to teach elementary school so he could more easily move into administration, which he did after three years of teaching. In 1981, he was hired by the school district in the city of Irvine. Other than touching on the subject of racism in its various forms such as police profiling, this oral history mainly focuses on educational subjects such as teaching and administration, as relating to Santa Ana and Irvine.

GEORGE WILLIAMS

OH No. 2358. Interview date: April 8, 1994. Interviewer: Dan Phillips.

George Williams was born and raised in Tyler, Texas, and he came to Orange County in 1989 to work for the Urban League and as a pastor at Friendship Baptist Church. He tells about the Urban League in Orange County, as well as nationally, and his work for the organization in other cities. He mentions that in 1981, Bernice Hurd and Earl Fields were among the founders in Orange County.

EVERETT WINTERS

OH No. 1684a. Interview date: November 12, 1974. Interviewers: Glen Ford and Maria Gutierrez.

This is an excellent interview of Everett Winters that covers much of the same material as Professor Larry de Graaf's interview in Chapter 3, which was conducted eight years later. This oral history is found in the book *Harvest*.

Appendix 2
Demographic Data from US Census 1920-2000

Until the census of 2000, those interviewed were asked to provide their race from a list of races or ethnic groups like white, Negro, Asian (or more detailed some years, like Chinese or Japanese). They could make only one choice. This could be a problem for a mixed-race person who, for example, had a white mother and a black father. This changed in the census of 2000. The interviewee could choose multiple races or ethnic groups. In Orange County, 47,649 people chose Black / African American as their single race. There were almost 12,000 other people who chose Black / African American as one of two or more races or ethnic groups. Looking at the year 2000 Orange County data below, this calculates to 25 percent more people than the single category of Black / African American. We don't have an answer to the question as to what number of people of the almost 12,000 would have chosen Black / African American in the year 2000 if they had been forced to choose only one race or ethnicity. But, using the racist created one-drop (and you are black) rule, there were at least 59,426 African Americans in Orange County in the year 2000. Having looked at the year 2000 city data, the 25 percent multiple-choice increase over the single-choice holds quite well for each city. The city data below corresponds to the single race or ethnicity choice and the only choice before the year 2000.

	Black Population	**Total Population**
Orange County		
1920	**139**	**61,375**
1930	**231**	**118,674**
1940	**287**	**130,760**
1950	**889**	**216,224**
1960	**3,171**	**703,925**
1970	**10,175**	**1,381,742**
1980	**24,560**	**1,932,709**
1990	**42,681**	**2,410,556**
2000[1]	**47,649**	**2,846,289**
2000[2]	**59,426**	**2,846,289**
Anaheim		
1920	**11**	**5,526**
1930	**25**	**10,995**
1940	**11**	**11,031**
1950	**74**	**14,556**
1960	**48**	**104,184**

1970	**170**	**166,701**
1980	**2,531**	**219,311**
1990	**6,780**	**266,406**
2000	**8,735**	**328,014**

Brea

1930	**0**	**2,435**
1940	**0**	**2,567**
1950	**2**	**3,208**
1960[3]	**-**	**-**
1970	**41**	**18,447**
1980	**130**	**27,913**
1990	**355**	**32,873**
2000	**447**	**35,410**

Buena Park

1950	**3**	**1**
1960	**1**	**46,401**
1970	**62**	**63,647**
1980	**705**	**64,165**
1990	**1,750**	**68,784**
2000	**3,000**	**78,282**

Costa Mesa

1950	**9**	**11,844**
1960	**66**	**37,550**
1970	**229**	**72,660**
1980	**539**	**82,562**
1990	**1,282**	**96,357**
2000	**1,520**	**108,724**

Fountain Valley

1960[4]	**8**	**4,282**
1970	**50**	**31,826**
1980	**408**	**55,080**
1990	**510**	**53,691**
2000	**611**	**54,978**

Fullerton

1920	**18**	**4,415**
1930	**41**	**10,860**
1940	**57**	**10,442**
1950	**77**	**13,958**
1960	**301**	**56,180**
1970	**678**	**85,826**
1980	**1,670**	**102,034**

1990	**2,479**	**114,144**
2000	**2,861**	**126,003**

Garden Grove

1950	**4**	**3,762**
1960	**34**	**84,238**
1970	**162**	**122,524**
1980	**1,039**	**123,307**
1990	**2,144**	**143,050**
2000	**2,168**	**165,196**

Huntington Beach

1930	**6**	**3,690**
1940	**0**	**3,738**
1950	**3**	**5,237**
1960	**2**	**11,492**
1970	**99**	**115,960**
1980	**1,218**	**170,505**
1990	**1,687**	**181,519**
2000	**1,527**	**189,594**

Irvine

1980	**916**	**62,134**
1990	**2,002**	**110,330**
2000	**2,068**	**143,072**

Laguna Beach

1930	**8**	**1,981**
1940	**28**	**4,460**
1950	**37**	**6,661**
1960	**102**	**11,303**
1970	**90**	**14,550**
1980	**96**	**17,901**
1990	**163**	**23,170**
2000	**190**	**23,727**

La Habra

1930	**0**	**2,273**
1940	**0**	**2,499**
1950	**0**	**4,961**
1960	**4**	**25,136**
1970	**23**	**41,350**
1980	**144**	**45,232**
1990	**485**	**51,266**
2000	**926**	**58,974**

Mission Viejo

1960[5]	**16**	**717**
1970	**36**	**11,933**
1980	**340**	**50,666**
1990	**680**	**72,820**
2000	**1,067**	**93,102**

Newport Beach

1930	**4**	**2,203**
1940	**2**	**4,438**
1950	**33**	**12,120**
1960	**47**	**26,540**
1970	**41**	**49,422**
1980	**144**	**62,556**
1990	**230**	**66,643**
2000	**371**	**70,032**

Orange

1920	**3**	**4,884**
1930	**6**	**8,066**
1940	**0**	**7,901**
1950	**3**	**10,027**
1960	**9**	**26,000**
1970	**213**	**77,374**
1980	**865**	**91,788**
1990	**1,551**	**110,658**
2000	**2,056**	**128,821**

Placentia

1930	**0**	**1,606**
1940	**0**	**1,472**
1950[6]	**-**	**-**
1960[7]	**176**	**6,780**
1970	**188**	**21,948**
1980	**381**	**35,041**
1990	**765**	**41,259**
2000	**821**	**46,488**

Santa Ana

1920	**22**	**15,485**
1930	**109**	**30,322**
1940	**158**	**31,921**
1950	**433**	**45,533**
1960	**1,759**	**100,350**
1970	**6,731**	**156,601**

1980	**8,232**	**203,713**
1990	**7,685**	**293,742**
2000	**5,749**	**337,977**

Seal Beach

1930	**1**	**1,156**
1940	**0**	**1,553**
1950	**2**	**3,553**
1960	**5**	**8,359**
1970	**13**	**24,441**
1980	**180**	**25,975**
1990	**245**	**25,098**
2000	**347**	**24,157**

Tustin

1930[8]	**1**	**4,076**
1940	**1**	**3,288**
1950	**2**	**1,143**
1960	**0**	**5,862**
1970	**40**	**21,178**
1980	**867**	**32,317**
1990	**2,895**	**50,689**
2000	**1,970**	**67,504**

Tustin Foothills

1960[9]	**6**	**12,261**
1970	**20**	**26,598**
1980	**61**	**26,174**
1990	**128**	**24,358**
2000	**134**	**24,044**

Tustin (El Toro and LTA Marine Corps Bases)

1960	**536**	**8,188**
1970	**733**	**9,076**

Westminster

1950	**1**	**3,131**
1960	**1**	**25,750**
1970	**48**	**59,865**
1980	**508**	**71,133**
1990	**868**	**78,118**
2000	**871**	**88,207**

(Endnotes)

1 The year 2000 census data included the mixed-race population. The number in this row for the black population is for black or African American race only.
2 This number is for persons claiming both black and any other race or races and this increases the total by almost 12,000.
3 Data was not found for this year.
4 Estimate based on Census Tract I-92.
5 Estimate based on Census Tract C-20, which includes Mission Viejo.
6 Population less than 2,500, therefore breakdown by race is not available.
7 Estimate based on Census Tract A-17.
8 1930 and 1940 are township data.
9 Estimate based on Census Tracts G-56 and G-57.

Appendix 3
Maps

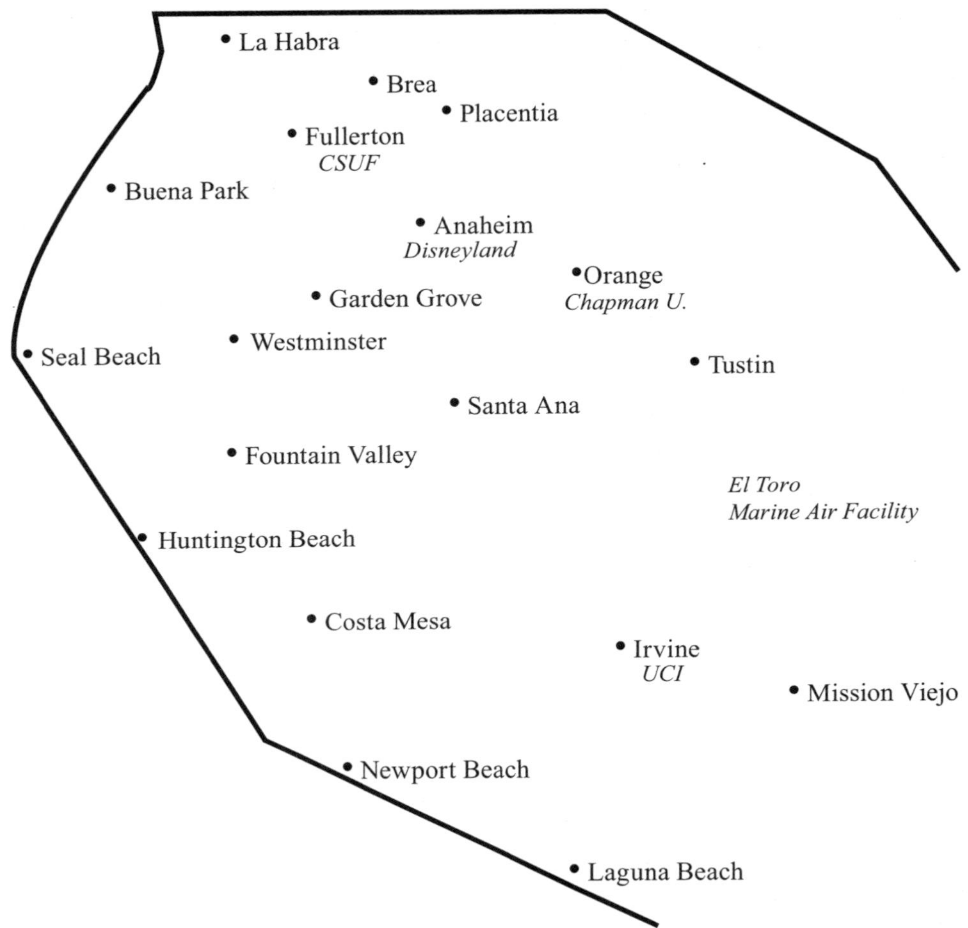

Northwest Orange County – This partial map, which covers most of Orange County, shows the approximate geographic location of inland cities listed in the demographic chart of Appendix II. The four beach city locations are shown along the Pacific Coast. Also shown are some often referred-to locations in the text. The distance from central Santa Ana to the Newport Beach coast is approximately 10 miles.

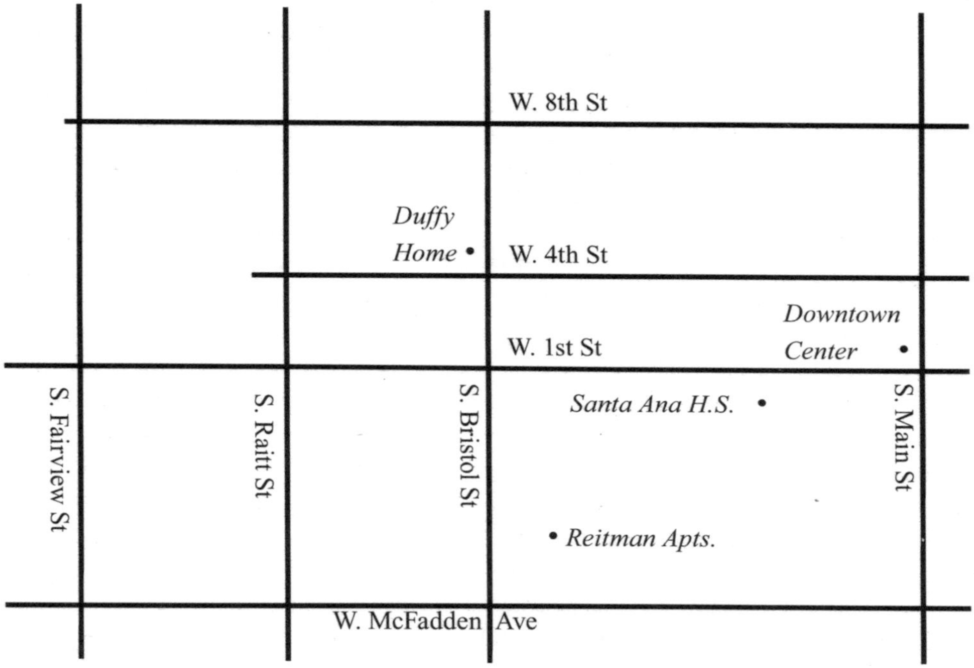

W. 8th St

Duffy Home

W. 4th St

Downtown Center

W. 1st St

S. Fairview St

S. Raitt St

S. Bristol St

Santa Ana H.S.

S. Main St

Reitman Apts.

W. McFadden Ave

West Santa Ana – Early black residents settled in the area bounded by 1st Street, 8th Street, Bristol Street, and Raitt Street (then named Artesia). By 1970 the majority of black residents had settled south and west to the area bounded by 1st, McFadden Street, Bristol, and Fairview Street. The 1970 Federal Census showed the greatest concentration of African Americans in Santa Ana was 48.2 percent in Census Block 46 bounded by 1st, Richland Street (between 1st and McFadden), Bristol, and Raitt. Most of West 4th Street became Santa Ana Boulevard. The distance from Main Street to Bristol is approximately 1 mile.

Bibliography

Other than newspaper articles and a few books, magazine articles, and academic papers, there has been little written about Orange County's mid-twentieth century African American community. The fact that this bibliography is quite short reflects this. The following are notes on the books, theses, and papers.

John H. Denton and Archibald Cox discuss Proposition 14 and *Mulkey v. Reitman.* Arnold Beisser talks about growing up in Santa Ana with a black friend, Bill Duffy. Sadie Benham and Dorothy Love tell their life stories, which include living in Orange County. Lawrence de Graaf, in the book chapter and the two papers, one co-authored with Emory Tolbert, discusses the history of the African American community in Orange County in the mid-20th century. Leo Friis presents an excellent general history of early Orange County. Ruby Goodwin, the well known writer, tells about her early life in Illinois before coming with her family to Fullerton in Orange County. Kling, et. al.'s book is an excellent history of Orange County covering 1950-1990. James Loewen includes only a small amount of material on Orange County but provides many examples of Orange County-like exclusion of blacks in other American communities. Lisa McGirr provides an excellent political-historical analysis of the libertarian, conservative, and anti-Communist movement that was so repugnant to the majority of black people in Orange County. Oaks and Gethaiga's book contains eight oral histories of African Americans in Orange County. General Frank Petersen provides almost forty pages to describing his El Toro base assignments in the 1950s. Molly Wampler's book includes the story of Korean American Olympic gold-medal diver Sammy Lee's being subjected to blatant housing discrimination in mid-1950s Orange County. Jean Mahlberg's master's thesis is an excellent history of black Santa Ana primarily based on her interviews of black pioneers. Ollie Whitaker, while drawing a great deal on Mahlberg, nevertheless provides the reader statistical data as well as material based on her own interviews of educators in Orange County.

Books

Denton, John H. *Apartheid American Style.* Berkeley: Diablo Press, 1967.

Beisser, Arnold R. *Halcyon Days: A Story of Growth and Social Change in Orange County, California.* San Clemente, CA: Davy Associates, 1994.

Benham, Sadie Reid and Cathy Maiden. *From Welfare to the White House: I Know Who Holds My Hand (The Sadie Benham Story).* Farrell, PA: Published by the Sadie Benham Foundation of Farrell, 2002.

Cox, Archibald. *The Warren Court: Constitutional Decision as an Instrument of Reform.* Cambridge, MA: Harvard University Press, 1968.

Friis, Leo J. *Orange County through Four Centuries.* Santa Ana: Pioneer Press, 1965.

Goodwin, Ruby Berkley. *It's Good to be Black.* Garden City, New York: Doubleday, 1953.

Kling, Rob, Spencer Olin, and Mark Poster. *Postsuburban California: The Transformation of Orange County since World War II.* Berkeley: University of California Press, 1991.

Loewen, James W. *Sundown Towns: A Hidden Dimension of American Racism.* New York: London: The New Press, 2005.

Love, Dorothy. *Love Has Something to Say.* Los Angeles: Inspiration 52, 1992.

McGirr, Lisa. *Suburban Warriors: The Origins of the New American Right.* Oxford: Princeton University Press, 2001.

Oaks, Pricilla and Wacira Gethaiga, eds. *Harvest: A Compilation of Taped Interviews on the Minority Peoples of Orange County.* Fullerton, CA: California State University, Fullerton, Oral History Program, 1975.

Peterson, Frank E., with J. Alfred Phelps. *Into the Tiger's Jaw: America's First Black Marine Aviator.* Novato, CA: Presidio Press, 1998.

Wampler, Molly Frick. *Not Without Honor: The Story of Sammy Lee.* Santa Barbara, CA: Fithian Press, 1987.

West, John R. *There are Always Blue Skies ... Over Dark Clouds*. Dubuque, IA. Kendall/Hunt Publishing, 2006.

Scholarly Articles and Master's Theses

de Graaf, Lawrence B. "African American Suburbanization in California, 1960 through 1990," *Seeking El Dorado*, edited by Lawrence B. de Graaf, Kevin Mulroy, and Quintard Taylor. Los Angeles: Autry Museum of Western Heritage in association with, Seattle: University of Washington Press, 2001.

de Graaf, Lawrence B., "From Virtual Exclusion to Limited Assimilation: Blacks in Orange County." Paper Delivered to the Western Historical Association, Oct. 19, 1990.

Mahlberg, Jean. "The Negro Community in Santa Ana." Master's thesis, California State University, Fullerton, 1967.

Tolbert, Emory J. and Lawrence B. de Graaf. "The Unseen Minority: Blacks in Orange County." *Journal of Orange County Studies 3/4* (Fall 1989/Spring 1990): 54-61.

Whitaker, Ollie L. *The History and Development of Educational Programs for the Negro in the Santa Ana Unified District.* Master's thesis, Chapman University, 1971.

Index